Britain's Iron Chancellor

Britain's Iron Chancellor

An Autobiography

Philip Snowden

Edited by Alexander Clifford

PEN & SWORD
HISTORY
AN IMPRINT OF PEN & SWORD BOOKS LTD.
YORKSHIRE – PHILADELPHIA

First published in Great Britain in 2024 by
Pen & Sword History
An imprint of
Pen & Sword Books Ltd
Yorkshire - Philadelphia

ISBN 978 1 39902 495 2

A CIP catalogue record for this book is available from the British Library

Typeset in INDIA by IMPEC eSolutions
Printed and bound in the UK by CPI Group (UK) Ltd, Croydon, CRO 4YY

Pen & Sword Books Ltd. incorporates the Imprints of Pen & Sword Archaeology, Atlas, Aviation, Battleground, Discovery, Family History, History, Maritime, Military, Naval, Politics, Railways, Select, Transport, True Crime, Fiction, Frontline Books, Leo Cooper, Praetorian Press, Seaforth Publishing, Wharncliffe, White Owl and After the Battle.

For a complete list of Pen & Sword titles please contact
PEN & SWORD BOOKS LIMITED
47 Church Street, Barnsley, South Yorkshire S70 2AS, United Kingdom
E-mail: enquiries@pen-and-sword.co.uk
Website: www.pen-and-sword.co.uk

or

PEN AND SWORD BOOKS
1950 Lawrence Rd, Havertown, PA 19083, USA
E-mail: Uspen-and-sword@casematepublishers.com
Website: www.penandswordbooks.com

MIX
Paper | Supporting responsible forestry
FSC® C013604

Contents

Editor's Introduction		vii
Chapter One	My Early Life	1
Chapter Two	My Early Socialist Days	16
Chapter Three	The Formation of the Labour Party	30
Chapter Four	My First Parliamentary Contests	36
Chapter Five	First Impressions of Parliament	48
Chapter Six	The Woman Suffrage Movement	58
Chapter Seven	A Review, 1906-1914	74
Chapter Eight	My Attitude to the War	81
Chapter Nine	Coalition and Conscription	86
Chapter Ten	The Russian Revolution	91
Chapter Eleven	Coalitions and Conferences	98
Chapter Twelve	The 1918 General Election	106
Chapter Thirteen	Communism in the Labour Movement	113
Chapter Fourteen	From Blackburn to Colne Valley	121
Chapter Fifteen	Labour a Parliamentary Party	124
Chapter Sixteen	Labour Forms a Government	131
Chapter Seventeen	First Experiences of Office	144
Chapter Eighteen	Difficulties of the New Government	149
Chapter Nineteen	The First Labour Budget	158
Chapter Twenty	The Fall of the Labour Government	174
Chapter Twenty-One	The "Red Letter" Election	184
Chapter Twenty-Two	Mr. Churchill as Chancellor	192

Chapter Twenty-Three	The General Strike	196
Chapter Twenty-Four	I Leave the I.L.P.	202
Chapter Twenty-Five	Formation of the Second Labour Government	205
Chapter Twenty-Six	The Hague Conference	216
Chapter Twenty-Seven	The Budget of 1930	249
Chapter Twenty-Eight	Internal Trouble about Unemployment	256
Chapter Twenty-Nine	The Serious Financial Position	260
Chapter Thirty	The First 1931 Budget	268
Chapter Thirty-One	Waiting for Dead Men's Shoes	271
Chapter Thirty-Two	The Story of the Crisis	276
Chapter Thirty-Three	The Story Continued	285
Chapter Thirty-Four	The Formation of the National Government	288
Chapter Thirty-Five	The Emergency Budget	295
Chapter Thirty-Six	The 1931 General Election	305
Chapter Thirty-Seven	A Constitutional Revolution	317

Appendix: Broadcast to the Nation on the General Election 333

Index 338

Editor's Introduction

Philip Snowden is one of the most remarkable and unusual figures in British political history. Born into poverty on the Yorkshire moors in 1864 and overcoming a paralysing illness in early life, he went on to be a founding father of the Labour Party and its first Chancellor of the Exchequer in 1924, an office he held three times. He would be reviled as a traitor for joining the National Government in 1931 and expelled from the party, spending his final years in the political wilderness. He had attained the second highest office in the land in spite of great disadvantages of birth and a severe physical disability.

Snowden was famous for his eye for detail, erudite speechmaking, cantankerous nature and caustic wit. Sometimes seen as cold and bitter, Snowden could also be warm and funny in private; he taught Lord Beaverbrook to sing The Red Flag during the General Strike of 1926. He would earn the moniker the 'Iron Chancellor' for his unbending, no-nonsense approach to international negotiations in the 1929 Hague Conference, which could drive his colleagues to distraction. Snowden was not without his faults, being aloof, prickly and dogmatic in his belief in free trade, balanced budgets, and temperance, all tenets that appeared outdated by the early 1930s. The perceptive German journalist Egon Wertheimer described Snowden as "a political thinker of crystal clearness" who "wields [sarcasm] like a shield between himself and the world". Churchill wrote of Snowden: "His fearlessness, his rectitude, his austerity, his sobriety of judgement, his deep love of Britain and his studiously-concealed, but intense, pride in British greatness, distinguish him as one of the true worthies of our age." Snowden's historical reputation has been severely damaged by his stubborn persistence with economic doctrines that hindsight deemed outmoded, his difficult personality and the venom he unleashed against his former colleagues in the 1931 election.

Indeed, 1931 overshadows the rest of Snowden's life and achievements in the historical record, with biographers being all too tempted to trace the roots of Snowden's 'betrayal' back to his brand of ethical socialism or his friendship with Lloyd George in the 1920s. Snowden and Labour's other founding fathers are frequently criticised for lacking any clear plan for the enactment of socialism beyond the notion that a socialist society would spring out of a prosperous capitalist one, with tax revenues being deployed to gradually eliminate social ills. Essentially their ideology of ethical socialism is seen as intellectually hollow. The record of the two Labour governments in which Snowden served as chancellor are generally held in very low regard. Certainly it is difficult to imagine any contemporary Labour politician citing Snowden as an inspiration.

Let us deal with these charges in reverse order. On the issue of the first Labour governments, one must bear in mind that Snowden and his generation of Labour leaders, born in the 1860s and 1870s, could never have anticipated that their tiny party would gain power in their lifetime. By the time they did, they were old men, without experience of government, or much in the way of a formal education. The performance of the first two Labour administrations must therefore be viewed in the context of the gigantic challenges, not least the Great Depression, that Snowden and his colleagues found themselves facing, and the huge barriers they had overcome merely to get into power. Besides, it is all too convenient to forget that both in 1924 and 1929-31, Labour was a minority government, with their hands tied behind their backs in parliament and reliant on Liberal backing. That they did not succeed is self-evident, but they paved the way for all future Labour governments. Someone had to go first.

As for their ideology, it is rather ironic to criticise the ethical socialists for failing to map a clear path to socialism given that, in the century since, it is hard to think of a Labour leader who has offered anything more substantive. It is true that, although the Labour Party of the 1920s aspired to nationalisation and universal healthcare, they did not have legislation ready to go, unlike in 1945. However, Attlee's undoubted achievements were built on the detailed work of a liberal civil servant, William Beveridge, and came on the back of five years of Labour in office as part of the wartime coalition. Whether one could accurately describe the 1945-51 Labour government as having 'achieved socialism' is a discussion for another time. The belief of the ethical socialists, that a prosperous capitalist society would generate the tax revenue necessary to tackle social inequality, appears, rather than being an aberration, to instead be a central plank that has underpinned generations of subsequent Labour ideology. Even the apparently radical programme of Corbynism was built on the precondition that Britain was a prosperous capitalist society that could generate tax reciepts sufficient to pay for nationalisation, free broadband and a National Care Service.

Finally, does Snowden deserve to be remembered as a villainous turncoat? During the 1931 crisis, a devastating run on the Pound in August-September of that year, Snowden faced the greatest challenge of his life. As readers will discover, he persuaded the majority of the cabinet to back his emergency budget plans, which included a controversial 10% cut in the dole. However, the nine cabinet rebels were too large a force to ignore and Prime Minister Ramsay MacDonald gave the king his resignation. Urged on by the monarch, and the other party leaders, MacDonald was persuaded to head an emergency coalition of all three major parties to face the crisis. Snowden was reappointed to the Treasury and his speech to the Commons presenting his emergency budget was practically Churchillian in its patriotic rhetoric. However, the Labour Party opted to oppose the National Government (as the coalition was labelled), amicably at first but soon with great hostility. MacDonald and Snowden found themselves thrown out of the party they had built. The chancellor's austerity policies have been derided as narrow-minded and economically illiterate by historians writing in the Keynesian age of the post-war years, who set the dominant narrative of British interwar history. While the Keynesian economic consensus is well and truly dead, the narrative remains. In truth, it is hard to see how a confidence crisis on the international financial markets could have been addressed with anything other than austerity measures. The British government had to convince the financial world of 1931 that they were solvent. An ambitious spending programme paid for through deficit financing would have done the exact opposite. Snowden always insisted that he acted in the best interests of working people; that had the value of Sterling truly collapsed, the masses would have borne the brunt of the hardship. Confidence had to be restored. Liz Truss's ill-fated economic experiment in 2022 put Snowden's actions in a different and more providential light; the opinion of international markets about a government's solvency truly does have a real-world impact.

The charge of treachery is harder to ignore when it comes to the 1931 election campaign, which saw the National Government coalition win the greatest landslide in British political history, attaining 554 seats to Labour's 52. Certainly, in an attempt to make himself indispensable to the National cause, and in settling some personal scores, Snowden threw himself into the offensive against his former colleagues. He wrote numerous articles attacking Labour's policy and the party's cowardice in not facing the crisis head on. Most infamously, he addressed the nation over the radio and decried the Labour programme as "Bolshevism run mad". This speech can be found in full in the appendix of the present volume. On the other hand, during the campaign Snowden and Ramsay MacDonald were the subject of a huge quantity of vitriol from their former colleagues and were falsely accused of plotting a coalition for years. Labour also did not fight entirely cleanly; they claimed impossibly that they would reverse the cuts Snowden had imposed while also balancing the books and not relying on borrowing. They touted the "Bankers' ramp" conspiracy theory that there had in fact not been a Sterling crisis at all, but rather that plotting foreign financiers had conspired to remove Britain's left-wing government. And Labour's Daily Herald stooped just as low as Snowden in the campaign, claiming at one point that a National Government victory would result in the establishment of a fascist dictatorship under MacDonald and, in another edition, used images of crowds gunned down in the Russian Revolution to depict Britain in the event of a Labour defeat.

All told, Philip Snowden's life and career is in urgent need of historical reassessment after years of neglect and slander. His autobiography is a highly readable eyewitness account of the first 40 years of the Labour Party and the great crises of British politics from the First World War to the Great Depression. It is a window into the lost world of rural life in 19th-century Yorkshire, a vivid and, at times, moving portrayal of the pioneering days of the Labour Party and an insightful narrative of the tumultuous political events of the early 20th century. It is also one of the most engaging memoirs of its age, packed with Snowden's characteristic wit, sarcasm and perspicacious pen portraits of Lloyd George, Churchill, Asquith, Ramsay MacDonald and Keir Hardie among others. Given that Snowden ordered all his personal papers be destroyed on his death in 1937, it is an invaluable source on his life, as well as the foundation and early years of the Labour Party, its path to power and first two governments. It is a key first-hand account of the 1931 crisis, the Labour split and the formation of the National Government.

Readers are to be advised on two counts. The first is that the original edition published in 1934 was made up of two volumes that weighed in at well over 1,000 pages. This new edition has been trimmed down considerably to create a readable and accessible volume that will appeal to a general audience. Many passages on issues that would be totally obscure to a modern reader, or where Snowden simply recounts historical events that he was not personally privy to but are otherwise well-documented, such as the foundation of the I.L.P. (Independent Labour Party) or the Versailles Treaty, have been removed for the sake of brevity. I have focused the narrative on the foundation of the Labour Party, the First World War and the first and second Labour governments, including the Depression and 1931 crisis. Students or scholars who require complete coverage of Snowden's life and career must, I am afraid, still seek out the original two-volume edition. Readers should also be aware that Snowden is extremely critical of most other Labour figures of his day, especially towards his bitter personal rival Ramsay MacDonald. His judgments are those of a man who had burnt his bridges first with Labour in 1931 and then with MacDonald's National Government in 1932. They are, by most historians' reckoning, rather on the harsh side.

After his departure from the National Government Snowden retired from public life, although he supported Lloyd George's 'New Deal' in 1935. His few appearances in the Lords, to which he had been elevated as Viscount of Ickornshaw, were almost solely dedicated to scathing attacks on MacDonald. Philip Snowden died of a heart attack less than three years after writing An Autobiography. He was survived by his wife Ethel, a suffragist and socialist activist in her own right. They had no children. His ashes were scattered on Ickornshaw Moor, a stone's throw from where he grew up, and a memorial cairn was erected there the following year. It still stands today, several helpful signs directing the rare visitor to this still isolated corner of Yorkshire. It is a dramatic, desolate yet arresting spot and, standing at it, one cannot help but feel that the unforgiving moorland on which he grew up reveals something of Snowden's character. The inscription on the cairn reads:

In this place
Mingled with the soil
And near the friends he loved
Are the ashes of
Philip Snowden
First Viscount of Ickornshaw
Who lived his whole life in the
Service of the common people
And died in the love of
His native land
On May 15th 1937.

Alexander Clifford
September 2023

Chapter One

My Early Life

I am a Yorkshireman. I was born in the moorland parish of Cowling in the West Riding on the 18th July 1864. In the days before the advent of modern means of communication the village of Cowling was isolated and remote. To the south hundreds of square miles of wild and desolate moors stretched away as far as the Derbyshire hills, and on the west the ridges of the rugged Pennines separated the parish from the neighbouring county of Lancashire.

Four miles beyond Keighley the wide valley of the Aire is divided by a chain of hills. The road to the left passes through Cowling. There is nothing attractive in what man has done to make this village. Grey stone houses, without even the relief of a garden, line the road. There has been very little change since I was a boy. But the natural situation of the village is very impressive. On the left there rises to the height of over a thousand feet a long and massive crag. The motorist with an hour to spare should, at the entrance to the village, turn into the old pack-horse lane by which the summit of the crag can be reached. He will be repaid by the sight of one of the finest views in England. Below is the wide and rich valley through which the river Aire slowly meanders. To the left the view extends far away to the Craven highlands, with Ingleborough and Penn y gant in the background. To the right Rombalds Moor stretches her wide expanse of heath and heather. Close behind is the vast extent of moorland where the silence is never broken except by the cries of the wild birds and the occasional bleating of sheep.

Returning to the main road and proceeding in the direction of Lancashire, shortly after passing through the roadside village, there comes into view, nestling peacefully in the deep valley through which the beck runs, the village of Ickornshaw, the place in which I spent the greater part of my boyhood. In the days before the main road was made, Ickornshaw was the centre of the life of the parish. On the hillside above the hamlet of Ickornshaw there is a row of old stone houses known as Middleton. It was in the top house of this row that I was born in a two-roomed cottage.

When does a child begin to remember? I am a little bit suspicious of persons who have vivid recollections of things that happened when they were two years old. Nothing that I saw or heard when I was so young fixed itself in my mind. The earliest recollection I have, and I must have been between three and four, was of being lifted by the doctor onto the long kitchen-table and told to open my mouth and put out my tongue. It appears that my mother had discovered that I was tongue-tied. I distinctly remember the doctor saying that he wouldn't cut it as I should probably break the tie when playing with something in my mouth, and in any case it was not likely to be a hindrance to me. It has not been! Another incident that happened when I was just short of six I mention for two reasons, because it is, I think, a good instance of how the very young child-mind can have events clearly and indelibly stamped upon it, and also because the incident illustrates the determined character of the village population. The houses in Middleton had to get their water supply from a well spring in a field behind the row. This spring had been freely used from a time beyond living memory. The agent of the local landowner demanded payments for its use. The villagers refused. One morning the news came that men were walling up the well. Off marched the women led by a powerfully built woman called Rachel, whose bare arms looked able to fell an ox. When they reached the well, Rachel, without any argument, picked up the agent and put him into the well. When he was sufficiently soaked she took him out. The work of closing the well stopped, for the workmen were not disposed to invite further attention from Rachel and her cohorts.

The housing conditions in the parish in these days, which were common to all hand-loom weaving villages, were terrible. My father had an uncle who had lived through these times. He was an old man when I was a boy, and I often sat for hours on a small stool at his feet listening to the stories he had to tell. Although the poverty of the people was extreme, they seemed to get a fair amount of enjoyment out of their lives. They were not subject to the discipline of the modern factory. They regulated their own hours of labour. It was the custom to send in their finished pieces once a fortnight, and it was the common practice to take things very easily in the first week, and then to work day and night the second week to complete the work they had on hand. It was quite a common thing for the bedroom of the cottage to contain five or six hand-looms, and in this room the weaving was done; and in this room the whole family, which was often very large, had to sleep. The death-rate must have been very high, but as a great deal of the time of the hand-loom weavers was spent in the open air this counteracted to some extent the appalling housing and sleeping conditions.

From what I learnt of these conditions from the stories told to me by the survivors of this period, I should think that the people of the village suffered less during "the Hungry Forties" than those who had come under the terrible factory conditions brought by the industrial revolution. The conditions in the parish were bad enough in all conscience. Their food was rough, but wholesome, and porridge was the staple diet. It was, to use a phrase I often heard to describe those days, "Porridge and Stop!"

By the time I was born hand-loom weaving had entirely ceased, both in the cottages and in the weaving-shops, although a few hand-looms were still to be seen in some of the cottages. I remember that my father had kept his hand-loom, and when we were children he sometimes worked it in the bedroom, buying remnants of woollen yarn from the factory and weaving them into cloth for family use. The yams, of course, were of various colours, and I remember a petticoat he made for my mother of such a variety of colours that Joseph's coat would have appeared a dull and drab affair by comparison. My father, whose name was John, was one of a family of five. His parents both died comparatively young, and these five young children were boarded out with farmers in the parish. This was in a sense very fortunate for these children, because they were sure of good food and enough of it. They all lived to grow up and to marry and have families.

The first Snowden came into the parish in the early part of the 18th century, and reclaimed a small farm from the moor. It was understood that he had come into this remote district to escape from justice, having been mixed up in a poaching affair. From enquiries I have made I believe he came from the neighbourhood of Goole. He reared a large family of lads. My father was a man of unusual natural ability, and if he had had opportunities I am sure he would have made his way in the world. He somehow managed to get some education as a boy, although I do not remember ever hearing him say how or where he got it. There were two or three "Dames' Schools" in the village, and it was probably at one of these that he learnt to read; but it is much more likely that it was the Sunday School that gave him his love of reading. He must have become a fairly fluent reader when he was quite young, for I have heard him relate how a number of hand-loom weavers contributed a halfpenny a week to buy a copy of the weekly Leeds Mercury, which was then sevenpence, and with these coppers he was sent to a village four miles away each week to get the paper; and then the subscribers to this newspaper met in a cottage and he read the news to them.

The Leeds Mercury in those days was a Radical journal. Those were times of great political and social excitement. The Chartist movement was affecting the industrial population, and the agitation for the Repeal of the Com Laws was at its height. They were dangerous times for those known to harbour Radical opinions. Throughout the West Riding, as well as in other parts of England, men were being arrested and sentenced to long terms of imprisonment for alleged sedition and political conspiracy. This group of Radical-Chartists in Cowling had to take precautions against the attentions of the constable, and when they gathered together to discuss politics and hear my father read the paper for them they shuttered the window and sometimes placed a scout outside to watch for the constable. I have heard my father relate that, as a youth, he was often taken with some of the older weavers to Chartist demonstrations as far away as Halifax and Huddersfield, walking the twenty miles each way. My mother, whose maiden name was Martha Nelson, was one of a family of eight, all of whom were reared and lived to old age. She, too, was an exceptional woman, full of shrewd common sense, and broad and generous in her general outlook. On her mother's side she was descended from a family named Emmott, who had been farmers in the parish for several centuries. The Nelsons were a comparatively recent importation into the district, and nothing is known of them beyond the belief that my mother's grandfather, the original Nelson, was a migrant from Scotland. My parents were closely associated with Wesleyan Methodism, and devotedly attached to the local chapel. Although these were days when narrow religions were very general, my father and mother were both liberal in these matters. My father had a brother who was a very strict Baptist, holding strong views about "election" and eternal damnation for the unrepentant. I remember many an ardent discussion between these two brothers on theological questions. After a discussion had been going on for some time, and my uncle had defended his Calvinistic beliefs, my mother would put an end to it by saying: "You say that

God loves us as we love our own children. Do you think I would put one of my children into hell fire? No! Not how bad he'd been!" There seemed to be little left to say after this statement.

I was the youngest of three children, the two elder being girls. In my young days our parents were very poor. In the early years of their married life, trade was very bad following the Crimean War. This long period of trade depression was known as "Owd Nick Panic". "Owd Nick" being the Czar of Russia.

My father did not earn more than 15s. a week. Having a young family, my mother was unable to work in the mill, but she supplemented the family income by spinning weft on a hand-wheel at home. Although we were so poor, I do not think that I ever lacked food. My mother saw to that. Our food consisted of porridge and milk, which in those days was sold by the local farmers at threehalfpence the quart, and boiled puddings, with what was called "sheep-head broth". When my elder sister was old enough to look after the house, my mother returned to the mill as a weaver, and this improved the financial position of the family. There was no money for buying newspapers or books, but by some means or other, how I cannot remember, I managed when I was able to read to get a collection of penny story-books. There was a library of two or three hundred volumes in connection with the Sunday School, but the books were mainly theological. My father in the days when we were young had little money to spend on books, but he managed to get a moderate collection. He was particularly fond of poetry, and possessed himself of copies of Burns, Byron, Shakespeare, Young and Milton. He knew all Burns' principal poems by heart, and he used to recite to me "Tam o' Shanter", "Man was made to Mourn", "The Cotter's Saturday Night", etc., and great parts of Byron's "Childe Harold" and other poems. My father had a remarkable memory, much better than I ever had. I never could remember much of a sermon, but he could go through the sermons he had heard point by point, criticising the argument and the form and the construction of them. He ought to have been a preacher, and probably would have been if the circumstances of the family had not prevented him from obtaining the necessary books. He had a remarkable knowledge of the Bible, and was always ready to illustrate an argument by the apt quotation of a verse from scripture. I owe much to him and to my years of Sunday School training of my own knowledge of the Bible, which is, I believe, above the average. The Sunday School and the chapel, and, I regret to add, the public-houses, were the centres of what there was of social life in the parish. There was a good deal of drinking in the village in those days, and far too many of the men were in the habit of going "on the spree". There has been a wonderful change in this respect, and the village is now a model of sobriety.

I cannot at all remember when I first began to attend the Sunday School in this place, but I have the happiest recollections of years of constant attendance there. I have still prize books in my possession, which show that I was never absent from the school once over a period of five years. In the early days of my Sunday School life the practice still survived of devoting half the time of the lessons to spelling. This was a survival of the days when the Sunday School filled to some extent the purpose of a day school. I am afraid that the religious instruction I received there did not altogether destroy the spirit of mischief which I possessed in a very large measure. On at least two occasions I got into serious trouble through my proclivity to play practical jokes. All the classes were assembled in one large room, and the noise of so many scholars reading and spelling at the same time made a deafening sound. One Sunday in the middle of the lessons I quietly stole up to the Superintendent's desk and rang his big bell. There was an instant hush, and before I had time to slip back to my place in the class the culprit was discovered. I was lightly let off with a severe reprimand. But my next delinquency was of a more serious nature. My father was then Superintendent of the school, and also took a class, in which I sat. Sitting behind him, I pinned up the two tails of his coat, and he, quite unconscious of the liberty I had taken with his garment, went away to discharge his duty as Superintendent in that undignified attire. I was, of course, discovered, and this was a matter too serious to be overlooked. A special teachers' meeting was called to consider what should be done with me. They considered my case, and finally came to the conclusion that I was hopeless, that I was "a limb of the devil", and that it was no use trying to exorcise the evil spirit which possessed me. They did not even hand me over to my father for chastisement, and I escaped with no greater punishment than the verdict of the teachers as to my spiritual depravity. I was not only a regular attendant at the Sunday School, but equally at the chapel services. I rather liked these religious services. I cannot say that the sermons were of a high intellectual order. They were generally given by local preachers, with an occasional visit from the stipendiary minister. My local preacher's sermons had what one might call the Hell Fire touch. For half an hour he dangled me and the others over the mouth of the pit of hell, and he did it so graphically as to make me actually smell the fire and brimstone. He left me in no doubt as to what my ultimate fate would be unless I departed from my evil ways. I am afraid I never missed much sleep through contemplating my future destiny. That was the advantage of having parents who were too liberal in their religious views to approve such a theology as that.

At the time I was ready to go to the day school there were two schools in the village. The one to which I went was conducted in the Church school, which had been hired by the schoolmaster. It consisted of one large room. The desks were fixed to the wall along the three sides of the room, and forms were placed in the middle of the floor for the younger children. It was a dreary place. There were no pictures or charts or any decorations on the walls. I well remember the day when I first went to school. I was put on the front form in the middle of the school - a form which stood about a foot high, and was called the "A.B.C. Form". I was not long on that form, and I clearly recollect the afternoon when I was promoted to the form behind, which stood about six inches higher. I do not remember much of the next three or four years I attended this apology for a school. The school fee was threepence a week for the older scholars, and two pence for the young ones, and we paid for our own copy-books. The curriculum was very limited. The schoolmaster sat at the head of the room on a high stool at an old-fashioned desk on high legs. The course of instruction was limited to reading, writing and arithmetic. I doubt if the master's knowledge extended beyond these subjects. Each class in turn was assembled round the master's desk for the reading lesson. We used the books for so long that the lesson became not a reading lesson, but a recitation we knew by heart. I must have made rapid progress from the infant form to the top desk, for I have no recollection of passing through the intermediate classes. It was about this time that I first went into the oratory business. I was a Band of Hope boy, and I was invited to give a recitation at one of the entertainments. My father, who was one of the best elocutionists I have known, took me in hand and trained me with some effect. My recitation extolled the virtues of bright, cold water, and its delivery was a tremendous success. But what impressed this occasion on my memory was not any oratorical triumph, but a very sordid reward. After the entertainment the crowd waited in the chapel yard and showered pennies upon me. When I got home I counted over five shillings in coppers. After this I became a regular star turn at the village entertainments, though I do not remember when my eloquence touched the pockets of my audience to the same extent. It has very often been said by those who have written about my early life that I used, when quite a boy, to make political speeches. I do not remember doing this, at least not my own speeches. It is true that at election times my sisters used to deck me out with yellow ribbons (the Liberal colours), and out I went, collected an audience and recited extracts from the speeches of contemporary politicians.

After the passing of Mr. Forster's Education Act, a few progressive persons in the village started an agitation for the adoption of the Act. It met with little opposition, except from the farmers who were terrified at the prospect of an increase in the rates. The Act was adopted, and the school I attended was taken over by the newly formed School Board. Steps were taken at once to build new school premises. A trained master was appointed, and a new era in child education in the village was opened up. I was between ten and eleven years old when this change took place. It brought me into a new world of learning. We were taught in a new schoolroom, which by comparison with the dingy old place we had left seemed like a palace to us. The walls were covered with maps and pictures. Our curriculum was extended to include grammar, geography, history, elementary mathematics, and the simple sciences. We were never troubled with the religious question, for, in order to avoid all controversy, the Board from the beginning banished the Bible from the school, not because they were irreligious, but because they believed that the teaching of religion was best carried out by the sects in their own Sunday Schools. I was always top boy in the school, and it may be of interest to those who have only known me limping along on sticks to learn that I could beat any boy in the parish three years older than myself at running and jumping. It was the usual thing for boys of my class to be sent half-time to the mill on reaching the age of ten. By that time the circumstances of my parents had so improved as to make that unnecessary. But, apart from that, my mother would never have allowed me to go half-time. She regarded the system as inhuman, and used to say: "No child of mine shall be dragged out of bed at half past five in a morning!" This half-time system has now happily been abolished, but I can remember when children began to work in factories at eight years of age. From every point of view the practice was an unmitigated evil. It was impossible to educate children who had been at work in a factory from six o'clock till noon. And in the economic sense the half-time employment of children did not pay either parents or employers. When I was twelve-and-a-half the School Board asked my father if he would like me to become a pupil-teacher. They caught them young in those days! I was appointed. It will throw some light on school conditions then if I relate that at that age I was at once put in charge of a class of forty boys and girls, not much younger than myself, in a separate classroom. I had seen so much of the master's efforts to enforce discipline that I felt I must emulate them. I had in my class a boy called Little Phineas, the son of John o' Phineas, who believed in ghosts. I do not remember what serious offence Little Phineas had committed, and whether I thought it was due to moral degeneracy following the banishment of religious teaching from the school. But I came to the conclusion that I must do a little of that on my own account. So I turned Little Phineas with his face to the wall and made him say his prayers. This breach of the regulations of the Board came to the ears of the head-master. He came into the classroom, and, before the boys and girls, conducted an enquiry into the charge against me. He found me guilty, and ordered me to take my cap and go home. A letter followed to my father saying that if he wished his son to remain in the service of the Board I must appear before them that night when a Board meeting would be held. Young as I was the seriousness with which my conduct was being regarded gave me a feeling of the ridiculous. I appeared before the Board, and mustered as much of an appearance of penitence as I could manage. I was gravely admonished, and informed that the Board would take my case into consideration with any extenuating circumstances which might be put forward, and that sentence would be promulgated in due course. My mother defended me, as mothers will, and told a member of the Board who lived opposite to us that it was a pity that a lot of men supposed to be intelligent had no more sense than to spend their time on such a silly business. My mother always had a fondness for mischievous lads. I have often heard her say: "I reckon nowt of these quiet 'uns. They'll never mak' owt aht. Give me a lad wi' some life and spirit in him. He'll get on in t' world." I don't think my mother's intervention in this affair helped me very much, but at any rate it relieved her feelings. A few days later I received the sentence passed upon me, which was that I be suspended from the service of the Board for fourteen days. I did not mind this at all. The weather was fine, and it was more agreeable to spend my time in the woods and on the moors. I returned at the end of a fortnight, but to safeguard Little Phineas from further outrage my class was put into the main room where I was under the eye of the master. The pupil-teacher in those days had a hard time of it. He had to take charge of a class for all the school hours. He had to be at school every morning at seven o'clock for instruction from the headmaster, and was given home lessons which occupied him all the evening. After the incident of Little Phineas I must have settled down and given no occasion for further complaint about my conduct, for I cannot remember that any further regrettable incident marred my career as an embryo schoolmaster. Three years later, however, circumstances over which I had no control arose which cut short my career as a pupil-teacher, and deprived the scholastic profession of my services. I have already reflected on the fact that events which at the time appear trivial often turn the course of our lives. If the firm by whom my father and sisters were employed had not become bankrupt, I should have been a schoolmaster, spending my life in the, to me, uncongenial work of teaching. It is a curious thing when you think about it that my future should have been shaped by the misfortunes of a firm with which I had nothing to do. And many people's lives are determined by happenings of an accidental nature.

The closing of the mill necessitated my parents' removal from the village. At that time the town of Nelson, five miles over the Lancashire border, then little more than a village, was attracting people from the West Riding, where the woollen trade was very depressed. I was taken there by my parents, and my school days came to an end. I was then fifteen years old. I had acquired a sound elementary education. I had a good knowledge of arithmetic, grammar, geography, history, elementary mathematics, a fair acquaintance with English literature, some slight knowledge of Latin, and enough French to read and write a letter. The problem of finding me something to do in Nelson at once arose. I had no desire to return to teaching. My father had the idea that I should make a lawyer, but the family means were not likely to run to that. He took me to see a local solicitor, who put an end to all ambitions in that direction by telling us that it would cost £2,000. My father would have been prepared to spend the few hundred pounds he had saved, but £2,000 was beyond the means of a poor weaver. This lawyer had some reason for discouraging us for I know now that he greatly exaggerated the cost. I eventually settled down to a job in an insurance company's office. It was a very good job. My wages were good and the hours were short. My life for the next few years was uneventful. Nelson was a hot-bed of Radicalism. The voteless condition of the working men made them the more determined politicians. Although still in my teens, I was a very keen politician, and never missed a meeting held in the district. I remember, when the House of Lords suspended the County Franchise Bill, walking in a procession holding aloft a banner with the words: "Down with the House of Lords" inscribed upon it. That was fifty years ago, and the House of Lords is still like Johnny Walker. It has not been my lot to help in "ending" this archaic institution, so I have made my personal contribution to "mending" it! At the Election of 1884, my father, who had been a keen politician all his life, was first entitled to vote when he was fifty-five years of age. Since then, by successive extensions of the franchise, the electorate has increased from three million to twenty-six million. It was about this time that I was first introduced to the Protectionist controversy. It had been "dead and damned" for forty years when a Nelson manufacturer made an effort to resurrect it. He was Mr. W. Farrer Ecroyd, a member of an old Liberal and Quaker family, who had become a Churchman and a Conservative. He became MP for Preston, and raised the question of Protection in many able speeches in the House. At that time there were too many people still living who knew from personal sufferings the evils of Protection, so Mr. Ecroyd hid this advocacy of the old Protection under the attractive name of Fair Trade and Reciprocity. Mr. Ecroyd's campaign fizzled out, but when Mr. Joseph Chamberlain revived it under the name of Tariff Reform twenty years later he often paid a tribute to Mr. Ecroyd's earlier efforts. My introduction to Mr. Ecroyd's policy came about in this way. He addressed a meeting on the subject in Nelson. I well remember his arguments, later so familiar in the speeches of Protectionists. He himself was in the Bradford light dress trade, and he gave a gloomy account of the way it was being ruined by French competition. He claimed that a duty of thirty shillings a piece was necessary to enable the Bradford manufacturers to meet the competition of their French rivals. The sequel to his address was crushing. When question time came there rose one Samuel Smith, himself in the same trade. "Mr. Ecroyd", he said, "tells us that he is being undersold by the French by thirty shillings a piece. If an English manufacturer is now making a profit of four pounds a piece couldn't he meet French competition by being content with a profit of fifty shillings a piece?" Mr. Ecroyd replied that if he were making a profit of four pounds a piece he could well afford to do so. Mr. Samuel Smith was ready with his retort. "It's no use Mr. Ecroyd trying to bluff me. I will give him chapter and verse about Nelson manufacturers who are today selling pieces in the Bradford market at four pounds profit."

Mr. Ecroyd said it was no use continuing the discussion, and the meeting closed. This was my first experience of a controversy in which I was destined to take a prominent part.

I was not so absorbed in politics in my young days as to be indifferent to my future. I was not content to be a clerk in an insurance office all my days. I began to look round. Somebody called my attention to the possibilities of the Civil Service. I looked up the examination papers. The Excise Service seemed to me to be within my educational attainments. I rubbed up my school knowledge, which had become rusty from four or five years of neglect, and passed the examination. I was first sent to Liverpool to be initiated into the mysteries of gauging and surveying breweries and distilleries. At the end of six weeks I was called before the Collector, a nice old man with a long white beard, and examined on my proficiency. I satisfied him that I was competent to assess the amount of duty a brewer or distiller should pay, and then received my parchment commission as a "gauger and surveyor of Inland Revenue". I was put to temporary work in the Tax Office, where I first learnt the difference between Schedules A and D. I little dreamt then that the day would come when I should have the unwelcome task of fixing the rates of Income Tax. Verily we never know what is in store for us! I much enjoyed my six months' stay in Liverpool, it is a city which possesses every attraction. It had Free Libraries, a fine Art Gallery, ran courses of scientific and literary Public Lectures and excellent Concerts. I was particularly interested in the theatre in those young days for I had ambitions to become an actor, and at one time seriously thought of running away from home to go on the stage. Only my ignorance of how to get into the profession saved me from carrying out my desire. My first appointment was to Aberdeen Revenue Collection. Nothing could have suited me better. I had never been fifty miles away from home. I had revelled in Scott's novels. From the pages of his romances I had pictured a Scotland of "wild heath and shaggy wood, of mountain and of flood" and of redhaired kilted outlaws. I had my first glimpse of Scotland from the windows of a railway carriage on a dull winter morning. I can well recall my sense of disappointment when I saw a country not half so beautiful as our own Airedale. My disappointment had deepened when I got to Aberdeen and I had not seen one kilt and only three redheads! The Orkney Islands are attached to Aberdeen for revenue purposes, and I spent two years in these regions. These years were among the happiest of my life. I had always a liking for out-of-the-way places, and the Orkneys gratified me in that respect to my heart's content. My revenue work carried me all over the islands, which provide the zoologist and the archaeologist with abundant material of interest. On every island there are Picts' houses, Runic inscriptions, and other relics of a prehistoric age, and the antiquarian can explore ruined castles, palaces and churches, each with a not inglorious past. The winters, too, had their attractions. There was a certain fascination in being, through stormy weather, shut off for days from communication with the outside world. This isolation throws the inhabitants on their own resources. The Orcadians do know how to be sociable. Dances, concerts and parties make the long winter nights pass pleasantly. We formed a Dramatic Society, and I made something of a reputation as an amateur actor. The local newspaper was quite eloquent about my performances. I left Orkney with real regret, and I shall always retain the happiest memories of the days I spent in these entrancing islands among the descendants of "the yarls and vikings who of old went forth under the raven banner of the North to fill the Southern Seas with wondering dread". I spent a couple of years in the city of Aberdeen. I was not then in the least interested in Socialism. Indeed, I doubt if I knew of the existence of the Socialist movement. There must have been a small Socialist organisation in Aberdeen at that time, for I remember, rather dimly, strolling into a small hall attached to a restaurant in Castle Street where a meeting was being held. The speaker was a short, burly man with a big, bushy beard, who spoke with a foreign accent. I learnt afterwards that he was Prince Kropotkin, a Russian exile, though at the time the name conveyed nothing to me. His address was on the philosophic basis of Anarchism, and so far as I can remember it advanced the arguments which he elaborated later in his great work Mutual Aid. But what I remember most clearly about this meeting was the audience, who seemed to me a queer-looking lot. They were mostly long-haired, unkempt and collarless. Years after, when I got to know some of these early Socialists, I understood. They were in revolt against all conventionalities and they regarded white collars, cropped hair and clean shaving as marks of bourgeois respectability. After this period in Aberdeen

I was moved south. Nothing noteworthy occurred during the remainder of the years I spent in the Revenue service, except an incident which is interesting because of the persons who were associated with it. One day I was strolling over Salisbury Plain on business bent when I heard shooting in the distance. I went in the direction of the sound, and came upon a partridge shooting-party. I asked to see their licences, and four out of the five members of the party were without. It turned out to be Mr. Walter Long's party. At that time Mr. Long was Financial Secretary to the Treasury in the Conservative Government of the day. It was not a very comfortable situation for Mr. Long, holding that position, to be discovered leading a party who were evading the Revenue law. He was terribly annoyed, and threatened to report me to the Chairman of the Board of Inland Revenue! The outcome was that the delinquents appeared later in the police court and were fined £5 each. Instead of receiving a reprimand from the Chairman, the Board made me a present of five pounds for my zeal. Over twenty years later this incident had its reverberations in the House of Commons. To relieve the tedium of an all-night sitting, my Parliamentary colleague, Mr. W. G. Anderson, to whom I must have told the story, related it. Mr. Walter Long was in charge of the Bill under discussion, and to my amazement he remembered the incident and had somehow for long known I was the person who had hauled his friends before the magistrates. He treated Mr. Anderson's disclosure with good humour, and said that he was annoyed with me, not for discovering that his friends had no licences, but because I had disturbed the birds! Strange things happen in the world, but I little thought when I first encountered Mr. Walter Long on Salisbury Plain that we should meet again as fellow-members in the House of Commons.

I enjoyed the years of my time in the Civil Service. The work was congenial. I should have been happy to spend my life in that occupation. The pay was poor in my days, but there were prospects of steady advancement to a man of capacity. The attraction of the Civil Service to a man without much ambition, and who is content with a moderate income, is the security of the employment. I seemed to be settled in life when again the fate which moves in a mysterious way ordained a change, which eventually brought me into the turbulent waters of politics where I have been tossed about for the last forty years. My father died in 1889 at sixty years of age. He died, as most of us would prefer to die, very suddenly. He had not been well for some weeks, but there did not appear to be anything serious the matter with him. He woke up during the night, gurgled, and died without speaking. Shortly after his death my mother went back to live in Ickornshaw. My sisters had married, and there was nothing to prevent her from going back to her old home, her old friends, and the chapel to which she was devotedly attached. My parents had always been thrifty, and she had managed to save enough to keep her in the modest comfort which satisfied her needs. Two years later I suffered a misfortune which eventually compelled my retirement from the Civil Service. When stationed at Plymouth I met with a slight accident. At first it seemed nothing serious, and the later developments were due to neglect. I had always been healthy and active, and I thought the trouble would pass away. An acute inflammation of the spinal cord supervened, and left me with the loss of the free use of my legs. I returned home to my mother. The idea that I was to be permanently crippled never entered my mind. In a little time I improved so far as to be able to walk laboriously with the aid of a stout stick. I found that walking was good for me. In all sorts of weather I hobbled through the lanes and over the hillsides of the Yorkshire parish. After a time I became convinced that full recovery was not likely to come. It is strange but true that this conviction brought neither grief nor despondency. I calmly resigned myself to what could not be helped. For two years my position in the Civil Service was kept open for my return. At the end of that time when it was evident I should never fully recover the use of my legs I was retired, to the regret of my superiors. How little one can forecast the future. Neither they nor I ever dreamt that in thirty years from that time I should be the political head of the State Department in which I had served for a time in the humblest position. I now began to think what I should do to earn a living. My material wealth consisted not in abundance of riches, but in the fewness of my wants. I might have settled down, with plenty of excuse in my condition, to an uneventful life in this quiet village, earning enough for my modest needs by occasional contributions to periodicals. But I had no inclination to waste my life, so I turned to an old love. I had kept up my education during my years in the Civil Service, so I began to read for the law examinations with the idea of going to the Bar. But that was not to be. I was caught up in a movement which was to absorb my interest and activities for the rest of my life.

Chapter Two

My Early Socialist Days

Amid all the political excitement aroused by the propaganda of the Independent Labour Party [founded at Bradford in January 1893], it was impossible for anyone interested in politics to remain unaffected by it. Isolated as I was in my remote village, my knowledge was derived from newspaper reports. But an opportunity soon presented itself to me of taking sides in the controversy. The Liberal Party in the village were very excited by what was going on, particularly by the I.L.P. attacks on the Liberal Party. Assuming that I should be in opposition to the new movement, being known as a good Liberal, I was invited by the local Liberal Club to speak on Socialism. I was wise enough to realise that I ought to know something about the subject ere I ventured to speak upon it. I began to read up the question of Socialism. I had all my time free, but I had little money to buy books. I first obtained a copy of Kirkup's *Inquiry into Socialism*. This was a fair and impartial statement of Socialism written by one who was sympathetic, but not an adherent. The reading of this work showed me that Socialism was not the stupid and unscientific thing it was represented to be by its opponents. I was not so much converted to Socialism by the book as clarified. I found in Socialism ideas and aims which I had for a long time held in a vague and indefinite form. My interest in the question had been keenly aroused. I was fervently anxious to study the subject fully. I sold two hundred volumes of literature I had accumulated, and bought books on Socialism. It was a revelation to me to discover that there was such a mass of literature on the subject, both American and English. I collected quite a library of old Radical and Socialist books and periodicals and pamphlets dating from the days of Hunt and Owen down to modern times. I obtained copies of all the early publications of the Social Democratic Federation and the Socialist League, and reports of the public debates on Socialism between Hyndman and Bradlaugh, and Hyndman and Henry George, and the famous four nights' debate between Annie Besant and Foot. All these publications I devoured with avidity, and in time became saturated with Socialist teaching. But, if I may say so, I owed most of my grasp of Socialism to thinking out these problems for myself. I used to lie awake for hours at night turning over the problems and trying to find the weak places in the solution until I felt assured the case was invulnerable. While I am on this subject of Socialist literature, I may make a confession which most Socialists would make if they had the courage to do so. I have never read Karl Marx. I have read many synopses of his teaching, and that has been quite enough for me. I have met a few men who claim to have read and studied the three huge volumes of *Das Kapital*, but the fact that they were still alive makes one inclined to cast some doubt upon their claim. Neither Keir Hardie nor William Morris derived their Socialism from Karl Marx. My late comrade, Bruce Glasier, in his fascinating book on *William Morris and the Early Days of the Socialist Movement*, relates an incident which shows how little materialistic philosophy and abstruse economic theories have done to inspire Socialist teaching. At a meeting addressed by William Morris in Glasgow he was asked: "Does Comrade Morris accept Marx's theory of value?" Morris' reply was emphatic, and has passed into the records of the movement as one of the best remembered of his sayings: "I am asked if I believe in Marx's theory of value. To speak quite frankly, I do not know what Marx's theory of value is, and I'm damned if I want to know." Then he added: "Truth to say, my friends, I have tried to understand Marx's theory, but political economy is not in my line, and much of it appears to me to be dreary rubbish. But I am, I hope, a Socialist none the less. It is enough political economy for me to know that the idle class is rich and the working class is poor, and that the rich are rich because they rob the poor. That I know because I see it with my eyes. I need read no books to convince me of it. And it does not matter a rap, it seems to me, whether the robbery is accomplished by what is termed surplus value, or by means of serfage or open brigandage. The whole system is monstrous and intolerable, and what we Socialists have got to do is to work together for its complete overthrow, and for the establishment in its stead of a system of co-operation where there shall be no masters or slaves, but where everyone will live and work jollily together as neighbours and comrades for the equal good of all. That, in a nutshell, is my political economy and my social democracy."

I have given this rather long extract because no words could better express the spirit and the aim of the early Socialist movement in Great Britain. It derived its inspiration far more from the Sermon on the Mount than from the teachings of the economists. Mr. A. E. Fletcher, who was editor of the *Daily Chronicle* in the nineties of the last century, and who was later a Socialist candidate for Glasgow, records an incident which shows the religious background of the Labour movement in those days. It happened during the miners' lockout in 1893. The police were informed that there was the likelihood of a riot in a Yorkshire mining village. A large body of police were hurried to the place. What did they find? There was a long procession of locked-out miners, not drawn up in battle array, but slowly wending their way to a meeting in the Methodist Chapel, and as they went along they were sending up to Heaven's throne the words of that grand old hymn:

"O God, our help in ages past,
Our hope for years to come…"

Oh that the Socialist movement of today could recapture the spiritual exaltation and religious faith of those early days!

I am afraid I have wandered far away from the invitation of the Cowling Liberals to address them. The outcome of this preparatory reading was that I gave my lecture; but, instead of its being the denunciation of Socialism which had been expected, it was an exposition and defence of Socialism. My chairman was the man who had conveyed to me the invitation to give the lecture, and at the end he professed his conversion to Socialism, though I am afraid he backslided later when I began to attack the Liberal Party. My lecture brought the discovery that there were a number of young fellows in the village who had been in the habit of surreptitiously going down to Keighley to attend Socialist meetings. There they had heard Ben Tillett and Tom Mann, and other fiery evangelists of the new gospel. Now they came into the open. My mother's cottage became the headquarters of the rebels. We used to meet every evening and talk of the "wonderful days a' coming". The neighbours began to be curious about these nightly gatherings and questioned my mother as to what was being said and done. She replied that all the talk she heard was about how to do folks good and make the world better. It happened that these young fellows were the mainstay of the Liberal Club in the village, and the management were unwilling to alienate their financial support. So I was again invited to speak in the Club, and gave them a stronger dose of Socialism. It was not our Socialism to which these Liberals mainly objected, but to our attacks on the Liberal Party. An incident occurred which brought me into wider notoriety. A young University woman named Enid Stacy, who was a travelling propagandist for the I.L.P., came to lecture in Keighley. She gave an address on the relation of the drink question to the poverty problem. She took up the attitude, which was not a distinctly Socialist position but quite in harmony with the teaching of the old political economists, that as working-class expenditure on drink entered into their cost of living, a sudden abolition of the drink traffic would result in a reduction of wages. Her address led to a correspondence in the local paper, in which her argument was vigorously combatted by the temperance people. One of the correspondents cited the case of Cowling, which he alleged proved that teetotalism had greatly improved the condition of the people. I was brought into the controversy, and in a series of letters to the Local Press I gave a graphic account of the social conditions of the village. I maintained with all the zeal of the new convert to Socialism that teetotalism and thrift had not solved the poverty problem there. I wrote of the children being taken out of bed at half-past five on wild wintry mornings to work in factories; of mothers who worked in the factories taking out their babies to be nursed by a neighbour; of the unending work of these mothers, who, after the factory hours, did their baking, washing, cleaning and mending. I was not opposed to temperance, for I had seen how its practice had improved the social life of the village. My point was that under capitalism it was greatly to the benefit of the individual to spend his wages on useful things instead of upon drink, though temperance alone would not touch the root causes of low wages and poverty. The way I put the case in after years, when I often publicly discussed this question, was that drink is an aggravation of every social evil, and, in a great many cases, the prime cause of industrial misery and degradation. The economic waste of expenditure on drink lowers the standard of living and reduces a great many families to destitution, who, if their incomes were usefully spent, would enjoy a reasonable degree of comfort. Universal temperance would undoubtedly bring incalculable benefits and blessings, but so long as the social system is based upon exploitation the mass of the people will remain comparatively poor. A sober democracy is necessary to achieve the great task of social reconstruction.

The letters I contributed to the local press created a great sensation in the district, and led to enquiries as to the identity of the writer. It was disclosed that "he was a Socialist chap up in Cowling". This discovery led the Keighley Socialists to hunt me out, and to invite me to come and address one of their regular Sunday evening meetings. I went. It was a great occasion. I was hailed even by the Liberal Press as "A New Prophet". "Here at last," it said, "was a man who could expound the Socialist cause with dignity and yet with fervour, with moderation and yet with vigour." That meeting at Keighley, the first I had addressed away from home, will forever stand out in my memory. It was an inspiration. It was like a revival gathering. Socialism to those men and women was a new vision, a new hope of relief from the grinding toil and hard struggle with poverty which had been their lot. To me it was the opening of a campaign which during many years I was to carry on throughout the length and breadth of the land. The news of this "find" spread among the branches of the Independent Labour Party, and invitations to address meetings poured in upon me. A year later the General Election of 1895 occurred. The Keighley Parliamentary Division Labour Party were determined to run a candidate. They had neither organisation nor money; but their enthusiasm laughed at such obstacles. I was to be their candidate. The National Council of the Labour Party, with an equal disregard of practical politics, gave their assent. I made a tour of the constituency and was well received. But, fortunately, my native caution led me to appreciate the situation. I knew that the enthusiasm of public meetings, mostly composed of unenfranchised men and women, would not be translated into votes on Election Day. I knew the deep-seated hostility of the powerful Liberal Party in the constituency. A Party only two years old could not in that time expect to have changed the lifelong political views of a majority of the electors. So I continued the campaign up to nomination day, and then persuaded my committee to be satisfied for the present with the propaganda work we had done during the election, save the money we had collected for another time, and not proceed to nomination. The I.L.P., nationally, at this Election (1895) was in the same position in regard to organisation and finance as our local Party. The party had been greatly encouraged by three by-elections at which it had put forward candidates the year before. The results of these by-elections gave a great shock to the Liberal Party throughout the country. It was clear that a new and powerful competitor for the working-class vote had come into the political field. These results encouraged the I.L.P. to put forward 28 candidates at the General Election which followed in July 1895. All the candidates were defeated. They polled an average of 1,592 votes per candidate. Eight of them polled more than 2,000 votes each, and seven less than 500 each. Mr. Keir Hardie lost his seat to a Tory at West Ham, a result which was hailed with great rejoicing by the Liberal Press. Mr. Ramsay MacDonald, who stood as an I.L.P. candidate at this Election for Southampton, polled 867 votes. The total cost of these 28 contests was £5,600, an average of £200, the greater part of this expense going in meeting the Returning Officers' charges. The enthusiasts of the movement were disappointed with the results of this General Election. They had been encouraged to expect something better from the enthusiasm of the election meetings, which far exceeded that of other Parties. It must be remembered that the I.L.P. was attracting in the main the young men who were not yet voters. The party was not yet three years old. From its formation it had had to face the open and bitter hostility of the Press, the platform, and the public, with few honourable exceptions. Although unsuccessful at this Election, when all the circumstances are taken into account, the difficulty of weaning the electors from inherited party allegiance, it was a remarkable achievement to poll such a vote against both the old political parties with their organisations and financial resources.

In spite of the disappointment of the Election, the membership of the I.L.P. continued to grow. At the Annual Conference of the Party after the Election it was announced that 77 new branches had been formed during the year, bringing the total number up to 381. These branches were located mainly in the industrial centres of the North. Open-air meetings were held every Sunday in fine weather, and in winter, when the branch could afford it, inside meetings were arranged. It was the invariable custom to take collections at meetings, though in those early days the sum realised was seldom sufficient to pay the railway fare of the speaker. The deficiency had to be made up from the pockets of the members. The Party quickly developed a large number of local speakers. Many young men who were Nonconformist local preachers were attracted to the movement by the ethical appeal of Socialism. Their experience in speaking was a great help to the Party propaganda. Working men who had toiled all day at arduous work went out at nights into the streets to preach in their simple way the new gospel of emancipation. Men who had never before attempted public speaking were given courage and the gift of effective oratory by the new passion for social justice which consumed them. The movement was something new in politics. It was politics inspired by idealism and religious fervour. Though the older Trade Union officials were as bitterly opposed to the new Party as the Liberals, there were many of the younger officials of the unions who were ardent supporters of the I.L.P. These men did great service to the party in these early years. They not only worked for the Party inside the Trade Unions, but gave their weekends generously to speaking from the Socialist platform. Among the number were J. R. Clynes, Pete Curran, George N. Barnes, Ben Turner, James Sexton, Ben Tillett and Robert Smillie. In those early days of the I.L.P. one of its propagandists was Jim Connell, the author of the revolutionary song "The Red Flag". Connell was a great, big, broad-shouldered Irishman with a delightful brogue, standing considerably over six feet. He had an enormous moustache, dressed in an Inverness cloak and wore a big-brimmed slouch hat. In this attire, with a large red scarf, he made a striking and picturesque figure. Connell had written "The Red Flag" when a member of the S.D.F., and it was taken up by that organisation, but it was not sung to the tune Connell had intended. He wrote the words to go with the tune of "The White Cockade", but that was not very suitable. It went with a better swing to "Maryland" or "Tannenbaum", and that is the tune to which the words are now universally sung. Bernard Shaw has described "The Red Flag" as "the funeral march of a fried eel", but that is, perhaps, due to envy because he has never given the Socialist movement a revolutionary hymn! Before I leave "The Red Flag" I must anticipate an incident which happened thirty years after the days I have been describing. About the time of the General Strike of 1926 I was dining one evening with Lord Beaverbrook and a few others in his room at the Daily Express office. "The Red Flag" was mentioned, and I enquired if they had ever heard it. Not one had. So I offered to sing it for them. It happens that I have only two songs in my musical repertoire - "The Red Flag" and "On Ilkla moor ba'at 'at". I sang "The Red Flag", and Lord Beaverbrook was enthused by its revolutionary fervour. He would have me teach him the last verse and the chorus, and in a few minutes he had the words. Then he stood in the middle of the room, and with arm uplifted, with dishevelled hair and blazing eyes, he bellowed forth:

"With heads uncovered swear we all
To bear it onward till we fall;
Come dungeon dark or gallows grim
This song shall be our parting hymn."
"Then raise the scarlet standard high,
Within its shade we'll live and die;
Though cowards flinch and traitors sneer,
We'll keep the Red Flag flying here."

I quite expected to see the newspapers come out next morning with flaring headlines: "The Social Revolution Breaks Out". "Lord Beaverbrook leads the mob to the barricades singing 'The Red Flag'." But the walls of the room were sound proof!

After Hardie's defeat at West Ham he devoted himself to platform propaganda, editing his weekly paper *The Labour Leader* in railway trains and in the cottages of comrades. This is not the place in this volume to give an appreciation of Hardie's work. To him more than to any other individual the bringing of the British working classes to a consciousness of their own power is due. Like all pioneers, he suffered in his lifetime, especially in the early years of his public work, from misunderstandings, misrepresentation and persecution. It is impossible for those who have no personal knowledge of the early days of the Independent Labour Party to understand how bitter was the hostility by which it was assailed from every quarter, and especially by the old leaders of the Trade Unions. I remember Hardie saying to me that when he first entered the House of Commons as member for South-West Ham the only insulting language he received there was from Liberal-Labour members. Against Keir Hardie, as the outstanding figure of the new movement, this hostility was mainly directed. To a lesser degree every man and woman who joined the I.L.P. had to endure persecution and ostracism. This opposition had the effect of creating a bond of brotherhood between the members of the new Party, which was far more than a compensation for the sufferings inflicted by political opposition. Only those who had the glorious privilege of fighting in those days against formidable odds can ever understand the joy which comes from braving all things, enduring all things for a great vision and a great cause. In the years between 1895 and

1900 when he was out of the House of Commons, Hardie's picturesque figure became well known throughout Great Britain from his platform appearances. He had naturally, one would think, a strong physical constitution, but the work of those years undoubtedly undermined his strength. At fifty he looked like an aged man. He died before he was sixty.

In the early years of the I.L.P. Tom Mann became General Secretary of the Party. He was at that time a well-known figure in the Labour movement. He had come into prominence in connection with the Dockers' Strike. He was the most volcanic speaker I have known, and a man of marvellous physical vigour. If Tom Mann had possessed one thing he lacked, namely, steadfastness of purpose, he would have been undoubtedly one of the most prominent men in the Labour Party of today. But he never could remain long associated with one movement. He had not the gift of settling down to one job and pursuing it to success. He was one of the most charming men personally I have known, kind-hearted and generous and tolerant. I never heard him speak an unkind word of anyone. He did not long remain Secretary to the I.L.P. His restless spirit kept him on the move. He left the I.L.P. to organise an international union of transport workers. After a short time he left that work to form a new union of unskilled workers in Great Britain. It would make a long list to give all the movements with which Tom Mann has been associated. At one time he was on the point of being ordained a clergyman of the Church of England, but he abandoned the idea, and took a public-house. That occupation he soon gave up, and went off to Australia, and became associated with the Syndicalist movement. He returned to England to carry on his Syndicalist propaganda, but his agitation met with no success. Later he drifted into the Communist Party. Having exhausted his association with every possible movement, there he has remained, but his influence had been destroyed by his lack of consistency. His life has been something of a tragedy, for there has been no man associated with the Labour and Socialist movements who could have rendered greater service to the working classes if he had possessed the essential gift of stability. The I.L.P. was fortunate in its early days in enlisting the services of a number of men and women of great ability who gave up promising careers to devote themselves to the Socialist movement. Prominent among these were three young University women whose names are still spoken of with affection akin to reverence by the older members of the Party. Their names were Enid Stacy, Caroline Martyn, and Katharine Conway. The Socialist movement in these days had nothing to offer these eager young women but a life of hardship and ill requited toil. Miss Stacy afterwards married a clergyman of the Church of England. She died shortly after. Her early death was, no doubt, brought about by the hardships she had to endure in the years in which she spent her days travelling from place to place and her nights addressing meetings in ill-ventilated rooms. Miss Caroline Martyn died after a few years of this work; but Miss Conway, who afterwards became Mrs. Bruce Glasier, still lives after forty years of active propaganda for Socialism. The husband of Miss Conway, Mr. Bruce Glasier, abandoned his profession as an architect to devote himself wholly to the Socialist movement, although it had nothing to offer him beyond the wages of an unskilled labourer. Mr. Glasier gave thirty years of his life to Socialist propaganda, and he died at an age when, in the natural course of events, many more years of activity might have been expected. Mr. Glasier was one of the most brilliant men I have ever had the pleasure of knowing, and as a conversationalist he surpassed any man of my acquaintance. He never received the popular recognition of his ability and services to which he was entitled. These are some of the men and women to whom the Labour Party of today owes a debt, the magnitude of which it does not realise. They were pioneers "who did their deeds and went away before the bright sun brought the day". But we, who knew their sacrifice and devotion, will always remember with gratitude the work they did.

After my debut at the Labour meeting in Keighley, I began to receive invitations to speak from branches of the Party in the West Riding and East Lancashire. When the places from which these invitations came were within easy travelling distance I accepted them; but when the requests became so numerous and from places a considerable distance away, it became a question of whether I should make up my mind to devote myself wholly to the work. My enthusiasm was unbounded, and my desire to serve the cause was intense. There were no financial attractions in making this decision. Up to that time I had taken no payment for my speaking services–not even my out-of-pocket expenses. I had saved a little money when in the Civil Service and was living on that. I was unmarried. There was just my mother and myself. We had a good cottage for an inclusive rent of 2s. 9d. a week, and we could live comfortably on a pound a week. But if I were to give my whole time to the Party I should have to accept some slight remuneration for my services. The charge usually made to branches for a lecturer was 5s. and travelling expenses, but I soon learnt from experience that the 5s. fee often went in necessary expenses beyond the railway fare. The usual thing was to take two meetings on Sunday, and one on each of three or four week-nights. This involved a good deal of travelling, and I find on referring to my engagement books that I seldom travelled less than 100 miles in the course of a week, and I often covered twice that distance. This went on for some years, during which I visited every part of Great Britain. As time went on the movement grew in strength, and correspondingly in financial resources. My popularity increased, and I was able to command large audiences, and branches with an eye to business had the temerity to make a charge for admission to my meetings. This was usually successful, and helped the finances of the local branch. For these meetings I raised my fee to 10s., but never during the ten years I was wholly engaged on this work did I average more than 30s. a week from it. But these were very happy days. It was a joy and an inspiration to meet the men and women of the movement who were so full of enthusiasm, who hoped that the cause for which they were giving their best would be realised in their time, or in their children's days. I usually was given hospitality by one of the comrades, and many touching evidences have I seen of the trouble they had taken to make me comfortable. Often the branch had difficulty in providing accommodation, for most of the members had no spare bed. In those days the branches were composed almost exclusively of working people. It was rare indeed to find a middle-class person associated with it. In those years of propaganda, constantly moving about among the branches, I was kept in close personal touch with the membership. I knew every branch of the Party, and it is hardly an exaggeration to say that I was personally known to all the members. I remember so well the happy times we used to have after a successful meeting when I met some of the active workers in the branch at the home of the comrade with whom I was staying. They listened to my stories of the progress of the movement in other parts of the country, and derived encouragement in their own difficulties and disappointments by the knowledge of the progress of the Party in other places. They were really poor, and what they gave to the movement involved real sacrifice on their part. There was little of the materialistic spirit in the Socialist movement in those days. Socialism to them was like a religion - the promise of a full spiritual life.

My experiences were often enlivened by incidents of a humorous character. My chairman was usually a local comrade who was quite unaccustomed to public speaking. It was the invariable practice at all our meetings to invite questions from the audience, and an inexperienced chairman would say at the conclusion of my address: "Well, now we are coming to the interesting part of the meeting. We are going to ask you to put questions to the speaker, and he will answer any questions you can put. What Liberals and Tories say is not open to question, but everything a Socialist says is open to question." I had an amusing experience when addressing an open-air meeting in Bradford. At question time a man would insist that I should give a simple "Yes" or "No" to his question. I pointed out that it was not always possible to do that. "Nonsense," he said, "I can do that." So I used the old chestnut on him and asked him to say "Yes" or "No" to this question: "Have you given up beating your wife?" I was surprised at the hilarity with which this was received by the audience. In the laughter the man slunk away. The chairman told me that the man, who was well known to the audience, had just come out of prison after doing fourteen days for ill-treating his wife. It is not often that a speaker unconsciously so effectively settles his hecklers. I met in my peregrinations many original and entertaining characters. One of them was a working man who lived near Bradford. His name was Johnny Coe. He used to say to me sometimes: "I have read about these old martyrs who went to the stake for their religion. I used to have my doubts about that, but since I became converted to Socialism I can understand it. I'd be willing to go to the stake for my Socialism." Johnny was a man who used to meet the speakers and take charge of them until the meeting was over. On one occasion he had to meet Mr. Fred Bramley, who was afterwards Secretary to the Trade Union Congress, but in those days was a humble Socialist propagandist. The place where Johnny Coe lived was called Wibsey, and Wibsey had a reputation among its neighbours for not being quite so smart as they were. So when Johnny Coe met Fred Bramley he gave him this admonition: "Now, look here, Fred. Tha' knaws they're an ignorant lot at Wibsey, so don't be trying any of that scientific Socialism. We want no Karl Marx and surplus values and that sort of stuff. Make it plain and simple. Tha' can put in a long word now and then so as to make them think tha' knaws a lot, but keep it simple, and then when tha'rt coming to t' finishing up tha' mun put a bit of 'Come to Jesus' in like Philip does." That was Johnny's way of describing my perorations.

I had, as I have said, ten years of this continuous propaganda work before I entered Parliament. When I look back on these years and recall the hardships I endured I marvel how I stood it. I walked with difficulty, with the aid of a stick, every step a deliberate effort, carrying my bag in the other hand. I made all the journeys alone. I spoke in practically every large town in Great Britain, in most of them very often, and in hundreds of smaller towns and villages. I often had to travel long distances between meetings, and frequently was unable to get food between breakfast-time and evening, except sometimes a railway refreshment cup of tea and a sandwich. Cabs were a luxury we seldom could afford, and I usually had to walk considerable distances to and from the meetings. In later years I did my propaganda under more comfortable conditions. My meetings then brought a financial profit to the branches, and they could afford to pay me more liberal expenses. It was the usual thing for our meetings in summer to be held in the open air. I liked speaking in the open air. If a speaker has knowledge of how to use his voice open-air speaking is a healthy exercise. During each summer I addressed on an average five meetings a week, and I went through the season without the slightest hoarseness or voice strain. The secret is in never shouting, always keeping the voice under control, and especially making a pause of a few seconds between each sentence. I have known many of our open-air speakers who have completely ruined their voices by not practising these little arts. From my experience of years of open-air speaking I would like to pay a compliment to the English summer. I don't think that in ten years I had to abandon half a dozen meetings through rain. Often, of course, there was rain, but seldom enough to prevent the meeting from being held.

Open-air speaking requires a different style and technique from indoor meetings. Outside, you must be more familiar with the audience, more conversational, not so serious, and must introduce more jokes and funny stories. Inside, you can argue, present a complete case. You know that your audience has come to hear you, whereas in the open air you have largely a scratch crowd which has to be held by arousing and keeping their interest. I always tried to adapt my addresses to the type of audience and to the local conditions. When breaking new ground for Socialism I followed Johnny Coe's advice and made it plain and simple. When speaking in towns where a lot of Socialist propaganda had been done, I dealt with special aspects of the subject, such as "The Evolution of Socialism", "Socialism and the Individual", "The Land Question", "The Moral Basis of Socialism", "How Socialism can be Established". I always encouraged questions at the end of the address, and often found, as the chairman put it, that this was the most interesting part of the meeting. There never was any interruption at my Socialist meetings, and the audiences were invariably of the "enquiring mind" type.

About 1899 the members of the Keighley Labour Party were anxious that I should come to live in Keighley in order to contest seats for the Town Council and the School Board, but mainly to act as editor of a local Labour paper they were running. My mother and I, therefore, removed to Keighley. I stood for the Town Council and the School Board at the first opportunity, and was elected to both positions. I enjoyed this work very much, and I often thought, after I got into Parliament and saw how few were the opportunities of a private member to do any practical work, that service on a local governing body was more useful than very largely wasting one's time walking through the Division Lobby at the behest of a Party Whip.

I had some rather interesting experiences in connection with my running the Labour Party's weekly journal. I may say that I undertook this work for the handsome remuneration of 8s. a week, which was paid very indifferently. The paper had a circulation of about 5,000 copies a week. I wrote practically all the matter myself, so it kept me fairly well occupied between my lecture engagements. I hope there is no file of this journal in existence apart from my own, for I am sure that a good deal of the matter I wrote was more entertaining than instructive. I was in the habit of writing reports of the meetings of the local bodies in a somewhat satirical vein. On one occasion at a meeting of the Town Council I attended, the Mayor, in reply to some aspersions that had been cast upon his accuracy, appealed to any man in the Council who had known him from childhood to say if he had ever told a lie. I felt that plain prose was not capable of doing justice to this modern George Washington, so, for the first time in my life, I burst into poetry, and wrote a poem on "The Man who Never told a Lie". It created quite a sensation; and the Mayor died shortly after. My constant lecturing had made me well known in the I.L.P., and in 1898 I was elected to the National Administrative Council. This began over twenty years' official connection with the Party.

Chapter Three

The Formation of the Labour Party

It had always been the aim of Keir Hardie to form the Trade Unions into an independent political Party in alliance with other democratic bodies. As far back as 1887 he raised this question at the Trade Union Congress. He was known then as a Socialist firebrand, and the Congress gave him little support. The Socialists then organised to capture the Congress, and the next year they nearly carried a motion refusing electoral support to any but Socialist candidates. The following year a motion by the Social Democrats was actually carried by a big majority, pledging the Congress to give support only to candidates who stood for the collective ownership and control of the means of production, distribution and exchange. I well remember the sensation the passing of this resolution made throughout the country. The Socialists thought they had captured the Trade Unions, and the plutocrats believed that the Social Revolution was at hand. It all came to nothing. It was an illustration of the practical worthlessness of Conference resolutions passed by engineering a vote which has not behind it the support of rank-and-file opinion. How often have I seen this happen. My experience of Conferences has taught me to attach very little importance to their resolutions. Of the hundreds of resolutions I have seen passed by Labour Conferences outlining a drastic programme of reform, I can hardly call to mind one which has had any practical result. Conferences will talk; let them talk. Governments, including Labour Governments, dispose of Conference resolutions. There is all the difference in the world between the licence and irresponsibility of a Conference and the position of a Government which has to face practical difficulties and knows that no Government can move far ahead of public opinion. Nobody knows that better than members of the Labour Cabinets. The rank and file of the Labour Party ought to have learnt that lesson by now. They have had enough experience of the futility of Conference resolutions. Every four years the Party is presented with a new programme, while not one item in the old one has been carried into effect.

We had the New Social Order, Labour and the Nation, and we are now being presented piecemeal with another more revolutionary than the last.

Keir Hardie had always regarded the I.L.P. as preparing the way for his aim of a political union of Socialists and the Trade Unions. From the formation of the I.L.P. in 1893 he had worked quietly to that end. The young and active members of the Trade Unions had become Socialists, and they were working in the Trade Union branches with the same object. By 1899 the time was considered ripe to test the Trade Union Congress on this issue. Accordingly the following resolution was put down on the Agenda of the Congress in the name of the Railway Servants Union. It is no secret now that the resolution was drafted by Keir Hardie. I quote it in full as a historic declaration:

"That this Congress, having regard to the decisions of former years, and with a view to securing a better representation of the interests of Labour in the House of Commons, hereby instructs the Parliamentary Committee to invite the co-operation of all Co-operative, Socialistic, Trade Union and other working-class organisations to jointly co-operate on lines mutually agreed upon in convening a special Congress of representatives from such of the above-named organisations as may be willing to take part to devise ways and means for the securing of an increased number of Labour Members in the next Parliament."

This resolution was carried by 546,000 votes to 434,000 against. The majority was small. The opposition realised that this question of Labour representation was now a practical issue. It will be noted that the terms of the resolution did not mention a separate Labour Party. It left that vaguely indefinite. But the delegates knew what was behind it. The real opposition, however, was to the operative part which instructed the Committee of the Congress to seek the co-operation of all Socialist, Co-operative, Trade Union, and other working-class organisations. The Trade Union Congress has always been an exclusive body, jealous of encroachments upon what it considers its own sphere, but always ready to encroach upon the provinces of other organisations. It was never more so than it is today. There is no political question upon which it does not feel required to express its views. This has been a bone of contention between the Trade Union Congress and the Labour Party ever since the Labour Party was formed. Attempts have been made to divide the functions of the two bodies without success. The Labour Party is not likely to quarrel with the

Trade Union Congress so long as the income of the Labour Party is derived from the Trade Unions. In accordance with the instructions of the Congress the Conference was called, and it met at the Memorial Hall, London, on the 27th February 1900. The three Socialist societies – the I.L.P., the Fabians and the Social Democratic Federation – were represented. The Trade Unions had 500,000 members represented, which was but a small proportion of the total Trade Union membership. I was present at the Conference representing the I.L.P. Other I.L.P. delegates were Keir Hardie, J. Ramsay MacDonald, F. W. Jowett and J. Burgess. This was the first time I had come in contact with the Trade Union leaders. They struck me as being a very commonsense lot, probably quite competent at their own job, but hardly the kind of men you would expect to find at the barricades when the Social Revolution came. Among the platform men was big, genial Will Thorne, whose intervention in the debates I remember chiefly because of a remark he made, that they only kept men in the Unions by putting the screw upon them. I met John Burns for the first time at this Conference. He was a delegate of the Engineers' Society. By this time Burns had become quite a respectable politician. He was living down his Socialist and Trafalgar Square reputation. His relations with the Socialists were very bitter, and his denunciations of the movement for an independent Labour Party lacked nothing of the vigour which he could command. He was soon on his feet. A resolution had been moved that "the Conference was in favour of the working classes being represented in the House of Commons by members of the working classes as being most likely to be sympathetic with the aims and demands of the Labour Movement". To this an amendment was moved by Mr. George Barnes of the Engineers' Society to the effect that the Conference was in favour of working-class opinion being represented in Parliament by men sympathetic with the aims of the Labour Movement and whose candidatures were promoted by one of the bodies included in the organisation about to be formed. John Burns made a forceful protest against the narrow and exclusive proposal that working men only could represent the working classes. He was "getting tired of working-class boots, working-class trains, working class houses and working-class margarine. The Labour and Social Movement should not be prisoners to class prejudice, but should consider parties and policies apart from class organisations". There was a good deal of sound sense in these observations, and the Conference emphatically rejected the proposal that only working men should be regarded as competent to represent the working class.

An attempt was made by the Social Democrats to commit the Conference to a declaration that the new Party should be based on the recognition of the class war, with Socialism as its ultimate aim. This was an illustration of the tactlessness of the Social Democrats, which explained the reason for the failure of their propaganda to make any impression on public opinion. At this stage to commit the Trade Unions to an extreme Socialist programme would have made the co-operation of the bodies represented at the Conference impossible. Keir Hardie, with a true appreciation of the situation, and of the importance of carrying the Trade Unions by stages to the ultimate goal, moved on behalf of the I.L.P. an amendment to the effect that the Conference "approve the formation of a distinct Labour Group in Parliament whose policy must embrace a readiness to co-operate with any Party engaged in promoting legislation in the direct interests of Labour, and an equal readiness to oppose any Party promoting legislation of an opposite tendency". Keir Hardie's amendment was passed unanimously, but not before John Burns had intervened to tell the Conference that such a group of Labour members as it was proposed to form already existed. "They had not called themselves Independent, they had not worn Trilby hats and red ties, but they had done the work."

It was decided that the name of the new organisation should be The Labour Representation Committee. An Executive of twelve was appointed, seven representing the Trade Unions, two the I.L.P., two the Social Democratic, and one the Fabian Society. The large representation of the Socialist bodies was an unexpected act of generosity on the part of the Trade Unions, who had a membership of over half a million represented at the Conference compared with only twenty-three thousand membership of the three Socialist Societies. The Socialists received further recognition by the appointment of Mr. J. Ramsay MacDonald as Secretary. There was no Trade Union nominee for the position. Mr. MacDonald's appointment came as a surprise. At that time he was little known. I remember the circumstances very well. There was no interest in the election. In fact the post went a-begging, two other persons having refused it before Mr. MacDonald was nominated. The Conference did not realise the importance of the position in the hands of an energetic man. It considered the post as merely a clerical one. Mr. MacDonald did not so regard it. He saw the possibilities of the new movement, and set to work to organise it. He freely gave his time and energy to the work. He had one great advantage. An ordinary Trade Unionist would never have made a success of the task. He would have been looked upon by his fellow Trade Unionists as one of themselves, and would have been treated by them with that lack of respect which equals show to one another. But Mr. MacDonald was not one of themselves. They regarded him as a superior person and their "inferiority complex" treated him as such.

What did this Conference actually accomplish? It agreed that it was desirable to set up a Central Committee to which Trade Unions and Socialist Societies could affiliate. It was not intended that this Committee should itself promote Parliamentary candidatures. That was left to the separate organisations affiliated to the Committee, who would be responsible for the election expenses and for the support of the candidate if elected. The Committee should endorse the candidatures thus promoted. The members elected should agree to join a Labour Group in Parliament for the purposes stated in the resolution already quoted. The Committee was to be financed by the payment of an annual subscription of 10s. per thousand members of the societies affiliating. It will be seen that at this time there was no idea of forming a Labour Party. The name of the new organisation and its declared purpose show that to be the case. The far-sighted promoters of this new body hoped that a Labour Party would grow out of this timid beginning, but the rank and file of the Trade Unions, and more particularly the leaders, needed a lot of political education before they grasped that possibility. The new movement did not begin auspiciously. At the end of the first year only 40 Trade Unions out of about 1,200 then existing had affiliated, with a membership of 353,000. The three Socialist bodies had joined up. The great organisations of the miners and the textile workers stood aloof, looking on the new movement with suspicion and regarding it with undisguised hostility. The first Annual Conference was held in Manchester in February 1901, and I well remember the feeling of despondency which prevailed. It looked as if this new effort was going to share the fate of previous attempts to secure the direct representation of Labour. During the previous year (1900) a General Election had taken place. It came before the new Committee had had time to get into its work. The I.L.P. had nine candidates in the field, and the Trade Unions four. Of these only two were successful: Keir Hardie at Merthyr and Mr. Richard

Bell at Derby. The votes of the I.L.P. candidates showed a remarkable advance over those reached at the previous General Election in 1895, the average vote being 4,030 compared with 1,572. The large vote polled by the I.L.P. candidates is all the more striking when it is remembered that the General Election was fought during the Boer War. That shameful episode in our history has been driven out of memory by the infinitely more awful tragedy of the Great War. The I.L.P. was the backbone of the opposition to the Boer War. It incurred the treatment which is always meted out to those who take the unpopular side when passions are excited. I think the Jingo spirit was more rampant at this time than during the Great War. Meetings, public and private, were broken up; peace advocates assaulted and their houses and business premises wrecked; editors of Liberal newspapers who deemed it their duty to oppose the war were dismissed; Christian ministers were hounded from their pulpits for daring to affirm that Christianity and a war of aggression were incompatible. It was a pathetic thing to see a great nation in such a state of terror because a small State of farmers was gallantly defending its independence against the might of the British Empire. It was in such a national temper as this that the General Election of 1900 was held. Keir Hardie was again the solitary independent Labour member of the new Parliament. He used to describe himself as the United Labour Party. His return raised a financial problem for the National Council of the I.L.P. There was no payment of members of parliament from the National Exchequer in those days. Hardie had no Trade Union behind him, and the newly formed Labour Representative Committee had no funds. The National Council of the I.L.P. set to work to raise by a private appeal a sum of £150 a year towards his support. Hardie had no private means. He was running *The Labour Leader*, but that was a burden rather than a source of income. I have a letter from him written to me at this time in which he puts his financial position frankly before me. He paid fourteen shillings a week for rooms in London, his food and other expenses he put at a pound a week, secretarial help and postage cost him fifteen shillings. In addition he had to provide for his home in Scotland, and for clothing and railways fares. To meet these necessary expenses, which his £150 allowance was far short of meeting, he was obliged to take meetings at weekends and almost nightly during the Parliamentary recess. These were the circumstances of the first Independent Labour M.P.

Chapter Four

My First Parliamentary Contests

It was at this General Election of 1900 that I first became a Parliamentary candidate. The National Council of the I.L.P. were anxious that I should contest a constituency where there seemed to be a reasonable chance of success. So they got in contact with the local branch in Blackburn, which on the face of things seemed to be one of the most hopeless constituencies in the country. I was well known to the members of the party in Blackburn, where I had frequently addressed meetings on the Market Square. There was no electoral organisation in the borough, but the Socialists had obtained some success in contesting the local elections, and they had at that time four representatives on the Town Council. The constituency had the reputation of being invincibly Conservative. It was a two-member constituency, and had never returned a Liberal member except once some twenty years before; and the success of the Liberal candidate on that occasion – he was a local man – was not due to his politics, but to the fact that his dog had just before the Election won the Waterloo Cup! At the time of my entry into the field the prospect of making a successful inroad into the Tory predominance was so hopeless that the Liberals had given up the fight. It was in this unpromising field that I made my first effort to enter the House of Commons. I was adopted in July 1900, when it appeared that the General Election would not long be delayed. I waited until the holiday season was over before appearing in the constituency in the capacity of Parliamentary candidate.

On the 10th September I held my first Election meeting. At that time Mr. A. G. Gardiner, the well-known journalist who later became editor of the *Daily News*, was on the staff of the Blackburn Liberal Newspaper. Mr. Gardiner wrote up my election campaign for his paper; and, in order to protect myself against the charge of immodesty, I am going to call upon Mr. Gardiner very largely to describe this extraordinary Election. My adoption meeting was held in the largest hall in the town. It was crowded and unanimous. Describing this meeting Mr. Gardiner wrote: "A remarkable impression was made by the Socialist candidate for Blackburn at his first meeting. Mr. Snowden, whether one agrees with him or not, is a man who cannot be ignored. He spoke for an hour and a half without note or pause, and the speech merely as an oratorical triumph was the best deliverance heard in Blackburn for a long time past. It is not probable that he will enter Parliament as the representative of Blackburn, for Blackburn does not like strong meat, but that he will be heard up at Westminster is highly probable." The Election came within a fortnight, and I at once began my campaign by addressing ward meetings. The impression made by my first meeting had spread throughout the borough, and from the beginning of the campaign my meetings were crowded and enthusiastic. The two sitting members for the constituency were both local men, and one of them – Sir Harry Hornby – was a member of a family which for long had been popular in the borough. Neither of these gentlemen had made any impression on the House of Commons, Sir Harry, I believe, never having so much as asked a question. But that did not detract from their popularity in a borough where local connections were of more importance than political knowledge. As the contest proceeded the enthusiasm and the excitement increased. Near the end of the campaign Mr. Gardiner wrote:

"Whatever be the result of the present Election, the Snowden campaign will remain one of the most memorable events in the history of Blackburn. I can compare it to nothing but those tides of spiritual revivalism that periodically sweep over the land touching the emotions of the multitude to an ecstasy that is as poignant as it is unfortunately short-lived. Mr. Snowden's campaign has touched the lost chord in the heart of Blackburn, and the people have responded to the touch with unbounded enthusiasm to which in my experience neither here nor elsewhere offers any parallel. It is as though the sleepers had awakened, as though a new heaven and a new earth have dawned upon them, as though a great light has burst upon them, dazzling and blinding them. They crowd to Snowden's meetings, not as to a political gathering, but as to a revivalist mission. They tread lightly, sit mute, almost transfixed, rarely applaud until the close, when the enthusiasm breaks forth. They seem entranced like men silenced by the impact of great truths. Ridiculous, you say. Perhaps. And yet there is that about this gathering that refutes the sneer of the cynic. Never in the history of Blackburn has there been such a succession of political meetings, night after night, meetings crowded to the doors and overflowing with men, not loafers, not rag and bobtail, but sober, serious men from mill and workshop, forge and warehouse. They are the most significant gatherings I have ever witnessed. They have filled me with the sense of the gigantic power that lies dormant in these silent thousands. What is the secret of this new phenomenon? A month ago Philip Snowden's name was practically unknown in Blackburn. I went to hear him for the second time on Tuesday night. In the meantime the snowball of his popularity had assumed gigantic proportions. The tale of his wondrous meetings, of the crowds that were present and of the crowds that were turned away, and of the speeches that he made and the enthusiasm they raised, had become the staple of conversation. In the light of developed events I went to take a second inventory of Philip Snowden, and my first impression was emphasised. I have said that Snowden's only stock-in-trade is himself. He has all the qualities that move great bodies of men. Personal magnetism, idealism, conviction, and a strong foundation of practical common sense. There is a further factor that is largely, perhaps chiefly responsible for the extraordinary influence that Mr. Snowden exercises. It is what I venture to call the spiritual quality of the man. He has touched politics with morality, and morality with religion, and has raised the whole subject to a plane above the normal littleness and screeching of Party warfare. Nor is there the faintest trace of portentousness or unreality in this. It rather permeates his speech than intrudes itself in definite phrase. It may be that Philip Snowden is only the comet of the season, a meteor flashing across the dark sky of Blackburn Toryism, but for the moment he is the most striking personality in Blackburn."

As the Election campaign went on, the hope with which we started of polling a moderately good vote gave place to a feeling that a miracle might happen, and we might be successful. Our meetings had shaken Toryism to its very foundations. By way of encouraging the Tory candidates, a speaker at one of their meetings said: "The Tory candidates would each receive 10,000 votes, and Mr. Philip Snowden perhaps 500." This immediately incited the audience to ridicule, and moved Sir Harry Hornby to jump up and declare: "Mr. Snowden will poll thousands of votes, and if we are over-confident we shall be beaten." We had not, as I have said, any electoral organisation, but voluntary workers flocked to the committee rooms. The Tories, on the other hand, had one of the best organisations in Lancashire. They relied for success on the local popularity of their candidates, and certainly not upon their public meetings, which were very thinly attended. The appeals they made to the electors were not on political but on local grounds. The following is a copy of an election bill widely posted on the hoardings: "Vote for men who have known you all their lifetime, and have contributed to almost everything in the town, from the boys' football and cricket clubs to bazaars of all denominations, and not for a youth of the romancing socialist type." A short time before this Election the two members had issued a statement regretting their inability to make any further contributions that year to football and cricket clubs and the like as they had contributed to 900 bodies within twelve months! The Liberals did not put forward a candidate. The local Liberal paper gave me strong support. The Liberals in the main supported my candidature, though not officially. There was no alliance between ourselves and the Liberals, though the absence of a Liberal candidate tended to identify my candidature with that Party. I made it quite clear during the contest that I was in no sense the candidate or the nominee of the Liberal Party. I appreciated support from all parties, but I wanted the support only of men who believed in me and would generally agree with me. If returned I should owe no allegiance to the Liberal Party. If I went to Parliament I should go independent of Liberal Party or Tory Party. I should go to champion the principles in which I believed against opposition from whatever quarter it came.

I did no personal canvassing during the Election. I never in all the elections I have fought, ever made a personal appeal to a voter to give me his vote. There came to my knowledge from our own canvassers a number of amusing experiences they encountered. A canvasser was trying to get the vote of a stubborn Tory. He would only repeat: "It's no use talking to me. I shall not vote for him." They had a parrot in the room, and after a repetition of this remark the parrot said: "Yah, do!" The wife turned round to her husband and said: "Just harken to t' parrot. It's more sense than tha' has!" An elector who was visited by one of our canvassers said: "Ah, lad, that's t' chap I'm going to vote for," when his missus said: "Tha'rt doin' nowt o' t' sort! Thou were born a Tory, and thou'rt to stop a Tory." The man replied to the canvasser: "Tak' noa notice o' her. She doesn't know what she's talking about." It had been the practice in previous elections for the Tory Party on the morning of the poll to cover the hoardings with two dialect placards. One ran "Voat for t' two owd 'uns," and the other "Voat for t' owd gam' cock". This had a reference to the father of Sir Harry Hornby, who was familiarly called "t' owd gam' cock". Knowing that these appeals would be forthcoming, we were ready with our reply, which appeared on the hoardings simultaneously. It ran: "We want a gam' cock thad con feight. Snowden con! He's all reight!" Small incidents of this sort tend to enliven the proceedings of an election contest.

The result of the polling was as follows:

Hornby (Con), 11,247
Coddington (Con), 9,415
Snowden (Soc), 7,095.

The vote polled for the Socialist candidate staggered the Conservatives. The much larger vote polled by Sir Harry Hornby than by his Conservative colleague Sir William Coddington is explained by Sir Harry's personal popularity. No less than 1,700 votes were split between Hornby and myself. I had 5,335 plumpers [voters who chose to use only one of their two votes in two-member constituencies]. My vote was by far the largest which up to that time had been polled by a Socialist candidate in Great Britain. It is interesting to note that of the 700 members returned at this Election only 16 polled a higher vote than mine. I had carried the whole platform campaign on my own shoulders. I have never felt the strain of electioneering. I have gone through a month's campaign, speaking at two or three meetings every night, and come out of it as fresh at the end as at the beginning. I attribute this to long experience of public speaking, and to the knowledge of how to use my voice. But even more perhaps to the fact that I never had the exhausting task of preparing speeches. I always trusted to the inspiration of the moment, drawing from the stock of accumulated material, and to matters that always arise in the course of a campaign. My long training as a propagandist had made me expert in handling public meetings and in dealing with the hecklers.

My Election campaign in Blackburn, and its striking result, increased the calls upon me for public meetings, and the next six years, up to the Election of 1906, I spent in propaganda. We were now getting large meetings everywhere, and interest in the Labour movement was rapidly growing. Mr. MacDonald was unceasing in his activities to get the Trade Unions to affiliate to the Labour Representation Committee, attending local conferences in all parts of the country for that purpose. The affiliated membership of the Committee would not, however, have grown as rapidly as it did in the next few years, but for an incident that caused great excitement in the Trade Union ranks. In 1902 the Courts decided in the famous Taff Vale case that Trade Union funds were liable for certain actions of individual members committed in pursuance of a trade dispute. This was a momentous decision. It deprived Trade Unions of a protection they had enjoyed for thirty years. In effect this decision meant that it would be impossible to conduct a strike without exposing the funds of the unions to legal confiscation. This incident provided effective propaganda for Labour representation. In a year the affiliated membership of the Labour Representation Committee doubled, reaching nearly the million figure. I now turn to describe a by-election contest in which I took part in Wakefield. This was one of those fights that the I.L.P. had to undertake, not with any hope of winning the seat, but for the purpose of propaganda. At the previous General Election the Conservative candidate had been returned unopposed. There seemed a likelihood that this would happen again, for the Liberal Party in the constituency was in a parlous condition. The National Council of the I.L.P. met to consider the situation, and decided to run a candidate. We had no branch of the Party in the constituency, and did not know of a single supporter of ours in the whole of Wakefield. My Council colleagues urged upon me to be the standard-bearer of Socialism. I undertook the job, regarding it as part of the general propaganda work upon which I was engaged. Keir Hardie went down to the constituency to look into the situation. He brought back a dismal report. He had not been able to get in touch with a single sympathiser in the town. However, we were adventurous in those days. We sent one of our organisers; he engaged the largest hall in the borough, and I went down to address the meeting in the character of a prospective candidate. We had to import a chairman, and there was not a Wakefield man on the platform. The meeting, however, was crowded and very enthusiastic, and the motion inviting me to come forward as candidate was carried with one dissentient only.

If the Liberals had had any intention of putting forward a candidate they were placed in a difficulty when we jumped the pitch. They finally decided to leave the field clear for myself and the Tory candidate. The Tories selected a Mr. Brotherton, a local man, who afterwards became well known in Yorkshire for his munificent gifts to Leeds University and to local charities. He was a charming man personally - gentle, kind and generous. He knew nothing whatever about politics, and his platform appearances were described by a local newspaper, strongly opposing my candidature, as a gross exhibition of political ignorance. That they may have been, but they were certainly the most entertaining speeches I have ever had to deal with in a political contest.

At that time there were two matters rousing a good deal of public interest – one in connection with the purchase of remounts for the South African War, and the other, contracts for meat. A question was put to my opponent at one of his meetings about the remounts and the meat scandals. He said he had seen something in the paper about this, but he did not understand it. He would look into the matter and give his answer at the next meeting. His carefully meditated reply is a gem. He said: "I presume that the question implies some grievance against the Government, and I stand here to declare that the present Government is the best of all Governments, and if anybody questions that, I say here that the complaints put before me have been grossly exaggerated. I have seen something about these complaints in the paper, but I have also seen statements explaining them all away. Some complaints have been made that the price of meat was too high; but if a man wants a nice piece of meat, so long as he gets what he likes, even if the price is a bit too high, you are not going to complain if you get the right stuff. And about these horses that went wrong. I wish they would give me the names of the horses that went wrong. I have not been given a single name. I had a horse that went wrong myself only a few days ago."

I had a delightful time in dealing with Mr. Brotherton. I admitted that his demand for the names of the horses was a perfectly reasonable one. These horses must have had names, and we cannot admit complaints against anonymous remounts. I demanded to know the name of Mr. Brotherton's horse that had gone wrong before I would believe that a horse belonging to a respectable gentleman like Mr. Brotherton would behave itself in such a way. This was the first Election where the support of the Liberal-Labour Members of Parliament was given to a Socialist candidate. I had personal letters of good wishes from all the Liberal-Labour Members of Parliament, including John Burns. The result of the Election was, of course, a foregone conclusion; but I polled much better than we had ever expected, the figures being:

Brotherton (Con), 2,960
Snowden (Soc), 1,979.

My vote included a considerable proportion of Liberals, though it was admitted that many voted Tory. The work of this Election laid the foundations of a Labour Party in the city, and since then it has been represented on two or three occasions by a Labour member.

In the spring of 1905 I was married. I was then forty years of age. I first met my wife at a Fabian meeting in Leeds. Our wedding took place at Otley-in-Wharfedale on the 13th March 1905. I don't think it ever occurred to either of us that we were tempting fate by being married on a "thirteenth". At any rate our experience of thirty years of married life has proved that if there is any truth in the "thirteen" superstition there are exceptions to it. We were married quietly and without advertisement, because it had come to our knowledge that the West Riding Socialists, who were expecting the wedding to take place, were preparing to turn it into a Socialist demonstration. There were present at the wedding my wife's sister, Miss Isabella and Miss Bessie Ford, my cousin and boyhood friend John A. Whitaker of Bradford, and my close Socialist comrade Fred Jowett. That day there began a married life which for thirty years has been a perfect partnership.

At the Annual Conference of the I.L.P., held at York at Easter in 1903, I was unanimously elected National Chairman of the Party. I presided at the next year's Conference held at Cardiff. The chairmanship was an annual appointment, but there was an unwritten rule that the same person might hold the position for three years, subject to re-election by the Annual Conference. I served the full term of three years, when I returned to the position of an ordinary member of the Council. I earned the reputation of being rather an autocratic chairman from the firmness with which I ruled the Annual Conference. It required a strong hand to deal with some hundreds of delegates, most of whom were gifted with a capacity to talk on any topic for any length of time. The agenda of the Conference was crowded with resolutions on every conceivable subject. It was only by curbing the loquacity of delegates that any progress could be made. There was at the Cardiff Conference a delegate from Huddersfield who was quite a character. When I cut short his speech on the ground of irrelevancy, he asked me if I called myself a democrat. When I answered in the affirmative, he retorted: "So then is the Czar of Russia!" The whole of the propaganda for Labour representation in the first years of the L.R.C. fell upon the I.L.P. It was not till the Conference at Liverpool in 1905 that a resolution was passed unanimously declaring "the ultimate object of the L.R.C. to be the overthrow of the present competitive system of Capitalism and the institution of a system of Public Ownership of all the means of Production, Distribution and Exchange". The Socialist leaven had done its work in the L.R.C., and the new movement from this date became a Socialist Party. At this Conference the important step was taken of changing the name from the Labour Representation Committee to the Labour Party. This change meant a great deal. The Labour group had now declared itself to be a Party. I had attended all the Annual Conferences of the L.R.C. from its formation. I had seen the movement grow in membership and increase its influence in the Trade Unions, its conception of the purpose of Labour Representation expanding, but this Conference at Liverpool marked an advance in all these respects greater than any previous Conference had shown. The original idea of the L.R.C. did not go beyond the formation of a group of Labour members in the House of Commons, who would exercise an influence upon the Government on industrial legislation. The Trade Unions had not at the inception of the movement any idea of a Labour Party which would compete with the other political parties for supremacy in the House of Commons. The possibility of Labour becoming strong enough to form a Government did not then enter into the imagination of the Trade Unions. That, of course, had been in the mind of the Socialists from the formation of the L.R.C.

This wider view of the aim and possibilities of the movement was now shown in the fact that a far larger number of Labour candidates had been adopted to run at the next General Election, which could not now be very long-delayed. At the previous Election fifteen candidates only had been run under the auspices of the Committee, but at the next Election in 1906 fifty candidates were put forward, out of whom twenty-nine were successful. The miners were still outside the Labour Party, but they returned twelve members at this Election under the old arrangement with the Liberals. The majority of the

Labour candidates returned at this Election had not to face opposition from the Liberals. There was no arrangement between the Liberal and Labour Parties, but Mr. Herbert Gladstone, who was Chief Liberal Whip, used his influence in some constituencies to give the Labour candidate a straight fight with the Conservative. The emergence from the Election of 1906 of an independent Labour Party twenty-nine strong in the House of Commons caused the easy-going politicians of the old school, who had complacently imagined that politics would forever continue to be a game of ins and outs between the Liberals and Tories, to wake up and begin to take notice. Everybody was asking what it all meant, and what the new Labour Party would do. A Party which could win seats in industrial centres like Bradford and Glasgow against the nominees of both Liberals and Tories had clearly a future before it. Organised Labour had begun to realise its power, and was learning how to use it.

Shortly after the previous General Election I had been adopted again as candidate for Blackburn. In the interval I had paid a good deal of attention to the constituency, frequently addressing public meetings there. We had now got together a fairly efficient Party organisation, and we entered upon the contest with high hopes of success. Blackburn is a two-membered constituency, and on this occasion the Liberals decided to put forward a candidate. One of the old Tory members discreetly retired. The result of the previous Election had shown that in all probability he would be defeated if he ventured to appeal again to the constituency. The Tories selected Mr. Geoffrey Drage as their second candidate; the popular Sir Harry Hornby was again their first choice. There was no understanding or arrangement between the Labour Party and the Liberals; but in the circumstances, with each voter having two votes and only one Liberal and one Labour candidate, a large number of voters divided their votes between the Liberal candidate and myself. The result of the Election was:

Hornby (Con), 10,291
Snowden (Lab), 10,281
Drage (Con), 8,932
Hamer (Lib), 8,892.

The explanation of the fact that I polled over 1,000 votes more than the Liberal candidate is this. Blackburn had been in the past overwhelmingly Conservative, and the Labour Party had drawn its support very largely from Conservative working men. It was always taken for granted by the Liberals that the Labour Party drew its support only from men who had been Liberals. This was quite a mistake. Many of my most enthusiastic workers were men who had been active Conservatives. I had over 1,500 plumpers at this Election, which represented Tory converts, who were not willing to vote for a Liberal. Sir Harry Hornby had 600 splits, which represented the votes of the Liberals, who in no circumstances would vote for a Socialist candidate. To her own and my great regret my wife was prevented by illness from taking part in this Election. She had already become very popular in the constituency, and was a great attraction whenever she was announced to speak. This Election, like the one I had previously fought in Blackburn, aroused great enthusiasm, but there was more liveliness on this occasion than at the former Election. The Tories realised that they were fighting for their very existence, and in consequence they imparted a good deal of bitterness into the contest. The old cry of "Socialism and Atheism" was raised, but I had been too long before the constituency for this to have any influence with the electors. The second Tory candidate, as I have mentioned, was Mr. Geoffrey Drage, who had opposed Mr. Will Crooks at his first contest in Woolwich. Some years later a rather amusing incident occurred at a Labour meeting in Derby I was addressing with Mr. Will Crooks. Mr. Drage was at that time the Tory candidate for Derby, and the chairman, Mr. J. H. Thomas, made a reference to him: "We have beaten him once in Derby, and we will beat him again". Crooks interjected the remark: "And I beat him at Woolwich!" and then I remarked: "And I beat him in Blackburn!" Victors over Mr. Drage seemed to be well represented on that platform.

In those days the pollings at the General Election were spread over about ten days. The pollings in the boroughs were taken on two or three days. The counties followed quite leisurely. The results of the first elections had a considerable effect on the later ones. If the early elections went decidedly in favour of one Party, that considerable number of electors which liked to be on the winning side helped to swell the victories of the Party which appeared to be winning. This spreading out the Election gave the candidates who had been elected in the early days of the polling the opportunity to go to the assistance of candidates where the elections had still to take place. After my election at Blackburn I spent the next few days assisting Labour candidates where the polling had not taken place. After I had finished helping candidates in their constituencies I paid a visit to my native village of Cowling, where my mother was again living. Somehow the news of my homecoming had reached the village before my arrival. I did not know what was afoot, but the driver of the bus from the railway station to the village four miles away behaved very suspiciously when I alighted from the train. He left his passengers in the bus and disappeared for some time, and it was only later that I learnt that he had been to the post office to announce the fact that I was coming up by the bus. The result was that I was met by the local brass band, who played the usual "See the Conquering Hero Comes"; and I was taken to the Assembly Hall, where a packed audience was waiting. I had to give them an address, in which I recounted the changes which had taken place in the village from the days when the few Socialists were looked upon as hare-brained curiosities who wanted to pile up all the wealth of the country into a heap, and then distribute it share and share alike among everybody. The vicar of the parish, who was a Tory, offered the congratulations of the meeting to me, and proposed that the school children of my old school should be given a holiday to celebrate the return to Parliament of one of the old scholars. The general result of this Election was an overwhelming victory for the Liberals. The country had had twenty years of unbroken Tory Government. After the Election of 1906 the Tories went back to the House of Commons with a mere remnant of their former strength. They numbered only 158 members in the new Parliament. The Election was a victory for Free Trade, and an overwhelming condemnation of Mr. Chamberlain's Tariff policy, but the enormous Liberal majority was due in the main to a feeling of disgust with the Tory Government. Of the twenty-nine Labour members returned at the 1906 Election, six were nominees of the I.L.P., and of this number five were members of the National Council of the Party. They were Keir Hardie, J. R. MacDonald, F. W. Jowett, James Parker and myself. The rest of the Labour members were nominees of the Trade Unions; but of the Trade Union members six had been for long active members of the I.L.P.

Chapter Five

First Impressions of Parliament

It is difficult to recall my first impressions of Parliament after nearly thirty years, but I would like to set them down so far as I can remember them, subject to this reservation – that later experience has in some respects modified first impressions. Before my return I had only been in the House of Commons once or twice, and I was wholly ignorant of its ways and proceedings. The new Parliament was called together for the 13th of February 1906. I went across to the House of Commons the day before Parliament was to meet and was taken in charge by Mr. Shackleton, who showed me round the building and introduced me to such old members as were about the place. The next day Parliament met for the election of the Speaker. My first experience was very commonplace and unexciting, and when I really became a Member of Parliament I do not know. Neither have I any idea of what particular one of the several little formalities through which I went constituted me a qualified legislator. I know I went through a hard-contested election. I learnt from the newspapers that I had been successful. I had no credentials to show. At the opening of a new Parliament members are taken on trust. They assemble for the election of the new Speaker without having taken the Oath of Allegiance. If anyone of an audacious spirit who could not get through an election successfully is very anxious to have a few days' experience of the life of a Member of Parliament, there is nothing to prevent him at the beginning of a new Parliament, except the fear of penalties he may invoke, from carrying out the experiment.

The first day of the sitting we crowded the benches, 670 members struggling for seats in a chamber which accommodates only half that number. This sitting is devoted to the election of a Speaker. The new Labour Party appropriated the two first benches below the gangway on the Opposition side. The Irish Party occupied the seats behind. The attenuated ranks of the Tory Party found ample accommodation on the benches above the gangway. Sir Henry Campbell-Bannerman, the new Prime Minister, in congratulating the Speaker on his election, betrayed a nervousness which was painful to see. Whether it was the emotion of his first effort as Prime Minister, or whether it was due to the terror with which the presence of the new Labour Party had filled him, I was unable to decide. After the election of the Speaker the House adjourned until the next day. The next few days were occupied in the swearing-in of members. I took my place in a long queue of members, and eventually reached a table where I made a declaration of fealty to the Constitution, and wrote my name in a huge book. I was then free until the following Tuesday, when the House formally met to hear the King's Speech. I used the interval to make myself acquainted with the geography of the House. I met one or two very old members of the House who claimed to know how to take the nearest course from one part of the House to another, but the new members during the first week or two almost gave up hope of ever understanding the intricacies of the innumerable corridors and lobbies. In the course of time, however, we overcame these initial difficulties, and became well enough acquainted with the bearings of the place to act as guides to our constituents who came up to London and looked upon a visit to the Houses of Parliament as a necessary part of a visit.

The staff of the House of Commons were very much interested in the appearance of this strange phenomenon of a Labour Party. I daresay they thought the respectability of the place was in danger, or that some of the nice jobs there were about the House would soon disappear. The policemen were particularly friendly to the new Labour members. I discovered a number of Labour men among them, and we exchanged mutual confidences. One of them told me that he had been collecting the pictures of the new members which had appeared in the illustrated papers, and he produced from one of his capacious pockets a compact scrapbook into which he had pasted portraits arranged in alphabetical order. "There is a great change in this Parliament, Mr. Snowden", another policeman remarked to me in the corridor the first day. "You know me then?" I answered. "Yes, sir. I've been looking for this time coming for many years. We police ain't expected to have politics, but I can talk to you, sir. Your Party's needed here." "They may need you for us before long", I suggested. "Oh well, sir, if it comes to that, you will find that we shall carry you out very gently!" In the smoke-room and in the inner lobby, in the corridors, wherever members congregated the topic of conversation was the new force in Parliament. The surprise and curiosity so evident in the country at the return of the Labour members were manifest in the House of Commons too. There seemed to be a general feeling among members akin to that which one experiences before an impending great change. Old members confessed that they did not expect things to go on as before; that for weal or for woe we were beginning a new era in Parliamentary history. It was some weeks before I paid my first visit to the Members' dining-room, as I had been warned by an old member that the prices there were beyond the means of a Labour member. He accordingly put me in the way of obtaining refreshment in a very comfortable tea-room where a meal was beautifully served at the democratic price of one shilling. I may here anticipate developments by mentioning that prices in the dining-room were soon reduced, and a good luncheon or dinner was served for two shillings and six pence.

A number of the Trade Union members had shocked their colleagues by appearing in what in those days was regarded as the head gear of conventionality, namely a silk hat. One well-known Liberal, who had previously worn a silk hat, put on a soft hat, and when reproached for this exclaimed that he did not want to be taken for a Labour member! The Parliamentary Labour Party met at the beginning of the session for the purpose of electing the officers of the Party. There was a keenly contested election between Keir Hardie and David Shackleton for the Chairmanship. It was expected that with the strong Trades Union element in the Party, an element which at this time had no wish to be identified with Socialism, Shackleton would easily be elected. It turned out, however, that Hardie was chosen by a majority of one. A number of Trade Union members must have voted for Hardie, and they had done so, no doubt, because they felt that his great services in building up the political Labour Party deserved recognition. Shackleton was appointed Deputy Chairman, MacDonald Secretary, and Arthur Henderson Chief Whip. Hardie was not a success as chairman. Nobody recognised this more than himself. Speaking on this matter some years later, he said: "Nature never intended me to occupy an official position. I think I have shown you that I can be a pioneer, but I am not guided so much by a consideration of policy or by thinking out a long sequence of events as by intuition and inspiration. I know what I believe to be the right thing, and I can and will do it. If I had twenty-one years ago stopped to think what the future would bring I would not have dared to accept the responsibility of entering the House of Commons."

Hardie had not the accommodating spirit that is essential in a successful Parliamentary leader. The humdrum everyday work of the House of Commons was never to Hardie's taste. During his chairmanship of the Party he left the arrangement of business, which must necessarily be carried through by conversations with the Government Whip, largely to Mr. Henderson.

In those days the House of Commons met at 2 o'clock in the afternoon and went on until midnight, except for an interval of one and a half hours for dinner. After the swearing-in of the members had been completed, the House met for business, and this gave me my first experience of Parliament as a Debating Chamber, and also introduced me to the new Ministers. The Government Front Bench in that Parliament was the ablest I have known in my Parliamentary career. Sir Henry Campbell-Bannerman looked the part of a Prime Minister. The other Ministers included such outstanding Parliamentary figures as Mr. Asquith, Mr. Haldane, Mr. John Morley, Mr. Lloyd George, Mr. Birrell, Sir Henry Fowler, Chancellor of the Duchy of Lancaster; and last, but not least, Mr. John Burns, "the first of the ancient lowly to reach the position of Cabinet Minister". The Under-Secretaries were a particularly strong team, and included Mr. Herbert Samuel, Mr. Churchill, Mr. Runciman and Mr. McKenna. The only weak Minister in this Government was Mr. Herbert Gladstone, who had been appointed Home Secretary, more, I should think, as a recognition of his services as head of the Liberal organisation in the country than as a mark of his fitness for office. He was supported by Mr. Herbert Samuel as Under-Secretary, who very soon in the new Parliament showed those strong administrative qualities which have distinguished him through all the following years. Though no rival of Mr. Winston Churchill's in the business of letting off fireworks, he was in those days that gentleman's immeasurable superior in the capacity for grasping and expounding details. I had not seen Mr. Asquith until then for over twenty years, and the change in his appearance was very striking. Although only a little over fifty years old, his hair was quite white. He had lost the pallor of his younger days. My first impression of Mr. Asquith as a Minister has been modified by subsequent events, but at that time he seemed to lack human sympathy, which alone could touch the responsive chord in those who listened.

The first impression made upon new members by the Debate on the Address was that of interminable talk, all with no practical end or aim. It was, of course, far too early to form definite views about Parliamentary proceedings, but one's first impression has been strengthened by all the years of later experience, and that is, that the House of Commons is a place given to much talk and little work. I remember so well that in the early days of this new Parliament, men who had come there for the first time with experience of municipal work contrasted the business methods of these bodies with the unending and unfruitful talk of the House of Commons. Old members smiled at the impatience of the new members. They reminded us of the time when they first came to Parliament full of an earnest enthusiasm to achieve some good purpose; but despair had entered into their hearts, and before the advent of the Labour men, they had resigned all hope of ever being able to move that cumbersome machine at any reasonable rate along the path of reform. The new members, the Labour members especially, listened with curiosity and interest to the speeches of the leaders of the several Parties. We estimated their fighting weights and their strategic skill. Mr. Chamberlain, in the temporary absence of Mr. Balfour through his defeat in Manchester, was leading the Opposition. I had not heard Mr. Chamberlain since the days of his matured powers twenty years before. I was amazed and pained by the decline of these powers. The hand of death was already upon him. In voice and vigour and skill he was but a shadow of the Joe Chamberlain of former days. There were times when he made an effort to score from an interjection or a weakness in an opponent's views, the thing in which Mr. Chamberlain was once an unrivalled master; but the failure of his effort only served to make more tragic the decline from his former skill. A member of the Government who aroused a good deal of curiosity was Mr. Winston Churchill. Mr. Churchill was a recent convert to the Liberal Party. He had left the Conservatives ostensibly on the fiscal issue, but with that mental agility which has characterised him through all his political life, he had accepted the whole Radical programme. Up to the General Election he had sat in the House of Commons as a Conservative member for Oldham, while at the same time he was the Liberal candidate for North-West Manchester. The new House soon had an opportunity of hearing him in debate. Mr. Churchill was Under-Secretary for the Colonies, and in the absence of the Colonial Secretary in the House of Lords it fell to him to defend the Government's policy on Chinese labour in the debate on the Address. The subject of Chinese labour was one on which he had spoken a great deal in the country, and he had, therefore, a large mass of material from which he was able to draw. This first speech on the Address was quite a success. It was a far better speech than I had heard him give on a public platform. His voice, his mannerisms, his style, were more in harmony with his surroundings. The slight stammer from which he still occasionally suffers was more pronounced in those days. It has always been Mr. Churchill's practice to prepare his speeches with great care, practically committing them to memory. A few weeks after this speech on the Address, Mr. Joseph Chamberlain again raised the question of Chinese labour on the Consolidated Fund Bill. He had only given Mr. Churchill very short notice of his intention to do this, which left very little time to prepare a speech in reply to Mr. Chamberlain. Mr. Churchill told me afterwards that this was the first speech he had ever delivered without committing it to memory.

In a new Parliament there is always competition among the new members to get in their maiden speeches as soon as possible in order to impress their constituents. In the Debate upon the Address which I am now describing there was the usual number of maiden speeches, all of which it was quite clear had done service on the Election platform. From a long subsequent experience of Parliamentary debates, I think it is a mistake for a new member to be too eager to impose himself upon the House. I have seldom known a case where a new member has made a success of a maiden speech who has subsequently lived up to the impression first created. There have been, of course, exceptions to this, but they are very rare. What makes an impression on the House of Commons is not eloquence or rhetoric, but a knowledge of the subject on which the member speaks. Eloquence and rhetoric are things which the new member should studiously avoid. Some of the most impressive speeches I have heard in Parliament have been delivered by men who made no pretensions to oratory, but who stated the case in a quiet manner on a subject of which they had full knowledge. The Tory Opposition, though small in numbers, made a gallant fight. The Tory Front Bench contained a number of experienced Parliamentarians like Mr. Joseph Chamberlain, Mr. Balfour, Mr. George Wyndham, Mr. Austen Chamberlain and Mr. Alfred Lyttelton, and they were admirably supported by the Back Benches. The Tory Opposition in this Parliament was, I think, the best I have known in my experience in the House of Commons. It played as a team, and every man took his part in the game.

The Labour members quickly adapted themselves to the customs of the House of Commons. There was a practice in those days that when a member left the Chamber he stopped at the Bar and made a profound obeisance to the Speaker. It was rather amusing to see the Labour members, whose advent to Parliament was expected to outrage all the conventionalities, performing this custom with more correctness than the Tory members. The Labour Party established a practice of holding a meeting of the Party every Thursday, after the business for the following week had been announced, to decide what its course of action should be. Under the constitution of the Party, members were required to vote on all questions in a solid body. At one time there was a clause in the constitution that a member who felt conscientiously obliged to vote against the decision of the group must resign from the Party.

This rigid condition of the subordinating of the individual opinion to the decisions of the majority was a cause of constant friction in the Party. A year or two before the 1906 Election, the Annual Conference of the Labour Party approved a scheme by which an allowance of £200 a year from the funds of the Party was made to each member elected. This, of course, was far from meeting the expenses of a member of Parliament, and the Trade Union members had an additional allowance granted to them by the Trade Union responsible for their candidature. I should have found it to be very difficult to exist if I had not been able to supplement my Parliamentary allowance by my earnings as a journalist. During the first years I had to maintain a home in the North of England, as well as to meet the expenses of living in hotels and lodgings in London. I had a good deal of sympathy with a few of my colleagues who had no means beyond the £200 provided by the Labour Party. I do not know how they managed to exist, and I am afraid they suffered a good deal of privation.

I had been in the House of Commons three weeks before I made my first speech. A private member had won a place for a private member's motion. He put down a motion by arrangement with the Government, affirming the fidelity of the House to Free Trade. This memorable debate took place on March 12 and 13, 1906. This motion was intended to put the Opposition in a difficulty. Mr. Balfour had not yet openly come down on the side of Mr. Chamberlain on the question of Protection. On the day this motion was down for discussion, Mr. Balfour returned to the House of Commons as member for the City of London after his defeat at the General Election. His introduction to the House at the end of Questions was a very interesting event. This was the first time I had seen Mr. Balfour. As he stood at the Bar, waiting to come forward to the table to take the Oath, he looked rather grave. He had come back to a very different House of Commons from that he had left a few months before, and which he had dominated for many years. His Party was now reduced to a mere remnant of its former members. As he advanced to the table, Mr. Jerry MacVeagh, the licensed wit of the Irish Party, cried out amid loud laughter: "Welcome, little stranger!" Immediately Mr. Balfour had taken his seat he took over from Mr. Chamberlain the duties of leadership of the Opposition. After the mover and seconder of the Free Trade resolution had spoken, Balfour rose to continue the debate. His speech was admitted on all sides to be "poor stuff". He was evidently depressed by the new circumstances in which he found himself. When Mr. Balfour sat down it was expected, following the usual practice, that the leader of the Opposition would be followed by a Minister. But no member of the Government rose, and the Speaker called upon a private Liberal member. The Opposition resented what they pretended was a slight upon Mr. Balfour. When the Liberal member had finished his speech, Mr. Chamberlain rose and excitedly complained that the Government had declined to define their own motion. This led to a scene the like of which I became very familiar with in my subsequent Parliamentary experiences. Mr. Chamberlain concluded by moving the adjournment of the debate. This brought up Sir Henry Campbell-Bannerman, who delivered a speech which was long remembered as one of the most delightful and brilliant little speeches heard in the House of Commons. He reminded Mr. Balfour that he had come to a very different House of Commons from that which he had left. While the Government were ready to treat the Opposition with respect, they could not be expected to treat seriously such futile and frivolous questions addressed to them. Sir Henry Campbell-Bannerman concluded his speech with the remark that has become as famous as Mr. Asquith's "Wait and see!" saying: "Have done with this foolery! It would have answered very well in the last Parliament, but it is altogether out of place in this. The tone and temper of this Parliament will not permit it. Move your amendments, and let us get to business." This telling speech occupied only four minutes, but it was one of the most effective I have ever heard in the House of Commons. It roused the House to a frenzy of enthusiasm.

It was later in the evening of this day that I made my maiden speech. I would prefer to pass over the event in silence, but I suppose I shall be expected to make some reference to it. I was so dissatisfied with it that I have never looked at the report of the speech from that day to this. I had a crowded House, and I have no complaint to make about the way in which I was received. I had, unfortunately, come into the House of Commons with the worst handicap from which a new member can suffer. The newspapers had boomed me as the orator of the Labour Party, and the House was expecting me to live up to the reputation which had been given to me by the Press. There is all the difference in the world between the style of speaking which appeals to the popular audience, and that which makes an impression on the House of Commons. The subject of the debate was one on which I had been speaking in the country for years; and I had in consequence become very familiar with the case for Free Trade and the arguments of the Protectionists. I did not prepare the speech, but trusted to my knowledge of the subject. In view of my own dissatisfaction with my maiden effort, I was surprised next day to see how undeservedly generous were the Press comments upon it. With one or two exceptions the papers were loud in their praise of the speech. One leading London newspaper attributed to me "the quality of the silver tongue which often the critical and not too indulgent House of Commons could not resist". Another paper described the speech as being "a contribution to the debate which had all the wider evidence of finished speech-making and sound ability". A further important London paper remarked that "one of the redeeming features of the evening sitting was the maiden speech of Mr. Snowden, one of the most eloquent of the Labour members. This frail-looking man, thin of face and form, striking because of his sharp features and his preponderating brow, held the attention of the House unbroken." Mr. John Foster Fraser was at that time the writer of a Parliamentary sketch for a number of provincial newspapers. Mr. Foster Fraser's comment upon my speech was to my mind a more correct criticism than the fulsome comments of the majority of the newspapers. He said: "We heard Mr. Snowden the other evening, and I think I am reflecting the opinion of the members who heard the speech when I say it was the poorest contribution which Parliament has had from any of the Labour representatives. I dare say Mr. Snowden with his undoubted abilities can sway a mass meeting. The qualities, however, which turn a mass meeting are not those which appeal to the House of Commons, and rather reluctantly we come to the conclusion that however much we are willing to admire him, Mr. Snowden could bore the House of Commons." Mr. Foster

Fraser fully atoned for these true, but uncomplimentary remarks by writing of a later speech of mine these words: “It was a speech which revealed Mr. Snowden as the most able spokesman in the ranks of Labour. He began speaking in an almost empty House, but he drew men away from their drinks, their cigars and their evening newspapers to hear him. There is no other Socialist in Parliament who comes within miles of him as an eloquent orator.”

Chapter Six

The Woman Suffrage Movement

The privilege of helping women to win the vote is one that I now look back upon with pride and satisfaction. To the young men and women of today the story is practically unknown and of faint interest; but in view of the possibility, in a world rapidly turning from democracy and personal freedom, of the loss of many of their hard-won liberties, the young women at least should interest themselves in their own political history.

From 1906 to the outbreak of war neither Parliament nor the country was allowed to forget the question of woman suffrage. In the last thirty years of the previous century a band of able and devoted women, mainly of the middle class, had been working for the emancipation of their sex from the educational, professional and social, as well as the political disabilities under which they lived. Their efforts resulted in the opening of the Universities and of the medical profession to women, and their admission to posts in the State and Local Government services. From 1870 woman suffrage commanded a majority of professed supporters in the House of Commons. Seven times a Woman Suffrage Bill had passed its second reading. These parliamentary majorities had been obtained through the strenuous work of the National Union of Women's Suffrage Societies which had continuously brought pressure to bear upon parliamentary candidates in their constituencies; but it cannot truly be said that, despite the academic support in the House of Commons, there was a popular demand for the vote for women. It had never been a main political issue. Men on the whole were hostile to it from the selfish dislike of sharing with women the privileges they had won for themselves. Even working men, in arms against their own oppressors, liked to feel there was something a little lower than themselves. The great mass of women were either indifferent or opposed. They had been taught to regard voting as a "man's job", and were inclined, through age-long training, to meekly adopt the Pauline view of their duties of silence and obedience.

About the beginning of this century the Woman Suffrage Movement suddenly sprang into great activity. The women textile workers of Lancashire and Yorkshire had been roused to a knowledge of the poverty of their labour conditions. This awakening was due in a large measure to the rise of the Labour Party, which was carrying on at this time a vigorous propaganda for political action amongst trade unionists. The women of the unions were called upon to contribute to the political funds, but had not votes themselves. The absurdity of this soon struck them. The campaign of the men gave points to the women. If the use of the vote could give all these things to men it could do the same for women. A strong suffrage movement grew up amongst these women textile workers. It was helped by the older suffrage societies whose members renewed their hope and faith through it, and by the men and women of the I.L.P. which had placed woman suffrage in its programme. Mr. Keir Hardie and myself, both of us keen suffragists, gave a great deal of our time to this movement. It directed its efforts largely to pressing the new Labour Party to give a prominent place in its programme to votes for women.

Mrs. Pankhurst was at this time living in Manchester, and she and her daughter Christabel threw themselves into this agitation with great energy. This was before the formation of the organisation which became so notorious. I knew Mrs. Pankhurst very well; we were colleagues for years on the National Council of the I.L.P. She and her husband joined that organisation soon after it was formed. Dr. Pankhurst was a Chancery Barrister and a great figure in the public life of Manchester – great in the spiritual sense, for, like his wife, he was small of stature, with a high-pitched, thin voice which, on more than one occasion when he was heard but not seen, caused him to be mistaken for a woman. He stood as a Socialist candidate for Gorton at the General Election of 1895 and polled 4,261 votes. When Mrs. Pankhurst was on the Council of the I.L.P. she was a suffragist, but by no means a fanatical one. At that time she was more Socialist than suffragist, and placed high hopes on the Labour Movement as an instrument for securing better conditions for women. In view of her later development this is interesting, for, as we know, she became a jingo-nationalist in the War and a Conservative candidate for Parliament towards the end of her days. The memorial erected to this one-time Socialist and Pacifist was unveiled in 1930 by a Conservative and former anti-suffragist Prime Minister, Mr. Stanley Baldwin. I have always thought that the development of Mrs. Pankhurst into a law-breaking militant was due to the influence of her daughter Christabel, whom she worshipped fanatically. Christabel was a very strong-minded young woman with a dictatorial manner. She had great organising ability and was a good, though not an eloquent, speaker. It was her sincerity which compelled respect even when her impertinence irritated. She had a profound belief that all politicians were insincere, that not one of them was to be trusted to keep his pledged word, and that they never gave a reform from conviction of its justice, but only under the compulsion of force. Christabel changed her views about politicians during the War, and at the General Election of 1918 stood as a Conservative candidate for Smethwick and was nearly elected. After this defeat she abandoned politics, and took up lecturing about the Second Coming of Christ.

Mrs. Pankhurst formed the Women's Social and Political Union in 1903. It carried on its work unostentatiously for two years, organising small meetings and interviewing Parliamentary candidates. Mrs. Pankhurst had no faith in the Liberal Party, but, after many disappointments, she still had a lingering hope that the new Labour Party might be forced to adopt woman suffrage in its programme. She kept up her membership of the I.L.P. The Labour Party up to that time had made no declaration on the subject. At the Labour Party Conference in Liverpool in 1905 it was brought forward for the first time in the terms of the following resolution:

> "That this Conference heartily approves of adult suffrage and the complete emancipation of both sexes, and endorses the Women's Enfranchisement Bill introduced into Parliament last session believing it to be an important step towards adult suffrage."

The terms of this resolution require some explanation. The position taken up by all the woman suffrage societies was that the disability of sex should be removed. Whatever entitled a man to vote should entitle a woman to do so. This was a very clear and simple formula. Its adoption would ensure that further extension of the franchise would apply to men and women equally. The Women's Enfranchisement Bill referred to in the above resolution was framed on these lines. It was true that the Bill would not have enfranchised a large number of women, but it conceded the principle of sex equality. This was what was known as the women's point of view; and it was the right one for women to take. Politicians, however, looked at it from the point of view of party interests. To give the vote to women on the then existing qualifications for men would, it was said, enfranchise women property owners, women graduates, women lodgers, women joint occupiers as well as women householders. Hence there arose much opposition from certain Liberal and Labour men on the ground that it would lead to an increase in the Tory vote. Prejudice was created by the widespread allegation that the Bill was deliberately designed to enfranchise well-to-do women while leaving working women voteless. This was not true. With all its imperfections the Bill would have given votes to four times as many working women householders as property owners. It was such prejudice which defeated the resolution submitted to the Liverpool Labour Conference. An amendment to the resolution was carried in the following terms:

> "That this Conference, believing that any Women's Enfranchisement Bill which seeks merely to abolish sex disqualification would increase the political power of the propertied classes by enfranchising upper- and middle-class women, and leaving the great majority of working women still voteless, hereby expresses its conviction that Adult Suffrage-male and female is the only Franchise Reform which merits any support from the Labour Members of Parliament."

This amendment was carried by 483 votes to 270. Mrs. Pankhurst, who was an I.L.P. delegate to this Conference, spoke in support of the resolution, and I also supported it. Mrs. Pankhurst declared that for her this question had resolved itself into a life and death struggle. She was terribly grieved at the defeat of the resolution. She wrote the following letter to me a few days after the Conference:

> "DEAR MR. SNOWDEN,
>
> 2nd February, 1905.
>
> I felt deeply grieved at our defeat for I felt so confident we should carry the composite resolution up to Saturday morning. I had not sufficiently

> realised the forces working against us. But I now feel that our temporary defeat is more than compensated for by the adhesion of yourself and other men who are now giving earnest support to this question.
>
> If you knew how I long to get this vote question settled so that women may get to real social work. I am so weary of it and the long long years of struggle first against ridicule and contempt and now of indifference and apathy.
>
> Still I feel more hopeful than I have ever been for the defeat at Liverpool has aroused much interest among men and women alike.
>
> We are working to make the Free Trade Hall Meeting a success. Is it possible to arrange for a full report of your speech and later publish it for distribution? We want more literature. In conclusion I do want to say how much my daughter and I felt your kind manner on Saturday morning and your understanding words of sympathy. Believe me with all my heart I welcome your help.
>
> Sincerely yours,
> EMMELINE PANKHURST.

In October of this year the Women's Social and Political Union came unexpectedly into wide public notice. Sir Edward Grey was to address a great Liberal meeting in the Free Trade Hall on the eve of the Liberal Government's assumption of office. He was to declare the programme of the new Government. Mrs. Pankhurst naturally wanted to know what place woman suffrage had in the Government programme. She arranged that her daughter and Annie Kenny – a factory-worker from Oldham – should attend the meeting and question Sir Edward Grey on the subject. The two girls sat quietly through the speeches, and at the end Miss Kenny rose to put her question. This was an innovation in a Liberal meeting which could not be tolerated, and especially in a meeting addressed by a front-rank statesman. Those of us who have had experience of public meetings can easily visualise what happened. The stewards and the audience made a pandemonium of what would have been a mere incident if they had had the sense to keep quiet. The two girls were seized by the stewards and the whole audience stood on the chairs and shouted: "Turn them out!" The stewards did so, twisting their arms and kicking them before they hurled them down the steps. Outside they held an indignation meeting, which came to an ignominious end with their arrest for obstruction by the police. Next day they were brought before the magistrates and fined, with the alternative of imprisonment. They chose to go to prison. This incident acted like a match to paper and began the real militant agitation. Thousands of people who had never heard of woman suffrage before had their attention drawn to it and began discussing it. The value of this sort of publicity was quickly recognised, and the presence of the "suffragettes" was henceforth an expected feature of every important Liberal meeting in the Manchester district. The organisation at that time had very little money and few members, but in 1906 the Pankhursts migrated to London and then began a struggle the like of which the political history of this country cannot show. The results of the General Election of 1906 had given great encouragement to the suffrage societies which worked on constitutional lines. The spirit of reform was abroad. A large majority of the members of the new Parliament were pledged to support the enfranchisement of women. At the opening of the new session, Mrs. Henry Fawcett, President of the National Union of Woman's Suffrage Societies, whose whole life had been spent in working for the Cause, called together a number of M.P.s who were known to be in earnest on this question, to discuss with them the proper line of action for bringing woman suffrage before the new House of Commons. Out of this meeting a suffrage committee was formed, of which the Hon. Geoffrey Howard, a Liberal member, and myself were joint secretaries. Early in the new Parliament an opportunity came for testing the House of Commons on this question. A Liberal member, Mr. Dickinson, had won a place in the ballot for private members' Bills, and at the request of the constitutional suffrage societies he introduced a Woman Suffrage Bill. Enormous interest had been aroused both in and out of Parliament, and I cannot remember there having been in my time such a large attendance of members on a Friday afternoon as were present on this occasion. The Bill was a simple measure which proposed to extend the vote to women on the same terms as men. A number of Liberals pledged to woman suffrage found an excuse for opposing this Bill because of its limited character. Members of the Government were divided on the question.

Mr. Asquith was opposed to, Mr. Balfour was in favour of woman suffrage. Immediately after the second reading of the Bill had been moved and seconded, Sir Henry Campbell-Bannerman, the Prime Minister, who was an ardent supporter of votes for women, rose to explain the position of the Government. He spoke in his personal capacity only, as his Government was too divided for him to be able to be its spokesman. He defended the claim of women to the vote on the ground that an increasing number of questions coming before the House of Commons were questions on which the women of the country should be able to express their views. He declared his intention of voting for the Bill, although he disapproved of its limited character. The discussion which followed was one of the best I have heard in the House of Commons. It was afterwards described by an opponent as a debate never to be forgotten.

The opponents of the measure pursued the tactics usually employed on a private member's Bill. They talked it out. The last five minutes of the debate was carried on in a House electric with expectancy, and in the hearing of women in the gallery agonising over the result, by a speaker who carried buffoonery to the point of extremely bad taste. Great indeed was the excitement when just before four o'clock the member in charge of the Bill moved the closure. The Speaker declined to accept it. The Bill was once more "talked out". Mr. H. W. Massingham in his "Pictures in Parliament" in the *Daily News* next day gave a generous report of my own part in the debate, which perhaps it is not unsuitable that I should quote: "Mr. Snowden's speech," he said, "was without question the finest he has yet delivered in St. Stephen's. Mr. Snowden's pleas drew loud applause from every side of the House. He appealed to the axioms of faith in man and in God with a fervour which came strangely after recent slanderous suggestions that Socialism and Atheism are synonymous."

The following Session (1908) another private member's Bill was introduced which passed its Second Reading by a majority of 179, but it got no further. The attitude of the Government was unsympathetic and very irritating. The House of Commons continued to pass the Second Reading of Woman Suffrage Bills by large majorities, but nothing ever came of them. Even Mr. Asquith, a strong opponent, was forced to admit that it was a disgrace to representative government that the House of Commons should repeatedly declare its desire to enfranchise women and no practical result follow. For four years of this Parliament, the Government with a large majority of its supporters pledged to this reform, paid no attention to it. Meanwhile, the agitation in the country grew formidable. The old constitutional societies enormously increased their membership and extended their activities. An increasing number of sympathetic men enrolled themselves for every sort of service for the Cause. Mrs. Pankhurst's organisation pursued its militant activities with ever-increasing violence. It had attracted the support of a large number of very wealthy women and money rolled into its coffers. The tactics of this group soon passed beyond the stage of merely interrupting meetings, baiting Cabinet Ministers, raiding the House of Commons, causing disturbances in the Ladies' Gallery, sending unwanted deputations to Downing Street, and smacking the faces of policemen. These minor acts of rowdyism, which were "pie" for the newspapers, obtained for the women the notoriety they desired. Hundreds were sent to Holloway Gaol, where they embarrassed the authorities by refusing to take food. Forcible feeding was resorted to, but was made dangerous and difficult by the struggles of the prisoners. They were kept in prison to the point of physical collapse and then released. Subsequently an Act was passed to deal with these cases of defiance. It was called the "Cat and Mouse Act" because it empowered the Home Secretary to release a prisoner at the point of death through hunger-striking and when she had recovered, to send her back to prison to go through it again. This cruel law had no deterrent effect on the women. I was once asked to go and see two women who had just been released after prolonged hunger-striking. They were a ghastly sight, apparently dying of their suffering. I was filled with a wondering pity. These women quite clearly were prepared to die – for what? Was it through some strange hypnotic power exercised over them by their leaders? Had they been convinced that the Cause was worthy of martyrdom? Was it a case in which reason had been displaced by emotions and desires transcending reason? I don't know to this hour; but the impossibility of answering these questions to my own satisfaction tempered my criticism of their actions, even when these were foolish and indefensible.

So long as these women confined their activities to such ingenuous performances as tying themselves to street lamps and park railings, throwing leaflets from the Gallery of the House onto the heads of members, or getting themselves arrested for causing obstruction, the public were more amused than angry, though the opponents of woman suffrage never failed to point to these antics as proof of the unfitness of women to vote. When they began to destroy property and risk the lives of others than themselves the public began to turn against them. The National Union of Woman's Suffrage Societies, whose gallant educational and constitutional work for women's freedom had been carried on for more than fifty years, publicly dissociated themselves from these terrorist activities. But it was little use. The ill-informed public lumped all suffragists together. Politicians, looking for an excuse to withdraw their support, exulted in the disorders for which only a fraction of the whole women's movement was responsible.

But, while depressing the spirits of the real friends of the Cause in Parliament, our efforts to secure the passage of a Woman Suffrage Bill did not lessen on account of these violent actions. We formed in 1910 a committee of members of Parliament drawn from all Parties with the Earl of Lytton as Chairman. An acceptable Bill was drafted and put into the hands of Mr. David Shackleton, the member for Clitheroe. We secured from the Government two days of time for the debate. It was a great occasion, and the Second Reading was carried by 299 votes to 190. It was opposed in debate by Mr. Lloyd George and Mr. Churchill on the ground that it was not sufficiently democratic. The Bill got no further that Session. We had prevailed upon Mrs. Pankhurst to call a truce to militancy, and all the suffrage organisations united in intensive propaganda in the country in favour of this Bill. In connection with this, the largest and most beautiful and impressive procession of women ever seen in this country marched four abreast through the streets of London. The procession was four miles long. The second General Election of 1910 came, and still women were unenfranchised. This, as things turned out, was the last General Election in which women were voteless. At this Election the Liberals had in their programme the promise of a Manhood Suffrage Bill. Mr. Asquith gave a pledge that the Bill would be so drafted that it would be open to the House of Commons to amend it so as to include women; and if it were so amended Mr. Asquith would accept the decision. In May 1911 we re-introduced the Conciliation Bill. It was again carried on the Second Reading by a still larger majority. Its further progress was stopped when the Government announced their intention to introduce a Manhood Suffrage Bill. No attempt was made to redeem their pledge till July 1912, when a Bill was read a second time. It was not possible to proceed to the Committee stage till the following January. It will be remembered that Mr. Asquith had given a pledge that the

Bill would be so drafted that an amendment to give votes to women would be in order, and that if such an amendment were carried on a free vote of the House, the Government would accept the decision. At the opening of the Committee stage the Speaker hurled a thunderbolt which destroyed the Bill and dashed the hopes of the woman suffragists to the ground. He ruled that if the woman suffrage amendments were carried they would so alter the Bill as to convert it into a new Bill. In these circumstances it ought to be withdrawn. Accordingly the Bill was withdrawn, and not re-introduced in an amended form. The truth probably was that the Government had believed the Bill to be so drafted that the woman suffrage amendments would be in order. The Parliamentary draughtsman had blundered.

Be these things as they may, nothing could relieve the Government from responsibility for the unfortunate catastrophe. They had been considering the Bill for two years, and such an oversight or stupid mistake was unpardonable. Nothing could convince the women that they had not been deliberately tricked. Mr. Asquith's bitter hostility to woman suffrage was cited in support of their behalf, and Mr. Lloyd George had never been trusted on this question by the suffrage societies, although professedly a strong supporter of the Cause. To make matters worse, Mr. Asquith declined to introduce another Bill in place of the one which had been withdrawn, and he refused to see the women whose cause he had betrayed. He added insult to injury by offering to allow time for a Private Member's Woman's Suffrage Bill, after seven such Bills had passed a Second Reading in four years! The constitutional suffragists were justifiably outraged. This was the treatment they had received for pursuing peaceful methods of agitation! The attitude of the Government was a disgrace to its members. It was a defiance of the oft-expressed will of the House of Commons! The militant tactics of Mrs. Pankhurst's organisation were resumed with redoubled violence. Mrs. Pankhurst was sentenced to three years' penal servitude for incitement to riot. By resorting to the Hunger Strike she evaded this sentence. She was released and re-arrested almost times without number. Her "martyrdom" aroused her followers to a frenzied emulation. But after six years of this policy the public were getting a little tired of it. A reaction against woman's suffrage set in. For the time being, the outrages which these women were daily perpetrating – burning buildings, slashing pictures in public galleries, cutting telegraph wires – had put back the chances of woman's enfranchisement. The great work of the non-militant suffragists over a generation seemed to have been destroyed.

The Conciliation Bill again came before the House of Commons. After two days' debate it was refused a Second Reading by 268 to 221. Two years before it had been approved by a majority of 67. The decline of support must indubitably be laid at the doors of the militant women. It had been the practice of the militants to harass Liberal Ministers by interrupting them at their public meetings. This practice was now extended to certain Labour members, and strangely enough, considering our unswerving loyalty to the Cause, in particular to Keir Hardie and myself. The reason they gave for this piece of illogicality was our refusal to subordinate every question in which our constituents were interested to woman suffrage, and to vote steadily against the Government no matter what our views on other questions might be. In 1913 and 1914 almost all my meetings were invaded by these women, and some of them were broken up. Attempts at personal violence were frequently made, and my wife has among her souvenirs of our public life several formidable weapons taken from suffragettes on the warpath. One is a lead disc weighing at least a pound, which was flung at me by a half-demented youth whom the women brought with them to a meeting in Manchester. After leaving another meeting, at which I was actually speaking on woman suffrage, a bottle was hurled at my head. Happily for me, it went past me and through a shop window. I think the women who upset meetings were a corps specially set apart for this work, for the faces became quite familiar to me in time. It was an awkward business for men to handle rowdy women, and like the police, they detested it. The suffragettes took advantage of this in places where men were of gentler mould than those of the Free Trade Hall gathering; but I recall an amusing occasion when the women were outmatched. The Chairman of the meeting was a woman doctor and a non-militant suffragist - for be it remembered these fanatics frequently broke up the meetings of the older suffrage societies. Anticipating trouble, she engaged as stewards a number of wardresses from a local mental institution who were trained to handle refractory patients. When the trouble started each woman steward quietly took a suffragette in hand, threw her over her shoulder and carried her out of the hall. I never saw anything more neatly done. The interrupters had not expected professional treatment.

The attitude of the National Labour Party remained for four or five years as laid down in the Liverpool resolution I have quoted. The resolution was reaffirmed by an even larger majority two years later at the Belfast Conference. This led to a striking declaration by Keir Hardie. Rising and speaking under obviously deep emotion, he said:

> "Twenty-five years ago this year I cut myself adrift from every relationship, political and otherwise, in order to assist in building up a working class party. I had thought the days of my pioneering were over. Of late I have felt with increasing intensity the injustice which has been inflicted on women by the present political laws. The intimation I wanted to make to the Conference and friends was that if the motion they had carried that morning was intended to limit the action of the Party in the House of Commons, I should have seriously to consider whether I could remain a member of the Parliamentary Party. I say this with great respect and feeling. The Party is largely my own child, and I would not sever myself lightly from what has been my life's work. But I could not be untrue to my principles."

These Conference resolutions did not as a matter of fact limit the action of the Labour M.P.s, who solidly voted for the limited Bills. In 1910, however, the Conference took a step forward by adopting a resolution moved by Miss Bondfield that any Government Reform Bill which excluded women would be met by the uncompromising opposition of organised labour. It was at the Labour Party Conference of 1913 that the great fight on this question took place. This was one of the most dramatic episodes in my career; and for that reason I may be pardoned for referring to it at some length. I will let the newspapers of that date tell the story of the incident. The resolution before the Conference "called upon the Parliamentary Party to do all in its power to expedite the passage of a Bill during the coming session giving votes to women on a broad and democratic basis". To this the I.L.P. moved to add "It further calls upon the Party in Parliament to oppose any Franchise Bill in which women are not included". This amendment brought the question to a definite issue. Were the Labour Party willing to accept a Reform Bill that gave manhood suffrage and refused votes to women? The opposition to this amendment was led by Mr. Stephen Walsh, the miners' leader. The newspaper report of the debate may now be quoted:

> "Mr. Stephen Walsh made a forceful appeal to the Conference which might be paraphrased thus: 'Don't embarrass the Labour members by forcing them to take up an entirely new policy inconsistent with the pledges given by the M.P.'s to their constituents. Were they to be compelled to oppose a Franchise Bill from which working men might derive great benefits simply because it did nothing for the women?'

"Mr. Philip Snowden sprang to his feet at the back of the hall and made a memorable speech. Mr. Snowden swept the Conference away with him. Before he spoke everyone said that the resolution would be carried. When he sat down it was felt that the Walsh party had lost the day. He spoke with passionate earnestness and with driving force. Turning fiercely on Mr. Walsh he accused him of being willing to allow the Labour members 'to steal more votes for men at the expense of the women'.

As Mr. Snowden hammered his points home, every sentence full on the bull's eye, the hum of conversation ceased and everyone in the big room turned towards the speaker. Here was an effort out of the ordinary run. They listened in a silence that could be felt. Not only so, but there was an instinctive movement - a surging up towards him. Every delegate turned in his seat. All those standing moved close-up. Viewed from the gallery, it was like nothing so much as the sudden placing of a magnet on a board covered with scattered bits of steel.

Mr. Snowden had gone far beyond his allotted five minutes, and again and again the Chairman perfunctorily tapped with his pencil; but the Conference was determined to hear Snowden out, and the close of his speech was greeted with an outburst of overwhelming applause. When Mr. Snowden sat down the Chairman called for the vote. 'For the amendment, 870.' 'Against the amendment, 437.'

Who shall describe the scene which followed? Hats waved, delegates sprang to their chairs, women in the gallery clapped hands, and cheers were renewed again and again. It was several minutes before the Conference could proceed to the next business. For this result thanks are due to the noble, enlightened and absolutely convincing plea from Mr. Philip Snowden. It was one of the greatest speeches in the career of a great man; an event to be marked on the toilsome way to freedom with a white stone."

This was one of those rare occasions when one feels inspired. I had no intention of speaking until provoked by Walsh's speech. I realised that to the women in the gallery, some of whom had been working on constitutional lines for fifty years, the issue was of more account than life or death.

When the War came the woman's suffrage societies, both constitutional and militant, suspended their agitation. Women turned their activities into helping the War in various ways, and in very large numbers performed tasks which had been regarded as quite outside a woman's sphere. This made a great impression upon male opinion, and removed largely the opposition to woman suffrage. When the question of Electoral Reform came to be dealt with in 1917 it was impossible any longer to deny the claims of women to political enfranchisement. Mr. Asquith, who had always been a strong opponent of woman's suffrage, announced that he had changed his attitude on the question. He said he had been influenced by two considerations. First the work which women had done during the War, and second the need for women's voices to be directly heard upon the questions of reconstruction which would arise when the War was over. Other life-long opponents of woman's suffrage also announced that they had changed their attitude on the question.

The Reform Bill, which was passed in February 1918, conferred the Parliamentary vote upon all males over twenty-one years of age, and gave both the Parliamentary and Local Government franchise to women on more restricted conditions. A woman was to be entitled to the Parliamentary vote if she had attained the age of thirty years, and was entitled by her own occupation to be registered as a Local Government elector, or if she was the wife of a husband entitled to be registered as a Local Government elector. The woman's franchise on these conditions entitled about nine millions of women to qualify as Parliamentary voters.

Thus, after fifty years of agitation, the sex barrier to political enfranchisement was broken down, and the long-delayed claims of women to justice were conceded. Ten years later the work was completed by the passing of a measure which equalised the franchise qualifications of men and women, and gave adult suffrage to all persons over twenty-one years of age – except lunatics and peers! Many of the women pioneers who had toiled so hard to remove the political disabilities of women did not live to see the final consummation of their devoted labours. It had fallen to a Conservative Government to complete this work. I had the satisfaction of following the Home Secretary, Sir W. Joynson-Hicks, in the debate on the second reading of this Bill, as one of the few surviving members of the House of Commons who had taken an active part in the Parliamentary demand for the enfranchisement of women in the days before the War. I may be allowed to quote the concluding sentences of my speech on this occasion:

> "I wholly agree with the Home Secretary with regard to the falsification of all the objections raised to the enfranchisement of women in the days when this was an academic question. These objections now seem, after ten years of the partial enfranchisement of women, and when women have sat in the House of Commons for some years, to be amusing, if not grotesque. We were told that women's enfranchisement would destroy the home, would break up family life, would destroy chivalry towards women, that women would all vote together, and the men's vote would be completely submerged. Nothing of that sort has happened. This Bill consummates sixty years of valiant work on the part of woman's suffrage organisations. It has involved a great effort and much suffering on the part of many devoted women who have felt the indignity of their political disability and the lack of opportunities of rendering public service. We support this Bill because we believe it will widen women's interests and inspire them with a greater sense of responsibility. We support it not merely in the interests of the women themselves, but because we believe it will bring a truer comradeship and closer co-operation of men and women in the common task of grappling with the grave national questions which it is the duty of the enfranchised democracy to solve."

The day after this Bill became law, I received from Mrs. Fawcett the following letter, which I deeply appreciated:

"MY DEAR MR. SNOWDEN,

4th July 1918.

Now that an equal Franchise Bill has become an Act of Parliament I am writing a few lines to convey to you the deep gratitude of the Societies with which I am connected for the invaluable support you have given us all along. I am thinking more especially of the way you held the fort for us in the meetings of the Labour Party, many members of which needed a good deal of converting, but it was largely your influence that made the Labour Party definitely a supporter of woman suffrage. That was a very great step in advance for us. When I am thinking of you I am thinking of your wife and of dear Isabella Ford and am thanking them both. Bless you for all you have done for women's freedom.

"Yours sincerely,
"MILLICENT G. FAWCETT."

Chapter Seven

A Review, 1906-1914

The end of July 1914 marked the close of an era in the political, economical and social life of Britain. The War came, and when it was over and our minds were free to look around, we saw all things had assumed a new form as though a great earthquake had changed the face of the land. When I look back to the years from 1906 to 1914 it seems as though these years belonged to a former life. Many of the men who then took a prominent part in public affairs have passed away, and their places have been taken by new men who were then unknown. It is supposed to be a common failing of old age to regard the present times as decadent. But I think no one with a knowledge of pre-War days will deny that they were in many respects happier than those in which we are now living. Life was less strenuous and more free from cares and anxieties. Some of the things we have today, which are regarded as evidence of the progress of civilisation, were then unknown. When I first came to London in 1906 there were no motor-buses on the streets, and the taxi-cab was rarely seen. The horse-drawn buses lumbered leisurely along streets far less crowded than they are today. The hansom cabs added a picturesqueness to the streets.

But the country in the decade before the outbreak of War was not in stagnation. Progress was being steadily made in all directions. In his Budget speech, three months before the calamity of August 1914 occurred, Mr. Lloyd George was able to report an unprecedented state of national prosperity. Trade was expanding, unemployment had touched the lowest point in the records, wealth was increasing, and the national revenue was bounding. In the eight years before 1914 our exports had increased by nearly 40 per cent. The assessable incomes of the income tax-payers had risen from £925,000,000 to £1,167,000,000. The wages of the workers, it is true, were very low, but in the years under review there had been substantial additions to their standard of living - Pensions, Health and Unemployment Insurance Grants, and a considerable improvement in National Education. The problem of the poverty of great masses of the population was being attacked, if not courageously, at least in a new spirit and with more energy. Before the outbreak of War there were evidences that all Parties were impressed by the need of social reform, and financial and trade conditions were favourable for carrying out such a policy.

The years 1906 to 1914 were productive of a larger output of beneficial legislation than in any similar period in our history. Much proposed legislation was mauled or destroyed by the House of Lords, but a fine record still remained. The legislation actually passed included the Trades Boards Act, a measure which has done immeasurable good in improving the wages and conditions in what were called the Sweated Industries; a Miners' Minimum Wage Act; the Act establishing the Labour Exchanges; the Old Age Pensions Act, and the National Unemployment and Health Insurance Schemes; the incorporation in our Taxation System of the important principle of graduation and differentiation of the Income Tax. These measures, when first adopted, were not ambitious, but they provided a foundation on which a great system of social services has been built.

When I close my eyes and picture a full House of Commons in 1906 I see many faces which deserve to be remembered. On the Labour benches I recall the striking figure of Keir Hardie in the corner seat below the gangway; the burly form of Mr. Shackleton sitting beside him; the black hair and beard of genial Will Crooks; the diminutive figure of Mr. Clynes modestly retiring into some inconspicuous seat; "Little Steve" Walsh, the Wigan miner, the most intellectual of the miners' members; John Hodge, the steel-smelter, and one of the greatest trade union organisers; Mr. Fred Jowett, the Member for Bradford, whose head always attracted attention in the Strangers' Gallery, where they thought he was some German professor who had wandered into the House of Commons; Mr. George Barnes, admired and respected by all for his sound common sense and practical knowledge; and others who are not forgotten by their living friends and comrades.

I am very often asked if I think the House of Commons has improved or deteriorated in the last thirty years. It is difficult to say. In many respects it is just the same. It contains quite as many bores, and members are just as prone as ever to talk for talking's sake. Members dress in a much more free-and-easy way than formerly. Thirty years ago the frock-coat and silk hat were very generally worn. The advent of the Labour members did a good deal to break down conventions.

I remember an old member telling me that before 1906 he had never seen a pipe in the smoke-room. In the 1906 Parliament Tommy Bowles outraged tradition by appearing in the House in a suit of white ducks. I find this item of news in the Press of the 12th June 1906: "This afternoon a new sartorial milestone was passed. Mr. Philip Snowden, the Labour member for Blackburn, sat among his political confreres wearing with entire unconcern the first ordinary straw hat ever seen within the precincts of the Mother of Parliaments." I am inclined to think that on the whole the speaking today is not up to the average level of thirty years ago. Most certainly the number of good speakers is smaller than in the pre-War Parliaments, and I add, without hesitation, that in all the post-War Parliaments there have been far fewer men of outstanding qualities. Providence has evidently, in the composition of the House of Commons, answered that part of Browning's prayer: "Oh, God, make no more giants," but has forgotten to fulfil the other part: "but elevate the race".

Keir Hardie's Parliamentary career ended with the outbreak of war. With one interval, he had been in the House of Commons for twenty years. He was not a success in Parliament, and that he fully realised. He never captured the House of Commons. It was not his place. He was not the politician, but the prophet and the seer. Compromise was not in the man's nature. He was the unsparing iconoclast who sought to break the illusions and conventions of his generation. He had set before himself an ideal which he pursued regardless of the hostility and opposition of enemies, and often with scant regard for the criticism and advice of his friends. But, withal, he was the greatest product of the democracy of our times. I had the great privilege of being intimately associated with him for over twenty years, and that acquaintance is one of my most cherished memories. I am proud to believe that I enjoyed his confidence in an unusual degree. He wrote to me once when I had been away from the House of Commons for two or three days. "What has become of you? You are the only man whose presence here I miss." He usually wrote to me when he was on a speaking tour, telling me of his experiences and how he found the movement. Keir Hardie owed nothing to the schools and Universities. He had no schooling as a boy. He taught himself to read from the chapbooks in the stationers' shop windows. He told me once what drove him to learn to write. When a youth, he went to join the Good Templars. He was unable to sign his name on the membership pledge, and he was so ashamed that he set to work to learn to write. Later, when working in the pit, he taught himself shorthand by marking the characters with bits of coal on the whitewashed walls. Yet, in spite of his early disadvantages, he became a well-educated man. Although he had a marked Scottish accent, his English, both in conversation and in public speech, was perfect. He used none of the solecisms which so often mar democratic oratory. His speeches were not those of the politician, but of the man with a mission and a message. His fine, rugged appearance, his powerful and resonant voice, the character of his popular addresses, brought to one's imagination the old Hebrew prophets thundering forth denunciation of the evils of their day and prophesying the coming of a better time. The moving impulse of Keir Hardie's work was a profound belief in the common people. He believed in their capacity, and he burned with indignation at their unmerited sufferings. He was no theoretic dogmatist. He never argued on the platform the economic theories of Socialism. His Socialism was a great human conception of the equal right of all men and women to the wealth of the world and to enjoyment of the fullness of life. Though he repudiated the dogma of the "class war", his appeal was invariably to the workers as a class. The fact of the class war he admitted, but he did not believe that its ruthless prosecution was the way to establish Socialism. He appealed to the working classes to realise their duty to act their part as citizens; and this, he believed, they could best be taught by organising themselves in a Labour Party. It was his class-consciousness which made him contemptuous of any attempt at patronage from the well-to-do. I remember on one occasion meeting a West Riding manufacturer in the Lobby of the House of Commons in a state of great indignation. He told me he had just tried to speak to Keir Hardie, who had cut him dead. "Think of that!" said this plutocrat. "And I once subscribed five pounds to the election expenses of a Labour candidate!"

"The apparel oft proclaims the man." Keir Hardie's dress was characteristic. His unconventional attire was worn for several reasons. I have heard it said that in his younger days he was something of a dandy, and the dress he assumed in his later lifetime – the flannel shirt and collar, the rough tweeds (the coat, vest and trousers usually of different patterns), the big slouch hat and Inverness cloak was worn as much probably because it made him conspicuous as because it marked him off from the conventional. A well-known Quaker thought fit, when Hardie first entered Parliament, to offer him some practical advice and to warn him against the temptations to which he would be exposed in the House of Commons, and he concluded by saying: "And above all, James, never alter your clothes". There was a wealth of wisdom in that advice. If Keir Hardie had changed into conventional dress it would have been regarded as a falling from grace. I have often wondered what he would have done if he had lived to become a Minister, and what his response would have been to the Command to go to Buckingham Palace in "frock-coat and silk hat". I am sure if he had dressed up in these symbols of respectability he would have looked handsome and dignified. Once, however, I did see him in a starched collar. He apologetically explained that he had been to his brother's wedding, and he had made that limited concession to conventionality. Once, too, he did discard the tweeds and flannel shirt. He was in Paris with a friend, and Jaures sent them tickets for the opera. They assumed that evening-dress would be essential. His friend was equipped in that respect, but the problem of providing Hardie with dress clothes was difficult. They took the head waiter into their confidence and asked him if he had a spare suit. He had a coat and trousers, but no vest. That difficulty was overcome by Hardie wearing a broad silk sash. In that attire he went to the opera, and he and his friend were the only two men in the theatre in evening-dress!

It is said to be impossible to argue with an optimist. It is more difficult to shake the faith of a prophet. Hardie profoundly believed himself to be inspired with a mission. After the declaration of the poll in an election in which he had been an unsuccessful candidate, he said to a gathering of his supporters: "I come from a race of seers, and I see clearly in prophetic vision the day, not fifty years ahead, when the cause for which we stand will be triumphant". He lived to see the Labour Party grow to such strength as to make others with duller intellects and clouded vision see the probability of his prophecy being realised. He had a strong grain of superstition in his nature. He was the only man I have known who claimed to have a certain conviction that he had lived in a former incarnation, and who had some remembrance of incidents of his former life. He had a touching sympathy for the helpless. I have seen his eyes fill with tears at the news of the death of a devoted dog. He carried to his end an old silver watch he had worn in the mine, which bore the marks of the teeth of a favourite pit pony, made by a futile attempt on its part to eat it. Though thirty years had gone, he still spoke of that dumb friend with an affection one shows to the memory of a lost child.

He never talked of religion, though I believe he retained his Church membership to the end. He had no sympathy with the pretences and unrealities of mere religious profession. It was not necessary for Keir Hardie to parade his religion. His life was the expression of a deep religious faith. A mutual friend once said to me: "If Hardie were the most blatant atheist I should still regard him as the most religious man I have ever known". "I do not know", Hardie once said to me, "what they will say about old Keir Hardie when he is dead and gone. But this at least I hope they will be able to say that, with all his faults, he always fought for his own class." And that, indeed, those of us who knew him can say.

The strenuous life which Hardie lived after he took up public work undermined a naturally strong constitution. At forty he looked twenty years older than his age. At fifty he was old and grey, almost white. At times in the eight years before the outbreak of war he had serious attacks of illness which necessitated long absences from the House of Commons. The shock of the War was too much for his enfeebled body. At first he called up all the resources of strength left to him, and spoke and wrote against the War with something of his old energy. The merging of the Labour Party in the war-mad crowd, the personal attacks of his old friends and comrades, and the temporary destruction of all he had worked for and hoped for finally broke him down. After six months of lingering illness, he died on the 26th September 1915, having just passed his fifty-ninth year. Few men have crowded so much into a short life. Few men have had so great an influence on the political life of the country. In the day when the common people enter into the Promised Land no name deserves to be more affectionately and gratefully remembered than Keir Hardie.

Before leaving recollections of the pre-War Parliaments, may I make a comment on the prospects of the Labour Party as they appeared before the outbreak of War. Between 1906 and 1914 there had been three General Elections and twenty-eight by-elections in which the Labour Party had put forward candidates. The results of all these elections showed little indication that the Labour Party was making headway among the electorate. At the two General Elections of 1910 the Party lost eleven and gained eight seats. At the twenty-eight by-elections, nearly all three-cornered fights, the Party won three seats, and lost two seats they had previously held. In the eight years from 1906 to 1914 the Labour Party had not increased the strength of its parliamentary representation. It looked as if the Party was destined to remain a mere group, depending for what representation it had upon the goodwill of the Liberals in a number of constituencies. As far back as 1903 Mr. Sidney Webb, whose political prophecies were usually very accurate, had expressed the belief that the British Labour Party was not likely ever to become so strong as to be a successful competitor with the Liberals and Conservatives for office. Even up to 1914 it looked as though Mr. Webb's forecast would prove to be true. But the War completely changed the situation. The Coalition of 1916-22 practically destroyed the Liberal Party, and gave Labour its opportunity.

Chapter Eight

My Attitude to the War

On our arrival in Liverpool at the end of January 1915 we went straight to Blackburn [Snowden and his wife had been away on a world speaking tour at the outbreak of war]. I was very anxious to meet the Labour Party there in order to get some understanding of the actual state of affairs. During my seven months' absence I had been completely out of contact with the British Labour Movement. What information I had been able to acquire had come to me from garbled and unreliable reports in the Dominion and American Press. As I think I have stated elsewhere, I had not seen an English newspaper since the outbreak of war, nor had I had any letter from England. I had gathered from what I had seen in the newspapers that there were divisions of opinion in the Labour Party upon the question of the War, and that the Independent Labour Party were not supporting it. I should have been surprised if the attitude of the I.L.P. had been otherwise. From the time I first learnt of the outbreak of the War I never had a moment's doubt as to what my position would have been if I had been at home. For fifteen years I had criticised the foreign policy of the British Government, and had declared that if it were pursued a European War would certainly break out sooner or later. When, after my return, I had the opportunity of studying the documents relating to the alleged causes of war, and when I had read the speeches of Sir Edward Grey and other British statesmen, my attitude was confirmed by everything which I read.

These facts, relating to the foreign policy of Great Britain, were the reasons why the Executive of the British Labour Party at the outbreak of war passed the following resolution, which was subsequently endorsed at a joint meeting with the Parliamentary Labour Party:

> "That the conflict between the nations in Europe, in which this country is involved, is owing to Foreign Ministers pursuing diplomatic policies

for the purpose of maintaining a balance of power; that our own national policy of understandings with France and Russia only was bound to increase the power of Russia both in Europe and Asia, and to endanger good relations with Germany.

That Sir Edward Grey, as proved by the facts which he gave in the House of Commons, committed, without the knowledge of our people, the honour of the country in supporting France in the event of any war in which she was seriously involved, and gave a definite assurance of support before the House of Commons had any chance of considering the matter.

That the Labour movement reiterates the fact that it has opposed the policy which has produced the war, and that its duty is now to secure peace at the earliest possible moment on such conditions as will provide the best opportunities for the re-establishment of amicable feelings between the workers of Europe.

That without in any way receding from the position that the Labour movement has taken in opposition to our engaging in a European War, the Executive of the Labour Party advises that, whilst watching for the earliest opportunity of taking effective action in the interests of peace and the re-establishment of good feeling between the workers of the European nations, all Labour and Socialist organisations should concentrate their energies meantime upon the task of carrying out the resolutions passed at the Conference of Labour organisations held at the House of Commons on August 5th, detailing measures to be taken to mitigate the destitution which will inevitably overtake our working people whilst the state of war lasts."

Mr. Ramsay MacDonald, who at that time was Chairman of the Parliamentary Labour Party, on the instructions of a meeting of the Parliamentary Labour Party spoke after Sir Edward Grey on the 3rd August. He made only a short speech, and reading what he said today many of his statements have proved prophetically true. He said:

"I think the Foreign Secretary is wrong. I think the Government which he represents and for which he speaks is wrong. I think the verdict of history will be that they are wrong. We shall see. The effect of the Rt. Hon. gentleman's speech in this House is not to be its final effect. If the nation's honour were in danger we would be with him. There has been no crime committed by statesmen of this character without these statesmen appealing to their nations' honour… So far as we are concerned whatever may happen, whatever may be said about us, whatever attacks may be made upon us, we will take the action that we will take of saying that this country ought to have remained neutral, because in the deepest parts of our hearts we believe that that was right and that that alone was consistent with the honour of our country and the traditions of the Party that are now in office."

Being absent from the country, I cannot write from my own knowledge of the state of public opinion in the days immediately following the outbreak of war. But from what I learnt there was little of the ignorant flag-waving jingoism. Men and women who had spent their lives in preaching peace; ministers of religion, who by their profession were expected to oppose war; Liberal newspapers which had protested magnificently against intervention before war was declared – all now threw themselves wholeheartedly into supporting the Government, calling loudly for the vigorous prosecution of the War – as though a threatened crime becomes a virtue when it has been committed. The majority of the Parliamentary Labour Party could not escape the influence of this great national surge, and as soon as war was declared they forgot their declarations, forgot the causes of the War, and decided to adopt a policy which conflicted with the resolution quoted above, which they had passed two days before. In these changed circumstances Mr. MacDonald could no longer speak in the House of Commons as Chairman of the Parliamentary Labour Party, and he accordingly resigned the position. All but two of the Independent Labour members of Parliament remained true to their principles, but the rest of the Labour Party from that time to the end of the War gave an unswerving support to the Government, and were not one bit behind in using all the usual methods of war propaganda.

So far I have written only of those reasons for the opposition of the I.L.P. members to the War which have dealt directly with its causes, but we had one other ground of opposition which far transcends all those other reasons in importance. That was our fundamental opposition to war as a national policy. We objected to war, not only because of its barbarity and of the universal suffering and ruin which it inflicts, but because of its futility. I have never taken up the attitude of the extreme pacifist who objects to war in all possible circumstances. I can imagine that in the present half-civilised state of humanity there may be occasions when war cannot be avoided if a nation is to preserve its existence, but it may be confidently asserted that war between modern nations never achieves its declared purpose. War invariably sows the seeds of future wars, and war itself never can destroy militarism and establish universal peace. Surely if the Great War has taught us any lessons at all it is that. In the war which so many people in Europe are now talking about as inevitable we shall find all the old reasons, all the old justifications, put forward, and the end will be the same as at the end of the last war – all the seeds of enmity will be left to ripen for yet another war.

When I went down to Blackburn immediately upon my return from abroad, I found that my Executive had taken up the position with regard to the War which I had expected they would take, and which was wholly in harmony with my own view. Although the great majority of my constituents had accepted what had been told to them by our politicians as to the origin and objects of the War, I found no evidence of the warlike spirit in the town. The members of the Party, I afterwards learned, were almost unanimous in their opposition to the War; there were only two or three exceptions. But all but one of these exceptions, during the four years of the War and the General Election which came at the end of it, never expressed publicly any opposition to my views. They came on to my platform at the public meetings, and worked heartily for my candidature at the Election. Like most places, I found there had been a great response to the appeal for recruits for the fighting services. I made arrangements to go back to the constituency in a fortnight to address a public meeting. It was an open meeting, and I had a packed audience of two thousand men and women. I had a very hearty welcome, and the meeting was quite unanimous. There was not a murmur of opposition, and at the end of my address when questions were invited none was put. I placed before the meeting a frank statement of my attitude to the War, very much on the lines I have already stated. I took advantage of the occasion to explain my attitude to the recruiting campaign. I had been invited by the Mayor to speak in the recruiting campaign, and had declined to do so. I could not ask men to fight in a war I did not approve. Moreover, I believed that no man had any right to use any influence he might possess to induce other people to take a serious risk which he was not prepared, or was not able to undertake himself. The consequences being so serious, enlistment was entirely a matter for the individual's own conscience. If men believed that liberty called them to fight for liberty, then they would go, and if they went under a noble impulse like that they were deserving of honour.

During the early part of 1915 I and my pacifist friends felt that it was little use publicly agitating for Peace Negotiations. The temper of the people was such that at that time an appeal would have had little effect upon the mass mind. It needed a longer experience of the horror and suffering inflicted by the War to bring them into a frame of mind where such appeals would receive consideration. So, in the meantime, I turned my activities into other channels.

Chapter Nine

Coalition and Conscription

In the early part of May 1915 it was widely rumoured that there were serious differences in the Cabinet. Some members, led by Mr. Lloyd George, were said to be gravely concerned about the ineffective prosecution of the War. Talk became general about the need for a reconstruction of the Government, and the idea of a Coalition Government began to be mooted. The circumstances which led up to the formation of the first Coalition Government have been described by those who were intimately associated with the events. I am able to write with knowledge only of the association of the Labour Party with this change.

One afternoon during this crisis I was leaving the House after the close of a sitting when I encountered Mrs. Asquith at the exit in the Speaker's Court. She said that she wanted to have a chat with me. Her car was at the door, and as I was making for Charing Cross Station she insisted that she should drive me there. When we got into the car she slapped my knee and said: "We're in an awful mess!" She went on to explain that the Tories had got information about the shortage of munitions and were insisting that they should be admitted into the Government. She said that Lloyd George was at the bottom of the whole trouble. Mr. Asquith was strongly opposed to the idea, which he regarded as an undeserved slight upon his administration.

A week later the Coalition Government had been formed. It consisted of twelve Liberals, eight Unionists, Lord Kitchener, and one Labour member – Mr. Arthur Henderson. Mr. John Redmond [the Irish Nationalist leader] had been offered a seat in the Cabinet, but was unable to accept it. His action was supported by a meeting of his party. On the day Mr. Asquith announced that a Coalition Government was in contemplation, Mr. Arthur Henderson intimated to the Executive of the Labour Party and to the Parliamentary Labour Party that he had received an invitation to join a Coalition Government with a seat in the Cabinet. The Executive of the Labour Party agreed that the

Prime Minister's invitation should be accepted. But when the matter came before the Parliamentary Labour Party on the same day the invitation was rejected by nine votes to eight. A joint meeting of the Executive of the Labour Party with the Parliamentary Party was then held, and the proposal was very freely discussed. This joint meeting decided to accept the Prime Minister's proposal by seventeen votes to eleven. The majority of the members of the Parliamentary Labour Party again opposed the acceptance of the offer. Since the outbreak of war there had been no Conference of the National Party. The Annual Conference was due to be held in January 1915, but the Executive of the party, after taking a postal vote of the affiliated organisations, decided that it should be postponed, especially as the social and industrial activities occasioned by the recruiting campaign made it inadvisable to hold it. Such a step as joining in a Coalition Government was so opposed to the constitution of the Labour Party that it was felt a decision ought not to be taken without the sanction of a Party Conference. It was not within the powers of the Executive of the Parliamentary Party to take such a step, and even the exceptional circumstances at the time did not warrant it. Notwithstanding the strong opposition of the Parliamentary Labour Party, as shown by the vote upon the question, Mr. Arthur Henderson acted upon the majority decision and joined the Coalition Government as President of the Board of Education with a seat in the Cabinet. Two other members of the Labour Party were appointed to subordinate offices – Mr. W. Brace as Under-Secretary for Home Affairs and Mr. George Roberts as a Junior Whip.

Shortly after the formation of the Coalition Government the question of Conscription became prominent. It was alleged that the voluntary system and Lord Derby's scheme of attestation were not bringing in a sufficient number of recruits. The Trades Union Congress in September had passed a resolution strongly opposing Conscription, but at the same time it realised that if Conscription were to be avoided increased efforts would have to be made to secure the necessary number of recruits under the voluntary system. On the 27th September a meeting of the Executives of the various Labour bodies, and including members of the Parliamentary Labour Party, met in London and conferred with Lord Kitchener and the Prime Minister on the situation. It was decided that the Labour organisations should undertake a special recruiting effort on Labour platforms through the organisations of the Labour movement only. The Government, however, did not wait for the outcome of this campaign, but proceeded to take steps for the introduction of a Conscription Bill. When it became definitely known at the end of 1915 that the Government were about to introduce a Conscription measure, the three National Labour Committees and the Parliamentary Labour Party met to consider the situation. Before this Conference had time to meet a Conscription Bill was introduced into Parliament by Mr. Asquith on the 5th January 1916. The House of Commons, of course, by overwhelming majorities supported the Conscription Bill. But the votes of the House of Commons in favour of the Bill did not reflect a united opinion in the country. Married men generally supported the measure as it applied only to unmarried men. They hoped that the number of men recruited from this class would supply sufficient men to render it unnecessary for the married man to be called to the colours. The votes of the Labour Conference provided further evidence of the lack of national support for the measure. There was a great deal of opposition to the measure among Nonconformists, but it never took an organised form of expression. Sir John Simon, who had been Home Secretary in the Coalition Government, resigned his office as he was unable to give his approval to the measure. His accession to the ranks of the anti-conscriptionists in the House of Commons was a great acquisition to their debating strength. He delivered some powerful speeches in opposition to the Bill. On the First Reading the Irish members voted against the Bill because it would apply to Ireland. The Government withdrew these provisions, and the Bill as passed did not extend to Ireland. It was believed that it would have been impossible to enforce a conscription measure in Ireland, and if attempts had been made to do so, very serious trouble would undoubtedly have arisen. After the Irish Nationalists had secured this concession they did not vote in the further stages of the Bill. The anti-Conscriptionist Party in the House numbered thirty-nine. Three or four of the Labour members who were not in opposition to the War joined us in voting against this Bill. Though the strength of the opposition to conscription in the House of Commons was small, the Bill was far from being popular in the country. Mr. Asquith had said a short time before the measure was introduced that there could be no measure of conscription except by general consent. General assent to this Bill certainly did not exist. This declaration by Mr. Asquith was like many others which he made during the War which he was at a later date compelled to repudiate through the pressure brought to bear upon him.

At the request of the little group of thirty-nine, I spoke on the Second Reading of the Bill. *The Times*, in its account of the debate, said that my speech was quite the ablest onslaught that had been made upon the Bill. This was a compliment which I did not deserve, for there had been in the four days' debate upon the Second Reading a considerable number of speeches in opposition of very high merit. The Bill, as I have mentioned, applied only to single men between the ages of eighteen and forty-one, and contained a number of provisions for exemption in certain circumstances such as business obligations, men in key positions in munition factories, physical incapacity, and the conscientious objectors to military service. We directed our attention during the Committee stage mainly to safeguarding and strengthening these provisions.

There was an incident in connection with the treatment of the conscientious objectors in prison which I must relate, because it answers the charge so often made against Mr. Asquith that he was always slow in making up his mind to take definite action. A large number of these resisters had been concentrated in one of the London prisons and placed in charge of a military officer as commandant. This man was, I think, mentally unbalanced. He treated the men in a shameful way, and wrote long letters to them of a most abusive nature. Some of these letters came into my hands, and I at once set out to place them before Mr. Asquith, who at that time was acting temporarily as Secretary for War in place of Lord Kitchener, who had just been lost in the *Hampshire*. When I reached Downing Street, Mrs. Asquith was just coming out. Her car was at the door. She asked me if I was coming in to see Henry. She thought he was engaged at the moment, but she would like to have a talk with me until he was ready to see me. So we went into the secretary's room, and for half an hour she gave me a most entertaining time. The intrigues of Mr. Lloyd George and Lord Northcliffe which had led to the overthrow of Mr. Asquith's first Government were still going on, she said. She saw them walking and conspiring at six o'clock in the morning in the garden of No. 11. Her great desire at that time was to see both of them dangling from lamp-posts in Whitehall!

When I was called into the Cabinet room to see Mr. Asquith he apologised for keeping me waiting. I told him I had been talking to Mrs. Asquith, and he said

"Oh!", in a tone which implied "I wonder what she has been saying now!" She had said nothing indiscreet, unless it were an indiscretion to tell me such family secrets as "Henry" coming home from the House every night to hear "Puffin" (Anthony) say his prayers before he went to sleep. Without any preliminaries I put these letters before him. I had carefully arranged them so that he read the milder ones first. The last letter I put before him had this sentence: "You say you are going to make a complaint to the War Office. You can do what the hell you like. I do not care a damn for Asquith or anybody else!" When Mr. Asquith read those words he collected all the letters, put them into his pocket, and said: "I am going across to the War Office now, and you will hear later what I have done". In half an hour that official was dismissed from his post.

Before leaving the conscientious objectors I may mention a strange incident that happened during a debate about them in the House of Commons. A young Conservative member, Mr. Harold Smith, a brother of "F. E.", was denouncing these resisters with great vigour as cowards and shirkers. I quietly interrupted him by asking: "Seeing that the Hon. Member is himself of military age, will he kindly tell us why he is not serving in the Army?" For a moment he was completely confounded, and then made this amazing answer: "That is a matter for my own conscience". The House was aghast at the inanity of this remark. The member stumbled through two or three more sentences and then sat down. I do not think he ever spoke again in that Parliament.

Chapter Ten

The Russian Revolution

In March 1917 the news burst upon the world that the long-awaited Russian revolution had come at last – quite suddenly and without warning. The revolution had been precipitated by the action of the Czar in issuing a Ukase dissolving the Duma and the Council of the Empire. But this action on the part of the Czar was the outcome of the internal state of Russia, where starvation was almost universal, and the army was virtually in a state of mutiny. Widespread corruption in the Government, and the misappropriation of money voted for the equipment of the army, had led to the soldiers being driven into battle with scarcely any arms at all, where they were mown down like rye. It was calculated that by this time over eight million Russians had been killed, and other casualties amounted to over twenty million.

During the first few weeks of the first Russian revolution there was an embarrassing division of power between the Provisional Government and the Soldiers' and Workers' Committee, which was a very powerful organisation of Socialists. M. Kerensky, who had taken office in the Provisional Government as Minister of Justice, was the only Socialist member of that Government. Eventually a compromise was reached about the middle of May under which the Socialists got six seats in the newly constituted Government. M. Miliukoff, who had been Minister of Foreign Affairs in the first Government, was dropped because he was considered to be too imperialistic. This new Coalition Government at once issued a declaration of its policy. It repudiated any intention of making a separate peace, made a promise to develop the principles of democracy in the army and to strengthen military power, but at the same time it laid down in very explicit terms that the peace at which Russia aimed must be a peace without annexations or indemnities, and must be based upon the rights of nations to decide their own affairs. On the 16th May, immediately after this declaration by the Russian Government, I opened a debate in the House of Commons on behalf of the peace group on the following resolution:

> "This House welcomes the declaration of the new democratic Government of Russia, repudiating all proposals for militarist conquest and aggrandisement, and calls upon His Majesty's Government to issue a similar declaration on behalf of the British democracy, and to join with the Allies in restating the Allied terms in conformity with the Russian declaration."

This motion led to a most interesting debate which occupied the whole sitting. Our amendment was, of course, lost, 32 members voting for it and 238 against. As a response from the British democracy to the declaration of the Russian Government, we formed a Committee, of which I was the chairman, to arrange for the holding of a great Convention at Leeds, "to follow Russia in her demand for the repudiation of all materialistic War aims, and the establishment of a peace without annexations or indemnities." As the purpose of this Convention was misrepresented at the time, and is still being misrepresented, I would like to state the facts relating to this great gathering. I was, as I have said, chairman of the organising committee, and have a clear knowledge of all that happened in connection with it. The organising committee of the Convention consisted of representatives of the Independent Labour Party and the British Socialist Party with the addition of Mr. Robert Smillie and Mr. Robert Williams. Circulars were sent out to Trades Councils, Trade Unionists, local Labour Parties, Socialist Parties, Women's Organisations, and other democratic bodies.

It was the most democratically constituted Labour Convention ever held in this country. It was held in the huge Coliseum at Leeds on the 3rd June 1917. At that time railway travelling was very difficult, but no less than 1,150 delegates came to the Convention, hailing from every part of Great Britain. If there had been any strong popular feeling against the holding of such a Convention it would certainly have organised itself. For weeks before the date of the Convention the Press had been denouncing the Convention and inciting the rowdy elements to opposition. There was not the slightest evidence of any opposition either inside the theatre or among the crowds outside. The delegates went about the streets wearing their red ribbons without the slightest molestation. The delegates had been sent from Trades Councils and local Labour Parties, Trade Unionists, Socialist Bodies, Women's Organisations, Co-operative Societies, Adult Schools, and the Peace Societies. Unlike the Trade Unions and Labour

Party Conferences, there was no "block vote". Every delegate had equal voting power. The Convention was a strange contrast to the Labour Conference held at Manchester in the previous January. Then the war spirit dominated the majority of the delegates. They would not listen to any talk about peace. The demand was for the ruthless prosecution of the War until a victory had been achieved. In the intervening five months the leaven of peace had worked a wonderful change in the minds and attitude of many of the leaders of the Trade Unions and Labour movement. The Russian Revolution and the magnificent appeal of its leaders to the democracies of the world to work for an early peace with no annexations and no indemnities had done much to bring about this change.

The great gallery of the theatre was crowded to suffocation with freely admitted visitors. The chair was taken by Mr. Robert Smillie, the miners' leader, who received a welcome which showed how warm a place he had in the hearts of those to whose service he had devoted a long life. The slogan of the Convention had been "Follow Russia", and as this has since been misrepresented as a demand for a revolution in Britain which would overthrow the monarchy and the constitution and establish a Communist State, it would be well to make clear what was the purpose of the Convention, and in what respect this country was called upon to "follow Russia". The Bolshevik Revolution which overthrew the Democratic Government did not occur until the November following, five months after the date of this Convention. The first resolution was moved by Mr. Ramsay MacDonald in a speech of passionate power, which roused the delegates to a high state of enthusiasm. The resolution was carried with complete unanimity. The second resolution on Foreign Policy and War Aims was entrusted to me. I had repeatedly to appeal to the delegates against applause as tending to waste of time. After a magnificent debate the resolution was carried with only two dissentients. The resolution on Workmen's and Soldiers' Councils needs a little further explanation. This proposal for the establishment of Workmen's and Soldiers' Councils was the idea of Mr. W. C. Anderson. For some days before the Convention the Press had seized upon this resolution and had grossly misrepresented its purpose. It was described as an incitement to the subversion of army discipline and military authority. It was in effect a very harmless resolution as a careful reading of its terms will show. It was largely unnecessary, for the work of looking after the interests of the workers in industry and of the disabled soldiers was undertaken by an organisation conducted by the Labour Party and the Trade Unions. Nothing came of this resolution, as, when the committee which had organised the Conference met afterwards, we considered it was unnecessary to carry out the proposal.

A number of local conferences had already been called to take up the question of forming local branches of Workmen's and Soldiers' Councils. Most of these were carried out quite peacefully, but at two or three of them there was organised rowdyism which broke up the conferences. At a conference which was going to be held at the Brotherhood Church, Southgate, the worst riot seen in London for years occurred. The Press had been for some days inciting soldiers and others to turn up at the meeting-place and prevent the conference from being held. A great crowd collected before the time of the meeting, which soon showed that it was bent on mischief. Conspicuous among the rioters were a considerable number of Canadian soldiers. The crowd rushed the church and, once inside the building, the work of destruction began with vigour. Every piece of furniture in the church was smashed to atoms, the chairs were used for the systematic battering of the leaded windows to pieces, water pipes were hacked away from the walls, and water drenched the attackers and for a time quenched their ardour. The promoters of the meeting, including a number of women, kept their seats, and passively defied the attack of the rioters. This seemed to have some effect upon the violence of the intruders, who made no attack upon them. Nobody was seriously hurt, but in the general scuffle three people received minor injuries and had to be taken away to hospital. At the time this incident was taking place I was addressing a Conference in Leicester, which passed off without the least interruption.

Some time after the outbreak of the Russian Revolution a deputation of four came to England from the Workmen's and Soldiers' and Socialist Councils to try to get the British Labour Party to take part in an International Socialist Conference of all the belligerent countries to attain peace on the conditions laid down in the manifesto of the new democratic Government of Russia. I had a number of acquaintances among the Russian political refugees in London, and through them I became well acquainted with the four delegates from Russia. With the help of Mr. H. W. Massingham, then editor of the *Nation*, who was giving strong support in his journal to the Russian Revolutionary Government, we were able to get the case of these Russian delegates put forward in a number of sympathetic British newspapers. Our house at Golders Green became the centre from which this propaganda was conducted. These delegates belonged to the Menshevik, or moderate section of the Russian Socialists. I believe that when the Bolshevik Revolution occurred some of these delegates, like Kerensky, were exiled from Russia.

In the days before the Great War there often came to see me a small, thin man, with the stooping shoulders of the scholar. He was always neatly dressed in well-worn black clothes, and his brown beard was always neatly trimmed. He spoke quickly in excellent English, jerking out his words, his hands always moving nervously. He was one of the band of Russian refugees who had found an asylum in England from the tyranny of the Czarist regime. Like many of his class, he seemed to have no occupation, and no visible means of subsistence. He lived in a tenement in the Euston district, and though I was never able to discover what his circumstances really were, I saw no evidence that he was in want. That he had ample leisure I had proof in the frequent and voluminous written epistles he sent me on the dogma of the "class struggle" and the theory of "mass action". This man was George Tchitcherine (so he always spelt his name). I little dreamt in those days that he was destined to become an historic figure, one of three men holding the fate of Russia in their hands. His main interest in those days was the fate of the revolutionary exiles in Siberia. He first came to me to enlist my help on their behalf. We formed an English committee, of which I was chairman and he secretary, to raise funds to get some comforts for these exiles.

When the first Revolution came Tchitcherine was not a Bolshevik. He did not, however, approve of the action of Kerensky and the Mensheviks in forming a Coalition with the Cadets, though he remained on friendly terms with them, and when a delegation of Mensheviks came to England he acted as guide and interpreter. When legislation was passed to send Russians of military age resident in this country into the Russian army, he organised resistance to it. He became the leader of a No Conscription Movement. Up to that time, as a citizen of an allied nation, he had been immune from the inconvenient attention which the British Government had bestowed upon so many foreigners of doubtful patriotism. What his views were about the War I never knew from any confession he ever made to me. But when he became prominent in opposition to British policy in the matter of recruiting, he was not long left to pursue his activities. He was arrested and interned in Brixton Jail. I had not seen him for a considerable time previous to this, and was surprised to get a request from the Committee, before which appeals against internment were heard, to appear before them and tell them what I knew of him. It was very little I could tell the Committee. My association with him had been solely confined to the object I have mentioned, and he had always been singularly reticent about his other activities. But I discovered from the Committee that he had not been interned ostensibly because of his alleged pro-German activities, or, in the official charge, for "hostile associations". It appeared that he had been a member and a frequenter of a foreign Communist Club in Clerkenwell, which was a notorious centre of revolutionary activity and of hostility to all existing Governments. The Committee confirmed the internment order, and he was kept in Brixton Jail for, I think, five months, and then deported under every circumstance of humiliation.

Immediately on his return to Russia, the Russian Bolshevik Revolution having in the meantime taken place, he was appointed to the high office of Commissar for Foreign Affairs. It came as a great surprise to me, and I think to all who had known this mild-mannered and apparently inoffensive individual, to discover that he was so important a person in the Russian revolutionary movement. As Foreign Minister, Tchitcherine soon began to show mettle we had little suspected he had in his nature. His offensive dispatches to the British Government, which would not recognise him, but could not ignore him, shocked the taste of our Foreign Office. I remember an interview I had with Mr. Balfour, who was then acting as Foreign Secretary, about some Russian matter, just after Lord Robert Cecil, then Under-Secretary, had sent a particularly dictatorial Note to Tchitcherine, and Mr. Balfour had complained that Tchitcherine had ignored it. "Would you have sent a reply to such a Note addressed to you ?" I asked Mr. Balfour. "Well", he replied, "I would not ask the man who sent it to me to dinner."

Another of the Russian refugees in London before and for a few years after the outbreak of war was Litvinoff, the present Russian Foreign Minister. He used to come occasionally with Tchitcherine to see me. He was at that time working in a warehouse in the City. When the Bolshevik Revolution occurred he was appointed by Lenin the Russian representative in London. He was not recognised by the British Government, and after many unpleasant experiences he was deported. I was not in sympathy with the Bolshevik regime, but I saw a good deal of Litvinoff in those days, as he came to live near us in Golders Green. He had married an English lady - a niece of the late Sir Sidney Low. One evening in September 1918 he called to see me, and said that he had heard that his house and office were likely to be raided by the police within the next few days. There was little or nothing among his papers of any importance, but he had a small packet he was very anxious should not fall into the hands of the police. He asked me if I would oblige him by taking charge of it for a day or two. I did not altogether like it, but I could not refuse to oblige him. I was not to give up the packet to anybody but himself or to a person holding his written instructions. He came for it himself two days later. A remark he made when I handed it back to him led me to believe that it contained money. I was at the time Chairman of the I.L.P., and he said he would like to make a donation to the funds of the Party. I thanked him, but added that on no account could the I.L.P. accept money from Communist sources. Litvinoff was a very different character from Tchitcherine. He seemed hard and unsympathetic, the sort of man who would pursue a purpose with relentless determination. I have not seen him since he was deported, but from his public actions as Russian Foreign Minister I assume that he has changed somewhat and become less extreme and more practical. If he ever did entertain the ideas held and preached by Russian Communists in the early years of the Bolshevik regime of Russia's isolation from the outside capitalist world and the pursuit of the aim of world revolution, he has abandoned these ideas and aims. It is, perhaps, the common experience of responsibility and the knowledge of practical affairs changing a person's outlook, for in recent years Litvinoff has shown himself to be the most international of statesmen and the most skilful and successful of diplomats.

Chapter Eleven

Coalitions and Conferences

Early in December 1916, a political crisis reached its climax with the resignation of Mr. Asquith of his office of Prime Minister. This was the culmination of a conspiracy which had been going on for some time, the principal conspirators being Lord Northcliffe and Mr. Lloyd George. For some time the Northcliffe newspapers had been violently attacking Asquith every day, and demanding his resignation. Matters were brought to a head by a demand presented by Mr. Lloyd George to Mr. Asquith that the War Committee of the Cabinet should be reconstituted and should consist of three members, one of the three being the Chairman. The Prime Minister was not to be a member of the Committee. This, of course, was an insulting suggestion that no self-respecting Prime Minister could possibly entertain, and it was no doubt put forward with the intention that Mr. Asquith would be driven to resign. Consequently Mr. Asquith offered his resignation to the King. Mr. Bonar Law was in the first instance invited by the King to form a Government, and upon his intimating that he could not do so, Mr. Lloyd George was offered and accepted the Premiership, and the duty devolved upon him of forming a new Government. All the important Liberal members who had been in the first Coalition under Mr. Asquith declined to serve under Mr. Lloyd George, including Lord Buckmaster, Lord Crewe, Lord Grey, Mr. McKenna, Mr. Runciman and Mr. Herbert Samuel. The Liberals whom Mr. Lloyd George retained or brought into his Government were a motley crew. There was not a single one who had the least political standing in the country. An additional number of Conservative members, mostly nonentities, were brought into the Government. The circumstances under which Mr. Asquith's Government had been overthrown and in which Mr. Lloyd George's Government was formed were such as to preclude a self-respecting Liberal or Labour man from participating in it.

Mr. Arthur Henderson had been a Cabinet Minister in Mr. Asquith's Coalition Government, and two other Labour members had held minor offices. When Mr. Lloyd George was forming his new Government he sought the help of Mr. Henderson to get the Labour Party's participation. On the Friday before Mr. Asquith resigned, Mr. Arthur Henderson spoke at a public meeting in Northampton. It was then publicly known what was going on in the Cabinet, and Mr. Henderson must have been well aware of the efforts which were being made by Mr. Lloyd George and the Conservative members to force Mr. Asquith's resignation. Mr. Henderson took the opportunity in his speech at Northampton to pass an eloquent eulogy on Mr. Asquith. "No statesman in the country", he said, "possesses the same power to reconcile and unite divergent interests as Mr. Asquith, and in my opinion he is the man to lead us to the end of the War." Mr. Asquith was then, in his opinion, the indispensable leader to carry the country successfully through the War. During the weekend Mr. Henderson had been thinking the matter over, and he came to the conclusion that it was not Mr. Asquith who was absolutely indispensable, but Mr. Arthur Henderson. On the Tuesday following, when Mr. Asquith resigned, Mr. Henderson was perfectly ready to follow a new leader who "might go faster, but where he will go there is not the same certainty as following a tried leader like Mr. Asquith." On the Thursday Mr. Henderson conveyed to the Labour Party an invitation from Mr. Lloyd George to associate itself with the new Ministry. The National Executive of the Labour Party were in London at the time, and it was agreed that Mr. Henderson's message from Mr. Lloyd George should be considered at a general meeting of the Executive and the Parliamentary Party. I was present at this meeting. Mr. Henderson told us that Mr. Lloyd George was prepared to offer a larger number of offices in the Government to Labour, and also to carry out a number of reforms which were upon the Labour programme. The meeting was not satisfied with Mr. Henderson's explanation, and decided to request Mr. Lloyd George to receive the whole of the members present in order to go further into the invitation and its conditions. The request was made to Mr. Lloyd George by telephone, and he responded to it with alacrity.

We all trooped off to the War Office, and there we found the new Prime Minister in the most exuberant spirits. He told us that the new Government had been formed for the ruthless prosecution of the War, that every consideration should be subservient to that aim, and that he was very desirous of securing the co-operation of the Labour Party. He indicated the offices and departments to which the proposed Labour members should be appointed. He announced his intention to institute State control of mines and shipping, important developments in the production of home supplies of food, and the establishment of a Ministry of Labour. As we were leaving the room, Mr. Lloyd George said to me: "I see you have managed to keep out of prison so far." I replied, "I do not suppose I shall keep out much longer now that you have the power to put me there." "I shall not do it", he said, "You'd be much more dangerous in than out." After this Conference with Mr. Lloyd George we all went back to the House of Commons and resumed our meeting. The announcement by Lloyd George that six or eight more Labour members were to be given posts in the Government had considerably reduced the opposition to accepting the invitation. To bring the matter to an issue the Chairman asked for a Resolution, and it was at once moved that the invitation be not accepted. A number of speeches followed, every one of which was opposed to accepting the invitation. Then Mr. Henderson rose, and began by complaining that no speeches in support of the invitation had been made. He said that this was a case where feeling pulled one way and national interests another. He had made up his mind to serve under Mr. Lloyd George, and justified this from the point of view of the national interest. "If Labour were to take no part in the new Government it would give to the Allies the impression that the country was divided and was not behind the new Government." He said nothing about the impression which the Allies would get from the fact that Mr. Asquith and every prominent member of the Liberals had withdrawn from the Coalition. After a long discussion, in which the weight of the argument was on the side of those who were against accepting the invitation, the resolution was put and defeated by 17 votes to 12. By this narrow majority Mr. Henderson and half a dozen of his colleagues were authorised to join the Government.

Six weeks later (in January 1917) the Annual Conference of the Labour Party was held in Manchester, and this action on the part of the Parliamentary Party and the Executive came up for decision. This Conference was the liveliest Labour Party Conference I have ever attended. Mr. Henderson had the warmest time of his life. There had been a good deal of disaffection among the engineers on the Clyde through schemes for the dilution of labour. Mr. David Kirkwood, who was the chief shop steward at one of the works, had come into notoriety through the prominent part he took in heckling Mr. Lloyd George, then Minister of Munitions, when he paid a visit to Glasgow about Christmas 1915. Three or four months after this visit a strike took place in several of the works, and this interfered with the output of munitions. Mr. Kirkwood, who disclaimed all responsibility for the strike, was deported without trial under the Defence of the Realm Act with eight of his fellows, and up to the time of this Conference he had been in Edinburgh. Mr. Kirkwood attributed his deportation to his attacks on Mr. Lloyd George when he had visited Glasgow, but there did not appear to be any ground for this assumption. As Mr. Henderson was a member of the Government it was assumed that he had a measure of responsibility for the deportation of Mr. Kirkwood. When the Chairman called Mr. Kirkwood the great body of delegates turned their heads in surprise, and the speaker was greeted by a loud cheer from those who knew the facts. As soon as it spread through the hall that Mr. Kirkwood was the representative of the Clyde deportees the cheering became general, and as Mr. Kirkwood proceeded with the narrative of his treatment the Conference was roused to a great state of indignation, which led to one of the wildest scenes that have been witnessed in a Labour Conference. He related in graphic style how he and his eight comrades were arrested one morning early, placed in prison cells, and deported in the evening from their native district. No charge was made against them. They were given no chance of proving their innocence of any offence which had led to this treatment. After keeping them in banishment for nine months, the Government now offered to set them free if they signed documents undertaking to work regularly and loyally and behave obediently to their Trade Union. They declined to sign what they considered to be a humiliating pledge. They demanded that the Government should state the reasons they had been deported, and that they should have a fair trial. When he left that Conference he said he would not return to deportation, but would go straight home to Glasgow, or to prison.

When Mr. Kirkwood sat down the Conference was in a state of pandemonium. Delegates jumped on chairs and yelled frantically for Henderson. Mr. Henderson rose, but for a time could not get a hearing. He faced the storm with coolness, and when he was allowed to state his case he repudiated any responsibility for an administrative act on which he was not consulted. He asked that the Conference should appoint a committee of investigation. "If I am to be condemned, then let me be condemned after a full investigation, which is the birthright of every Englishman." The Conference at once seized on this statement, and yelled out: "This is what you have refused to Kirkwood." However, the Conference finally gave Mr. Henderson his committee, but passed a resolution condemning deportation without trial as a thing that savoured of that Prussianism which we were fighting to destroy. The delegates followed this up by a telegram to Mr. Lloyd George, demanding the immediate withdrawal of the deportation orders against Mr. Kirkwood and his friends, and it fell to Mr. Henderson as Secretary to the Conference to send this telegram to his fellow-member in the War Cabinet!

The next exciting incident in the Conference arose on the action of the Executive Committee and the Parliamentary Labour Party in accepting by a majority the invitation of Mr. Lloyd George to join his Government. Mr. Henderson made a long statement, setting out the reasons which had induced these two bodies to recommend acceptance of Mr. Lloyd George's invitation. I followed Mr. Henderson in opposition to the course which had been pursued. I had one of the most entertaining experiences in my career. At this time the majority of the delegates were still ardent supporters of the "knock-out blow" policy. I knew that it was hopeless to get a vote in the Conference repudiating this action, so I just let myself go! For forty-five minutes, as the *Manchester Guardian* put it, "I exercised my dangerous gift of irony". Another newspaper described the incident as follows:

> "Mr. Snowden stood on the floor for forty-five minutes pointing a long menacing forefinger at the Labour Members of Parliament who had lined up in coalition with the Tories and Lloyd George. He skinned and flayed them, and rubbed salt in the sore places. When they howled, Mr. Snowden only dangled his spectacles and waited. He was in no hurry, he told them, but they had to take the medicine that he, as a good physician, had prepared for them."

The resolution approving the action of the Party in joining the Coalition was, of course, carried by a large majority - 1,849,000 for the Coalition, and 307,000 against it. This majority was obtained by means of the block vote, and it was likely that had an individual vote of the delegates been taken the majority would not have been nearly so large.

When the Conference met the following January (1918), at Nottingham, a great change had taken place. Mr. Henderson had been driven out of the Coalition Government by his Cabinet colleagues because of his support of the proposal for a Conference of the Socialist Parties of the neutral and belligerent countries. Special Conferences had been held to formulate Labour's peace proposals. By this time the British Labour Party had become widely infected with the rapidly growing desire for peace. The conversion of the Labour Party to the policy of peace negotiations brought them into line with the attitude which the I.L.P. had assumed from the beginning of the War. We recognised that when once the War had been entered upon, when passions had been aroused, and when the question of national honour and prestige became involved, it was impossible to stop it until time and the tragic sufferings had cooled these passions and brought about a change of mind favourable for the employment of reason. We believed that at any time after the first year of the War diplomacy should have been employed for the purpose of trying to bring it to an end. This was the policy which the I.L.P. advocated vigorously from the end of the first year of the War to its conclusion. During the years of the War the I.L.P. as an organisation passed through very difficult times. It was no pleasant experience to be in opposition to so many of our friends in the Labour Party. When we take into consideration the fact that the War position of the I.L.P. was supported only by a small minority of the nation, it is remarkable that the organisation was kept so well together. In the first year of the War the I.L.P. was undoubtedly very unpopular. It was the object of persistent and violent attacks and malevolent misrepresentation in the Press. In the face of all this it maintained its organisation and continued to hold public meetings. In the first year of the War the income of the Headquarters was maintained, and the number of the branches of the Party increased. In the second year of the War the I.L.P. intensified its propaganda, and a larger number of meetings was held on the subject of peace by negotiation and the conscription of wealth. This propaganda was carried on under considerable difficulties arising from the restrictions on the Press and upon public speaking, and also from the fact that the imposition of conscription had taken away many of the active workers in the local branches. The year ended with an increase of members, an increase of branches, and a financial position improved as compared with twelve months before.

At the first I.L.P. Conference after the outbreak of War, which was held at Norwich, we experienced some difficulty in obtaining a hall for the Conference. The owners of the hall, which had been engaged for the purpose for some time, cancelled the hiring just before the date of the Conference. When this became known two religious bodies in Norwich offered the use of their buildings for the Conference. At this Norwich Conference Mr. Keir Hardie made his last appearance on the platform of an I.L.P. Conference. His health had been for some time failing, and the shock of the War aggravated his illness, causing his death six months later. I shall never forget his last speech near the end of the Conference. Although he was weak, and the hand of death was obviously upon him, he spoke with great passion on a resolution protesting against the action of the Russian authorities in passing severe sentences upon the members of the Duma. His concluding sentence was: "We register our protest against the infamies of the bloody cruelties of Russia". These were the last words he addressed to a Party he had been largely instrumental in making, and of which for more than twenty years he had been the honoured leader.

During the last two years of the War there was a remarkable increase in the membership of the I.L.P., which reflected the change of public opinion in favour of bringing the War to an end by negotiation. At the Annual Conference of the Party at Leeds in 1917 I was elected Chairman of the Party. On taking office I ventured to express the hope and the confident belief that the year upon which we were entering would see the Party grow in strength and interest. This hope was realised far beyond all expectations. When I presided at the Annual Conference held next year at Leicester I was in the proud position of being able to present a report of progress during the year which had surpassed all previous records in the history of the Party. Our income at the Headquarters Office had increased by 50 per cent, and one hundred and fifty-eight new branches had been formed. The reported membership of the Party was 90 per cent higher than the year before. The following year's Conference assembled at Huddersfield. I was in the position to report that the progress of the Party had been maintained. One hundred and thirty-nine new branches had been formed during the year. This increase in the membership of the Party had not been recruited wholly from the working classes, but also from men and women of influence and reputation whose faith in the old political Parties had been destroyed by the War, and who recognised in the I.L.P. a movement which expressed the economic, political and international ideals and needs of the age. This Huddersfield Conference was the largest the Party had ever held, consisting of three hundred and seventy delegates. The Conference was held a few months after the General Election of 1918, when the five I.L.P. Members of Parliament who had taken an anti-War attitude were defeated. These defeats had not in the least depressed the Party. We realised that it was the result of a temporary state of public opinion which was already rapidly passing away, and that when the next Election came the electors would reverse this decision, as indeed proved to be the case.

Chapter Twelve

The 1918 General Election

Immediately after the announcement of the Armistice, rumours spread that Mr. Lloyd George was contemplating a General Election. He wanted to get a popular verdict before disillusionment and the inevitable reaction which follows every period of strain came to the electors. In view of the likelihood of a General Election, the Labour Party held a Special Conference on 14th November to decide what its election policy should be. The Labour Party still had its representatives in the Coalition Government, and the point at issue was whether Labour's part in the Coalition should be continued, or it should go back to its former position of political independence. The delegates were almost wholly the same persons who had attended the various Labour Conferences during the War, and who had opposed all proposals for peace negotiations and who had given enthusiastic support to the Coalition Government. I could not help contrasting in my mind the tone and temper of this Conference with the experiences of the minority in former Conferences when we were howled down for advocating the attitude which this Conference was prepared to approve. It was quite evident from the opening of the Conference that the majority of the delegates had made up their minds to have nothing more to do with Mr. Lloyd George's Government. The Executive of the Party submitted a resolution declaring that the General Election would terminate the conditions under which the Party entered the Coalition, and the Party should resume its independence and withdraw from the Coalition at the close of the present Parliament. Mr. Clynes, who was a member of the Coalition Government holding the office of Food Controller, moved an amendment that Labour should remain in the Coalition Government up to the end of the War, and when the Peace Treaty had been signed the Party should resume its freedom of action. He put forward the plea in support of his amendment that if Labour remained in the Coalition Government up to the end of the Peace Conference it might be able more effectively to influence the terms of the settlement.

Mr. Clynes' Amendment was defeated by a huge majority, and the resolution of the Executive was adopted.

In the evening of the day on which this Conference was held, Mr. Lloyd George announced the dissolution of Parliament; and the Labour members of his Government, with the exception of Mr. Barnes and two minor Ministers, resigned their offices. In speeches in which Mr. Lloyd George defended the Coalition he made use of arguments, and in almost identical language, similar to those which are being now employed in defence of the present (1934) "National" Government. The problems of reconstruction before the next Parliament were so grave that only by sinking former political differences could they be satisfactorily solved. The condition he had laid down, that only those candidates should be approved who gave a definite pledge to support him and his Government in the new Parliament, put Mr. Asquith and those Liberals who had remained outside the Coalition under Mr. Lloyd George's ban. This ostracism dealt a blow at the Liberal Party from which it has never recovered. A meeting had been arranged to open the Coalition Election campaign before the Labour Party's decision to withdraw had been made. It was expected that at that meeting the Labour Party would be represented in an official capacity, but the Conference decision of the Labour Party had upset this plan. It was evident from Mr. Lloyd George's remarks, at this meeting, that the action of the Labour Party had deeply annoyed him. He described the decision to withdraw Labour members from the Government as the height of folly, and he could not imagine whatever inspired men to come to such a decision. A few days after this meeting a joint manifesto was published, signed by Mr. Lloyd George and Mr. Bonar Law. This manifesto appealed to every section of the electorate without distinction of Party to support the Coalition Government for the furtherance of the general good. The manifesto contained no allusion to matters which became the popular topics of the election. The only reference to peace was contained in two or three lines in these few words: "Our first task must be to conclude a just and lasting peace, and so to establish the foundation of a new Empire that occasion for further wars may be for ever averted."

As the election proceeded, candidates began to feel that they needed something with more blood and thunder in it than these platitudinous statements. In Mr. Lloyd George's early election speeches he said no word about hanging the Kaiser, or making Germany pay. Mr. Lloyd George was in a great difficulty. He had to give his candidates something with a bite in it by which they could satisfy the appetites of their audiences, and at the same time he was restrained by his own knowledge of the impracticability of obtaining a large indemnity from Germany. It is quite true that Mr. Lloyd George never committed himself to any definite sum which Germany would be compelled to pay. But in his public speeches he dealt with the subject in such a way as to encourage his more irresponsible supporters to make the electors believe that they were going to be relieved from bearing the cost of the War, and that Germany would have to shoulder the burden of the British National Debt.

Mr. Lloyd George in his campaign speeches was specially bitter against the Labour Party for this desertion of the Coalition. On the eve of the poll he made a speech at Camberwell in which he said that the Labour Party was being run by the extreme pacifist Bolshevist group.

"It was they who pulled Labour out of the Government. They pulled it out - why? What they really believed in was Bolshevism. Who are these men? They are the outstanding figures of that Party, I name one or two of them - Mr. Ramsay MacDonald, Mr. Snowden and Mr. Smillie and others.... Supposing the Labour Party won. The moment they got in these are the men who would run the Government. That is exactly what happened in Russia."

This was rather hard on men like Mr. Henderson and Mr. Clynes, who had been associated with him for two or three years during the War; and his denunciation of the Labour Party as aiming at Bolshevism found little justification in the programme upon which the Labour Party fought this General Election. Its programme demanded a peace of international co-operation, freedom for Ireland and India and democratic rights, the repeal of the Defence of the Realm Act, the complete abolition of conscription, and it urged land nationalisation as a vital necessity. It demanded that a million new houses must be built at once at the State's expense and let at fair rents. It stood firm against Tariffs and for Free Trade, and it declared that in paying for the War, Labour would place the burdens on the broadest back by a special tax on capital. It also advocated the immediate nationalisation and democratic control of the vital public services, such as mines, railways, shipping, armaments, and electric power. This was the "Bolshevik Programme" on which Labour appealed to the country for support!

I sought re-election in Blackburn, a constituency I represented for thirteen years. The Liberals and Conservative Parties solidly united in opposition.

They used a common platform, and issued joint literature. The Tories adopted as their candidate a local man who had won the V.C. for distinguished naval service in the Zeebrugge affair. He had no knowledge of politics, but it was expected that his War service would make a special appeal to the electors. Both my opponents had Mr. Lloyd George's coupon. It was the most strenuous contest that I ever waged. The local Labour Party were solid in my support. The Trades Council issued a manifesto on my behalf, and the local Trade Union leaders gave me their whole-hearted assistance. Blackburn was a two-membered constituency, each elector having two votes. I had at previous elections obtained the bulk of the Liberal vote, the Liberals giving one vote to their own candidate and their second vote to me. At former elections the Conservatives had put forward two candidates, but at this Election there was one Liberal and one Conservative candidate combined for the purpose of defeating me. Against such a combination as this my prospects from the outset seemed hopeless, or at the best very doubtful. That, however, was not the impression given to newspaper correspondents who visited the constituency. Public meetings are never a reliable guide to forecasting the result of an election. My meetings were by far the largest and the most enthusiastic in the campaign. My wife threw herself into the campaign with great energy, and addressed three or four meetings every day. All my meetings during the contest were packed to the doors, crowds being turned away; and at all of them - including the overflow meetings which were frequently necessary – the enthusiasm was extraordinary. We filled the large theatre half a dozen times during the contest. At the beginning of the campaign I made my position perfectly clear. I said in my opening speech:

> "If there be those in the constituency who expect that I shall recede by one inch from the position I have maintained during the whole War they will be grievously disillusioned. I shall fight this Election on the record of my past work. Not to get ten thousand votes will I apologise for anything I have done, nor modify my attitude, nor sacrifice my principles in the slightest degree."

My opponents' canvassers carried out a thorough house-to-house visitation, and made in this way all sorts of untrue statements, and, as is usually the case, circulated statements that they had not the courage to make publicly. In some cases, however, these statements came to my knowledge through questions asked at public meetings. This gave me an opportunity to answer them. There was one statement which was circulated by the Coalition of a specially ignorant and scurrilous character. It was to the effect that I had charged £1 for every case of separation allowances or discharged soldiers' pensions which I had undertaken. This is the sort of slander that one always gets at Election times, and it is a humiliation to have to refute it. But I suppose there are electors who can be influenced by such patently absurd statements. This particular slander, however, was answered by a Tory speaker who said he was bound to admit that Mr. Snowden had done much so far as pensions and allowances of soldiers' dependants were concerned.

At this Election I had a larger measure of outside support than at any previous contest in which I was engaged. Mr. Bernard Shaw came down to address a meeting for me, but I doubt if he did me very much good for he made the blunder of recommending that the electors should give their second vote to the Liberal Coalition candidate, who happened to be an acquaintance of his! Mr. A. G. Gardiner, then Editor of the *Daily News*, who had strongly criticised my War attitude, wrote a letter appealing to the Liberal electors of Blackburn to vote for me because "I know you to be a man who can be neither bribed nor bought, and who seeks only the general good, the reign of justice, and the establishment of a clean world." One other interesting platform supporter I had in this Election was Mr. Siegfried Sassoon, the poet. Defying all army regulations, Mr. Sassoon spoke on my platform dressed in his army uniform. He was no orator, but he became immensely popular during the contest through his transparent honesty and sincerity.

The result of the Election, which was declared a fortnight after the polling (the counting having been delayed to give time for the soldiers' votes to arrive), showed that the two-party combination in the Election had been even more solid than we had expected. The figures as announced by the Returning Officer were as follows:

Norman (Coalition Liberal), 32,076
Dean (Coalition Tory), 30,158
Snowden (Labour), 15,274

Each elector had, as I have said, two votes, and 12,994 electors who voted for me did not use their second vote. I had 2000 splits with the Coalition Liberal. My election expenses were nearly three times heavier than at any previous contest I had in Blackburn, though we kept them well within the statutory limits. The grand total amounted to £962, and the fact that this sum was raised mainly by contributions from the constituency is evidence of the enthusiasm of my supporters. Although I may not be believed, it is true to say that my defeat caused me neither disappointment nor misery. I did not lose a wink of sleep through it. I was out of Parliament for four years, and during that time I never visited the House, nor felt any desire to do so. The House of Commons had never gripped me. I had no personal ambition to be a member of Parliament, nor did I ever feel to be a superior person because I was one. Why then, it will be asked, did I take the trouble to fight my way into Parliament. The answer is simple. I was a leading member of a political organisation and an advocate of great causes, and when I was asked to stand for Parliament and carry my advocacy of these causes to the floor of the House of Commons I felt it to be my duty to respond to the request.

The result of the General Election in the country gave Mr. Lloyd George an overwhelming Parliamentary majority. But an analysis of the votes cast shows that his huge Parliamentary majority did not represent a corresponding support in the country. As a matter of fact, taking the circumstances of the Election into consideration, remembering that he had forced the Election at the height of his popularity as the man who had won the War, the small amount of support he actually received from the electorate was very remarkable. The result was described by every section of the Press as a cataclysm, a landslide, a catastrophe, and an overwhelming victory for Mr. Lloyd George. It was none of these things. With every favourable advantage Mr. Lloyd George had not carried the country. Through the anomalies of our electoral system, Mr. Lloyd George obtained four out of every five seats in Great Britain, though out of every nineteen votes recorded nine were given against him and his Coalition. At this Election the Labour Party put forward 361 candidates, which was greatly in excess of the number run at any former General Election. Out of this large number only 61 were successful. All the pacifist members who had sat in the previous Parliament were defeated at the Election, and the same fate was shared by 66 Liberals who had refused to accept Mr. Lloyd George's coupon.

Mr. Asquith and all his former Cabinet colleagues, including Mr. McKenna, Mr. Runciman, Mr. Herbert Samuel, Sir John Simon, were defeated. The total number of independent Liberals was only 33, while Mr. Lloyd George's mixed party contained 131 ex-Liberals who had been returned as Coalition candidates. At the previous Election in December 1910, the Labour Party put forward 56 candidates, who polled a total vote of 370,802. At this Election the total poll of 361 candidates was 2,375,202. This large aggregate vote was the promise of what actually did happen at the following General Election in 1922. Deprived of the services of many of its most experienced debaters, the Labour Party in the new Parliament was rather poorly equipped to stand against the serried ranks of the Coalition, which, as somebody said, was largely composed of "hard-faced men who had done well out of the War". The Opposition was further seriously weakened and rendered largely ineffective by the defeat of Mr. Asquith and all the former Liberal Ministers who had refused to follow Mr. Lloyd George.

Chapter Thirteen

Communism in the Labour Movement

During the four years I was out of Parliament I found plenty of congenial work which fully occupied my time. In 1918 I was re-elected National Chairman of the Independent Labour Party, a position which I held for three years. These were rather critical years in the history of the Party. Young men, full of enthusiasm but with little knowledge of Socialism, were coming into the party in very large numbers, and a steadying influence was needed to keep their activities within reasonable bounds. A considerable number of men and women who had been attracted to the I.L.P. by its peace policy joined the Party, and they were exerting themselves to influence the policy of the Party in a measure which their knowledge of the movement did not entitle them to do. A number of pacifist M.P.s who had been associated with us in peace work in the previous Parliament, and who had been defeated as Liberal candidates at the 1918 Election, realising that there was no prospect of a political career in the Liberal Party, now allied themselves with the I.L.P. The National Council of the Party had a very difficult task in those years in keeping the I.L.P. on its traditional lines as a constitutional instrument for the propagation of Socialism.

In addition to my work as Chairman of the Party, I undertook the direction of its Publication Department. We had established in connection with the Party a printing plant from which we issued pamphlets and books, and did a good deal of printing work for the Labour and Trade Union Movements. *The Labour Leader*, the official organ of the I.L.P., had now attained a large circulation, and had a considerable influence outside the membership of the Party. At the request of my colleagues on the National Council I agreed to accept the position of Supervising Editor of this journal. Each week I wrote a page of comments on political events over my own name, and also contributed the leading articles. In addition to this I resumed my platform work, and during the winter months travelled all over the country addressing large meetings.

I also wrote a number of pamphlets and two or three books on Socialism and social questions. All these activities kept me fully occupied.

I had always taken a keen interest in the Temperance Movement, and often spoke at Temperance demonstrations. At one of these meetings in Cardiff I had an amusing experience. It was a great meeting in one of the largest churches in the city, which was crowded and enthusiastic. The Chair was occupied by the late Lord Aberdare, who, in his speech, expressed surprise that he should have been invited to preside at a Temperance meeting. He explained that he was the chairman of a brewery company, and was not a teetotaller. "As a matter of fact," he said, "I had a bottle of wine before I came to this meeting." Among my fellow-speakers at this meeting was the present Bishop of London. He spoke before me, and the argument of his speech was the effect which even a small dose of alcohol had in confusing the mental faculties. When the Bishop sat down, the Chairman called upon "The Rev. Philip Snowden" to speak. I began by saying that we had not had long to wait for a practical illustration of the truth of the Bishop's argument. The audience were quick to seize upon this point, and there was prolonged laughter at the Chairman's expense, which, I am afraid, he did not altogether like. After the meeting Lord Aberdare said that he thought I had been a little too hard upon him, but it was impossible for me to resist the temptation to draw the connection between the Chairman's bottle of wine and his description of me as "Reverend".

The I.L.P. at that time had a good deal of trouble with the extreme section. The Bolshevik Revolution had made a great impression upon the younger members of the Party, who were enthused by the spectacle of a great country overthrowing the capitalist system and establishing a Communist Republic. Their sympathy with the Russian Communists was more emotional than intellectual, and they were not in the least critical of the methods which were being employed in Russia to fortify the Revolution. The Russian Communist Party, which for all political purposes was an instrument of the Russian Government, had established in Moscow what they called "The Communist [Third] International", and were spending large sums of money in other countries to prepare for "The World Revolution". The I.L.P. was acutely divided upon this question of the re-establishment of a Socialist International. We had a moderate section which was prepared to let bygones be bygones and to give their support to the building up of the [pre-war] Second International.

We had a not inconsiderable section, composed in the main of young men and women, who were prepared to throw in their lot with the Moscow Communists and join the Communist International. We had a third section dissatisfied with both the moderate policy of the Second International and the extreme policy of the Communist International; they wanted to join up with other sections of Socialists in the continental countries by forming still another International. It was a very complicated state of affairs, and it looked at one time as though these divisions would disrupt the I.L.P. Matters came to a head at the Annual Conference of the I.L.P. which was held in Glasgow in April 1920. I had to preside over this Conference, and my task was a very difficult one. The majority of the National Council of the I.L.P. were opposed to joining up with the Moscow International, and I, personally, felt so strongly upon this matter that I had made up my mind if the Conference decided in favour of affiliating with Moscow I should leave the Chair. However, the necessity for carrying that decision into effect never arose. After a debate which occupied the greater part of two days - a debate which was conducted in excellent temper and with great ability - the Conference decided by a large majority to disaffiliate with the Second International. But when the question of affiliating with the Moscow International was put it was defeated by 472 to 206 votes. The Minority vote on the matter did not so much represent Communist opinion as a desire for the linking up of the whole world Socialist Movement in one inclusive International.

The Conference instructed the National Council to gather information on the International situation, particularly to address a communication to the Moscow Communists asking for a full statement of the basis of that organisation. The reply of the Moscow Communists was the submission of the text of the Theses upon which the Communist party was based. This information put an end to any further consideration by the I.L.P. of associating with the Communist International. Neither the policy nor the principles of the Communist Party were in accord with the attitude of the I.L.P. There remained, however, a section of the I.L.P. who, while not daring to publicly approve all the Theses of the Communist Party, gave so much support to the Bolshevik Government as to convey the impression to the public that they were in sympathy with its methods. This semi-Communist propaganda did great harm to the I.L.P., and in order to counteract its evil effect I used my platform in the *Labour Leader* to dissociate the I.L.P. from Communist methods. My attitude was resented by the Left-Wing members, and eventually led to my stopping my weekly contributions to the *Labour Leader*.

This conflict between the two wings of the I.L.P. continued. But the controversy was by no means confined to the I.L.P., but existed in the wider Labour Party. The British Communists, acting on instructions from Moscow, used their membership of the Trade Unions to carry on a Communist propaganda inside the unions, and to agitate for the admission of the Communist organisation to the Labour Party. The question of their affiliation was discussed at many Annual Conferences of the Labour Party, and it was finally decided that the declared methods of the Communist Party debarred them from admission.

My opposition by speech and writing to the methods of the Communist Party brought me a good deal of abuse from that Party and from the Left Wing of the I.L.P. I could foresee then what has since actually happened, namely, that this conflict between the democratic and the revolutionary sections of the I.L.P. would ultimately lead to the disruption of the Party. This conflict between two sections of a Party which had fundamental differences on the method of achieving a common object was no new experience in popular movements. The difference between the advocates of moral persuasion and revolutionary methods wrecked the Chartist Movement. It broke up the First Socialist International. It has now disrupted the I.L.P. and made that once influential body a thing of shreds and patches. The conflict between Democracy and Dictatorship has now (1934) assumed a world significance. Democratic government has been overthrown in several European countries, and others are seriously threatened with the same fate. There is no difference in principle or in methods between a Dictatorship of the Right and a Dictatorship of the Left. Both attain power by force and maintain it by ruthless suppression of all opposition and the practice of tyranny and torture and persecution. The Communists openly advocate the Dictatorship of the proletariat and the abolition of Parliamentarian forms of government. The Theses of the Communist Party declare that:

> "only a violent defeat of the bourgeoisie, the confiscation of its property, the annihilation of the entire bourgeois government apparatus from top to bottom, parliamentary, judicial, military, bureaucratic, administrative, municipal, up to the individual exile or internment of the most stubborn

> and dangerous exploiters, the establishment of a strict control of them for repressing all inevitable attempts at resistance--only such measures will be able to guarantee the complete submission of the whole class of exploiters."

My quarrel with the Communists is not so much with Communism as a theory as with the methods by which they seek to establish the Communist State. The pure Communist ideal - each for all and all for each - is a great conception. It is the Christian ideal of the perfect Society. Some day humanity may have reached a state of moral development where such a society will be possible. But it can never be forced by methods of violence and by the suppression of individual liberty. No social system will ever endure which is based on class antagonism and upon hatred and selfishness. Extremism on the one side inevitably begets extremism on the other. The history of the countries of Central Europe since the War provides abundant evidence of this. Social evolution is a growth, and if progress is to be permanent moral development must proceed parallel with economic change. That is the reason I have always been an advocate of what is called "Gradualism" in social progress.

One can understand, and, indeed, in a measure sympathise with those who, realising the misery and hardship to which the masses are condemned today by the injustice of the social system, think that a call to the distressed to unite and by some great catastrophic uprising overthrow the existing order will not fail to meet with a response from the victims. But, reluctant though we may be to abandon the hope that the agelong misery and subjection of the masses can be removed by one great dramatic stroke, we must recognise facts as they are, and learn the lesson of all history, which is that violent revolution is always followed by reaction and by the arrest of ordered progress. Ordered progress is the law of life; it is the living principle which carries men and nations forward. The method of democratic progress may be dull and unexciting, but it is the only sure and certain road to the final goal. "Gradualism" does not mean that progress must necessarily be slow. The rate of advance will depend upon the intelligence of the democracy. But I do insist, and have done so from the earliest days of my Socialist teaching, that every step forward must carry with it the approval of public opinion, and that every change must be consolidated before the next step is taken. Progress cannot be too rapid for me provided it carries with it the support of democracy and is in accord with the other conditions I have laid down. I think it was Lord John Russell who said that "reform is the surest preventive of revolution." At the present time (1934) there is a real danger that the complacency and procrastination of the Government in dealing drastically with economic and social problems may drive the masses into unconstitutional methods. If the Parliamentary form of Government does not function effectively, if it will not redress keenly felt grievances, it cannot survive. The greatest danger to democracy is the failure of democratic institutions to respond to democratic demands.

These are the reasons I have always opposed a revolutionary policy and preached a democratic Socialism. I have never objected to a forward movement within the Labour Party. I have often been at variance with my colleagues when I thought the Party was not pursuing a more vigorous fighting policy. My rebellious conduct was frequently the subject of complaint in the Party meetings. On one occasion a special meeting of the Party was called to consider a particularly outrageous act of indiscipline on my part. I had written an article in the *Labour Leader* vigorously criticising the Party for its moderation. This caused great offence, and I was summoned to defend myself before a Party meeting. I was not in the least disturbed. Indeed, I anticipated the meeting with considerable pleasure. The case against me was stated by the chairman. When he had finished I was expected to rise. I sat still. A dead silence continued for some minutes. Then Will Thorne said: "What can we do with him? He won't speak!" Then I spoke – for forty minutes, and at the end of my speech the meeting adjourned *sine die*.

At the end of my three years' tenure of office as Chairman of the Independent Labour Party at Easter 1920, I accepted the position of National Treasurer rendered vacant by the resignation of Mr. Benson, who had held the office for many years. This carried with it a seat on the National Council. I was becoming more and more discontented with the Left Wing tendencies of the I.L.P., and at the end of the year I declined to accept renomination. This severed twenty-five years of official association with the Party. I retained my membership of the Party but took little part in its work. My resignation was the occasion for a number of laudatory speeches on my work for the I.L.P. which came from old members of the Party, and which touched me deeply. I was anxious not to harm the Party by my resignation, for I knew that the great majority, though less vocal than the extremists, were loyal to the constitutional methods which had been the policy of the Party from its beginning; so I excused my action by saying that I thought it time, after a quarter of a century of office, to make way for younger men. I had attended every Annual Conference of the I.L.P. (which was held at Easter) for twenty-seven years. This annual event was always a very happy occasion. There gathered active Socialists from all parts of the country. It was a reunion of old comrades and congenial spirits. After the day's work in the Conference was over we spent the evening in jolly companionship. Certain items in our programme became an annual institution. Keir Hardie was always expected to sing "Annie Laurie" and "Bonnie Mary of Argyle". We looked to Bruce Glasier to give us "The Battle of Stirling Bridge", which he rendered with a fiery patriotism quite unbecoming the editor of an *Anthology of Peace Songs and Poems*. Perhaps the happiest part of these convivial gatherings was when a few of us gathered round the fire and recounted our propaganda experiences. The stories had been often told, but were always fresh. We insisted that Wallhead should tell us again of his Cockney chairman who introduced him with these few remarks:

> "Kumarades and Fellow Workers. Before I call on our Kumarade what has come here to eddicate you I want to say something about these here Liberals and Tories. Now, it's my firm belief - it's my firm belief - that Arthur James Balfour takes 'Enery Campbell-Bannerman by the arm, and they goes behind the Speaker's chair, and Arthur says to 'Enery:' 'Enery, what shall we do next to dish these bloody workers?'"

The stories of Jimmy Sexton – now Sir James Sexton – on such occasions were very popular. We always called for the old ones we had heard so often, but which were never stale as Jimmy told them. The favourite ones were about his election contest at Ashton-under-Lyne in 1895 when he was an I.L.P. candidate and polled 415 votes. Jimmy fought this election on the economic basis of Socialism and on Marx's theory of surplus value and methods of Socialist exchange. There was a man who followed him round his meetings and seemed very interested in these abstract theories. Jimmy was flattered by this attention, but a bit disconcerted when the man explained at the end of a meeting what he understood by what Sexton said. The man said:

> "About this means of exchange under Socialism. I understand that a man will exchange what he has for something he wants. Well, I'm a tripe dealer, and so under Socialism if I want to go to London I shall go t' station and plank a yard o' tripe on t' ticket sill and say 'Gie me a ticket to London'."

And so we spent our care-free evenings. These were happy days.

Chapter Fourteen

From Blackburn to Colne Valley

Shortly after my defeat at Blackburn in 1918 I was invited by the Labour Party in the constituency to become their candidate for the next Election. Although I had been heavily defeated by the combination of the other two Parties against me, neither my supporters nor myself had any doubt that in the changed circumstances at the next Election I should recapture the seat. I was very much attached to Blackburn. I had been associated with the borough as candidate and member for twenty years, and my relations with it had always been of the best and most friendly character. I, therefore, had no hesitation in accepting the cordial invitation to once more become the Labour candidate. For three years I kept in close touch with the constituency as the prospective candidate, making frequent visits and addressing public meetings, all of which gave evidence of a revival of the old enthusiasm.

However, in the autumn of 1921 circumstances arose which brought my long political association with Blackburn to an end. The National Council of the I.L.P. received a request from the Colne Valley Division of Yorkshire to provide them with a candidate. My colleagues were anxious to make a certainty of my return to Parliament at the next Election, and they did not share my optimism about my prospects at Blackburn. They pressed me hard to accept this opening in Colne Valley. The constituency had certain attractions. It was in Yorkshire, not far away from my native place, and the nature of the constituency and the character of the people there were quite familiar to me. In the previous thirty years I had done a good deal of propaganda in the constituency, and I was on intimate terms of friendship with all the leading Socialists in the Division. After a good deal of anxious thought, I agreed to fall in with the appeal of my colleagues on the National Council and to accept the invitation from Colne Valley, provided my friends at Blackburn would agree to release me. The Blackburn Labour Party were extremely reluctant to do so, and the private meeting I had with the Executive there was a very painful ordeal. Shortly after this decision arrangements were made for a farewell public meeting, at which my wife and I were presented with valuable tokens of goodwill.

After my release from Blackburn, I went down to Slaithwaite, which is the centre of the Colne Valley Division, for a meeting with the Labour Council. I was formally invited to become the candidate. I accepted the invitation. Arrangements were made for me to address meetings in each of the polling districts. Colne Valley is a widely scattered constituency. There are thirty-eight small towns and villages, but the bulk of the population live in the two narrow valleys which fork from Huddersfield and which take their names respectively from the rivers Colne and Holme which run through the valleys. These valleys still retain evidence of the handloom weaving times in the bare stone cottages with a third storey which had been built to accommodate the handlooms. These cottages are built on the steep hillsides, and access to them, now that the workers find their occupation in the factories in the valley, is a laborious task. Colne Valley is a very hard constituency to work. To reach the electors a candidate must be prepared to travel long distances for comparatively small meetings, and to address three or four of these each night during the Election. My first experience in the Division as a Parliamentary candidate would have driven me from the constituency if I had not known the people. My preliminary tour of the Division, a year before the Election, was most depressing. I found the electors sunk in appalling political apathy. The meetings were sparsely attended and wholly devoid of enthusiasm. There was only one place in the Division where any political propaganda had been done for years. When I complained about the deadness of the electorate I was told:

> "it'll be all reight when t'Election comes; they'll wakken up then; they doant think it worth bothering naah; they say 'We sall 'ev plenty chances of hearing him at t'Election'."

I knew there was a good deal of truth in this, and that induced me to stick to it. When the Election came they "wakkened up", though they never were roused to wild enthusiasm. This reticence in expressing opinions or feelings in public is a trait in the character of the people in this part of the West Riding. At my first Election, after the declaration of the poll announcing my success had been made I left the Town Hall at Slaithwaite to drive to the Socialist Hall. I passed through the street. There were numbers of people about, half of whom must have voted for me, but there was not a single cheer! It might have been a funeral procession!

There was a particular reason many of the electors hesitated to make known their support of the Labour Party. There had been some persecution of active Socialists by employers in the early days, and the recollection of this still lingered. However, "it was all reight" when the Election came in November 1922. I was returned by a comfortable majority. This result was due in a large measure to the help of my wife, who had worked like a Trojan in the contest and had made a great impression on the electors, particularly upon the women. I fought three Elections in Colne Valley in three years – four altogether including the Election of 1929 – and at each successive Election I increased my majority and raised the enthusiasm of the electors until in 1929 my meetings were enormous, and the enthusiasm equal to the memorable Election meetings in Blackburn. But they had been a difficult lot to move!

Chapter Fifteen

Labour a Parliamentary Party

The General Election of November 1922 marked the final disappearance from British politics of the old Two-Party system. In all the previous Parliaments from 1906 the Labour members had been so small in number as hardly to be entitled to be regarded as a Party. As I have pointed out, their electoral successes from 1906 to 1918 gave little support to the hope that the Labour Party would become a serious menace to the older political parties. The practice of alternating Liberal and Conservative Governments seemed to be firmly established in our political system. The Labour Party had been slow in reaching the position of a full-sized Parliamentary Party. From the Election of 1922, however, it emerged as the second largest Party in the State. The Liberals had entered upon this Election as a divided Party. Mr. Lloyd George kept his National Coalition Liberals, and Mr. Asquith's group fought the Election as an independent Party. The platform recriminations between these two sections of the old Liberal Party showed the bitterness of feeling with which they regarded each other.

The result of the General Election, November 1922, gave the Conservative Party in Great Britain 305 seats; the Labour Party 140; the Independent Liberals 55; and Lloyd George's Liberals 50 seats. The Labour vote exceeded the combined votes of both sections of Liberals, and was only 1,162,000 votes below that of the Conservative Party. The Labour Party in the new Parliament was remarkable in another respect. In previous Parliaments the Labour members, with few exceptions, were Trade Union nominees and representatives. Of the 140 members returned to the new Parliament not less than 50 were I.L.P. candidates or the nominees of the local Labour Parties. The new Party contained a larger element of middle-class people and professional men. The ex-Liberals who had recently come into the Party, including Mr. Trevelyan, Mr. Lees-Smith, Mr. Arthur Ponsonby, Mr. Roden Buxton, Mr. Noel Buxton and Mr. E. D. Morel, had been returned as I.L.P. candidates. We had doctors, lawyers and a parson!

The main reason for the success of the Labour Party was that the country was sick of the Coalition, and "fed up" with the old political parties. I fought my Election in Colne Valley on four planks: the record of the Coalition, the Revision of the Peace Treaties, a Capital Levy, and Public Works for dealing with Unemployment. The new Parliament met on Monday, the 20th November 1922, for the election of the Speaker. Parliament was formally opened by the King three days later. The King's Speech contained not one word about a legislative programme beyond saying that the measures prepared by the late Government would be examined afresh. The absence from the King's Speech of any legislative proposals was in harmony with Mr. Bonar Law's Election Programme. He had declared that what the country most needed was tranquillity, and that the new Government proposed to give them. "The policy I put forward", he had said, "would be regarded as one of inaction. It is my aim that it should be so regarded. There are times when it is good to sit still and go slowly!" The day before Parliament assembled, the Labour members met to elect the Party officers for the session. The I.L.P. section of the Party had met previously to decide whom they would support for the Chairmanship. Mr. Clynes, it will be remembered, had held that office for two years, and it was known that he would be put forward for re-election by the Trade Union members. I attended the meeting of the I.L.P. members, which was held at the office in Fleet Street, and took part in the conversation as to whom we should support. I was opposed for several reasons to Mr. MacDonald accepting the position at that time. He had been out of Parliament four years, and Mr. Clynes had held the position of Chairman in very difficult circumstances, and had on the whole done as well as anyone could be expected to do under the conditions prevailing. I felt that it was not quite fair to oppose his re-election to the position, at least for the forthcoming session. My other objection to Mr. MacDonald taking the chair at this time was that I did not think it likely he would give the Party a vigorous lead. I had seen a good deal of him in such a position when he was Chairman before the War, and his passion for intrigue and compromise, and his desire to be regarded as a "gentleman" by the other parties, disqualified him to lead a party which contained so many members who had come into the House of Commons filled with enthusiasm for a fight. It had come to my knowledge that Mr. MacDonald had been actively canvassing among his friends for support, and he had been especially concerned to get the support of the new Scottish members. During the time that he had been out of Parliament he had contributed a weekly article to the Glasgow Socialist paper *Forward*, in which he had played up to the Left Wing, an attitude strikingly different from that he had pursued when in the House of Commons in previous Parliaments. At this meeting of the I.L.P. members the Scottish contingent were strong in support of Mr. MacDonald, and even more strongly opposed to the re-election of Mr. Clynes, against whom they remembered many occasions during the previous four years when he had not come up to their standard of leadership. When the party meeting took place both Mr. Clynes and Mr. MacDonald were nominated, and the election of Mr. MacDonald was carried by a majority of two votes. This meeting was not very fully attended. Many of the Trade Union members who would have given their support to Mr. Clynes were unable to reach the Party meeting in time on account of some Trade Union work which detained them. The Scottish members to whom MacDonald owed his election were not long in being disillusioned with his leadership, and within two months he became the object of persistent and bitter criticism. I had opposed Mr. MacDonald's election because I was convinced that he would have been far more useful and far more effective in Opposition if he had not had the responsibility of leadership at that time. Mr. Arthur Henderson was appointed Chief Whip, although he was not then in Parliament. He had been defeated at the General Election. It was expected that he would very soon find an opportunity to return to the House of Commons at a by-election. This hope was soon realised.

The divided state of the Opposition led to a difficulty about who should be regarded as the official Opposition. The Labour Party, as the largest of the Opposition sections, put in a claim to be recognised as the official Opposition, carrying with it the exclusive occupation of the Front Opposition Bench. The Speaker had to be called in to settle the difficulty. He decided that he must take into account the existence of other Parties in Opposition, and it was ultimately agreed that the seats on the Front Bench should be divided between the Labour Party and the Independent Liberals. The Lloyd George Liberals put in no claim to be regarded as a section of the Opposition. This arrangement, though probably the only thing that could be done in the circumstances, led to some inconvenience. The ex-Cabinet Ministers among the Independent Liberals, who were now led by Mr. Asquith, made little use of the privilege of sitting on the Front Opposition Bench. So far as I can remember, Sir John Simon was the only one who regularly sat among us. Mr. Asquith usually sat on the front bench below the gangway, and only came to the box on the Front Opposition Bench when he had a speech to deliver. Mr. Lloyd George sat "remote, a melancholy man", in the corner seat on the second bench below the gangway, surveying in silence the House which for nearly twenty years he had dominated, and over which for some years he had been virtual dictator. It was some time before he began to take an active part in the debates. Coming back to the House of Commons after four years of absence I experienced no new sensations. The membership of the House had greatly changed. In former Parliaments the Labour Party had occupied a rather inconspicuous position on two benches below the gangway. It now required all the benches above the gangway to accommodate them. Mr. Balfour and Mr. F. E. Smith had been translated to the House of Lords. Mr. Winston Churchill was temporarily absent from the House, having been defeated by a Labour member at Dundee. Mr. Baldwin - an inconspicuous member of the House in my last Parliament - now occupied the important post of Chancellor of the Exchequer. The only new member who had attained Cabinet rank in the meantime was Sir Philip Cunliffe Lister.

The greatest change from former Parliaments I had known was not merely the increase in numbers but in the character of the Labour members. From the first day of the new session they displayed a militancy which had been lacking in the Labour Party hitherto. The General Election had returned a large contingent of Socialist members from Scotland, and they were all members of the Independent Labour Party. Glasgow had contributed eight of these members, the County Divisions of Lanarkshire five, and from the whole of Scotland there were twenty-nine members. It may be mentioned that all the Scottish Labour members, with one exception, were teetotallers. Their activity in the House of Commons attracted a good deal of attention in the country. Dundee had returned Mr. Scrymgeour, a fanatical prohibitionist, who was not a member of the Labour Party, but he sat with the Labour Party and acted with them during all the time he was in the House of Commons. His burning zeal and high personal character won for him the respect of all parties in the House, although the majority of the members had little sympathy with many of his views. The Scottish Labour members - who became known as "the

Clydeside Group" - began from the first day to take a prominent part in the Parliamentary proceedings. In the debate upon the King's Speech, which was the first business of the new session, they competed with each other to catch the Speaker's eye. They had all been active Socialist propagandists before coming to the House of Commons, and it was a great opportunity for them to be able to make their speeches with the serried ranks of the capitalists in front of them. To those of us who were well acquainted with the character of outdoor Socialist propaganda, their speeches had a familiar ring. We recognised their speeches as having done duty on many previous occasions. The other parties in the House were very tolerant of these speeches, and were more entertained than indignant at the thundering denunciation of the capitalist system, which was something new to them. By the end of the debate upon the Address most of the Scottish Labour members had made their maiden speeches, and it was possible to form some idea of their quality. The outstanding man amongst them was Mr. John Wheatley. His first speech marked him out as a man of exceptional ability, an impression which was sustained and enhanced by his later interventions in debate. Mr. Maxton from the beginning was prominent in the proceedings, but in those days he made little impression upon the House of Commons. But, apart from Mr. Wheatley and Mr. Morel, the Scottish Labour members did not impress the House of Commons with their ability. They delivered countless platform speeches filled with vague generalities. They would perhaps have done better if they had waited until they had gained a little Parliamentary experience. But their constituents in Glasgow were expecting them to stir things up, and that they certainly succeeded in doing.

The first debate in the new Parliament centred largely round the question of unemployment. On the second day of the debate I made my first speech in the new Parliament. I had no reason to be dissatisfied with its reception either in the House or in the Press next day. This was the occasion when, after speaking for more than an hour, members called upon me to "go on." One of the leading newspapers, in describing this incident, remarked that "Memory could be ransacked without result for an occasion when any man of lesser rank than a Prime Minister was shouted at by the House of Commons to 'go on' when he had been speaking for an hour and had hinted that he ought to stop." The points of my speech, in which I analysed the causes of normal and abnormal unemployment, were at that time unfamiliar, but they have since become the commonplaces in all discussions on the unemployment problem. I expressed the view that normal unemployment would in the future become greater, if tendencies at work were to be allowed to continue to operate without control, because of the fiercer international competition and the rationalisation of industry. I advocated the development of our national resources, such as land, transport and housing, and insisted on the expenditure of money only on immediately or prospectively remunerative schemes. As to abnormal unemployment which was largely due to the conditions left by the War, I admitted that the remedy was not wholly within our own control. The first remedy was the establishment of peace in Europe and the recovery of foreign trade. I advocated the abandonment of reparations and war debts, which were a curse to the country which paid them and a curse to the country which received them. I advocated the recognition of the Soviet Government, not from any sympathy with Bolshevism - which I described as a "rotten thing" - but because I believed that Russia offered great possibilities for British trade. After I sat down I received a note from the Speaker which read: "Allow me to thank you very warmly for your speech. Such a contribution raises our debates to a higher standard." And my friend Mr. J. H. Thomas also passed along a note with these characteristic words: "Dear Philip, if you never made another speech rest satisfied!" I had spoken from Mr. Lloyd George's corner seat on the second bench below the gangway. I always regarded this as the best position in the House from which to speak, and I always tried to get it when I was going to make a speech. One is better able to command the House from this position than from any other. The Chamber of the House of Commons is very badly constructed from the point of view of both the speaker and the audience. Wherever one stands he is bound to have a fairly considerable part of the House behind him. I had taken Mr. Lloyd George's seat on this occasion because it happened to be vacant. Mr. Lloyd George came into the House shortly after I had started speaking, and took the corner seat just across the gangway. When I sat down he leaned across and shook me warmly by the hand. Next day Mr. MacDonald invited me to occupy a seat on the front Opposition Bench.

Sir Laming Worthington-Evans, who followed me, remarked upon the change in my style of speaking since I was last in the House. Next day all the newspapers took this line of comment. "Those with memories", said one journal, "marvelled at the change which had come over this Labour orator. They recalled the acidulous attack made on capitalism, the passionately cold sarcasm with which he formerly inveighed against established order, the contempt he poured on old forms of political thought. Time has brought its mellowing influence." I was not conscious of any change in my style. The explanation of these comments was that the occasion did not call for an aggressive style. There had been no provocation, and my purpose in this speech was to convert the other side, and not to criticise them.

Chapter Sixteen

Labour Forms a Government

Few incidents of importance occurred during the Parliamentary Session of 1923 apart from the death of Mr. Bonar Law and the appointment of Mr. Baldwin to the Premiership. The emergence of Mr. Baldwin from what I have described as the comparative obscurity of a private member to the Premiership and leadership of the Conservative Party is one of those strange incidents which is difficult to explain. I was not in Parliament during the Coalition Government and I cannot say, therefore, whether he made any impression on the House as President of the Board of Trade, but he certainly was not a well-known political figure in the country. His case is similar in many ways to that of Sir Henry Campbell-Bannerman. Both owed their elevation to Party leadership to existing divisions within their respective Parties, and both displayed a capacity in their high positions far beyond what had been expected. In October of this year (1923) Mr. Baldwin sprang a surprise upon the country with a speech at Plymouth which indicated that he was thinking about a General Election on the question of Protection. The Conservative Party at that time were under a pledge given by Mr. Bonar Law at the previous General Election that within the lifetime of the existing Parliament no steps would be taken to fundamentally change the fiscal policy of the country. In his Plymouth speech Mr. Baldwin said that he had come to realise that the unemployment question was the most crucial problem before the country. He was willing to fight it, but could not fight it without weapons. Five days later at Swansea he went a step farther and elaborated his declaration that protection of the home market was the only remedy for unemployment.

When Parliament met on the 13th November Mr. Baldwin informed the House of Commons that he had reached a definite conclusion on the subject of unemployment. He was not prepared to continue in office unless he could get a mandate from the country for a Protectionist policy. Two days later he defined his Protectionist policy in greater detail to the House of Commons, and concluded by announcing that he had advised the Crown to dissolve Parliament. A momentous General Election followed: an Election which was fought solely on the question of Protection, and which led to a result which made the Labour Party the Government of the country. The General Election following Mr. Baldwin's decision to appeal to the country on the question of Protection was held on the 6th December 1923. The Labour Party manifesto on which its candidates fought this Election challenged the Tariff policy and the whole conception of economic relations underlying it. "Tariffs", they declared, "are not a remedy for unemployment. They are an impediment to the free interchange of goods and services upon which civilised society rests. They foster a spirit of profiteering, materialism and selfishness, poison the life of nations, lead to corruption in politics, promote trusts and monopolies, and impoverish the people. They perpetrate inequalities in the distribution of the world's wealth won by the labour of hands and brain."

The Liberal Party were, of course, equally opposed to Protection. The result of this General Election was that the Conservatives lost nearly 100 seats and returned 255 members; the Liberals (who had now become nominally united) won about 40 seats and returned 158 members; and the Labour Party increased its membership of the House of Commons from 144 to 191. This result was an overwhelming defeat for Protection, and the magnitude of the victory is seen even more strikingly than in the number of seats won by Free Trade candidates in the total number of votes recorded for Free Trade and Protection respectively. The Conservatives polled 5,544,540 and the Free Trade candidates 8,722,706 votes. Never in the history of this country, when a definite issue was submitted to the electors, had they given a more decisive verdict.

It will be noted that the position left by the General Election gave no Party a majority of votes in the House of Commons. If His Majesty's Government were to be carried on under these circumstances it was obvious that some arrangement or understanding would have to be made between Parties. There were four possible courses - a Conservative Government relying for support upon an arrangement with the Liberal Party; an arrangement between the Conservatives and the Labour Party; an arrangement between the Labour Party and the Liberals; a National Government where the Ministry was drawn from members of all the three Parties. The second and fourth of these possibilities were clearly out of the question. The Labour Party would not for a moment enter into arrangements with the Conservatives, and it seemed equally improbable that the Liberals would agree to keep in office a protectionist Conservative Government. After the recent experience of the Coalition Government a return to anything of that sort was equally improbable. There remained, as the only course, a Labour Government maintained in office by some understanding with the Liberal Party. In view of the closeness of the aggregate votes of the Labour and Liberal Parties, neither Party could afford to treat the other with superiority.

It is difficult to convey an impression of the sensation which was created in political circles, and indeed throughout the country, at the possibility of a Labour Government. Two years before such an event seemed far remote. No change in the political situation had ever before in such a short time happened in British politics. The Conservative newspapers made frantic appeals to Mr. Asquith to save the country from such a disaster. The situation was clarified in a speech made by Mr. Asquith on the 18th December to the Liberal members of Parliament. He declared that the Liberal Party would not make any alliance or arrangement with the Conservatives. When Parliament met the Liberals would take the first opportunity of dismissing the Conservatives from office. He expected that the Labour Party, as the second largest Party in Parliament, would assume the responsibility of governing, and in that event he could assure them that the Liberals would do nothing wantonly to hamper the course of government. Mr. Lloyd George expressed his complete agreement with the position as stated by Mr. Asquith. The National Executive of the Labour Party had met on the 12th December, and adopted a resolution declaring that should the necessity arise the Party should undertake the responsibility of forming a Government. It is difficult to see what other course could have been adopted by the Labour Party. If they had declined to take office, and stepped aside to permit the Liberals to do so, it would obviously have been regarded as an act of cowardice indicating that they felt themselves incompetent to undertake such a responsibility.

The Conservative Government decided not to resign in consequence of the Election results, but to meet Parliament. This was, no doubt, the correct constitutional thing to do, as the Conservatives were the largest Party in the House. The evening before the day when the National Executive of the Labour Party decided that the Labour Party should take office should the opportunity arise, a few of us met at dinner at Sidney Webb's house to discuss the situation. There were present Mr. MacDonald, Mr. Henderson, Mr. Webb, Mr. Clynes, Mr. Thomas and myself. The news was in the evening papers that Mr. Baldwin had decided to meet Parliament. Mr. MacDonald expressed intense relief at the news, as it left open the possibility that arrangements might be made by which he would not have to accept the responsibility of forming a Government. He said that he was dismayed at the prospect of having to take office. This probably explained why, since the Election, he had taken the line in his writings and speeches of doing what he could to antagonise the Liberal Party. He told us that he had been looking through the list of Labour M.P.s, and was appalled at the poorness of the material. I had a good deal of sympathy with him in the tremendous task which seemed likely to fall upon him. It was a prospect which nobody could envy him. The Labour Party was composed in the majority of new and undisciplined members who would expect the Labour Government to do all sorts of impossible things. We discussed at great length the question of whether, if called upon, we would form a Government, and ultimately agreed, for the reasons I have already stated, that we had no choice but to do so. The talk then turned upon what our policy and programme as a Government should be. There was a general agreement that the Capital Levy had now become an electoral millstone, and that the financial and trade condition of the country was such as to make the proposal impracticable. We agreed that something would have to be done with the National Debt problem, and we considered that the best course to take would be to appoint a Committee to enquire into the whole problem. If this Committee reported against the Capital Levy we should drop it; but if the report was favourable to such a scheme we would give a pledge not to adopt it until the country had given a Parliamentary majority in favour of it.

The conversation turned upon what we might be able to do in the first session. There would be two courses open to us. We might use the opportunity for a demonstration and introduce some bold Socialist measures, knowing, of course, that we should be defeated upon them. Then we could go to the country with this illustration of what we would do if we had a Socialist majority. This was a course which had been urged by the extreme wing of the Party, but it was not a policy which commended itself to reasonable opinion. I urged very strongly to this meeting that we should not adopt an extreme policy, but should confine our legislative proposals to measure that we were likely to be able to carry. It was no use getting swelled head and imagining that we were omnipotent. We must remember that we were less than one-third of the House of Commons. We must show the country that we were not under the domination of the wild men. Mr. MacDonald was afraid that we should have a good deal of trouble with the extreme section, who would press upon us and expect us to do all kinds of impossible things. Mr. Thomas emphatically agreed with my view. Mr. Henderson pointed out that we should be bound by Conference resolutions, and particularly by the resolution to increase unemployment pay to £2 a week. We tentatively agreed that we should recognise the Soviet Government, but we left over the consideration of the conditions until we were in office. We agreed that we must at once take administrative action to remove certain injustices in the Unemployment Insurance Act, particularly to remove the gap. In regard to finance, I was asked what I thought were the possibilities of reducing taxation. If I went to the Exchequer I was anxious not to raise expectations which I might be unable to fulfil, so I said that possibly we might be able to reduce the food taxes. Nothing was said about the allocation of Ministerial offices beyond that this should be left to the Prime Minister, Webb urging that we should follow in this respect the usual constitutional practice. In the course of general conversation, Henderson, who was not then a member of Parliament (having again been defeated at the General Election), expressed willingness to go to the House of Lords as a life peer. That raised the question of our representation in the House of Lords. Under the law there would have to be at least two Secretaries of State in that Chamber. It would be necessary to create peers to meet that condition, and we all agreed that in the selection of men for that elevation we should try as far as possible to choose men who would not have an heir so that the peerage should not be permanent.

Henderson and I went home together, as we lived within a few doors of each other. When we parted, Henderson expressed some misgiving about leaving the appointment of Ministers wholly to MacDonald, and hoped that he would consult us freely upon this important matter before finally coming to a decision. After this meeting Mr. MacDonald went to Lossiemouth, which is a small fishing village on the Morayshire coast. Here he spent his time drawing up draft after draft of his Ministerial appointments. At Christmas-time Mr. Henderson and his son came down to see us at Tilford and stayed for the weekend. Henderson was very full of the political situation, and had apparently been in correspondence with MacDonald on the formation of the probable Labour Government. MacDonald had written to him to say that he had drafted two preliminary lists of Cabinet and Ministerial offices. In one he had left Henderson out altogether on the understanding that he should devote himself to organising the Party in the country. In the other list he put Henderson down as Chairman of Ways and Means! This latter suggestion outraged Henderson. It certainly was offensive, and I considered that Henderson's indignation was justified. It showed what tactless things MacDonald could do sometimes. The office of Chairman of Ways and Means was not even a Ministerial post. We talked about possible men to fill the various offices. It had been generally assumed that Lord Haldane would be a member of the Labour Government. I believe he was not a member of the Party, but he had shown considerable sympathy with it, and had addressed a few Labour meetings in the country. Henderson said that he understood that Lord Haldane had expressed a preference for the India Office. Henderson, who appeared to have been very busy consulting various people, said that he had suggested the Colonial Office to Sidney Webb, who had turned it down as not good enough. Thomas had told Henderson that he would not take the Air Ministry because it was not a first-class Secretaryship. MacDonald had told Henderson that he had definitely decided to combine the Premiership and the Foreign Office, and that Clynes would be given the post of Lord Privy Seal in order that he would have leisure to lead the House in MacDonald's absence. So far as Henderson knew, MacDonald was going to appoint non-Trade Unionists to all the best offices, and he anticipated that there would be strong resentment from the Trade Union section, who would consider that their numerical strength in the Party and their financial contributions to it entitled them to a large share in the Ministerial posts. Both Henderson and myself in these conversations expressed our resentment at MacDonald's secrecy, and thought that he ought to be in London in regular consultation with his colleagues. Henderson thought that we ought to have sought from MacDonald that night at Webb's some indication of how he proposed to fill the particular offices. Henderson's temper is mercurial, and at this time he was not very friendly towards MacDonald. But the relations between the two have never been very cordial. On each side there is some excuse.

Mr. Lloyd George, who is a near neighbour of mine in the country, called in the afternoon of 3rd January 1924. The talk naturally turned on the political situation. The name of Lord Grey cropped up, and Lloyd George said that Grey was not being consulted by Asquith about the action of the Liberal Party. In regard to the political crisis and the likelihood of a Labour Government, Lloyd George said that MacDonald's vanity might ruin the Labour Government. This expectation was fulfilled within twelve months. As an indication of the fear with which the Conservatives regarded the advent of a Labour Government, it may be mentioned that the City of London Conservative and Unionist Associations sent to the Press on 2nd January a letter they had addressed to Mr. Baldwin urging that the Conservative Party should support a Liberal Government in order to exclude Labour from office. Mr. Baldwin replied that co-operation was impossible in view of Mr. Asquith's speech at the National Liberal Club on the 18th December, in which he had stated that the Liberal Party would enter into no sort of alliance or arrangement with the Conservatives. The meeting of the new Parliament had been fixed for the 8th of January. Mr. MacDonald had returned to London a few days before this date, and although I had no communication with him I learnt from other sources that he was busy putting the finishing touches to the draft of his Cabinet. On the morning of this date Mr. Henderson looked in on his way to his office to tell me that he had seen Mr. MacDonald. It was definitely fixed that I was to go to the Exchequer. I had had no intimation from Mr. MacDonald of this. Webb would probably be Minister of Labour, with Miss Bondfield as Under-Secretary. MacDonald had offered Henderson the War Office. Henderson was indignant at this because to face a by-election as a War Minister when he held the office of President of the Socialist International would provide the enemy with material for attack. Moreover, he did not want the War Office job. He would prefer the Home Office, which would leave him free to supervise the Labour headquarters in Eccleston Square. Thomas, said Henderson, had changed his mind about the Colonies. He had been looking up precedence, and he thought that the post of the Colonies was higher in precedence than the War Office or the Admiralty. But Thomas had said that if he could not have the Colonies he would demand the Home Office. MacDonald proposed to put General Thomson into the Lords as Air Minister, and might make Cecil Wilson, the member for Attercliffe, an Under-Secretary in the Lords in order to give Henderson a by-election at

Attercliffe. In the sketch Cabinet MacDonald had left out Tom Shaw altogether from any office. This seemed incredible, but Henderson assured me it was a fact. MacDonald had also the idea of making Trevelyan Health Minister. I could not accept this rumour, knowing as I did what MacDonald thought of Trevelyan's capacity. Stephen Walsh had been put down as Chancellor of the Duchy of Lancaster. I thought there was little foundation for some of these rumours, and as the events turned out this proved to be the fact.

Parliament met in the afternoon of this day (8th January). I saw MacDonald for a moment in the Lobby, but he said nothing at all to me about Ministerial appointments. The next few days were occupied by the swearing in of members, and it was not until 15th January that the Commons got down to business. Two days later, on 17th January, Mr. Clynes moved the Labour Amendment to the Address, which was very brief. It read: "It is our duty to submit to Your Majesty that Your Majesty's present advisers have not the confidence of this House."

Mr. Asquith followed Mr. Clynes, and made a speech which settled the fate of the Conservative Government and prepared the way for the coming of the Labour Party into office. Mr. Asquith took it for granted that the Amendment would be carried, that Mr. Baldwin would resign, and that the King would summon Mr. MacDonald to form a Labour Government. The vote of lack of confidence in the Government was carried by 328 to 256 votes. Next day, the 22nd January, Mr. Baldwin announced to the House of Commons that he had tendered his resignation to the King and that His Majesty had accepted it, and the House adjourned to 12th February. The King sent for Mr. MacDonald, who became Prime Minister, and with unprecedented expedition the Labour Government was formed. The same day the list of names of the Labour Cabinet was issued. It had come at last! Few of us who had toiled through the years to achieve this object had expected to see it realised in our lifetime. It was true that the first Labour Government was brought into existence by accidental circumstances and not by the will of the majority of the electorate. Labour was in office, but not in power, and it depended for its continuance in office upon the good-will and support of a Party with which it had been in political conflict from the time of the inception of the Labour Party. The future of the Labour Government depended upon whether it realised the difficulties and the limitations of its position. It did not, as I have said, owe its accession to office to the support of a majority of the electorate to a Socialist policy. It had no mandate to carry out far-reaching Socialist schemes, but it was in the position to carry through the House of Commons schemes of social reform which were common to the Liberal and the Labour Parties. The immediate future would decide how far such co-operation was possible.

Two days before Mr. Baldwin resigned, Mr. MacDonald called into his room at the House those members of the House of Commons he proposed to include in the Cabinet. Up to that time I had had no formal invitation to join the Government, but it had been assumed that I should take the office of Chancellor of the Exchequer. At this meeting Mr. MacDonald threw across the table to me a pencilled note written on an envelope which said: "I want formally to ask you to accept the office of Chancellor to the Exchequer." I nodded my acceptance. I should think there would be no precedent for such an informal offer and acceptance of a Cabinet post. The question we had to decide at this meeting was our visit to Buckingham Palace to receive our Seals of Office. Sir Maurice Hankey, the Secretary to the Cabinet and the Clerk to the Privy Council, now came upon the scene. He was very much concerned that we should go through the ceremony at the Palace with due regard to all the conventional proprieties. The first difficulty which arose was about dress. The instructions were that we should put on frock-coats and wear silk hats. Several of the prospective Cabinet Ministers lived in the provinces and had no residence in London. They had no clothes in London except the suits in which they stood. There was no time to get new clothes; there was nothing for it but to go to the Palace in their working attire. The situation was placed before Lord Stamfordham, the King's Private Secretary, who was a great stickler for Court etiquette, but eventually he had to agree that the usual conditions should be set aside, and several of the new Cabinet Ministers went to the Palace in ordinary lounge suits. Other members appeared to have been successful and managed to drag from some obscurity a frock-coat and silk hat which might have been fashionable a generation before. Sir Maurice Hankey, who was extremely anxious that there should be no hitch in the proceedings, put us through two or three rehearsals of the ceremony. Everything, however, passed off without a hitch, greatly to Sir Maurice Hankey's relief. I was unable to conform to the condition of a frock-coat. I had once possessed one, but some time before I had sent it to a jumble sale. I managed, however, to find a morning coat and a silk hat.

Of the twenty members constituting this Cabinet thirteen belonged to the non-Trade Union section of the Labour Party. There were seven who were Trade Union members. The Trade Unionists regarded this small representation of their section of the Labour Party with a good deal of dissatisfaction, and their resentment was strong at the inclusion in the Cabinet of so many men who had no record of service in the Labour Movement and who had done little or nothing to create the Labour Party. The greatest surprise was the appointment of Viscount Chelmsford as First Lord of the Admiralty. This appointment had been kept secret until the announcement was made public. Lord Chelmsford had had a distinguished career as Viceroy of India. He had never in the slightest degree been associated in any way with the Labour Party. Indeed, I believe that during the time he held office in the Labour Government he was not a member of the Labour Party. Lord Haldane, as I have said previously, though he expressed sympathy with the Labour Party, was not a member at the time of his appointment. Lord Parmoor, General Thomson, Noel Buxton, Trevelyan and Colonel Wedgwood were all comparatively recent recruits to the Party. The publication of the names of the Cabinet had a reassuring effect upon that section of public opinion which had been in terror about the advent of a Labour Government. The most timid Conservatives and the most frightened capitalists took heart from the presence in the Cabinet of men like Lord Parmoor, Lord Chelmsford and Lord Haldane; they could not believe that these men would be the instruments for carrying out the Socialist Revolution. Something like consternation had reigned in aristocratic and financial circles at the prospect of a Labour Government. A countess rang me up during this time of suspense to ask me frantically (she had been reading the *Morning Post*) if it were true that the first thing the Labour Party would do would be to cut the throats of every aristocrat and steal all their property. I tried to pacify her by assuring her that the prospective Labour Government had not yet decided what its first administrative act would be, but if it should decide to realise her fears it would be able to plead a good many historical precedents on the part of her ancestors. I finally assured her, however, that it was not likely that her personal safety would be in jeopardy, and she went away happy. About half the minor offices were distributed among Trade Union members, and the other half were given to the non-Trade Union element. Some surprise was caused by the absence of the name of Mr. Lansbury from the new Ministry. I was told that Mr. MacDonald had offered Mr. Lansbury an Under-Secretaryship without a scat in the Cabinet, and Mr. Lansbury had indignantly declined the offer. I think, on the whole, Mr. MacDonald had made the best of the material at his service. Only one Labour member of the Government had previously held a Cabinet post. Mr. Henderson had been a member of the War Cabinet in the Coalition Government, and two other members of the new Cabinet had held subordinate positions in that Government. Mr. MacDonald was wise in including in his Cabinet one member who had had a long Cabinet experience, namely Lord Haldane. There was no member of the Labour Party who was qualified to take the position of Lord Chancellor. As it turned out, Lord Haldane's long experience proved to be of the greatest service to the inexperienced Labour Government. During the construction of the Cabinet he had expressed, he told me after, a desire to take the India Office, but his legal qualifications obviously fitted him for the post of Lord Chancellor - an office he had held in Mr. Asquith's Government. During the time Lord Chelmsford held office as First Lord of the Admiralty he did not concern himself with matters outside his own Department. I was brought closely in contact with him in the protracted negotiations which annually take place between the Admiralty and the Exchequer on the Navy Estimates. Lord Parmoor had only recently joined the Labour Party, and his conversion was something of a phenomenon. He had been a high Tory and a devoted Churchman - the last man in the world, one would expect, to ever become identified with the Socialist movement. He had become associated with our movement during the War mainly because of our opposition to conscription and our defence of civil rights. He had a very kindly and sympathetic nature. He held very strong Free Trade views, and I could always count upon him to support me in defence of that policy. General Thomson, who afterwards became Lord Thomson, was another member of the Cabinet who had come into the Socialist movement because of his strong dissatisfaction with the Peace Treaties. He had acted as one of the military advisers at the Paris Conference. I well remember my first introduction to him. He called at the Independent Labour Party's office one day shortly after the end of the War, when I was acting as editor of the publications department, to submit to me a manuscript of a book on the consequences of the Peace Treaties on the future relations of European countries. I published the book for him under the title *Old Europe's Suicide*. The only other member of the Cabinet to whom at this point I may make a special reference was Mr. Tom Shaw. Mr. Shaw was born within five miles of my native place, and had lived in that district up to the time of his return to Parliament in 1918. Mr. Shaw was an official of a Lancashire Weavers' Association and Secretary of the International Textile Federation. He had himself been a weaver. He was entirely self-educated, and had taught himself French and German, which he spoke, I am told by those who are qualified to judge, with remarkable fluency. His office in the Government - that of Minister of Labour - was not one which anybody would take except under a sense of duty. The Minister of Labour has very limited powers, and he has to bear the odium of a great deal of popular criticism on matters for which he is not directly responsible.

The Labour Party was very weak in the House of Lords, and it was necessary that it should have representatives of the Government in that Chamber. Immediately after the formation of the Government, peerages were conferred upon Sir Sidney Olivier, General Thomson, and Mr. Sydney Arnold (who had been appointed Under Secretary for the Colonies). Neither Olivier nor Thomson nor Arnold were members of the House of Commons. Their elevation to the peerage had been contemplated when they were appointed to office. The inclusion of Olivier in the Government as Secretary of State for India had caused some surprise. He was a member of the Fabian Society, and one of the original Fabian Essayists. He was a permanent Civil Servant attached to the Colonial Office, and for some years before the formation of the Labour Government he had been Governor of Jamaica, where he had been regarded as an outstanding success. He had not, however, since the early days of the Fabian Society taken any part in Socialist activities. He had, undoubtedly, considerable administrative gifts, but as a speaker he was hampered by a voice and articulation which made him almost unintelligible. His old Fabian colleague, Mr. Sidney Webb, had come into the Labour Government as President of the Board of Trade. Mr. Webb, too, had great administrative ability and had gained a wide experience as a member of the London County Council, where for many years he had been chairman of some of its important committees. Mr. Clynes had been appointed Lord Privy Seal, an office to which no departmental duties are attached. This leaves the holder of the office free to assist the Cabinet by taking up any special work which may arise. As Mr. MacDonald held the two offices of Prime Minister and Foreign Secretary, it was obvious that he would not have time to put in a full attendance on the Bench during the sittings of the House of Commons. So Mr. Clynes had assigned to him the duty of Deputy Leader of the House of Commons. Mr. Austen Chamberlain in the later days of the Coalition Government had held this office, and had also acted as Deputy Leader of the House. The usual salary attached to the office of Lord Privy Seal is £2,000 a year, but in view of the added duties of leadership Mr. Chamberlain had received £5,000 a year, and this precedent was followed in the case of Mr. Clynes. Mr. MacDonald held the two offices of Prime Minister and Foreign Secretary, but received the salary of one office only, so there was a saving of £2,000 a year in the total of ministerial salaries.

Chapter Seventeen

First Experiences of Office

After the members of the Cabinet had been sworn in on the morning of Wednesday, the 23rd January 1924, the first meeting of the Cabinet was held that day at 4 o'clock in the afternoon. After the ceremony at Buckingham Palace the Ministers went to their respective Departments to make the acquaintance of their permanent officials. I had often been in the Chancellor's room at the Treasury, and there I went to meet the officials. The only official with whom I was personally acquainted was Sir Warren Fisher, the Secretary to the Treasury, with whom I had been on friendly terms for some years. I had already arranged to take over as my two Private Secretaries the officials who had served the previous Chancellor. My principal Private Secretary, Mr. P. J. Grigg (now Sir James Grigg) is now the Financial Minister of the Indian Government, a high position he has reached by exceptional merit. My second Secretary, Mr. Donald Fergusson, was a man of sound judgment whose advice was always worth consideration. He is now the Chancellor's principal Private Secretary.

On the evening of the day I assumed office, a secretary came into my room to say that the Governor of the Bank would like to present his compliments to the new political head of the Treasury. I had not previously met Mr. Norman, but I had a vague idea of what a Governor of the Bank of England ought to look like. I had seen caricatures in the Socialist Press of the typical financier – the hard-faced, close-fisted, high-nosed individual whose active brain had worn off every trace of hair from the summit of his head. I wondered if the Governor of the Bank would look like that! There came into the room a man so different! He might have stepped out of the frame of a portrait of a handsome courtier of the Middle Ages. It took but a short acquaintance with Mr. Norman to know that his external appearance was the bodily expression of one of the kindliest natures and most sympathetic hearts it has been my privilege to know. I do not remember clearly what we talked about at that first interview. But the impression his character made upon me still vividly remains. A Chancellor of the Exchequer sees much of the "Governor", or perhaps it would be more correct to say that the Governor sees much of the Chancellor. It is well known that the relations between the Treasury and the Bank are close and intimate. They are probably much more intimate today than in the past, for great political problems and financial problems are now so closely interwoven. It was said of a great statesman in the Victorian Age that he had the "international mind". How truly that may be said of the present Governor of the Bank of England! To him, more than to any statesman of Europe, is the credit due for the partial restoration of the economic conditions of Europe from the utter collapse in the years following the War. I never hear uninformed remarks about the callousness of international finance but I think of the injustice done through ignorance to the high and unselfish motives of the Governor of the Bank. I think of the prolonged and herculean efforts he has exerted to bring international finance to aid the ruined countries of the Continent to re-establish their economic life. Whether Mr. Norman's policy and actions have been right or wrong, whether he has made mistakes or not, one thing is indisputable – no man with great responsibilities ever tried more faithfully to discharge them with the single aim of promoting national and international well-being. Mr. Norman has in abundant measure the quality of inspiring confidence. He is something more than a colleague to those with whom he is associated. He is a friend. I know nothing at all about his politics. I do not know if he has any. A man's real politics arise from his temperament and feeling. And the Governor's nature is essentially democratic. I should say that he hates snobbery and class distinctions. This is not the place to deal much further with Mr. Norman's work and policy, nor with the criticism of that policy, but I want to say, after four years of intimate and almost daily association with him, that I am sure his work as Governor of the Bank of England, especially in developing the principles of central banking and international financial co-operation, deserve the recognition which posterity will accord to him.

The Treasury buildings in Whitehall are the shabbiest of all the Government offices. In fact, their disreputable condition is a disgrace to the State. The offices of the Spending Departments, like the War Office and the Admiralty, are palatial by comparison. The room of the Chancellor of the Exchequer, which is reached through stone-flagged passages, is all right when you get there. It is a large room overlooking the Horse Guards Parade, and was formerly the room where the Council of State met. The gilded throne on which the Sovereign sat when he presided over the Council is still there on an elevated dais. The large table which occupies the centre of the room is said to be the table round which the members of the East India Company used to sit. There is a full set of William and Mary chairs, which I understand are very valuable. In the centre of this table there now rests the battered dispatch case in which Mr. Gladstone used to carry his Budget Speech to the House of Commons. This box has in the corner the letters "C. G.", and nobody appears to know what they mean. I have heard it suggested that the letters mean "Chancellor Gladstone".

After I had made the acquaintance of my principal officials I went downstairs to the Cabinet Room at No. 10 for the first meeting of the Labour Cabinet. No. 10 Downing Street, including the Cabinet Room, is a part of the Treasury buildings, and provides less accommodation for the Prime Minister's staff and work than even the Exchequer. I am sure there cannot be elsewhere in the world a Council of State Room so inadequate as the Cabinet Room at Downing Street. There are two or three rooms adjacent to the Cabinet Room for the use of the Prime Minister's Secretaries and staff. The Cabinet Room is occupied by an oblong table which fills the whole floor space, leaving just sufficient room for the chairs the Ministers occupy. There is scarcely room to pass between these chairs and the wall, and it is difficult for Ministers to see or hear any of their colleagues but those in front of them and in their immediate neighbourhood. There has been a revolution in Cabinet procedure from the days before the War. We have been told that in those days the Cabinet met without any agenda of business; it had no secretary; and no notes or memoranda were prepared as a record of the proceedings. It is said that Mr. Gladstone, when Prime Minister, always insisted that any pencilled notes which might have been taken by members of the Cabinet during the proceedings should be destroyed before the meeting was closed. If any record of the decisions of the Cabinet was kept in those days it must have been confined to the Prime Minister's letters to the Sovereign. I do not know how the Cabinet was able to conduct its business under the conditions which prevailed before the War. Everybody who has had experience of committee meetings where a large amount of business is considered must know how difficult it is to remember precisely what happened, and members of the committee in the absence of a record of the proceedings carry away with them various impressions. By the time the next meeting is held there are probably as many impressions of what was agreed to as there were members of the committee present.

There is no need for me to explain the system of Cabinet Records which is now in operation. It has been done by others quite as competent as I am. The Secretariat of the Cabinet is now a large office with a considerable staff. The old tradition of absolute secrecy on what takes place in the Cabinet has to some extent been relaxed in these latter days, and I do not see how this could very well be prevented in view of the fact that questions are being constantly asked in the House of Commons on Cabinet decisions to which the Prime Minister is expected to give a reply. Decisions of the Cabinet which have an operative effect must of necessity eventually be made public, but what it is important to preserve is the secrecy of the discussions in the Cabinet and of the various views which are expressed by Ministers. The Cabinet Minutes, as others have pointed out, are confined to a record of the decisions, and are not a report of the discussions. There are occasions when a Minister dissents very strongly from the majority, and asks that his dissent may be recorded. The Labour Government introduced an innovation in the reports given to the Press of Cabinet Meetings, which hitherto had been confined to the mere statement that a meeting of the Cabinet had been held, with a list of the Ministers present. But this brief report was amplified by a decision of the Labour Government to stating the business which had been considered. This practice has since been abandoned, and the former practice of circulating to the Press a mere notification that a Cabinet Meeting had been held, with the names of the Ministers present, has been revived.

Parliament at the time when the Labour Government took office was not in session, and did not meet until the 12th of February. In the meantime the Cabinet held frequent meetings to prepare its legislative programme for the session. The Ministers got to work in their respective Departments and, full of enthusiasm, began to draft schemes of reform which fell within their province. One of the first collective acts of the Government was the de jure recognition of the Russian Government. The Note intimating to the Soviet Government that the British Government was prepared to recognise them was dispatched on the 1st February and published in the British Press the following day. This Note laid down the conditions of recognition. The two principal ones were that it was of the utmost importance to come to an understanding between the two Governments on the problem of the settlement of existing claims by the Government and nationals of one party against the other, and the restoration of Russian credit; and the other had relation to propaganda. If genuine friendly relations were to be completely established, all suspicion must be removed that their Government was carrying on propaganda against our interests and directed at overthrowing our institutions. The British Government, therefore, suggested that the Russian Government should send over to London at the earliest possible date representatives armed with full powers to discuss these matters, and to draw up the preliminary basis of a complete treaty to settle all questions outstanding between the two countries. The British Government did not consider it to be necessary to wait the meeting of Parliament to confirm this act of de jure recognition, as both the Labour and Liberal Parties at the General Election had expressed their approval of such a course. When Parliament met, Mr. Asquith, on behalf of the Liberal Party, expressed much satisfaction at the announcement of the Government that they were de jure recognising the Soviet Government, and Mr. Baldwin, who, of course, as Leader of the Opposition, had to say something critical about the action of the Government in this matter, was very lukewarm in his objection.

Chapter Eighteen

Difficulties of the New Government

The Labour Government met Parliament for the first time on the 12th February 1924. It was something of an ordeal for Ministers, most of whom had had no previous experience in office, to meet the House of Commons, and to face a strong Tory Opposition, and a critical if sympathetic Liberal Party. At the opening of the sitting we had to face the usual barrage of questions. Answering questions is a severe test of a Minister's knowledge of the work of his Department, and of his alertness in dealing with supplementary questions. The practice of devoting the first hour of each sitting to questions to Ministers is one which, I understand, does not obtain in any other Parliament in the world. It is, I think, an invaluable institution. It has a restraining influence upon Ministers, who know that their actions are always open to possible criticism by questions in the House. It is well known that the replies to printed questions are prepared for the Minister by the officials of his Department, but a wise Minister never accepts the answers which are put before him without careful examination, and without preparing himself for any possible supplementary questions which may arise. A Minister with a sharp intellect and quickness of repartee, who has made himself fully acquainted with the subject-matter of the question, need never fear "Question Time". Members very soon recognise those Ministers they can badger and those who are more than a match for the questioner. It is very seldom indeed that a questioner is able to score off a Minister who knows his subject. There is, of course, a refuge for a Minister who is faced with an inconvenient question in the formula "I must have notice of that question". But the too frequent use of that formula gives the House the impression that a Minister is not too well informed upon the work of his Department. I always enjoyed Question Time as an exercise in intellectual alertness. Ministers got through their first experience of Question Time without any mishap.

After Questions had been disposed of at this sitting, the Prime Minister made a long statement on the legislative programme of the new Government. His speech was conciliatory, and he recognised the unprecedented circumstances in which the House was placed, since no Party had a majority. This situation necessitated some alteration in Parliamentary practice. Individual members would have to think less about Party and assume more personal responsibility. The Government which could not command the votes of a majority of the House could not expect to obtain a majority upon every proposal it submitted to Parliament. The Government would not resign as the result of a snap division on a petty issue. The Labour Government would not resign unless it was defeated upon some substantial issue of principle. He said:

> "I propose to introduce my business knowing that I am in a minority, accepting the responsibilities of a minority, and claiming the privileges that attach to those responsibilities. And if the House on matters non-essential, matters that do not strike at the root of the proposals that we make-and do not destroy fundamentally the general intentions of the Government in introducing legislation - if the House wish to vary our proposition, then the House must take the responsibility of this variation-then a division on such amendments and questions as those will not be regarded as a vote of no confidence."

The announcement was made that the Government intended to introduce Bills to improve the Old Age Pensions Act, and a Bill to amend the Factories and Workshops Acts. The most important measure of the session would be a Housing Bill aimed at producing decent houses at rents that could be borne by the average income of the working classes. The question of unemployment, the Prime Minister announced, had already been under the serious consideration of the Government. The Government aimed in this matter at doing two things - providing work, and amending the scale of benefits for the unemployed where work could not be provided. The Government approached this question somewhat with the idea of getting the unemployed back into their own work, and therefore, in so far as the Government could influence trade, that would be the first point of attack.

It is interesting to note, in view of the discussions which have since been insistently carried on about the problem of unemployment, that Mr. MacDonald in this speech declared that "the Government were not going to diminish industrial capital in order to provide relief." "I want to make it perfectly clear", he said, "that the Government have no intention of drawing off from the normal channels of trade large sums for extemporised measures which can only be palliatives. That is the old, sound Socialist doctrine, and the necessity of expenditure for subsidised schemes in direct relief of unemployment will be judged in relation to the greater necessity for maintaining undisturbed the ordinary financial facilities and the reserves of trade and industry."

It was not an ambitious programme, but it provided material for a full session's hard work. It disappointed those members of the Labour Party who had expected that the Minority Labour Government would put forward bold Socialist proposals. The Labour Government, as I have pointed out, depended for its continuance in office upon the good-will and the support of the Liberal members. There was no doubt that Mr. Asquith and the majority of the Liberal Party were prepared to keep the Government in office so long as they pursued a programme of social reform which was common to the Labour and Liberal parties. But very early in the session it became quite clear that there were a number of Liberals who were bent upon causing embarrassment to the Government, and, if possible, defeating them on some substantial issue. Within ten days of the opening of the session, the Liberal members brought forward two hostile motions which, had they been carried, would have brought the Labour Government to an untimely end. On the 21st of February, in reply to a question from the Tory benches, the representative of the Admiralty announced that the Government had decided, in view of the serious unemployment, to proceed with the laying down of five cruisers. Whereupon Mr. Pringle, a Liberal member who had never hidden his bitter hostility to the Labour Party, moved the adjournment of the House to discuss the question. Having obtained leave to do so, a debate took place, and upon a division the Government were saved by the votes of the Conservative members. The division list showed a division in the Liberal Party. Thirty Liberals had voted with the Government and seventy three against. The Liberals who had voted with the Government did so not because they were in favour of the building of new cruisers, but because they were unwilling to embarrass them at this early stage of the Labour Government's existence. A few days later, on the 26th February, a Liberal member brought forward a vote of censure upon the Government in respect of the action of Mr. Wheatley, Minister of Health, in cancelling an Order which had been made by Sir Alfred Mond restricting the Poplar Board of Guardians in the granting of Poor Law relief. This motion was brought forward with the approval of Mr. Asquith, who a few days before had declared in the House "in the plainest and most unequivocal terms that unless the Government would reconsider this action the Liberal Party would vote against them." From the point of view of the continuance of the Government in office this was a much more serious matter than the Liberal action on the cruiser question. Then the Government could rely on the Tory Party. In this case, if the motion were carried to a division, and if Mr. Asquith's declaration of unequivocal opposition to the Government on the matter were carried out, then the defeat of the Government was certain. This debate was looked forward to with much excitement for it seemed as though nothing could save the Government if the Liberals carried the motion to a division. As matters turned out, our fears were groundless. Mr. Wheatley made such effective and convincing defence of his action that when he sat down the Liberal case had been completely destroyed. Mr. Asquith rose to extricate his Party from a humiliating position. He stated that if he could be sure upon one or two points the Liberals would not press their motion to a division. There was no difficulty in the Prime Minister conceding these two points, which were of minor importance, and the Liberals thereupon announced that, as the Government had given such satisfactory assurances, their motion would not be pressed. Mr Wheatley's speech was a veritable triumph and raised his prestige in the House of Commons immensely. Mr. Asquith told me afterwards that in all his Parliamentary experience he had never heard a Minister make a more convincing defence of his action.

The first ten days of the Parliamentary experience of Labour Government showed that we had not fallen into a bed of roses. It was evident that our existence was very precarious, and that we should never know from day to day how long the agony of uncertainty would continue. These two hostile motions by the Liberals at the beginning of the session had embittered relations between the Labour and the Liberal members. The Labour members in their speeches in the country denounced the Liberals with all the old vehemence.

The Liberals were not behind the Labour members in abuse and recrimination. A situation had been already created which made cordial co-operation very difficult. Looking back over the nine months' life of the Labour Government, I am forced to the conclusion that both Parties pursued a policy which was more befitting a lot of irresponsible children than of responsible statesmen. The blame for this cannot be assigned wholly to one Party. The Labour Party had never really accepted the limitations of its Minority position, and on the other hand the Liberals were somewhat arrogant in saying, as Mr. Asquith did in a very unfortunate phrase: "the Labour Government must eat out of the Liberal hand". I wonder now that the Labour Government did not come to grief at an earlier stage of the session. It never showed that consideration to the Liberals to which they were entitled. The Liberal criticism that the Labour Government refused to adopt the co-operation which was necessary for legislative progress was to a great extent justified. There was little or no preliminary consultation between the Government and the Liberal leaders on legislation which it was proposed to introduce. I am not suggesting that there should have been anything of the nature of a Coalition. Neither of the two Parties would have considered that. I am not shirking my personal responsibility for this lack of more cordial co-operation between the two Parties. There were times when the attitude of certain prominent Liberals, obviously inspired by a desire to embarrass and humiliate the Government, made me resentful. But I confess that, indeed, I gave public expression to the feeling at the time that the majority of the Liberal members were genuinely anxious to help us to secure measures of reform. By the time we had been in office two months the relations between the groups had become so strained that in the Liberal Press and official publications and in the speeches of Liberal leaders the view was openly expressed that they could see no useful purpose to be served by keeping the Government in office. At Easter, two months after the Labour Government had first met the House of Commons, Mr. Lloyd George made a speech in his constituency which gave very emphatic expression to this view. He declared that the Government had already completely dissipated their stock of goodwill, and that the only thing which was keeping them in was that no one else was particularly anxious to take office under present conditions.

In the succeeding weeks we led a precarious existence. On several occasions we were defeated in the Division Lobby on matters which were not of much importance, but on other occasions we narrowly escaped defeat on crucial issues through the Liberal vote going against us. In the meantime the Government went on with its administrative work and its legislative programme under these discouraging conditions, and succeeded in passing into law a number of useful if non-spectacular measures. We were, unfortunately, handicapped in the first months of office by a number of serious industrial disputes. A strike of the railwaymen took place during the first week we were in office. But through the efforts of the General Council of the Trade Union Congress it was brought to an end. In February a strike of dockers took place which lasted for eight days; and later there was a serious threat of a strike of electricians which would have endangered the lighting services in London. These disputes gave the Government a good deal of trouble, and there was a wide public impression that they had been entered upon in the expectation that the Labour Government would give the strikers their support. There was, of course, no justification for such an impression. The Government, in every case, adopted an attitude of strict impartiality. It made great efforts within its legal powers to bring the disputes to an end by negotiation. In the Dock Strike, the Minister of Labour (Mr. Tom Shaw), who as a Trade Union leader had had considerable experience of industrial disputes, took the matter in hand at once, and appointed a Committee of Enquiry under the Industrial Courts Act. The purpose of this enquiry was to ascertain all the facts in order that the public might be fully informed. The two parties to this dispute were unwilling to maintain direct relations with one another after the strike had begun, but agreed that the Minister of Labour should keep in touch with both sides, and if the Minister thought a favourable opportunity offered for discussion with a view to a settlement they would both accept the invitation to talk things over. This Docks dispute threatened the distribution of essential foods and fuel, and it was essential for the Government to take steps to see that these necessaries were supplied. The attention of the Government was drawn to the fact that prices of food commodities were being raised in various parts of the country in consequence of the dispute, and the Government issued the following notice to the Press:

> "The Cabinet has had information from various parts of the country that meat and other prices have been raised from 33 to 50 per cent. There is no reason for this increase except the power of profiteers to extract from

> the public unjust prices. The Cabinet hopes that this notice will have the effect of stopping this increase, but in the meantime it has asked the law officers to consider the powers of the Government in this matter, and to draft such emergency measures as may be necessary to prevent the exploitation of the consumers owing to the Strike."

This notice had a deterrent effect, and the prompt action of the Government was much appreciated by the country. During the acute stages of this Dock Strike the Cabinet met every day, sometimes twice a day, to review the situation and to make preparations for dealing with any serious developments should they arise. The Prime Minister kept the House of Commons informed as to the steps the Government were taking to secure the transport of necessary food supplies, and stated that the nucleus of an organisation for that purpose had already been set up. He properly stressed the importance of nothing being said in the House of Commons which might tend to aggravate the serious situation. The negotiations between the two parties which had been initiated by the action of the Minister of Labour had a happy result, and terms were arranged which brought the strike to an end and removed the necessity for the Government to put into operation any of the machinery it had prepared to secure the maintenance of the essential services.

The settlement of this dispute, unfortunately, did not end the troubles of the Government in the matter of trade disputes. There seemed to be an epidemic of unrest and strikes, and threats to strike were of almost daily occurrence. Two or three weeks after the Dock Strike had been settled a strike in the transport services of London broke out which caused great public inconvenience. There was serious talk of the workers in one of the principal electric stations coming out on strike in sympathy with the transport workers. There was trouble in the coalfields which seemed at one time likely to lead to a stoppage, but fortunately that disastrous course was averted. There was a large number of sectional and unauthorised strikes, the cause of which could be traced to Communist activity within the Trade Unions.

It will be understood that all this trouble caused the Government great anxiety, and diverted its attention in a large measure from the work of preparing its legislative measures, in which it should have been wholly occupied. It will be realised that the situation of the Government was not one of ease with dignity.

The strike fever is infectious, and this outbreak, apart from Communist activity, was not caused by a desire to embarrass the Government, but was rather due to the release of a feeling of genuine discontent with the wages reductions which had been imposed in most industries over the preceding four years.

The general public have no idea of the amount of work which falls on members of the Government which never comes to their notice. A great mass of documents, memoranda and dispatches almost daily are circulated amongst Cabinet Ministers, and it is necessary that these should be carefully studied if the Ministers are to keep themselves fully informed upon questions on which decisions have to be taken. The departmental duties of a Minister vary very much according to the nature of the office. I think that the Minister of Labour and the Minister of Health have particularly hard departmental work. The functions of both offices bring them more closely in touch with the public, with the House of Commons, and with the country than the work of most other Departments. The Minister of Labour in particular has a very thankless office. He is exposed to constant criticism by members of Parliament, and however sympathetic he may be he can never satisfy all the demands which are made upon him. In peace time the departmental work of a Minister in charge of one of the Fighting Services is not heavy, and these Ministers are available when their services are required to assist on Committees dealing with other matters.

A week after the Labour Government had met the House of Commons, I was called upon to make my first speech as a Minister. A Labour member had secured first place in the ballot for Private Members' Motions, and he had selected the subject of Mothers' Pensions. This was a subject which had come into prominence in recent years, and all political parties had committed themselves to the principle. Mr. Dukes, the Labour member who put forward this motion, introduced it in an extremely able and reasonable speech. In my reply I expressed on behalf of the Government much sympathy with the motion, and mentioned that, although we had only been in office a month, we had already had this matter under consideration. We had called in to help us in framing a scheme some of the chief experts in their various departments, and they were already investigating the subject. I expressed the belief that the House of Commons would sympathise with my position. I doubted, however, if there were ever a Chancellor of the Exchequer in a position more unfortunate in one respect than that in which I found myself. I was expected to do all kinds of impossible things. The miracle of the loaves and fishes was a comparatively trivial thing compared with what I was expected to do. The Government was already committed to a large legislative programme. It had already submitted to Parliament social reforms which would involve a very large expenditure. We were pledged in this session to amend the Old Age Pensions Act, which would cost a considerable sum of money. The Minister of Labour and the Minister of Health were certain that I was going to lend a sympathetic ear to their demands, and provide the financial help to carry out the proposals they were making. We were committed to a Housing Bill and a not inexpensive Housing programme. I had not yet had sufficient time to overhaul the national finances and get them into a sound condition. When I found that I could provide the money I promised that Widows' Pensions would be one of the first measures to which I should apply the resources which would then become available.

This motion was carried unanimously. I may here anticipate events by mentioning that the following year our successors brought forward a contributory scheme for Widows' Pensions, which was based upon the Report of the Enquiry to which I have referred.

Chapter Nineteen

The First Labour Budget

The preparation of the Budget occupied what time I could spare from other activities during the month of March. Fortunately for me, the national finances as disclosed by the outturn of the year (which ended on the 31st March) proved to be very satisfactory. Mr. Baldwin's Budget of the previous year, when he estimated for a surplus of £1,884,000, resulted in a surplus of £48,329,000. It was very difficult in those days to estimate income and expenditure with approximate accuracy. This difficulty was owing to the dislocation of economic and social conditions caused by the War. Mr. Baldwin's surplus of £48,329,000 went automatically to the reduction of the National Debt, and did not help my Budget except in so far as it was an indication of the probable yield of taxes in the coming year.

The Estimates for the Supply Services for which I had to budget showed a reduction of £31,000,000 on the previous year's Budget Estimates. This saving of expenditure, of course, gave me a very good start; and as I felt justified in being rather optimistic as to the yield of the revenue, I was in a position to present a very favourable Budget to the House of Commons. With the help of my experts I went very carefully into the possibilities of the yield of the existing taxes, and of the probable income from non-tax revenue. This task of estimating the revenue for the coming year is a fascinating but difficult job. The least difficult part of the work is to estimate the probable yield of the indirect taxes on sugar, tea, tobacco and the liquor duties. The consumption of these commodities is very stable. The experience of previous years is available. If the consumption of any particular article is showing a steady increase, an increase in a yield is estimated. The growth of the population has to be taken into consideration, and, roughly assuming trade conditions are likely to remain normal, about 2 per cent rise in consumption is expected. There are other items of revenue which are much more difficult to estimate. A Chancellor can never tell with certainty how many millionaires will die next year. He does not know whether there will be boom or stagnation on the Stock Exchange and in Company Promoting which will affect the receipts from Stamp Duties. But the law of averages is a wonderful thing, and it helps the Chancellor to estimate the yield of the Death Duties and the Stamp Duties with reasonable accuracy. The Income-Tax is the main source of revenue, and a grave miscalculation of the probable yield will seriously upset the Budget. Generations of experience of the working of the Income-Tax have placed valuable material at the disposal of the revenue authorities. During the whole year a careful examination of the balance-sheets of all public companies, from which the greater part of the Income-Tax is derived, is continuously made, and when the time comes for the Estimates there is accumulated information from which a fairly accurate idea of how the profits on which the tax will be based compare with previous years. When the estimates of the probable yield of all the existing taxes in the coming year have been completed, the Chancellor knows whether his revenue from them will meet the expenditure to which he is committed.

When the Estimates are presented to Parliament in March the country knows what the expenditure on the Supply Services will be; but there is one large item of expenditure which is kept secret until the Budget is disclosed - that is, the cost of the Debt Services. This item includes the interest on the Funded Debt, which is not difficult to estimate. To estimate the cost of the Floating Debt is more difficult, because it depends upon the probable course of money rates during the coming year. Finally, the Chancellor has to decide what provision he will make for the redemption of the Debt. When all this work has been completed, when the full estimated expenditure is known, and when the estimates of revenue have been made, the Chancellor knows whether he has a surplus or a deficit. When I had the completed estimates before me I found that I should have a surplus to distribute of nearly £40,000,000. I was, of course, a very happy man, and my next task was a most agreeable one. What should I do with this surplus? I could not devote all this surplus to a reduction of taxation, as I was committed to considerable expenditure on account of the Government's legislation for which no provision had been made in the Estimates. In previous Budgets the Income-Tax had been reduced from 6s. to 4s. 6d. in the £1, and, although the rate was still very high, I felt that there were other classes of tax-payers whose turn for consideration had now come. In the previous two years the Income-Tax payers had had a total relief in the region of £85,000,000 a year. The main part of this remission had gone into the pockets of the wealthier portions of the community, and in my view these tax-payers had had their just share of previous reductions, and should expect no more relief this year. The Income-Tax payers would, of course, share with others in any remission of indirect taxation I might make, and there were two or three other items of taxation which I finally decided to repeal, which were taxes in the class which paid Income-Tax.

Budget secrets are generally well kept. This is highly creditable, for something like a score of officials must necessarily be taken into the Chancellor's confidence and made aware beforehand of the contents of the prospective Budget. Sometimes it is necessary for a Chancellor who is contemplating an alteration of some specific duty to take the leaders of that industry into consultation, and I know of no case where that confidence has ever been betrayed. When the Chancellor has got his Budget into its final form it is not immediately presented to the Cabinet, nor has there been any preliminary conversation in the Cabinet - unless some proposal likely to be highly controversial is suggested. What happened in the case of my first Budget was that I did not submit it to the Cabinet until the morning of Budget day. I shall never forget the impression made upon my colleagues as one after another I outlined reductions of taxation, and they were evidently so deeply impressed that they decided to place on record their warm approval of the first Labour Budget. I presented my first Budget on 29th April 1924. When I left Downing Street with the Budget in Mr. Gladstone's battered dispatch-box, there was the usual crowd of the public and of photographers, and all the way to the House of Commons cheering crowds lined the streets. It is always like this on Budget day, though on this occasion public interest and curiosity had been increased as this was the first time that a Labour Budget was to be presented to Parliament.

When I entered the House I faced a Chamber uncomfortably crowded in every part. Members were sitting in the gangways and filling the side galleries. I suppose that I ought to have felt a considerable nervousness at the ordeal which was before me, but I am not an emotional person, and I have to confess that I was as unperturbed as on an ordinary occasion. There were in the Strangers' Gallery some of my boyhood mates who had come all the way from Yorkshire for this unique occasion. Hidden away in a corner of the Speaker's Gallery was my wife, suffering from a state of nervous tension from which I was happily free, and for which there was no need. The text of a Budget Speech is always necessarily very carefully prepared. It is important that there should be no slip in any of the figures with which the Budget Statement abounds. A copy of the speech is held by the Financial Secretary, who sits beside the Chancellor ready to give him a nudge if he should make a slip in any of the figures. I can only remember one case where a Chancellor delivered his speech without the aid of voluminous notes. That was Mr. Bonar Law, who spoke for over an hour from two half-sheets of note-paper. I am sure if my dear friend Willie Graham had lived to present a Budget he would have spoken for a couple of hours without even the assistance of a sheet of note-paper. As I unfolded my proposals for a reduction of taxes, the enthusiasm of the Labour members grew in intensity. I had, as I have already stated, nearly £40,000,000 of revenue in hand, and this was how I proposed to distribute the relief. Before I passed on to the tax reductions I announced a few minor concessions. I made concessions on motor vehicle licences, which cost approximately £500,000 a year. I made a concession in the allowance on Income-Tax to a widower or widow for a housekeeper. I was not in a position to make any considerable changes in the postal rates. I had been very anxious, if possible, to restore the penny post, but I was forced to the conclusion that this was not at the time an economic proposition. The cost of such a concession would have wiped out the profits of the Post Office and required a subsidy from the general taxpayer. I did, however, by an arrangement with the Postmaster-General make a reduction in the telephone charges which would cost £ 1,000,000 in a full year. Both the Labour and the Liberal Parties had long been pledged to the abolition of taxes on food when the financial position of the country would permit that to be done. I proposed to reduce the sugar duty, which then stood at 2¾d. per lb., by 1½d. per lb., a reduction of just over half. This was a very expensive concession, and absorbed nearly half my available resources. The tea duty then stood at 8d. per lb., a wholly indefensible rate of taxation. I reduced this by half, at an estimated cost of £5,000,000 a year. This reduction brought the tea duty below the Pre-war rate. Similar reductions were also made on cocoa and coffee. I also reduced the duties on dried fruits, and abolished the duties on sweetened table waters. All these reductions I estimated would cost about £25,000,000 a year. Although these concessions were not a complete fulfilment of our desire for the abolition of duties on the breakfast-table, they went as far as it was possible in the financial circumstances. I then turned to the Entertainments Duty. I believe I was the only member of the House of Commons who opposed this duty when it was first introduced. I had never liked it, but unfortunately I was not in a position to propose its repeal. I had to be content with some modification. I proposed to give relief on the cheapest seats, which are used by the less well-to-do members of the community, by abolishing the duty on the payments for admission up to and including 6d. and by reducing the duty on payments over that amount up to and including 1s. 3d. I may say that I had experienced more difficulty in dealing with this question of the Entertainments Duty than with any other matter I had had under consideration in connection with the Budget, owing to the fact that a great part of the duty is derived from the cheaper seats, and, therefore, the abolition of the duty on these seats involved a sacrifice of a very large amount of revenue. The reduction that I proposed meant sacrificing nearly one-half of the annual revenue from these duties. The relief given was estimated to amount to £4,000,000 in a full year.

As I have already stated, I was not in a position, if relief were to be given to the indirect tax-payers, to make any reduction of the Income-Tax. I had, however, the satisfaction of removing from our revenue system a tax which had long ago become an anachronism. I refer to a tax the existence of which, I suppose, has now been forgotten. It was the Inhabited House Duty. This duty had been with us with an intermission of sixteen years for nearly a century and a half. It was the historic successor of the old Chimney and Hearth Tax. It was, in effect, a double and unnecessary addition to the IncomeTax, and it was paid by the middle and upper classes. It was supposed to be a rough-and-ready device for estimating a person's capacity to pay. I repealed this duty altogether at a cost of £2,000,000 a year. The most controversial part of my Budget was the proposal to remove what was known as "the McKenna Duties". These duties were imposed in 1915 on motorcars and motorcycles (other than commercial vehicles), musical instruments, clocks and watches, and cinema films. These duties had never been a permanent part of our fiscal system, but had been renewed from year to year. It was made perfectly clear when these duties were first introduced that they were intended purely as a temporary war-tax. Each year, when the duties were renewed, the reason put forward for their retention had been the need for revenue. This, however, was merely an excuse. It was the protective character of these duties which was the real reason they had been kept. The recent General Election had been fought upon the question of the imposition of duties upon imported manufactured articles, and the country had given a most decisive verdict against such duties. The Government, therefore, felt that they were bound to give effect to this popular decision. In order to avoid hardship to traders which might occur if the duties lapsed in two days without further notice, I proposed that the duties should be renewed until the 1st August next, when they must finally expire. I gave this extension of time to enable the trade to clear off their duty-paid stocks, and I thought that this concession was reasonable. The cost of the abolition of these duties was estimated at nearly £3,000,000 a year. As I anticipated, this proposal was the only controversial item in the Budget, and it roused violent opposition from the Conservative Party and the motor manufacturers. During the War a special tax had been imposed upon the profits of Public Companies, known as the Corporations Profits Duty. It was never a popular tax, although fairly remunerative. It was unloved by its parents and reviled by its subsequent guardians. It was condemned by every Party, and it had been quite obviously waiting for its final doom. The abolition of this tax made a considerable inroad into the revenue. It was estimated that in a full year it would cost over £12,000,000. Taking all these reductions in taxation together, I estimated that they would give relief to the extent of £40,000,000 in a full year.

I was, therefore, left with an estimated surplus of £4,000,000, which I felt bound to keep in hand, more particularly as I had made no other provision for supplementary expenditure. I would like to supplement this brief summary of the proposals of the first Labour Budget by quoting the final sentences of my speech. I said:

"I thank the Committee for the patience and interest with which they have listened to my speech. But I want very briefly to summarise the proposals contained in the Budget. The Budget imposes no new taxes. It makes no new additions to existing taxes. It proposes to abolish the Corporation Profits Tax; to abolish the Inhabited House Duty; to give concessions to the owners of motor vehicle licences; to extend the allowance for a housekeeper; to make certain Post Office concessions; to abolish the duties on imported manufactured articles; to reduce the entertainments duty by nearly one-half; to abolish the duty on sweetened table waters; to abolish the 50 per cent additional duty on dried fruits; to reduce the tea duty by 4d. per lb.; to reduce the duties on cocoa, coffee and chicory by one-half; to reduce the sugar duty by 1½d, per lb.; and to leave over the funds necessary to improve Old Age Pensions.

This is the first Budget of the first Labour Government. This is the best I have been able to do in the short time we have been in office. I think we can confidently appeal for the support of the majority of Members of this House. These proposals are the greatest step ever made towards the realisation of the cherished Radical ideal of a free breakfast-table. (Hon. Member: 'Hear, hear!'). They will, I am sure - those cheers show-be heartily welcomed by Hon. Members below the Gangway, as well as by those of my own Party. They will give some benefit to every man, woman and child in the country. The Budget is vindictive against no class and against no interest. Though I have always held and declared that the State has the right to call upon the whole of the available resources of its citizens in case of national need, I have equally held and declared that the State has no right to tax anyone unless it can show that the taxation is likely to be used more beneficially and more economically. I have distributed the relief that I have been able to afford in such a way as to confer the greatest benefit upon the greatest number. I have done it in a way which, I believe, by increasing the purchasing power of the people, will stimulate trade and industry; and I have kept in mind always the vital necessity of maintaining unimpaired the national credit on which the very existence of the country depends. I am glad to have been able to propose this substantial relief of the burden of taxation which, for the last ten years, has been borne with such commendable fortitude by every class of the community."

When I sat down there was a great demonstration by the Labour and the Liberal members. The usual brief complimentary speeches followed. The Conservative ex-Chancellor Sir Robert Horne spoke on behalf of the Conservatives. He said: "If I might venture my own personal word of commendation, I do not think, certainly during the time I have been in the House, we have ever heard a more clear or perspicuous statement with regard to our national finance." Mr. Asquith said: "I desire, if I may, to express on behalf of myself and my colleagues our extreme satisfaction, not only with the admirable lucidity and cogency which I have rarely heard surpassed in the introduction of this most complicated and difficult of all discussions, but also on the fact - so far as I can form a judgment - that the Budget proceeds on sound financial lines." According to the usual practice, the general debate upon the Budget Statement was postponed until next day.

The reception of the Budget by the Press of the country was everything that I could have desired. It relieved the feelings of the rich, who had feared that there might be drastic impositions upon their class. The Liberal Press and the Liberal speakers claimed that it was based upon sound Liberal principles, and in it I followed in the footsteps of Gladstone. The Labour Party were in high spirits and some of them were talking about having an immediate General Election, when they expected the Labour Party would sweep the country and get a majority in the House of Commons. The Conservative newspapers found nothing in the Budget they could criticise except the proposal to abolish the McKenna Duties. Indeed, the Tory Press and the Tory speakers said, apart from this proposal, it was a Budget that might well have been introduced by a Tory Chancellor of the Exchequer! If all these comments were true, I had achieved a remarkable, indeed a unique, success in presenting a Budget which had pleased everybody! The Budget certainly had the effect of improving the relations between the Liberal and the Labour Parties, and gave us the promise of a more certain life, at least until the Budget had been passed into law. I had, of course, the usual shoal of letters and telegrams of congratulation, none of which pleased me more than a most cordial letter from Mr. Walter Long, then Lord Long, with whom I had had so many encounters when he was in the House of Commons. I would like to quote the opinion of Mr. T. P. O'Connor upon the Budget, because he had an experience of Budget speeches extending over half a century. He wrote in one of the London papers:

> "I listened to the speech of Mr. Snowden the other night. I say nothing here about his proposals - this is not the place for such a discussion - I limit myself to a judgment upon it as a Parliamentary performance. I unhesitatingly say that it was the best Budget speech since Gladstone. It had light and shade most delicately contrived, with none of the forced humour of a Hicks-Beach or a Ritchie; it was so lucid that a child could follow the figures; it was serene and unprovocative in temper; and, above all, it was modestly done. I think everybody in the House was delighted with him, and that from every quarter he had compliments which he well deserved."

It is not a difficult thing to deliver a carefully prepared Budget Speech. The test of the Chancellor comes in replying impromptu to questions in the general debate. For two days after my statement a general discussion on my proposals took place, and at the end of this time I was called upon to make a final reply to the criticisms which had been put forward. These criticisms were very mild, with the exception of the expression of the Tory exasperation at the repeal of the McKenna Duties. The only criticism of the Budget as a whole was that by Sir Laming Worthington-Evans from the Tory benches, and by Mr. Masterman, a very warm supporter of the Budget, from the Liberal benches. Their criticism was directed to what they called the insufficient reserve I had kept in hand to meet supplementary expenditure, and they both maintained that I had been far too optimistic in my estimates of revenue. They prophesied with confidence that I should find myself with a deficit of £100,000,000 at the end of the year. Even some usually intelligent and well-informed journals expressed similar opinions. I may anticipate the event by mentioning here that at the end of the financial year there was a surplus of £3,659,000, which was only £365,000 below the figure for which I had estimated. When I came to reply on the general debate I was in a very happy mood. The reception of the Budget and the weakness of the criticism had acted as a tonic. I adopted a light bantering tone which highly entertained the House. "As to this being an Election Budget", I said, "this is the first of a series of electioneering Budgets. I expect to be here next year, and I have sufficient regard to my own reputation not to produce a Budget this year the basis of which will be falsified in twelve months' time. It is not only a democratic but a sound Budget, and, indeed, I hear that there is a movement in the City of London to erect a statue to me." Amid roars of laughter I sat down, and the first stage of the Budget was adopted without a division. I felt considerable compassion for the Conservative Opposition in the difficulty in which they were placed in criticising the Budget. So, having little to criticise in the Budget itself, they fell back upon what was not in the Budget, and they complained that it was not a Socialist Budget, and they wanted to know what had become of our programme for taxing unearned incomes to extinction and the appropriation of rents for Socialist extravagances. Indeed, they prophesied that there must be some diabolical design behind it, and that it was a dose of soothing syrup to put the capitalists to sleep before robbing them later.

The passage of the measure through the House would have been a very humdrum proceeding had it not been for the proposal to repeal the McKenna Duties. As soon as my announcement of this was made there broke out what I later described as a ramping, raging propaganda against the repeal. The recklessness and dishonesty of this campaign exposed what I had always regarded as one of the greatest dangers of a tariff system, namely its corrupting influence on politics. The Lobbies at the House of Commons were crowded out with representatives of vested interests bringing pressure to bear upon members of Parliament to oppose the repeal of these duties. Such an experience as I had during these weeks would have made every honest Protectionist who had some regard for the purity of our political life and for the independence of Members of Parliament into a Free Trader. However, I had better leave this aspect of the question until I come to deal with the debate.

Although the ordinary procedure on a Budget provided ample opportunity for a debate on the McKenna Duties, the Tory leaders insisted upon a day being specially set apart for a full debate upon the question. The Government were quite willing to grant this request, as we were well aware of the weakness of the Opposition's case and the strength of our own position. Mr. Baldwin, on behalf of his Party, put down a motion which was practically in the form of a vote of censure, though he denied that he regarded it as such. Mr. Baldwin's speech in moving this motion was the utterance of an honest man. Much for him depended upon making a good impression upon his Party and of securing some concession from the Government. There had been for some time mutterings in the Tory Party against his languid leadership, and many people felt that this debate was for him a crucial action which might determine the future of his political career. He opened very well with some flashes of wit and sarcasm which delighted his supporters. He made one delightful confession which was typical of Mr. Baldwin, and which deserves to be preserved. He apologised for the moderation of his language, and said: "My style of oratory has always been singularly ineffective because I cannot exaggerate, and because I attribute more cleverness and honesty to other people than they deserve." He made a delightful hit at me by saying: "Mr. Snowden is one of those fortunate men who has what is described as a first-class brain. I have always noticed that when a first-class brain does something stupid it not infrequently happens that a stupidity of this kind is colossal." After this very entertaining opening Mr. Baldwin passed on to deal with the case for maintaining these duties. Mr. Baldwin is never good in arguing the concrete case. He is at his best with the emotional appeal, and some of his speeches in that key have been among the most effective I have heard in Parliament. But on this occasion, perhaps because there was little opportunity for sentiment, he delivered a very ineffective speech, which depressed his supporters. Before the debate was opened the general impression was that I should have a stiff battle. The Conservatives were confident that they would at least wring some concession from the Government. But by the time I had got through half of my speech the battle had been won, and won easily. The speech was described in the Press next day as "one of the most smashing pieces of destructive criticism that had been heard for some years in the House of Commons. It was like an irresistible tide sweeping all before it." The success of this speech was due to the fact that I had an unanswerable case to state. The outside propaganda against the repeal of the duties had overreached itself, and its exaggerations and absurdities provided abundant material for effective exposure and reply. Under this exposure the Tories squirmed and wriggled, and the more they did this the farther I pressed the rapier into their bodies. I described the nature of the propaganda, and the intimidation which the motor manufacturers were pursuing. I had received hundreds of printed postcards purporting to be signed by workmen which read: "Owing to the falling off of orders due to the proposed removal of the McKenna Duties we have been given notice that our services will not be required after the 9th of May." Grossly exaggerated statements had been made by the motor manufacturers as to the number of workers employed in the industry. They stated that there were 4,000,000 persons employed in the industry. The Board of Trade stated that it would be a full figure to take 200,000 men as the total number of men employed in the private motor-car industry and allied trades. Statements had been widely circulated in the campaign that if the McKenna Duties were abolished 2,000,000 British workmen would be thrown out of employment! I was glad to admit that these exaggerated and untrue statements were not supported by the more responsible motor-car manufacturers, who dissociated themselves from what they described as the colossal humbug of this Press campaign. I received letters from workmen employed in motor works who described the methods which were being employed by the manufacturers to intimidate the workmen into sending the postcards and signing the petitions. I have described this campaign because it is a good instance of the way in which a protected industry will fight against every attempt to abolish the privileged position given to it by tariffs at the expense of the community. The substantial reason the Government was proposing to abolish these duties was that the question had been submitted to the electors at the General Election, when they had by an overwhelming majority voted against tariffs. Acting upon this popular mandate, the Government were in honour bound to repeal the duties. "The Government will stand or fall on this proposal" I concluded. But we did not fall. The debate ended in the defeat of Mr. Baldwin's motion by a majority of 65 votes. After this decisive defeat of the Opposition the remaining stages of the Budget were carried through very quietly. The Report Stage was passed in one day - a feat that was without precedent for many years. Discussion on the Third Reading of the Finance Bill was a very formal proceeding, and it was passed without a division.

I cannot pass away from this account of the first Labour Budget without paying a well-deserved tribute to my colleague - Mr. William Graham - the Financial Secretary to the Treasury. He was the ablest and most competent holder of that office I have known. He had prepared himself for such a position by years of intensive study of economic and financial questions. These subjects had a strong attraction, and he was never happy unless he was immersed in some financial problem. He had made a mark in previous Parliaments by his speeches on financial subjects; he had served on the Royal Commission on the Income-Tax, and was thoroughly acquainted with every detail of the Income-Tax system. No man ever went to a political office more fully equipped for the work he had to undertake. To show how anxiously he desired to have the opportunity of engaging officially in work so congenial to him I may be pardoned reproducing portions of a letter he addressed to me when the Labour Government was under consideration. I had written to him to say that I had definite information that the office of Financial Secretary would be offered to him. This is what he said in reply to my letter:

"DEAR PHILP,

"I find it difficult to write to you, for I am so grateful for your message.

"The best reply I can give you is to mention the following. Nearly a fortnight ago, at one of our private meetings of the Central Labour

Party, the members were asking me chaffingly if, as reported in some of the newspapers, I was going to the Scottish Office. I told them that no man would willingly go there, as the Office is one of the most thankless in the Government, but I had an ideal, which I hoped would be realised. I told them that we all hoped and expected you would be Chancellor of the Exchequer, and I wanted to go there with you as Financial Secretary.

Your suggestion to stand aside for the higher post is characteristic of your great kindness to many of us. But it is too preposterous. All the members of the Parliamentary Party I know have singled you out for this work; we believe it to be beyond all doubt your task; and in fact in recent weeks we have assumed it in all personal discussion regarding the situation created by the General Election. Your long service to the movement, and the manner in which you have specialised in finance, are recognised by all of us, and I cannot believe there is one member of the Party who would have a word of criticism.

It is difficult to believe that our ideal is so near realisation. Even if we had only a short time in office it would be a great experience. Within recent years I have read little but economic problems and finance; it would be a great joy to me to work under you with all the energy I could put into it. If it comes to pass, I shall do everything I can to lighten the load for you both at the Treasury and in the House. Without any lack of modesty, I think we can say that the combination would be a very happy one in the eyes of the Parliamentary Party. We have both a number of critics, but they are negligible.

All kind regards to you, and the assurance of all my friendship and support through thick and thin in the work to which I trust we shall be called.

Yours sincerely,
WILLIAM GRAHAM."

My relations with Mr. Graham from the time I first knew him were more those of a warm personal friendship than a mere political association. Members of Parliament used to call us "the happy twins". He had those qualifications for Treasury work which I did not possess. He was a master of detail. My line was more that of dealing with broad principles. The function of the Financial Secretary when the Finance Bill is in Committee is to help the Chancellor, particularly on matters of detail which might arise. Very often, when a member raised some new and difficult point, I would say to Graham: "I don't know anything about all this. Do you?" He was sitting alert, listening to what the member was saying, and replied to me: "It's all right. I understand it." And when the member sat down Graham would rise, and in his clear style give a complete reply from the profundity of his knowledge.

As a speaker, Mr. Graham was something of a phenomenon. Whether he delivered a short or a long speech he never referred to a single note. His memory was prodigious, and a never-ending source of amazement to the House. When he had to make a long speech on a subject upon which an exhaustive brief had been prepared he could repeat the brief with hardly a verbal change. He told me that the explanation of this was that when he read a brief or a memorandum it made a photographic impression upon his mind, and from this mental impression he could speak as if he were reading the text of the memorandum. I am afraid, however, that this must have imposed a considerable strain upon him which affected his health, and probably was responsible for his early and deeply regretted death. As a speaker, his style was very different from mine. He was never provocative, never rhetorical, and always confined himself strictly to a business-like statement. During the time the Finance Bill was under discussion, Punch published a cartoon where the two of us form a cruet, the one labelled "Vinegar" and the other "Oil". If I had to be absent from the House during the debates on the Finance Bill I could always with confidence leave Mr. Graham in charge. I never knew a man so fond of work. He hardly ever took a holiday, and when he did he took away with him voluminous documents to study. He occasionally took a day off for a cricket match at Lord's, the only recreation he enjoyed, and even then he filled his pockets with official documents to read in case the game was dull. I tried sometimes to induce him to read a detective story as a change, but that was too frivolous an indulgence for him. When the Labour Government came to an untimely end, Mr. MacDonald recommended Mr. Graham for a Privy Councillorship, an honour which was never more deservedly conferred.

The proudest day of my life was not when I introduced my first Budget, but a month later when I went back to my birthplace in Yorkshire. The villagers felt that they must do something to show their pride in the fact that one of themselves had attained a high Ministerial office. The Parish Council, on which I had begun my first public work, had taken action and arranged for a celebration of my homecoming. The whole parish had taken up the movement with great enthusiasm. The celebration took place on the 17th of May. Cowling is four miles from the railway station, and my wife and I made the journey by car. At the entrance to the village we were first welcomed by the members of the Parish Council. Then the councillors marched in procession up the main street accompanied by the Cowling Temperance brass band, and followed by hundreds of people from far and near. Large parties had come from surrounding districts. The village was en fete. The main street was hung with bunting and banners expressing messages of welcome to "Awr Philip", mostly in the native dialect. We went along to the Methodist Sunday School, the largest hall in the village, where a wildly enthusiastic meeting was held, though only a small number of the crowd was able to gain admission. The Chairman of the Parish Council, who had been my colleague on that body thirty years before, presided at the meeting, and the platform was filled with my boyhood friends. The Chairman made a presentation to us of a silver rose-bowl and vases suitably engraved. Before I left the village we visited in their own homes a few of the old folks I had known as a boy, and called at the little cottage where I was born. This event was the grandest experience of my life, and the only regret I had was that my mother had not lived to see it. She had died two years before, in February 1922. Her death was the result of an accident. She slipped on a treacherous piece of ice and broke her thigh. At her age (she was nearly 90) it was impossible to repair the fracture, and after a fortnight she died. Up to the time of her death she had lived alone in a little cottage next door to my married sister. She was able to do all her housework, and declined outside help. All her life she had enjoyed remarkable health. I never knew her to be confined to bed for a single day. Up to her accident she had risen every morning not later than six o'clock. She was a woman of strong independence of mind and action. She was one of those rare individuals who become more liberal in their views with advancing years. Up to the date of her accident she maintained her interest in public affairs, and at nearly ninety years of age her memory of events of eighty years before was remarkably clear. She lived through the Great War, and was outspoken in denouncing all the horror and futility of this calamity. She had remained a widow from the time of my father's death thirty years before. She had the full flavour of the rich West Riding dialect, and her quaint dialect stories and recitations charmed and delighted her friends. There is preserved at Leeds University a gramophone record of her speech. I deeply regretted the accidental cause of her death, for, with her strong constitution, I believe that if this had not happened she would have lived to be a centenarian. She had a simple and touching religious faith, and her last words before she sank into a state of coma were: "I am going to be with Jesus."

Chapter Twenty

The Fall of the Labour Government

DURING the Recess two incidents occurred which changed the political situation, and which seriously damaged the prestige of the Government and threatened to bring its life to an ignominious and untimely end when the Autumn Session began at the end of September. One was a personal matter which I dislike to mention, but it is necessary to do so because of the material which this incident provided for the political opponents of the Labour Government.

On the 12th of September there appeared in the Press under a sensational double-column heading a story that Mr. MacDonald had become the holder of 30,000 shares in the well-known biscuit manufacturing firm of McVitie & Price. This transaction had taken place in the previous March, and until this Press disclosure it had been kept quiet. When this fact leaked out through the newspapers there was a violent Press attack upon Mr. MacDonald, and, if not openly, by innuendo, he was charged with political corruption. While the circumstances when they became known reflected no discredit on Mr. MacDonald, the blundering way in which the transaction was carried through lent itself to the meanest form of personal attack. The circumstances were these. Mr. Alexander Grant, the head of the firm of McVitie & Price, was an old acquaintance of Mr. MacDonald's family. Mr. Grant, as he was then, had been a very intimate friend of Mr. MacDonald's uncle, and, though opposed to Mr. MacDonald's politics, he had followed his political career with interest and with warm admiration. When Mr. MacDonald became Prime Minister, Mr. Grant expressed a desire to present him with a Daimler car as a contribution to his personal comfort. Mr. MacDonald at first demurred, but finally agreed to accept the generous offer. Instead of presenting Mr. MacDonald with the car and providing for its maintenance, he took the unfortunate method of transferring these shares to Mr. MacDonald. The understanding was that the income from these shares would be enjoyed by Mr. MacDonald so long as he kept a car, and at his death the shares would revert to Mr. Grant or his heirs.

But there was another unfortunate incident which political opponents, anxious to damage the Prime Minister's reputation, dragged into prominence. The shares had been transferred to Mr. MacDonald in March, and in the following June Mr. Grant's name appeared in the Honours List as the recipient of a baronetcy. Evil-minded people put the two things together and insinuated that the Prime Minister had recommended a baronetcy for Mr. Grant in consideration of the gift of these shares. It is within my own knowledge that Mr. Grant's name had been on the waiting-list for a baronetcy before Mr. MacDonald became Prime Minister. Taking into consideration the reasons for which public honours are conferred, Mr. Grant had a high claim to such a distinction. He had risen from the position of a poor working-man to the head of a large and prosperous business. He had used his wealth generously in the public interest; he had come to the rescue of the famous Advocates' Library with a large sum of money, and had received the freedom of the City of Edinburgh for his public benefactions.

But the whole transaction of the shares and the motor car could not have been carried out in a way better calculated to excite public suspicion and to give Mr. MacDonald's political opponents a better weapon to attack his personal honour. Things like this are not used so much on the public platform, although there was no lack of this form of attack, but in underhand ways. At the General Election which followed shortly after this exposure, there is no doubt that this was used with damaging effect by canvassers who carried the slander from door to door, and told it with exaggeration and described it as an instance where a Prime Minister had used his position to recommend a baronetcy for pecuniary consideration. Slanders of this sort by canvassers are difficult to combat, and often have a more damaging effect on political opponents than any amount of platform abuse and criticism.

This exposure was a terrible blow to Mr. MacDonald. He is keenly sensitive to adverse criticism and to personal attacks. Indeed, I think I know no man who takes things like this so much to heart. When the exposure appeared in the newspapers Mr. MacDonald was at Lossiemouth, and he was inundated with abusive communications from the "anonymous correspondent". These letters, the Press attacks, and the whole incident completely upset him. When he came back to London for a day or two a fortnight later a few of his colleagues who were in London met him for an informal talk about the political situation and the work of the forthcoming Autumn Session. We saw at once that he was in a highly nervous condition. He was not in a state to take a calm and reasoned view on any subject. Everything seemed black to him. The problems which were facing the Government had assumed a dark and hideous appearance, and he said that he felt unable to face the difficulties ahead. He would welcome a General Election as a way of escape from his troubles.

When we left this gathering every one of my colleagues were agreed that he was nerve-racked and in need of a long holiday. That, however, was out of the question as we were within a few days of the meeting of Parliament. When Parliament did meet on the 30th September it was clear to some of us that he had not recovered his nerve, and we feared what might happen when he had to face a merciless Tory Opposition and a Liberal Party by now no means friendly. Our fear, unfortunately, turned out to be fully justified, and ten days after the meeting of Parliament the Government was overthrown and the country plunged into an Election by one of the most ill-considered and tactless decisions in Parliamentary history.

At the end of July, just before Parliament adjourned for the Summer Recess, attention was called to a letter appearing in a Communist newspaper which was alleged to be of a seditious and treasonable character. Little notice was taken of this incident at the time, and nobody imagined that it was going to develop into a first-class political crisis, eventually bringing about the defeat of the Labour Government. Two days before Parliament rose the editor of this paper, a man named Campbell, was arrested on a charge of having written this article, and a charge of sedition was alleged against him.

In answer to a question in the House of Commons on the 6th August (and in view of subsequent developments this is an important date in the story of this incident), the Attorney General, Sir Patrick Hastings, announced that the editor had been arrested, and that he accepted responsibility for these proceedings. The Attorney General afterwards explained that up to the time this question appeared on the paper he had taken little interest in the case and had done nothing beyond giving his legal opinion as to whether the charge of sedition could be established on the article in the Communist paper. Before giving a reply to the question he thought it was necessary to inform himself more fully upon two points: first, whether on further reference to the article his former view that it was a breach of the law could be confirmed, and secondly, if there were other facts about Campbell he ought to know. He wanted to get hold of some person who knew Campbell, and as Mr. Maxton was the first member who asked a question on the case the Attorney General thought that he would be able to give him some information. He sent for Maxton, who told him that Campbell was not the editor of the paper, but was in the position temporarily while the editor was away ill. Maxton told him that he knew Campbell well; that he was a man who had fought through the War from beginning to end, and had been decorated for exceptional gallantry, and had been crippled in both feet. "I thought to myself", said the Attorney General, "What would I look like suppose this were true as the Attorney General of England putting into the dock at the Old Bailey as the only dangerous Communist I could find such a person as that!"

The result of the enquiries made by the Attorney General confirmed the account of Campbell which had been given to him by Mr. Maxton. Taking the man's record into account, together with the fact that he was beginning to have grave doubts whether the prosecution would be successful, the Attorney General came to the conclusion that the best course would be to withdraw the case. Before definitely deciding to do so, he and the Director of Public Prosecutions had an interview with the Prime Minister in his room at the House. At this interview the Prime Minister, according to the Attorney General, strongly expressed the view that the prosecution was ill-advised from the beginning, and he put the blame on the Director of Public Prosecutions. The Attorney General objected to that remark, and said that he could not allow any blame to be put upon the Director as the responsibility was entirely the Attorney General's. After this interview with the Prime Minister, the Attorney General stated that he was asked to attend a meeting of the Cabinet, and, without disclosing anything that transpired at this Cabinet meeting, he said that he left the meeting having definitely decided to withdraw the prosecution. These proceedings took place between five and eight o'clock on the evening of 6th August, nearly two months before the Prime Minister gave his inaccurate reply to the question addressed to him by Sir Kingsley Wood!

The case had been put down for hearing at the Police Court for 13th August, and when it was called the Treasury Counsel made a statement, when giving reasons it was not desired to continue the prosecution, which was open to the construction that political influences had been brought to bear in the case. He said:

> "It has been represented that the object and intention of the article in question was not to endeavour to seduce men in the fighting forces from their duty in the regiment or to induce them to disobey lawful orders, but it was a comment upon armed military force being used by the State to repress industrial disputes...."

> "It has been possible for the Director of Public Prosecutions to accept that alleged intention of this article more easily because the defendant is a man of excellent character with an admirable military record."

I think it cannot be disputed that this explanation of the withdrawal of the prosecution did give grounds for the suspicion that there had been influences at work which were not disclosed. The next day the Communist Party issued a statement that they had been anxious that the prosecution should proceed and that they had arranged that the Prime Minister, Mr. Henderson, Mr. Clynes and others should be subpoenaed as witnesses for the defence.

Sir John Simon was quickly on the war-path, and in a speech in his constituency he referred at length to the case, and intimated that he intended to raise the matter when the House of Commons reassembled. He asked who had made the representations that the article was of an innocent character, and contrasted this with the assertion made by Mr. Campbell and his friends that the prosecution had been withdrawn after severe political pressure had been applied by certain Labour M.P.s. When Parliament reassembled after the Summer Recess on the 30th of September, private notice questions were addressed to the Attorney General asking the reason for the withdrawal of the charge. The interest that was taken in these questions indicated that the Government were in for a warm time. Prominent members were hot on the Attorney General's track, including Sir John Simon, Sir Robert Horne, Sir Douglas Hogge and Mr. Baldwin. After the Attorney General's explanation of the reasons for the withdrawal of the charge, Mr. Baldwin intimated that in view of the seriousness of the incident an opportunity must be given to the

House to debate it at length. It was arranged that a day should be set apart in the course of the next week for a full day's debate.

That same day (30th September) the Prime Minister replied to a question on the subject, and his reply had very unfortunate consequences. Sir Kingsley Wood asked the Prime Minister "whether any directions were given by him or with his sanction to the Director of Public Prosecutions to withdraw the proceedings against Mr. Campbell, the editor of the Workers' Weekly, and whether he received any intimation that he would be personally required to give evidence on behalf of the defendant at the hearing?"

The Prime Minister said:

> "I was not consulted with regard to either the institution or the subsequent withdrawal of these proceedings. The first notice of the prosecution which came to me was in the Press. I never advised its withdrawal, but left the whole matter to the discretion of the law officers where that discussion properly rests. I never received any intimation or even hint why I should be asked to give evidence. That also came to my attention when the falsehood appeared in the Press."

The Prime Minister's reply was clearly at variance with facts which were widely known. A week later, on the day which had been set apart for a debate on this case (8th October), the Prime Minister rose at Question Time to offer an explanation of his inaccurate answer to this question, which, I am afraid, instead of removing the impression his reply had created, made the position still worse, and actually increased the impression of lack of frankness and candour which had been made by his reply. The Prime Minister's explanation was in these words:

> "I rise to ask the indulgence of the House, to make an explanation of a word that I wrongly used in replying to a question put to me on the 30th of last month. The hon. Member for West Woolwich (Sir K. Wood) put the question, which ended with these words:
>
> ... 'and whether he has received any intimation that he would be personally required to give evidence on behalf of the defendant at the hearing?'

It refers, of course, to the case we are going to debate today. The form and suggestion of the question concentrated the whole of my mind upon myself and upon my own personal and separate part in this affair. I have been accused in certain papers of having known that I was going to be summoned, and with that knowledge, and because of that knowledge, of personally interfering. I have felt that very warmly. It was absolutely untrue. The accusation was one of these things that made one feel most resentful, and in concentrating my ideas about a personal reproach, on account of personal reasons, I used an expression which, when my attention was drawn to it two days afterwards, I had to admit was a little further than I ought to have gone, because it implied not merely that I, as a person, was either approached by the Attorney General, or approached the Attorney General for personal reasons - a thing I had repudiated hotly - but it also implied that I had no cognisance of what was going on. I am very sorry. I did not mean to imply that. It was simply the concentration of my personal resentment at that gross imputation which made me for a moment forget that officially, and in conjunction with colleagues, the matter was talked about when no personal considerations were in our minds at all. If I have misled any hon. Members, I apologise for having done so."

This incoherent, evasive and prevaricating reply staggered the House, and made his colleagues who were sitting on the bench hang their heads in shame. This reply brought Mr. Austen Chamberlain and Sir John Simon to their feet, who submitted the Prime Minister to a severe cross-examination, under which he succeeded only in strengthening the suspicions that he was holding something back. The debate was to follow immediately after this cross-examination. The Prime Minister's lack of candour had seriously prejudiced the position of the Government.

Both the Conservative and the Liberal leaders had put down motions. The Conservative motion was a short and straight vote of censure on the Government. To this the Liberals, in the name of Sir John Simon, had put down an amendment in these words:

> "That a Select Committee be appointed to investigate and report upon the circumstances leading up to the withdrawal of the proceedings recently instituted by the Director of Public Prosecutions against Mr. Campbell."

Ickornshaw, photographed in the 1930s. (Reproduced from the original 1934 edition of Philip Snowden's *An Autobiography*.)

The cottage in which Snowden was born. (*An Autobiography*)

Cowling viewed from the crag. *(An Autobiography)*

Snowden's parents. *(An Autobiography)*

Snowden as an insurance clerk in 1880, aged 16. *(An Autobiography)*

Snowden as an I.L.P. councillor c. 1899, aged 35. *(Editor's Collection)*

Snowden addressing a meeting in Keighley, 1901. *(An Autobiography)*

Ethel Snowden (neé Annakin) at the time of her marriage in 1905. *(An Autobiography)*

Labour leaders 1906, from left to right: Arthur Henderson, G.N. Barnes, Ramsay MacDonald, Philip Snowden, Will Crooks, Kier Hardie, John Hodge, James O'Grady, David Shackleton. *(Public Domain.)*

Snowden as a Member of Parliament, c. 1906, aged 42. *(Editor's Collection)*

Snowden at the outbreak of war, 1914, aged 50. *(An Autobiography)*

Portrait of Ethel Snowden. *(Public Domain.)*

The First Labour Cabinet, 1924. All of Labour's 'Big Five' are on the front row, Snowden is three from the left and from right to left are Henderson, Thomas, Clynes and MacDonald. *(An Autobiography)*

James Ramsay MacDonald as Prime Minister, c. 1929. *(Public Domain.)*

Willie Graham, Financial Secretary to the Treasury in 1924 and President of the Board of Trade 1929-31. *(An Autobiography)*

Tense scenes at the Hague Conference of 1929. From right to left: Snowden, Louis Loucheur, Henri Chéron, Henri Jaspar. *(Public Domain.)*

Snowden is lauded in *Punch* magazine in the wake of the Hague Conference. *(Editor's Collection.)*

Snowden as Chancellor of the Exchequer, wearing his official robes of office c. 1929, aged 65. *(An Autobiography)*

The emergency cabinet of the National Government, August 1931. Seated from left to right are Snowden (Lab), Baldwin (Con), MacDonald (Lab), Samuel (Lib), Lord Sankey (Lab). Standing from left to right are Cunliffe-Lister (Con), Thomas (Lab), Lord Reading (Lib), Chamberlain (Con), Hoare (Con). *(Editor's Collection.)*

J.H. Thomas, one of Snowden's National Labour allies, campaigning in the contentious October 1931 General Election. *(Editor's Collection.)*

Philip and Ethel photographed in 11 Downing St, on his retirement from the Treasury, November 1931, aged 67. *(An Autobiography)*

After leaving the National Government, Snowden supported several causes, including temperance and Lloyd George's 1935 New Deal campaign. *(Editor's Collection.)*

The memorial cairn erected in 1938 where first Philip and later Ethel Snowden's ashes were scatted on Ickornshaw Moor. *(Editor's Collection.)*

The difference between the motion and the amendment will be noted. The Tory motion was a direct vote of censure which assumed that the case against the Government had already been established; while the Liberal amendment did not propose to censure the Government, but to appoint a Committee to investigate and report upon the circumstances.

After the Conservative vote of censure had been moved by Sir Robert Horne, the Attorney General rose to make his reply. His frank statement created a favourable impression on the House of Commons. But this effect was destroyed by the subsequent speech of Sir John Simon and by the speech of the Prime Minister who followed him. The Opposition were not in the least anxious to put the Attorney General in the pillory. They were concerned to discredit the Prime Minister and the Labour Government.

The Prime Minister's speech made a bad impression on the House. It was evasive, and strengthened the impression he had made at Question Time that afternoon that he was not being frank and candid. He had a perfectly good case if he had faced up to it fearlessly and honestly. During his speech, John Wheatley, who was sitting next to me, remarked: "I never knew a man who could succeed so well, even if he is telling the truth, in giving the impression that he is not doing so."

When the Prime Minister sat down the fate of the Government was sealed, and Mr. MacDonald realised this. He had concluded his speech in these words:

"I said on a former occasion that we should take advice from this House in the sense of rejection of the proposals which we made, provided that they were not regarded as essential, and provided that the rejection of our proposal or our defeat in the Lobby did not amount to a diminution of that sense of self-respect which every Government must have if it is justified in sitting for five minutes on the Treasury Bench."

"If the House passes the resolution or the amendment, we go. It is the end: it will be the end of what hon. Members on all sides of the House will agree as being a high adventure-the end of a Government which I think has contributed much to the honour of the country, to our social stability, and which, when the country has had an opportunity of passing a verdict upon it, will come again."

Mr. Asquith followed the Prime Minister, and his opening sentences dealing with Mr. MacDonald's peroration deserve to be quoted. He said:

> "I do not rise for the purpose of entering into the merits of the controversy which has been carried on during this debate, nor shall I do more than drop a sympathetic and tributary tear on the funeral oration which the Prime Minister has just pronounced. These obsequial tributes are generally reserved, if not until the corpse has been interred, at any rate until the doctor has pronounced that life is extinct. I confess that it is to me, a man of rather keen susceptibilities, a melancholy thing to hear the right hon. gentleman anticipate so comfortably his own early, and indeed almost immediate, decease."

When the division came the Tories did not persist in their motion of a direct vote of censure, but concentrated on the Liberal amendment for the appointment of a Select Committee. The Liberal amendment was carried by a majority of 166 votes. I met Mr. Asquith when we were leaving the House after this decision, and he seemed genuinely distressed. He said that in all his Parliamentary experience he had never known a case where the Government had so wantonly and unnecessarily committed suicide.

Next day the Prime Minister obtained the consent of the King for an immediate General Election. This is the story of the end of the first Labour Government. The Government had rejected the motion for an enquiry by a Select Committee into the circumstances leading up to the withdrawal of the Communist prosecution. The reason they assigned was that it would be a reflection on their honour to accept the proposed enquiry. I did not at the time agree with that decision. So far as I knew there was nothing the Government had to conceal. I would have given the Opposition twenty committees if they had asked for them, and this was the view widely held by the reasonable members of the Labour Party, who were shocked that the Government should have accepted defeat on what, after all, was a very trivial incident.

This view of the Government's action was not at the time publicly expressed by the dissatisfied Labour members, who were anxious that the Party should show a united front in the face of a General Election. Another excuse advanced in deciding the Government to take the line it did was that if it surrendered on this motion it was only postponing its downfall for a few days, as it would certainly be defeated on the Russian Treaty, which was to come up for discussion a few days later. There was no force in this reason, as the Prime Minister had already stated that on that question the Government would leave the House of Commons free to take what course it might decide. The Labour Party entered upon the Election under circumstances which made its defeat a foregone conclusion.

Chapter Twenty-One

The "Red Letter" Election

The Labour Party entered upon the General Election following upon the defeat of the Government under the heaviest handicap ever carried by a political party. The incident of the Campbell case and the Russian Treaty had caused the electors to forget the record of the Government, and the popularity which it had enjoyed up to September had largely been dissipated by these events. The Election had come unexpectedly, and the Labour Party's organisation was not prepared for it. The Party had fought two General Elections in two years, and this had been a severe strain on the resources of a poor Party. The dissolution of Parliament took place on the 9th October. In order to avoid clashing with the municipal elections, the General Election was hurried forward and polling took place on the 29th October. At the dissolution the Labour Party had 365 endorsed candidates, including sitting members. With an energy and determination which was marvellous, the headquarters of the Party set to work, and before nomination day, that is in nine days' time, 149 additional Labour candidates were placed in constituencies, bringing the total up to 514, an increase of 87 over the number put forward at the previous General Election. I doubt if any political party ever achieved such a feat as that.

This General Election was the most strenuous I remember. The Tories threw themselves into the contest with a grim determination to turn out the Labour Government. The Liberals, too, mainly concentrated their attack upon the Labour Party, and made the Russian Treaty the principal topic of their platform speeches. Mr. Lloyd George spoke every day in different parts of the country, and denounced the Labour Party and all its works.

Mr. MacDonald, unfortunately, permitted his friends to arrange for him a great motoring tour, which was to extend from Glasgow to South Wales. This involved making speeches at practically every town through which he passed. It was a task beyond human endurance, and one which the strongest man could not carry through without disaster. From the beginning of this campaign, which commenced with a great meeting in Glasgow, it was evident that he was in a highly nervous condition, and this became more marked as his tour proceeded. His speech to the great meeting at Glasgow was broadcast, and it was almost unintelligible to listeners. Early in the campaign, through addressing huge open-air gatherings, his voice gave way. During one part of the tour through the industrial districts of the North-east of England he spoke at twenty-seven meetings in one day. Before the end of the tour he was compelled to abandon a number of meetings. A week after the tour had begun he reached his constituency of Aberavon both physically and mentally tired out and quite unfit for the work in front of him. During the next ten days he would be required to make speeches which would be fully reported throughout the country, where an indiscretion was calculated to have serious consequences.

The campaign of the opponents of the Labour Party was carried on with a malice and unscrupulousness which surpassed the limits of decent political controversy. Mr. MacDonald was always keenly sensitive to criticism, and particularly when it was directed against his personal conduct. In such circumstances he was always liable to lose his temper and to say things which afterwards were regretted. On one occasion in the House of Commons, when the Tories were fiercely interrupting him, he turned round and hissed "Swine!" in a voice loud enough to be heard in the Press Gallery.

Speaking at Barry during the Election about the tactics of his opponents, he let drop a sentence which was seized upon by his enemies and used with the most damaging effect. Referring to the misrepresentation to which he was being subjected, he said:

> "A party who are on the verge of being beaten and disgraced always tell lies, as they are doing now.... Why can't they make a decent intellectual fight of it, lay down their principles, put them against ours, and have an honourable set-to? Why do they slander us? Why, instead of having a great battle on a political principle, do they go about sniffing like mangy dogs on a garbage heap?"

The Press pounced upon these words with avidity. The widely circulated newspapers quoted the sentence in black type. It had a great effect among a class of people who disregarded what his opponents said about him. The Prime

Minister had fallen from his pedestal. They felt that he had degraded the high office that he held by such statements. They began to wonder whether, after all, there might not be some truth in what his opponents said about him. Perhaps it did not change many votes, but, more important than that, it changed popular opinion about the man who had used these words.

But within a few days' date of the polling an incident happened which had a profound effect upon the result, and which by the polling day was the main topic of popular interest and platform speeches. On Saturday morning, the 25th October, Mr. Thomas, who had been speaking in my constituency the night before, came hammering at my bedroom door early, and shouted: "Get up, you lazy devil! We're bunkered!" He had a copy of that morning's Daily Mail which, in flaming cross-page headings, published the notorious Zinovieff letter. We found that this was also the main news feature of all the other morning papers. This letter came as a great surprise to both Mr. Thomas and myself. Neither of us had heard a hint that such a letter was in existence. We got on the telephone at once to the Prime Minister at Aberavon to enquire what it was all about. He did not seem to be very much concerned about it, and said that he did not know whether it was a fake or it was genuine. But he was making enquiries, and would refer to the matter in a speech.

The whole country was waiting expectantly to hear what Mr. MacDonald had to say about it. It was assumed that if the letter was genuine it would put an end to all further communications with the Soviet Government. The newspapers assumed that the letter was genuine, and its existence must have been known to the Government, or at least to the Prime Minister, all the time they were defending the Russian Treaty.

The evening newspapers came out without reporting any explanation from the Prime Minister. Every hour's delay in an explanation being forthcoming strengthened the public belief that there was something in it which the Government were anxious to hide. I knew of no justification for such an impression, but the country was in a state of panic and ready to accept the interpretation which was placed upon the incident by the Tory Press. The Zinovieff letter, and the Foreign Office Note to the Russian Ambassador upon it, had been supplied to the Press by the Foreign Office itself. But the reply to this was that the Foreign Office had been in possession of this letter for weeks. They had kept it secret, and had only given it publication when they knew that a newspaper already in possession of either the original letter or a copy was about to publish it.

Mr. MacDonald spoke that Saturday afternoon at Swansea, and made no reference at all to the letter, which was the one thing that was in everybody's mind. His silence was taken as confirmation of all that the Tory newspapers were saying. The Labour candidates who had to address meetings that evening were wholly at a loss what to say. Some of the more venturesome denounced the whole thing as a fraud; while others, more cautious, followed Mr. MacDonald's example and said nothing unless they were questioned upon it by the audience.

The Labour supporters opened their Sunday papers greedily, hoping that the Prime Minister had made an explanation which would dispose of the bombshell. There was nothing in the newspapers, and universal dismay prevailed in the Labour ranks. Monday morning came, and still there was no word from Mr. MacDonald. The Opposition Press for two days had had the field entirely to themselves, and had created a state of public suspicion which it was now too late to remove. The pollings were on Wednesday. On Monday afternoon Mr. MacDonald made a speech at Cardiff in which he dealt at length with the matter. This was reported in the Tuesday morning's papers, the last day of the Election campaign. It was now too late to undo the mischief, even if Mr. MacDonald's explanation had been satisfactory to every open-minded person. But, unfortunately, his explanation only made matters worse, and increased the suspicion that there was something shady about the whole question. There was some justification for Mr. Asquith's description of the Prime Minister's explanation "that he could not remember to have read a more distracted, incoherent and unilluminating statement in the whole of his political experience".

A friend of mine, one of the most prominent Socialists in South Wales, was recently talking to me about this meeting. He was on the platform, and he said that the Prime Minister's manner and his treatment of this question were so tragic and had such an effect upon the meeting that those on the platform fervently prayed that it would open and swallow them up and put an end to the distressing spectacle.

I had better state in chronological order the story of this letter as related by the Prime Minister in this Cardiff speech. The facts as stated by Mr. MacDonald were as follows:

The Government was defeated on the 8th October on the Campbell Case.

This Red Letter did not find its way into the Foreign Office until 10th October.

It was not taken in by the Department until the 14th October. It was sent to Mr. MacDonald at Manchester on the 15th October.

He received it on the 16th October.

On the morning of the 16th he commented that the greatest care would have to be taken in discovering whether the letter were authentic or not. If it were authentic it had to be published, and in the meantime, while investigations were going on to discover the authenticity, the draft letter to the Ambassador would be prepared so that when the authenticity was established no time would be lost in making a protest to the Soviet Government.

This Note from him was received at the Foreign Office on the 17th October.

On the 21st October the draft of the letter to the Russian Ambassador was sent to him for his observations.

Mr. MacDonald was away at the time, and did not receive it until the 23rd October.

On the morning of the 24th he looked at the draft, altered it, and sent it back in an altered form expecting it to come back to him again with proofs of authenticity.

The copy of the Zinovieff letter and the Note to the Russian Ambassador were sent to the Press by the Foreign Office on the 24th October.

The Foreign Office had had no reply from Mr. MacDonald to their draft letter of the 21st October to the Russian Ambassador on Friday evening, the 24th. The officials of the Foreign Office apparently appreciated the seriousness of the matter more than Mr. MacDonald did, for that evening, without waiting any longer for a reply from the Prime Minister, they issued the Zinovieff letter and the letter they had sent to the Russian Ambassador to the Press in order to forestall the publication of the Zinovieff letter next morning, that is 25th October, by the Press.

The amazing thing in these days of telephones and telegrams is that the communications between the Prime Minister and the Foreign Office were conducted by the slow method of postal correspondence. Knowing something of the conduct of Departmental matters, I am astonished that when Mr. MacDonald first received the letter on the 16th October he did not at once request the official in charge of the matter at the Foreign Office to come down to discuss it with him, or at the least to employ one of the staff of special messengers to expedite matters. He did not in the least seem to realise its importance, or the impression which would be created in the country if the contents of the letter were first made public by the newspapers.

The decision of the Foreign Office to publish the letters should not have been made without first informing Mr. MacDonald of the intention to do so, and of the reason for taking immediate action. The only comment I need make on that is that I doubt if there is any other Government Department where such a thing would be possible.

But however badly the Foreign Office may have blundered by not communicating with the Prime Minister (who it must be remembered was also Foreign Secretary), there could be no doubt that they took the course which with the knowledge in their possession they felt to be the best in the circumstances.

For days before the publication of the letter there had been rumours that such a letter was in existence and would be published before the Election Day. *The Times* Parliamentary correspondent stated on Monday, 27th October, that during the past week it was a matter of common gossip that a message from Zinovieff had been intercepted. If the Foreign Office officials had done what Mr. MacDonald apparently expected them to do, that is to return the draft letter to him for signature, they would have "missed the boat". A copy of the letter, which had been for a month in the possession of the *Daily Mail* (and it was later asserted that a copy was in the hands of the Tory headquarters), would have been published by the newspapers, and there would have been no conclusive answer to the charge that the Foreign Office did not intend to publish it.

Before the Labour Government left office they appointed a Cabinet Committee to examine the authenticity of the Zinovieff letter, and the conclusions of this Committee were afterwards communicated to the Press. The Cabinet statement read:

> "The Committee appointed on the 31st October to examine the authenticity of the Zinovieff letter, after hearing the Department concerned, find it impossible on the evidence before them to come to a positive conclusion on the subject. The original letter has not been produced or seen by any Government Department, and action was taken on what was not claimed to be more than a copy. Unfortunately, in the short time available the Committee find it impossible to obtain the evidence throwing further light upon the matter."

When the Conservative Government took office they made further investigations into the matter, and they stated to the House of Commons that they had had further evidence which had convinced them that the letter was genuine. The truth about the matter will probably never be known, but in my opinion it was not of much importance whether the letter was genuine or a forgery. My own view is that the letter was a clever forgery, but its genuineness is immaterial. If it had not been that the Labour Party was associated in the public mind with Russian Communism, the "Red Letter" would have had no effect.

The publication of this letter, and the Prime Minister's mishandling of it, undoubtedly had a considerable effect upon the result of the Election. It was not so much that it alienated votes which otherwise would have been given to Labour candidates. It whipped up a large number of indifferent electors to vote for Conservative candidates. Nearly two million more votes in the aggregate were polled than at the previous General Election twelve months before. The total Labour vote rose to 5,487,620 compared with 4,348,379, an increase of

1,139,241. But this increase in the total vote was accounted for by the fact that the Labour Party ran 87 more candidates than they did at the previous Election. The effect of the "Red Letter" showed itself in the enormous increase in the Tory vote, which rose by 2,265,000 over the 1923 figures. The Labour Party lost 64 seats and gained 22. The outstanding individual victory of the Labour Party at this Election was the success at Paisley after a long series of attempts to capture this constituency. This involved the defeat of Mr. Asquith, and was followed by his decision to retire from active politics. The Labour Party's Parliamentary strength was reduced from 193 to 152. The most remarkable feature of this Election was the reduction in the Liberal poll and the total number of seats obtained. The Liberal vote was reduced by 1,400,000, and they lost 116 seats, their Parliamentary strength being reduced to the insignificant number of 42. The explanation of this was twofold. They ran 111 fewer candidates; but of the number they did run no less than 311 were defeated. The second explanation of this Liberal disaster was that a large number of electors who ordinarily voted Liberal cast their votes for Conservative candidates in order to make sure that the Labour Government would be overthrown.

The result of the Election caused widespread dissatisfaction in the Labour Party. It was felt that the loss of 64 seats was due to the blundering tactics of the Prime Minister. The feeling against Mr. MacDonald was intense, and the view was widely held and given expression to within the Party that he had made his future leadership of the Party impossible. This feeling, however, gradually subsided as the disappointment wore off. So far as I was concerned in my contest at Colne Valley, I do not think that the "Red Letter" had the slightest effect on the Election result. Only once during the contest was the matter raised by a question at a meeting. My majority rose from 1,921 to 3,243. Mr. MacDonald's majority at Aberavon was reduced from 3,512 to 1,650. At this Election the Conservatives obtained 411 seats, which gave them a majority of more than 200 over all other Parties. The Election thus settled the fate of the Labour Government, which resigned four days later. Mr. Baldwin was sent for to form a Government, which held office for the next four and a half years.

Chapter Twenty-Two

Mr. Churchill as Chancellor

The most surprising of the Ministerial appointments made by Mr. Baldwin when he constituted his Government in November 1924 was the selection of Mr. Winston Churchill as Chancellor of the Exchequer. What induced Mr. Baldwin to offer Mr. Churchill this important post still remains an inscrutable mystery. Mr. Churchill had been out of the House of Commons for two years, having been defeated at Dundee at the Election of November 1922, when he stood as a Liberal candidate. In the meantime he had been making one of his periodic changes in his political allegiance. He had stood as a Liberal candidate at Leicester in 1923, and later had contested a by-election in Westminster as a Constitutional candidate. At the Election of November 1924 he had been elected as a Constitutional Free Trade candidate for the Epping Division of Essex.

It was said that when Mr. Baldwin sent for Mr. Churchill and offered him the Chancellorship Mr. Churchill had assumed that it was the post of Chancellor of the Duchy of Lancaster, and it only slowly dawned upon Mr. Churchill during the conversation that Mr. Baldwin was offering him the Chancellorship of the Exchequer. This was the second highest post in the Government, and Mr. Churchill could never have expected that, as a new recruit to the Tory Party, he would be offered that post to the exclusion of Sir Robert Horne and Mr. Neville Chamberlain, both of whom had already held that office in previous administrations. A further surprising feature of this appointment was the fact that Mr. Churchill was a Free Trader, and, although for the General Election Mr. Baldwin had promised that if he were returned he would not embark upon a scheme of general Protection, he undertook to consider applications for a tariff for particular industries by special Committees. If on examination of these applications the Committees came to the conclusion that a case had been made out for the "safeguarding" of these industries the Government would carry out these recommendations. Although holding an important office in a

Protectionist Government, Mr. Churchill lost no opportunity in speeches in the House of Commons of announcing his Free Trade views and his strong opposition to a general tariff.

At the end of April 1925, Mr. Churchill introduced his first Budget. He had been working, of course, on the estimates of income and expenditure which I had prepared in my Budget of the previous April. In that Budget I had estimated for a surplus of £4,024,000, and the realised surplus was £3,658,884. This was the closest approach to strict accuracy in Budget estimating that had been made since the War. In presenting his first Budget Statement, Mr. Churchill rose to the occasion and spoke for two hours and a half. He estimated that upon the existing basis of taxation he would have a disposable surplus of £26,600,000. This surplus he distributed by reducing the standard rate of Income-Tax by 6d., from 4s. 6d. to 4s. He made reductions in the Super-Tax which would cost £10,000,000 in a full year, and offset this reduction by an increase in the Estate Duties. He reimposed the McKenna Duties which I had repealed the previous year, but was very anxious to let it be understood that he was reimposing these duties not as Protective measures but purely for revenue purposes.

The Budget was memorable for two announcements which were not revenue proposals. The first of these was a return to the Gold Standard, and the second a scheme for the establishment of a system of Widows, Orphans and Contributory Old Age Pensions. The latter was not strictly a Budget proposal at all, but Mr. Churchill could not resist the temptation of personally claiming credit for this scheme. He spent a long time in his Budget Statement in elaborating this measure down to the minutest detail, and then left it to Mr. Neville Chamberlain to take charge of the Bill and to pilot it through the House of Commons. This Widows and Orphans Pensions Scheme was based upon a plan which the Labour Government had prepared, and which they would have introduced that year if they had remained in office. The announcement of the return to the Gold Standard came as a surprise, for although the policy of the Bank of England and of previous Governments had aimed at this object, the time for taking this important step was generally regarded as not having yet arrived. In view of the controversy on the Gold Standard which is still going on in 1934, it may be well to state what was the attitude of the Labour Party at that time. On the Second Reading of the Bill for the restoration of the Gold Standard, I moved on behalf of the Labour Party an Amendment in these words:

> "This House cannot at present assent to the Second Reading of a Bill which by providing for a return to the Gold Standard with undue precipitancy may aggravate the existing grave condition of employment and trade depreciation."

In moving this Amendment, I explained that I had always been in favour of a return to the Gold Standard, but we did not believe that the present was the time when such a step should be taken, having in view the grave and serious consequences that might ensue. There was a disparity between this country and the United States in the price value converted to a gold basis, the United States price-level being probably from 5 to 10 per cent lower than the price-level in this country. The Labour Party were of opinion that a return to the Gold Standard ought to have been delayed until the prices on a gold basis had been brought to the same level in the two countries. Later experience of our return to the Gold Standard tended to confirm the fears which we expressed. It undoubtedly had the effect of injuring our export trade, and the crisis in the mining industry which developed in the following year was rightly attributed to a great extent to this premature step. Mr. Churchill has since excused himself by saying that he did not know much about the problem himself, but he acted upon the advice which was given to him.

It would be tiresome if I were to deal at length with the innumerable encounters between Mr. Churchill and myself in the Budget debates of this year and of succeeding years. As an Ex-Chancellor it fell to me to lead the Opposition in the Budget debates, and I found Mr. Churchill a foeman worthy of my steel. The debates between us became quite a Parliamentary entertainment. They were regarded as the best show in London. When it was expected that we should both be speaking, the public galleries were invariably crowded. After a time I ceased to take very much interest in these duels, but I was expected to play the Parliamentary game of opposition and to provide entertainment for my supporters. During those four years we were in Opposition a large part of the burden of sustaining the Labour Opposition fell upon me. In those years my popularity in the Parliamentary Labour Party reached its height. This was shown by the fact that in the annual ballots for the Executive of the Parliamentary Labour Party I was invariably at the top of the poll. Mr. Churchill, during these years, gradually developed as a Parliamentary debater. He learnt to rely less on careful preparation of his speeches and more upon spontaneous effort. However much one may differ from Mr. Churchill, one is compelled to like him for his finer qualities. There is an attractiveness in everything he does. His high spirits are irrepressible. It was said of a French monarch that no one ever lost a kingdom with so much gaiety. Mr. Churchill was as happy facing a Budget deficit as in distributing a surplus. He is an adventurer, a soldier of fortune. An escapade has an irresistible fascination for him. It is related, with what truth I do not know, that when the Cabinet were waiting for the last stroke of twelve which brought Great Britain into the War, he alone of all his colleagues was full of a fever of excitement. When the last stroke came, he is reported to have said: "Now we are in it!" The War to him was a great adventure.

Mr. Churchill is a hard hitter in debate, but he is not unfair. He keeps his temper admirably, even under severe provocation. He has the Churchill spirit of the fighter. I have said many hard things to him and about him, but I am sure he has never borne the slightest malice or ill-will. "The purpose of our debates is to attack our political opponents," he said to me once, "and the harder we hit the better we are doing the job."

One cannot help liking a fellow you have hit or who has hit you in a fair fight, and that is, I am sure, how Mr. Churchill regards political controversy. It was in that spirit that we both conducted our Parliamentary fights.

Chapter Twenty-Three

The General Strike

In the Spring of 1926 an unprecedented event took place in the industrial history of Great Britain. This is not the place to attempt a history of the General Strike. Volumes have been written on this unfortunate episode, and all that I can attempt here is to give very briefly the impression of an interested outsider.

For years, as I have described, there had been an active section of the Trade Union Movement which had been advocating the General Strike as a method by which industrial warfare should be carried on. In May 1926 this policy was put to the test, and the experiment provided lessons of the greatest value to Trade Unionism and to the community generally. The General Strike was the culmination of a long series of closely connected incidents. For some reason the mining industry has always been the storm-centre of industrial trouble. I remember Mr. Baldwin saying once that he never entered a conference of mine-owners and miners' leaders without sensing an atmosphere of irreconcilable differences. It is not for me to attempt to apportion blame between the two parties; probably upon impartial investigation a measure of blame must be apportioned to each side. In the years immediately preceding the General Strike the fact cannot be disputed that the miners were very badly led. A serious crisis in the industry was only averted in July 1925 by the offer of the Government to grant a subsidy to the mine-owners which cost the taxpayers about £25,000,000. At the same time it was decided to set up a Royal Commission to enquire into the state of the mining industry. The Report of this Commission was made in March 1926, and during the month of April the recommendations of this Report were considered by the Government and by joint committees of the owners and the miners.

The main matters in dispute centred upon hours and wages, and incidentally whether working conditions and wages should be regulated by district settlements or on a national basis. These negotiations failed to reach an agreement. On the 30th April the subsidy came to an end. The whole of that day was spent in hectic conferences between Cabinet Ministers, owners, miners, and the Industrial Committee of the Trade Union Congress. In anticipation that all efforts to arrive at a settlement would be futile, the mine-owners had issued lock-out notices if the miners would not accept a longer working day and a reduction of wages. It was not until literally the eleventh hour that the hope of averting a stoppage of work was abandoned, for it was at 11.15 p.m. that it was announced that the conversations between Mr. Baldwin and the Trade Union Council had finally broken down. When it became clear that the owners and the miners would not come to an agreement, the Industrial Committee of the Trade Union Council took the matter in hand. The reasons the Trade Union Council intervened were that they were not satisfied with the way in which the miners were carrying on the negotiations, and there was a fear that if the miners were compelled to accept the drastic terms of the owners that would be an encouragement to employers in other industries to make a concerted attack upon the standard of hours and wages. The intervention of the Trade Union Council came too late. The mine-owners had that day presented their final terms, which they were determined to enforce by a national lock-out of miners. The Trade Union Congress had contemplated the possibility of a break-down of negotiations and the lock-out of the miners, and they had called a meeting of the Trade Union Executives for the next day (1st May) to consider whether the whole Trade Union Movement should give support to the resistance of the miners to the owners' demands. It was at this meeting that the decision was taken by an almost unanimous vote to call the General Strike for the following Monday midnight. I was not present at this meeting, but Mr. MacDonald, as Chairman of the Parliamentary Labour Party, attended and took part in the discussions. A feeling of suspicion that the Government were siding with the mine-owners and against the men was no doubt chiefly responsible for the decision which was taken at this meeting. That same evening a manifesto was issued by the Trade Union Council which laid on the Government the responsibility for the crisis which had arisen. When Mr. Baldwin learnt from this public announcement that the Trade Union Council had taken charge of the situation he invited the Council to meet him at 8 o'clock that night, and after five hours of talk no compromise was reached.

In the meantime the Government had taken steps to meet the impending General Strike. They issued a Royal Proclamation that a state of emergency had arisen, and they put in force the powers of the Emergency Act which gave the Government full authority to control food supplies, to commandeer all forms of transport, and to take necessary measures to preserve order. The next day was Sunday, the 2nd May, which according to custom was devoted to Labour demonstrations. I had arranged to go down to my constituency for such a demonstration, but in view of the critical situation I remained in London and joined in conference with Mr. MacDonald and Mr. Thomas. They were both deeply concerned about the prospects of a general stoppage of work, and neither of them had the least hope that it would be successful in its object in bringing pressure to bear upon the Government and the mine-owners. While the three of us were together, Mr. Thomas received a message which had been conveyed to the Trade Union Negotiating Committee to meet the Prime Minister that evening at Downing Street. Mr. Thomas left for this meeting, hoping that at the last minute the conflict might be averted. At this meeting with the Prime Minister, Lord Birkenhead suggested a formula which the Trade Union Council might be able to accept as a basis for negotiations. This formula read:

> "We, the Trade Union Council, would urge the miners to authorise us to enter upon discussion with the understanding that they and we accept the Report as a basis of settlement, and we approach it with the knowledge that it may involve some reduction in wages."

The Trade Union Council had no powers to accept this formula in the name of the miners, but they left Downing Street to consult the miners' leaders. Mr. Thomas sent up word to Mr. MacDonald and myself that he felt that they were within an ace of a final settlement. The Trade Union Council had some difficulty in getting into touch with the miners' leaders, who had dispersed to their various districts.

In the meantime an incredible thing happened. It appeared that after the Trade Union Council had left Mr. Baldwin to consult with the miners' leaders a full Cabinet Meeting took place, and the majority of the members of the Cabinet were against conducting any further negotiations with the

Trade Union Council. The reason for this attitude was stated to be that it was a wrong thing and a humiliation to a Government to continue peace talks under a threat of a General Strike. After this Cabinet Meeting, at 1 o'clock next morning an announcement was issued from Downing Street that negotiations had been broken off. The reason afterwards given by the Government for this abrupt action was that it had come to the Government's knowledge that specific instructions for the General Strike had already been sent out, and the strike had already begun by the action of employees of the *Daily Mail* in preventing the publication of the paper because they objected to a leading article on the situation. It was quite clear that the Government had decided to allow the General Strike to proceed, for when the Trade Union Council returned to Downing Street with the Birkenhead formula they could not get in touch with the Premier. The decision of the Government had already been taken. It is impossible to believe that the action of the employees of the *Daily Mail* had been the reason for the Government breaking off negotiations. Mr. Baldwin had been overruled by the majority of his Cabinet. He, himself, would have been willing to continue the negotiations, but he had the majority of his Cabinet against him, who threatened that if he yielded to the Trade Union Council they would adopt direct action and go on strike. The Trade Union Council were extremely anxious that a strike should be averted, and, as Mr. Thomas put it later, they would have been willing to "grovel for peace". But the majority of the Cabinet were determined to teach the Trade Unions a lesson. Had Mr. Baldwin been prepared to pursue the negotiations, it is very probable that a peaceful settlement at the last moment would have been reached and the disastrous strike averted.

The next day there was a debate in the House of Commons in which Mr. Baldwin, who was evidently suffering from the strain of the last few days, said the simple issue was whether the Government would capitulate to a General Strike which threatened the basis of ordered government. Mr. J. H. Thomas, who to my knowledge had done all he could to avert the strike, did not attempt to defend it, but with a good deal of justice put the blame upon the mine-owners and the Government, and asserted that if the Government had brought pressure to bear upon the mine-owners to withdraw the lock-out notices pending the further negotiations, the Trade Union Council would also have withdrawn the General Strike notices. He denied there was any other motive in calling a General Strike than to express sympathy with the miners. The outcome of this debate made it inevitable that the General Strike would take place as arranged at midnight that day. The Government had definitely made up their minds that the strike should be a contest of power between the Government and the Trade Unions.

I need not describe the nine days during which the strike continued. Success for the Trade Unions was hopeless from the first day. Although there was a considerable response to the call to "Stop Work", there was little or no enthusiasm for the strike among the Trade Unionists. Most of the Trade Union leaders had been keenly opposed to it from the beginning. The great mass of workers who were not Trade Unionists had no sympathy with the strike, though there was among all classes a good deal of sympathy with the miners. If the Trade Unionists had fully realised the forces that would be ranged against them they would never have embarked upon the strike. The Trade Union Council had made a serious mistake in making arrangements for the General Strike while the negotiations with the Government were still going on; and when these negotiations collapsed it was difficult for them to withdraw from the ill-considered position they had taken up. As events proved, it would have been better at this stage, even at the cost of some humiliation, to have withdrawn from a course of action which was certain to result in a still further humiliation after inflicting great inconvenience. During the nine days of the strike the Parliamentary Executive of the Labour Party met every day to consider the situation, and to be ready to use any influence they might have to bring the dispute to an end under conditions which would save the Trade Union Council from abject surrender. Our efforts were not altogether without avail. But the Trade Union Council had got themselves into such a hopeless position that it was impossible to bring the dispute to an end on terms which were not a confession of the failure and futility of the strike.

On the day before the final collapse a decision was given in the Courts that the strike was illegal, and that it had exposed the Trade Unions which had taken part in it to the forfeiture of their funds. This legal decision finally decided the Trade Union Council to bring the strike to an end, and next day they sought an interview with Mr. Baldwin and announced that from that day the General Strike would be terminated, in the hope that negotiations might be reopened. Other reasons than the judgment of the Court that the strike was illegal, no doubt, influenced the Trade Union Council in taking this step. It had become evident that a large number of strikers were beginning to stream back to work, and there was a fear that it would soon come to an inglorious end. During the nine days of the strike I remained silent. From one point of view I was not sorry that this experiment had been tried. The Trade Unions needed a lesson on the futility and foolishness of such a trial of strength. A general strike could in no circumstances be successful. A general strike is an attempt to hold up the community, and against such an attempt the community will mobilise all its resources. There is no country in the world which has proportionately such a large middle-class population as Great Britain. They, with the help of governmental organisation, with a million motor-cars at their service, could defeat any strike on a large scale which threatened the vital services. This General Strike had no revolutionary purpose. It did not seek in the least to overthrow the Government. It was a demonstration of sympathy with the miners, and the only purpose it sought to serve was to bring pressure to bear upon the Government to do justice to that deserving body of workers. Leaving aside the question of the wisdom of the strike, this at least must be conceded, that it was a magnificent demonstration on the part of millions of workers of sympathy with a section of their brethren. The lesson of this strike was learnt by the Trade Union leaders. Since then there has been no repetition of such a hopeless adventure, nor is it likely that there will be so long as the memory of this unfortunate experience survives.

Chapter Twenty-Four

I Leave the I.L.P.

At the end of 1927 I resigned from the Independent Labour Party. My reasons for taking this step are explained in the following letter which I addressed to the Secretary of the Party on the 28th December 1927:

"MY DEAR JOHNSON,

"My subscription as a member of the I.L.P. expires at the end of this year, and I am writing to you to say that I do not intend to renew it.

"It is a matter of the deepest regret to me to feel it necessary to sever my connection with an organisation of which I have been a member continuously for 34 years, and to which I have given the best years of my political life.

"I have not taken this decision hurriedly. For several years the conviction has been growing upon me that the I.L.P. as a separate body has served its purpose, and that its continued existence is neither necessary nor useful.

"The Labour Party, since it permitted individual membership and adopted a definite Socialist basis, adequately fulfils all the purposes for which the I.L.P. originally existed.

"The I.L.P. now unnecessarily duplicates the work of the Labour Party, and in doing so wastes money and effort which could be more usefully employed in the local Labour parties.

"The old I.L.P., by creating the Labour Party, has made a far greater and more powerful instrument for establishing the Socialist State than it could ever hope to be, and it might well be content now to merge itself in the larger life.

"I shall always cherish with affection the memories of my long years of association with the I.L.P. and with men like Hardie, Glasier and Benson. The joyful comradeship of the thousands of men and women of the I.L.P. who in the old days 'saw visions and dreamed dreams' which are now becoming realities through their work can never be forgotten.

"To you, personally, I would like to express my sincere respect and gratitude. I think I have had a longer official association with you than any other man now living, and I can testify that no organisation ever had a more devoted, capable and sincere servant.

"Believe me to remain, yours sincerely,
Philip SNOWDEN."

I do not think I can add much to what I said in this letter. The pain of leaving an organisation which had been so much to me during my political life was moderated by the fact that in recent years I had taken no part in the work of the I.L.P., not only for the reasons stated in this letter, but because I was not in sympathy with the policy of the Party, which was drifting more and more away from the traditional policy of the I.L.P. of evolutionary Socialism into revolutionary Socialism. This change in the I.L.P. policy has resulted, as I expected, in destroying the usefulness of the organisation, and now (1934) it has practically ceased to exist. The I.L.P. might have continued to serve a useful purpose if its activities had been confined to the propaganda of a reasonable Socialism, leaving the Labour Party to take charge of political work. My resignation was received by the leaders of the I.L.P. in a very good spirit. My reasons for leaving the Party were appreciated. They had realised for some years that I was out of sympathy with them, and that it was better for all sides that the separation should come. The official organ of the I.L.P., *The New Leader*, writing upon my resignation, said:

"Philip Snowden's resignation from the I.L.P. after 34 years' continuous membership will be regretted by thousands of Socialists throughout

> the country. New members coming into the I.L.P. will not understand this. They have only known him during recent years when his mind was obviously turned away from the I.L.P. But to the older generation his defection will mean the end of an epoch.
>
> "We cannot let Philip Snowden pass from our ranks without an appreciation of what he has done for Socialism, or without expressing the sense of joy that the I.L.P. has known in the high adventure it has shared with him.
>
> "These things, alas, belong to the past, but their memory endures."

Mr. J. Maxton, who at that time was Chairman of the I.L.P., in writing upon the topic made a confession which put upon me a great responsibility of which I had not been aware until that time. He said: "I want to say in as public a way as I can that while I have recognised this step as inevitable on Snowden's part for some time, it is going to cause me great personal regret. It was after hearing a speech by Snowden that I finally made up my mind that it was my duty to join the I.L.P. and play my part in this work."

I hope my responsibility for Mr. Maxton's adhesion to the I.L.P. does not extend to all his actions since I converted him to Socialism!

Chapter Twenty-Five

Formation of the Second Labour Government

The General Election of May 1929 was one of the most strenuously fought contests I have known. During the two years previous the by-elections had shown that the Tory Government had lost its popularity, and that when the General Election came there was very likely to be a change of Government. This Election was not marked by any such discreditable incident as the Red Letter of the Election of 1924. On the whole it was kept free from personal recriminations, and elevated to the platform of political controversy.

This Election will be historic as the first occasion on which broadcasting was introduced into an electoral campaign. The three political parties were given the opportunity through representative speakers to explain and defend their Party programmes. I followed Mr. Winston Churchill on the microphone, and criticised his financial record and expounded the taxation policy of the Labour Party. This broadcasting of political speeches is an innovation which in the future will play a great part in political controversy; and I expect to see it universally used to relieve the political leaders from the necessity of touring the country and making platform speeches.

The Tories fought the Election with the desperation of men who realised that they would have to put forth every possible effort to avoid a disastrous defeat. The Liberals, who had been almost wiped out at the previous Election, fought hard to rehabilitate the Party. The Labour Party entered the contest with high hopes. The Party put forward 570 candidates, an increase of 54 over the number which ran at the previous Election. In the confident expectation that the Party would have to form the next Government, they had cautiously issued a moderate programme - that is, moderate in the sense that it contained nothing which a Labour Government might not reasonably be expected to carry if supported by a majority in the House of Commons. The leaders of the Labour Party had gained experience from their previous brief tenure of office.

They were not going to commit themselves to schemes which they knew to be impossible of realisation in the immediate future.

I have already expressed the opinion that Election manifestoes have little influence in gaining votes, though they may lose a Party votes if they contain some extreme proposal upon which their opponents can seize and frighten a section of the electorate. I fought my own election mainly upon two questions - National Reconstruction and War Debts. I believe that my criticism of the American Debt Settlement and Mr. Churchill's War Debt concessions to France and Italy did as much to gain votes as anything else. I spoke in many constituencies during the Election, and usually devoted my speeches to this topic, and to the exposure of the way in which the British tax-payer was being burdened for the relief of other countries. Everywhere this made a tremendous impression. I believe that if all the Labour candidates had had the knowledge to deal fully with these matters the result of the Election would have been even more favourable to the Labour Party than it actually was.

The result of the Election, however, was a great victory for the Labour Party. The Conservatives lost 155 seats. The number of Conservative members returned was 260. The Labour Party increased the number of members in the House of Commons to 289, an increase of 137 over the number returned at the previous General Election! The Liberals, in spite of their strenuous efforts and the lavish expenditure of money, and the fact that they ran 512 candidates, returned only 58 members. But the number of seats they won grossly under-represented the number of votes recorded for Liberal candidates. The absurdity of our electoral system was strikingly illustrated in the results of this Election. In the new Parliament each Liberal member had behind him roughly three times as many voters as the average Labour and Conservative member! The Labour vote at this Election increased by just under 3,000,000, rising from 5,422,000 to 8,379,000. The most surprising personal result of this General Election was the case of Sir Austen Chamberlain, who just managed to scrape in with a majority of 43 over a Labour opponent at West Birmingham. In my own constituency of Colne Valley my majority was increased from 3,243 to 9,135. It may be mentioned that the increase in the total votes recorded at this Election was accounted for by the fact that there had been an increase in the total electorate of about 7,000,000 due to the passing of the measure which gave women the vote on the basis of adult suffrage.

The result of the Election made it clear that Mr. Baldwin could not retain office. The Labour Party was now the largest Party in the House, having a majority of 29 over the Conservatives (excluding Independents), and a combined Liberal and Labour vote gave a majority of 87 over the Tories. Mr. Baldwin on this occasion did not wait for the new House of Commons to turn out his Government. The Election had been held on the 30th May, and on the 4th June he went to Windsor and submitted the resignation of his Government to the King. The next day His Majesty sent for Mr. MacDonald, who accepted office, and three days later announced the names of his new Ministry. The day after the declaration of the polls Mr. MacDonald returned to London, and at once got in touch with his principal colleagues. I had a brief conversation with him on Saturday, the 1st of June, and we arranged that "the big five", that is MacDonald, Henderson, Clynes, Thomas and myself, should meet at his house in Hampstead on the following Tuesday morning. The night previous to this meeting it had been announced that Mr. Baldwin was going to resign. Mr. MacDonald rang me up at Tilford about 9.30, and said that he was to see Baldwin next day. I got an impression from what he said that he was trying to make a bargain with Baldwin to keep us in office. Mr. MacDonald's experience with the Liberals when last in office did not encourage him to approach them to form some working arrangement. The way in which Mr. Lloyd George and the Liberals generally had attacked the Labour Party during the Election did not offer much prospect of harmonious relations between the two Parties in the new Parliament. I had made up my mind, however, that I should not be a party to any arrangements with the Tories.

At the opening of our meeting on Tuesday morning Mr. MacDonald began by saying that he thought we might consider the personnel of the Labour Cabinet. I said that there was a prior matter, namely, what our attitude was to be to the other Parties, and I repeated what I had said to him in our telephone talk the previous evening. On that occasion he had said to me: "I suppose you are ready for your old job." I had answered: "I am not so sure about that. I must be reasonably certain that we can remain in office until we have done something, and that means more than two years" (referring to his public statement that he wanted two years of sure office). I continued that I could not take on the Chancellorship unless I had the reasonable assurance that we should remain in office for at least three years, because Churchill had left the national finances in such a desperate state that it would require at least three Budgets, even if trade were good, to get them into something like order, and before any reduction of taxation could be made.

Mr. MacDonald said at this Tuesday meeting that he had never any intention of trying to make any arrangement with Baldwin, and that his visit to him was just an ordinary courtesy visit of an incoming to the outgoing Prime Minister. At this meeting I repeated what I had said on the telephone - that before I agreed to take office I wanted to have this assurance. I could not possibly consider any understanding with the Tories, as we should then be quite unable to carry our own Budget, or hardly any of the items on our programme. There was an irreconcilable difference between the Tories and ourselves on the question of "safeguarding", for instance. Henderson and Thomas wholly supported my views, and MacDonald fell into line. We agreed that we should pursue our own course, and make no arrangements with either of the other Parties, depending for Liberal support on the nature of our measures.

We then proceeded to consider the Cabinet appointments. The question arose of giving Miss Bondfield a Cabinet post. Henderson was strongly in favour of doing this, as he thought it would be a popular thing to do and would be especially popular among the women. Both Thomas and I took the line that a person should not be appointed to the Cabinet because of sex but on merits and qualifications. Miss Bondfield had already held the minor post of Under-Secretary to the Minister of Labour in the previous Labour Government, and she had fulfilled her duties with outstanding ability. On her own merits she was entitled to Cabinet rank. MacDonald was in favour of Miss Bondfield's inclusion, and we decided to put her name down for the arduous and unpopular office of Minister of Labour.

A discussion on John Wheatley then arose. During the time we had been in Opposition in the previous Parliament, Wheatley had dissociated himself from his former Cabinet colleagues, and had gone to the back benches into the company of the Clydesiders. In the country, too, he had made speeches attacking his late colleagues. MacDonald was strongly opposed to offering him a post in the new Government. Wheatley had deserted us and insulted us, and MacDonald thought the country would be shocked if he were included in the Cabinet, and it would be taken as evidence of rebel influence. Henderson took the view, and I was inclined to agree with him, that it might be better to have him inside than outside. I took this view from my experience of him as a Minister. He was a man who, when free from the responsibility of office, would make extreme speeches; but as a Minister I had always found him to be reasonable and practical. However, we finally accepted MacDonald's view, and his name was not further considered.

What to do with Lansbury was something of a problem. He had been kept out of the previous Labour Cabinet, but we all agreed that some Cabinet office would have to be found for him in the new Government. But we also agreed that he could not be put in as head of an important Department. Merited or unmerited, the stigma of "Poplarism" still clung to him. I suggested that he might be given the Office of Works. I thought that this post would suit him admirably. He would not have much opportunity for squandering money, but he would be able to do a good many small things which would improve the amenities of Government buildings and the public parks. He was offered and accepted this post. He proved to be a very efficient and popular head of this Department.

Then a most distressing discussion arose about the Foreign Office. We knew that Henderson had set his heart upon this post. Thomas wanted this office, and I gathered that he and MacDonald had talked over the matter and MacDonald was favourable to giving him the appointment. Neither of them had very much love for Henderson. There were a good many past incidents, the recollection of which rankled on both sides. MacDonald made a very good suggestion that one of the Cabinet posts to which no official duties were attached should be given to an energetic person who would act as Minister of Employment to co-ordinate the Departments which might provide work and generally formulate plans for national reconstruction. He suggested that Henderson might take on this job. But Henderson was not having this. Thomas, who had been Secretary to the Colonies in the previous Labour Government, said that he would not take this office again. Henderson became very angry, and threatened to refuse to have anything to do with the new Government. He would keep to his work at the Labour Party Office. MacDonald seemed determined that Henderson should not have the Foreign Office, and eventually he said that he would take that post himself in addition to the Premiership for two years to get outstanding questions, like better relations with America, settled. The discussion ended with no reconciliation between Thomas and Henderson. On the way home

I had a talk with Henderson, who had cooled down, and seemed inclined to consider the suggestion of being Lord Privy Seal and Employment Minister if I would agree that he should act as Deputy Leader of the House in my absence. I agreed, and we parted with the impression on my part that he would accept this. The same evening he came in to see me (we were then almost next-door neighbours), and he had altered his mind again, and suggested that he would write to MacDonald to say that if MacDonald was determined to take the Foreign Office he would not enter the Government. I pointed out that if he did that he might strengthen MacDonald's determination to do so. Henderson was convinced that MacDonald and Thomas had agreed that the latter should be Foreign Secretary, and that MacDonald intended to take it just to keep Henderson out. He was still bitter about the letter MacDonald had written to him in 1924 when MacDonald was forming the first Labour Government asking him to be Chairman of Ways and Means. "If I had not been a good Wesleyan I should have sworn!" he said.

On Wednesday afternoon, the 5th June, a meeting was held at Transport House of the members of the National Executive of the Labour Party and of the Parliamentary Executive. We expected that there would be questions about the way in which the Government was being formed, and that the dissatisfaction which had been felt in 1924 at the large share of the appointments which had then been given to the non-Trade Unionist element in the Party would find expression. However, MacDonald made a brief and tactful opening statement. He revealed nothing, and there was not a word of enquiry as to the construction of the new Government. Everybody there who was an M.P. evidently hoped that he would be in the new Government, and was afraid to speak. The meeting showed a desire to leave MacDonald free in the appointment of his Ministers.

Two important matters were raised at this meeting. Henderson said that, as Secretary of the Labour Party, he had had a communication from Citrine, Secretary of the Trade Union General Council, asking for some liaison between the Labour Government and the Trade Union Congress. After a few words of opposition to this from Mr. J. H. Thomas, because it would give countenance to the idea that the Government was under outside dictation, it was unanimously agreed not to establish anything of the sort. Henderson also raised the question of the weekly Party meetings, and suggested that these should be abandoned, and a small consultative committee elected by the private members be formed to keep the Government in touch with the Party. This suggestion was accepted.

After this meeting the "Big Five" met again. At this meeting Thomas said that he had considered the suggestions made the previous day about offices, and he was now prepared to take the Dominions Office. Henderson immediately shook him by the hand, and said "That leaves me the Foreign Office." I was taken completely aback, and presumed there had been some private arrangement. MacDonald never said a word about his statement of the previous day that he would take that office. This confirmed my suspicion. Shortly after Henderson left for another appointment and then the matter of his going to the Foreign Office was raised. Thomas, like myself, appeared to have been wholly taken by surprise by Henderson's assumption that he was agreeing to go to the Dominions Office in order to leave the Foreign Office open to Henderson. In declaring that he would accept the Dominions he said that he assumed that MacDonald was going to the Foreign Office. Thomas was wild at being "tricked", as he put it. He threatened that he would not take office at all. He declared that he had said that he would take the Dominions under the belief that that would force Henderson to take the office of Lord Privy Seal and Employment Minister. It seemed that no compromise was possible. Thomas was irreconcilable, but eventually agreed to think the matter over until next day. So there the matter was left, Thomas promising to let MacDonald know his decision that evening. I rang up Thomas about nine o'clock and found him calmer, but still fiercely indignant with Henderson, and still undecided as to his action.

Next morning I had a telephone call from MacDonald to meet him and Thomas at Downing Street. I arrived first, and Thomas came in next, and we had a talk before MacDonald arrived. Thomas told me that he had slept over the matter of Henderson "tricking" him about the Foreign Office. He had decided to accept the post of Lord Privy Seal and Director-General of Employment Schemes. This was a surprising outcome of the events of the previous day. Henderson's stubborn pertinacity had won, and he became Foreign Secretary. I never knew why Mr. Thomas changed his mind and agreed to take the post of Employment Minister, for he must have known that he was taking on a very difficult job, and one which was bound to bring him more criticism than credit. He had already plans, and his chief concern at the moment seemed to be to get together a staff and an office. He was keen on Colonial development. He wished to announce that all contracts for this would be given to British workshops. We pointed out to him the unwisdom of making any such announcement as it would simply give protection to British firms, who would form rings, and prices would soar sky-high. We agreed that he might keep Preference in mind and give it where prices were not unreasonable. We decided that he must do something to let it be known that we would not tolerate rising prices on account of demand caused by public works, and that, if necessary, we would introduce an anti-profiteering Bill.

We discussed at length what Thomas's new duties would be, and what steps he could take to increase the volume of employment. Thomas was extremely popular among business men, and he had decided that he would get in touch with the leading men in the various branches of industry and discuss with them trade possibilities and new construction work. He seemed in the few hours since he decided to take on this job to have been thinking tremendously, and he had got a number of quite sound ideas in his mind. I promised that I would help him with as much money as he needed for sound ventures which promised ultimate returns, but with not a penny for subsidies to inefficient industries. We were in complete agreement on this policy, and during the harassing months he held this difficult post there were no differences at all between us on policy, nor did he ever submit to me for financial help any proposal to which I had any hesitation in giving my approval.

When I left this meeting I met Mr. Churchill coming out of the Treasury Office where he had been clearing up. He looked fresh and happy, and gave me the encouraging information that he had not left a penny in the till!

I found in the evening papers that Thomas had begun his work – his new appointment was the news feature, and it had lost nothing of its importance in the telling!

Mr. William Graham had been a conspicuous success as Financial Secretary to the Treasury in 1924, and he was obviously marked out for Cabinet rank. The Board of Trade seemed the most likely post for him, and he was appointed to this office. It had been suggested that Mr. Alexander might go to the Dominions Office, but Mr. Sidney Webb had made it a condition of his elevation to the House of Lords that he should carry a Cabinet appointment with him. So, when that office became vacant through Mr. Thomas's acceptance of the dual office of Lord Privy Seal and Employment Minister, Mr. Alexander was offered the post of First Lord of the Admiralty. Sir Oswald Mosley had been considered for this post, as it was thought he might be strong enough to fight the "gold braids" there. It was eventually decided, however, that Cabinet rank should not be given to one who had only recently joined the Party, and about whose Socialist orthodoxy there was at that time considerable doubt. He was, however, given the nominal office of Chancellor of the Duchy of Lancaster without Cabinet rank on the understanding that he would help Mr. Thomas with his employment schemes.

I asked that Mr. Pethwick-Lawrence should go with me to the Treasury as Financial Secretary - a position for which I considered him to be eminently qualified. He had not held office in the previous Labour Government. At the University he had had a distinguished career - a Wrangler and a Smith Prizeman - and he was a very able Economist. I never regretted this selection. He made an excellent Financial Secretary, both in his Departmental duties and in the conduct of financial measures through the House of Commons.

I need not go further into details of the constitution of the second Labour Government. It was composed overwhelmingly of the Right section of the movement. Of the fifty-four major and minor appointments the Trade Unionists were given twenty-one offices, and the remainder were filled from the non-Trade Union section. The composition of the new Government was on the whole favourably received by the Press. The appointment of Mr. Henderson as Foreign Secretary caused considerable surprise. It was generally assumed that the Prime Minister would continue to give close attention to foreign policy. General sympathy was expressed with Mr. Thomas in the almost impossible task he had undertaken. Mr. Lansbury's inclusion in the Cabinet was regarded as its most disturbing feature, but some consolation was derived from the fact that as First Commissioner of Works his opportunities for extravagance would be severely circumscribed. Mr. Herbert Morrison was brought into the Government for the first time, taking the post of Minister of Transport without Cabinet rank. He proved himself, however, in a short time to be such an efficient Minister that he was taken into the Cabinet.

On Friday evening, the 7th July, I received official notice to attend at Windsor Castle at 11.30 next morning to be sworn in as Chancellor of the Exchequer. The King had only recently recovered from a very severe illness, and was not fit to make the journey to Buckingham Palace. It had been arranged that a special train would take the new Cabinet from Paddington to Windsor on Saturday morning, the 8th July. The news of our journey had got abroad, and a great crowd assembled at the station to see us off. We had an enthusiastic reception, and the good wishes of the crowd were showered upon us. At Windsor five open landaus with postilion riders had been sent from the Castle to meet us. It was the first occasion in history when a new Cabinet had attended the Sovereign accompanied by a woman. Miss Bondfield, who had that unique distinction, was seized upon by the reporters, who asked her if she was frightened. "Oh, not the least bit," she said. "I am used to this sort of thing. There is only one thing that I am really conscious of, and that is that I am making history." At Windsor a large crowd lined the streets as far as the Castle, and again the new Ministers had a great reception all along the route.

The ceremony of swearing in the Ministers took place in the Audience Chamber of the Castle. The King looked remarkably well considering the severe illness through which he had recently passed. He apologised for having put us to the trouble of coming to Windsor on account of his illness, and asked to be allowed to remain seated. Lord Parmoor, as President of the Council, called each Minister before the King, taking the Secretaries of State first, then the Chancellor of the Exchequer and other Ministers. Each went to the King's chair and on bended knee swore to fulfil his office faithfully, and was then handed his seals, and kissed the King's hand. I was excused from kneeling on account of my physical infirmity. The ceremony went through without a hitch, and Sir Maurice Hankey, the Clerk to the Privy Council and Secretary to the Cabinet, afterwards described it as a brilliant success. The King complimented Miss Bondfield on being the first woman Privy Councillor. As we were leaving the room the King said to me: "I hope you are not too tired with standing." He was always most kind and considerate.

On our return from Windsor the Ministers proceeded to their respective Departments and deposited their seals. I found that Churchill had altered the position of the furniture in the room. I had it at once put back into its former position. I reappointed my two former Private Secretaries - Mr. Grigg and Mr. Fergusson. Churchill had had three, but I dispensed with the third and handed him over to Thomas, to whom he had acted as Private Secretary in the former Labour Government. I then returned to the Cabinet Room in Downing Street, where we had an informal talk. We fixed the first Cabinet Meeting for eleven o'clock on the following Monday.

On our arrival at Downing Street that morning we found a tremendous commotion in the court. There were some fifty photographers, talkie men and cinema operators. Henderson had arranged this for advertisement purposes. I disliked all this show business. We had to parade before the camera, and the Prime Minister introduced each with appropriate words. At this first Cabinet Meeting no business was presented beyond the Prime Minister initiating the new members into the mysteries of Cabinet procedure.

Chapter Twenty-Six

The Hague Conference

I come now to the story of what was perhaps the most sensational episode in my career; an episode which to my great surprise brought me for a time into world-wide notoriety. This was the Reparations Conference which was held at The Hague in the month of August 1929.

Perhaps I had better begin with a brief statement of the events which led to the calling of this Conference. Ever since the end of the War the question of Reparations and War Debts had caused considerable trouble. A great many International Conferences had been held on these matters, but no working and permanent settlement of Reparations had been reached. The Peace Conference met in Paris after the war in an atmosphere still charged with war passions. Fantastic ideas were then entertained as to the possibility of compelling the defeated Powers to pay the whole cost of the War. These ideas were soon found to be vain delusions, and the successive Conferences on the subject made unsuccessful efforts to reduce the amount of Reparations to be exacted from Germany to a limit which might be within her capacity to pay.

Three years after the end of the War some wiser heads began to realise that the whole idea of exacting Reparations and discharging War Debts was financially and economically impossible without inflicting injury upon debtor and creditor alike. On the 1st August 1922, the British Government made a bold and statesmanlike declaration on the subject, which was embodied in a Note addressed by Lord Balfour to our European Allies in the War. This document insisted upon the relationship between Reparations and Inter-Allied Debts; and set forth in plain language the British view of the problem. It was pointed out that up to that time the British Government had abstained from making any demands upon their Allies either for the payment of interest or the repayment of capital on the debts due to Great Britain. In the meantime Great Britain had been required to meet her obligations to the United States. In this Note the British Government announced that they were prepared, if such a policy formed part of a satisfactory international settlement, to remit all debts due to Great Britain by her Allies in respect of Loans, or by Germany in respect of Reparations. This magnificent offer met with no response either from the Allied countries or from the United States.

Further efforts were made to place the Reparations Payments on a more practical basis, culminating in the London Conference held in July 1924, to put the Dawes Scheme into operation. The Dawes Plan was never regarded as being of more than a temporary character.

No further step towards a revision of the Dawes Plan was taken until September of 1928, when during the sitting of the League of Nations Assembly at Geneva the German Ministers raised the question of the Evacuation of the Rhineland. The French Government insisted that the Evacuation of the Rhineland could not be considered until the matter of German Reparations had been placed in a more satisfactory position. It was finally agreed that there should be parallel discussions about evacuation and about a final settlement of Reparations, and that a Committee of Experts should be appointed to draw up proposals for a complete and final settlement of the Reparation problem. Negotiations on the matter took place between Mr. Churchill and M. Poincare.

It is important here to note, in view of the controversy which arose at The Hague Conference, that Mr. Churchill insisted that in any alteration of the amount of the Annuities to be paid by Germany the distribution of these Annuities between the different Creditor Nations should be based upon the percentage which had been fixed by agreement at the Spa Conference held in 1920, and which since then had been maintained in all the Reparation Plans. He also insisted that full cover from Reparations and Allied Debt payments should be assured under any new Plan. He pointed out that up to that time the British payments on her Debt to America had exceeded our receipts from Reparations and Allied Debts by £180,000,000, and he insisted that the British Government must reserve their right to deal with this deficiency and to recover supplementary payments over and above their current debt liabilities.

When I come to deal with the proposals of the Young Committee, which was the outcome of these negotiations, it will be seen that in demanding amendments to their Report at the Hague Conference I was doing no more than acting upon the policy of the British Government, with which the Allied Governments ought to have been familiar. The new Committee of Experts, charged with the duty of drawing up proposals for a complete and final settlement of the Reparations problem, was formally appointed on the 19th January 1929. Chairman of this Committee was Mr. Owen Young, an American, and it consisted of ten other members - two Belgians, two French, two Germans, two Italians and two British. This Committee sat for four months and, according to all reports, its proceedings were not of a very harmonious nature. Each of the Allied members of the Committee who had been appointed by their respective Governments, and who regarded it their duty to get as much as they could for their own country, put forward claims which, if satisfied, would have resulted not in a decrease in the amount of Reparations Germany would have to pay, but an increase in the full Dawes Annuity from £125,000,000 to £150,000,000.

It leaked out in the Press at the beginning of May, while the Committee was still sitting, that in order to reconcile difficulties and to meet the demands of the French, Italians and Belgians, the chairman had produced a fresh scheme. Under this scheme the average share of the British Empire was to be reduced to a figure which would fail to cover even our future Debt Payments. When this became known there was a storm of protest from all shades of opinion in this country, and Mr. Churchill was questioned upon it in the House of Commons. He stated that the British Government was in no way bound by the recommendations of the Committee of Experts, and he made it quite clear that there could be no chance of any such proposals being accepted by this country. Eventually fresh proposals for the distribution of the Annuities were made which slightly increased the share of the British Empire.

In order to get an understanding of the matters which caused such acute differences in the Hague Conference, I will try to make as plain as possible the objections of the British Government to certain proposals of the Young Report.

The Report fixed the amount of the payments to be made by Germany at an average of £100,000,000 a year over the next fifty-nine years. This was a reduction of about 20 per cent upon the Annuities under the Dawes Plan. This reduction in the German payments was accepted by the British Government, but we took the position that so long as Reparations were paid they must be fairly distributed amongst the Creditor Powers. This question of the distribution had been hotly debated in the earlier Conferences. Two years after the War, at a Conference at Spa in 1920 a scale of distribution among the Creditor Powers was agreed upon. The percentage of Reparations allotted to

Great Britain under the Spa Agreement was substantially below the percentage to which Great Britain was entitled on merits. But it was accepted, and although the system of German payments had been altered at least four times in the subsequent eight years, the Spa scale of distribution had been maintained. The Young Report recommended a change in the percentage of distribution of the Annuities which would reduce the shares of the United Kingdom, the United States of America, and some of the smaller Powers by £2,000,000 a year for thirty-seven years, and Great Britain's loss was to be distributed amongst France, Italy and Belgium, the major part of the advantage going to Italy.

There was a further feature of the Young Report to which the British Government took strong exception. It was proposed to divide the German Annuities into two classes - Conditional and Unconditional Annuities. About one-third of the total Annuities - equal to a sum of £33,000,000 - was to be placed in the category of Unconditional, and was to take priority of payment over the other two-thirds. Five-sixths of this prior charge was allotted to France. Italy was to get about £2,000,000 a year, and the remainder, amounting to less than £2,000,000, was to be distributed amongst all the other Creditor Powers. It was extremely unlikely that Germany would be able to maintain the regular payments of the whole of the Annuities, and, as practically the whole of Great Britain's share of the Annuities was to come from the postponable part, while half of the share of France was guaranteed against postponement, France in this respect was placed at a great advantage compared with Great Britain.

The other part of the Report to which the British attached importance was that dealing with the payments of Annuities in kind. This method of paying Reparations was especially disadvantageous to Great Britain, as these exports from Germany entered into competition with British exports.

These were the three principal matters in the Report to which the British Government took strong exception, and the British Delegation went to the Hague Conference with the authority of the Cabinet to insist on such adjustments of these matters as would secure justice to this country. A delegation to a Conference of this character must necessarily be given a certain measure of liberty, within their general instructions, to deal with matters which may unexpectedly arise, and with developments that cannot have been foreseen. It was understood that if the British Delegation found it impossible to secure the acceptance of their demands, and if the break-down of the Conference seemed likely, the British Delegation would refer to their Cabinet colleagues for further instructions.

The British Delegation left for the Hague on Sunday, the 4th August. We arrived on the Sunday evening, and were received at the station by the British Minister, and on behalf of the Dutch Government by M. Beelaerts van Blokland, the Foreign Minister. We had to submit to the usual infliction of being photographed, and then proceeded to our headquarters at the Grand Hotel, Scheveningen, a seaside resort two or three miles from The Hague.

The formal opening of the Conference had been fixed for Tuesday morning, the 6th August. The Dutch Parliament was not then in session, and the Government had very generously placed the Parliamentary buildings in the Binnenhof at the service of the Conference.

On the evening before the Conference assembled, the heads of the six principal Powers, including Germany, met at the hotel at which the French Delegates were staying for an informal talk about the proceedings of the Conference. This was the first occasion on which I had met M. Briand, and M. Jaspar, the principal Belgian delegate. I renewed my acquaintance with Dr. Stresemann, who, I was pained to see, was obviously in a very poor state of health. We discussed at this informal gathering the question of the Chairmanship of the Conference, and the appointment of a Secretary-General. In regard to the latter appointment there were no differences of opinion as to the man beyond all others best qualified to fill that important post. Sir Maurice Hankey was well known to the foreign delegates, who had met him when acting in a similar capacity at many previous international conferences. In regard to the Chairmanship of the Conference arrangements were made which, however, were never carried through, that the chair should be occupied successively by the heads of the principal Delegations.

M. Jaspar, the principal Belgian delegate, was selected to take the chair at the first plenary session of the Conference, a position he accepted in complete innocence of the onerous duties he was undertaking.

M. Jaspar had a head of hair which reminded one of Mr. Lloyd George, and this resemblance had led at a previous Conference at Cannes to an amusing incident. Two Englishwomen saw M. Jaspar, who they believed was Mr. Lloyd George, enter a barber's shop. They waited outside, and when M. Jaspar emerged they went into the barber's shop and begged for a lock of hair which had been cut from the gentleman's head who had just gone out. This was given to them, and it is very likely to this day two Englishwomen are wearing a lock of M. Jaspar's hair in the belief that they are treasuring a lock of Mr. Lloyd George's!

The arrival of the delegates for the opening session the following morning was watched by vast and cheering crowds. On this occasion the public were admitted to the galleries, as the proceedings were to be of a purely formal character. There were thirty-three chief delegates at the Conference, representing fourteen nations. The Dutch Foreign Minister welcomed the Conference on behalf of the Government and the Queen to the calm and peaceful atmosphere of The Hague. M. Briand, as the senior Minister among the delegates, followed with one of his appropriate little orations. He referred to The Hague as a symbol of peace, and "here", he added, "is a propitious atmosphere in which to serve the cause of humanity, and to make yet another effort to promote peace and good-will between the nations which have by sad experience learned that war is bad business, even for victors." Dr. Stresemann followed, and, though physically weak, made a bold speech in which he referred indirectly, but still quite pointedly, to the idea which M. Briand had recently put of a "United States of Europe". I followed with a very brief speech in which I expressed regret that M. Poincare and Herr Mueller, the German Chancellor, were prevented by illness from attending the gathering, and I congratulated Holland upon being free from the necessity of taking part in the proceedings, and expressed the conviction that though Holland was not directly concerned with such troublesome problems as Reparations, she, like all nations, would benefit by a just and satisfactory settlement of the problems before the Conference. After these formalities the opening session came to an end, to be resumed for business purposes at four o'clock that afternoon.

It had been decided that the business sessions of the Conference should be held in private, though it was soon discovered that it might have been better if the Press had been admitted. It was impossible to keep the proceedings and debates of the Conference secret. There were scores of press men from all parts of the world assembled at The Hague, and, being denied access to the meetings of the Conference, they were driven upon other resources for their information. With the exception of Great Britain, all the other Delegations had brought with them strongly staffed and highly efficient Press departments, and they had also perfect arrangements for meeting the Press representatives from their respective countries and putting them in possession of the news they wanted circulated in their own countries. Nothing transpired at the Conference which was not immediately conveyed to the foreign Press representatives, and, naturally, coloured by the impression they wished to make upon the people of their respective countries. The British Delegation were driven to adopt similar methods, although our Press department was never so elaborate as that of the other Delegations.

At four o'clock that afternoon the first business session of the Delegates assembled under the chairmanship of M. Jaspar. I thought it desirable that the British attitude towards the Young Plan should be stated at the outset of the proceedings, and I rose at once for that purpose. In view of the impression which my statement made on the Conference and the sensation it created throughout the world, it might be well if I reproduce the fairly full report of my remarks which was afterwards communicated to the Press. I began by saying:

"The experts had stated that the Young Report must be regarded as indivisible and must be accepted as a whole, but I was afraid that if the Conference accepted that statement and took the proposals as they now stood, they would have to follow in some respects an inconsistent and rather contradictory decision. The British experts were not Government servants, and the British Government was in no way committed to adopt the committee's recommendations.

"The views of the British Government were that the annuities which had been fixed were not beyond Germany's capacity to pay. If a difficulty should arise, it would not be in Germany finding it difficult to obtain the money, but because Germany could not pay the money into the creditors' pockets.

"The abolition of financial control was heartily welcomed by the British Government. As regards financial security, this was now based upon a solemn undertaking by the German nation, which also was a departure from that laid down by the Treaty of Versailles. There were a few safeguards in case of difficulties, which I hoped and believed would not arise, and I was glad that the sanctions had been removed.

"The British Government had no objection to the volume and the amount of the annuities, but it objected to the proposal to divide the amount into two categories. So long as conditional annuities were being paid it did not matter much, because all nations were getting their money, but unconditional annuities carried the right of mobilisation, and therefore attained greater security than the conditional annuities.

"The British Government objected to the present proposed division whereby France got five-sixths of the unconditional annuities and Italy had a very considerable sum amounting to £2,000,000 annually, which was much larger than her revenue under the Dawes Plan. There remained a perfectly negligible part to be divided among the other creditor Powers. I hoped they would forgive me for speaking frankly and firmly. The division was utterly indefensible, and the Experts themselves had made no attempt whatever to explain it or to justify or to defend it.

"The British Government attached the greatest possible importance to the proposed modifications which had been made in the distribution of annuities among the various creditor nations, and which was a departure from agreements which already existed, and, unfortunately, this division was very much to the disadvantage of certain creditor countries and very much to the advantage of other creditor countries. Great Britain was a very heavy sufferer from these suggested alterations in the distribution of annuities, and some of the smaller nations would also suffer. That was in one respect very unfortunate, because the small nations who were now asked to make sacrifices in their percentages were not represented at the Experts' Conference.

"This was the first time that a suggestion had ever been made that there should be a departure from the Spa percentages. There have been eight conferences since that of Spa on the Reparations problem, but this was the first time any suggestion had been made that there should be any change or modification in the percentages then decided upon. The question had never been raised by the Dawes Scheme, and the experts had no authority to interfere with existing arrangements for the distribution of annuities. When the Young Committee was convened, it was agreed among the chief creditor Powers that there should be no interference with the Spa percentages.

"The effect of the reduction was very heavy upon some countries which did not share at all in the mobilisable part of the annuities. Great Britain would lose under the proposed scheme 48,000,000 marks a year. France, in addition to five-sixths of the unconditional annuities, would gain 10,700,000 marks, Italy 36,800,000 marks and Belgium 12,200,000 marks. Japan, Serbia, Greece and Rumania, and the United States would also lose small amounts.

"We have paid to the United States £150,000,000 which, with accrued interest, is now £200,000,000 before we have received any payments from our debtors on account of their debts to us. It is estimated that if the scale is adopted Great Britain will get just her bare debt to the United States covered. But it must be remembered that it makes no allowance whatever for the sum of £200,000,000 which is due to Great Britain under the terms of the Balfour Note."

I then touched on the question of payments in kind, and said Great Britain attached great importance to this question, adding:

> "Our relations with Germany are very friendly commercially, and long may they continue so, but we compete in the markets of the world, and payments in kind therefore have assumed a great and serious importance.
>
> "Forgive me if I appear to speak with great firmness in regard to the distribution of annuities. The House of Commons would never agree to any further sacrifices of British interests in this matter. We are agreed - and as you all know, all parties in Great Britain are agreed upon this.
>
> "We are prepared to wipe the slate clean of all international debts and all Reparations. That was implied in the Balfour Note. It was the declaration of our Party before we came into power. But so long as Reparations are paid and received, so long as debts are payable, every Government in Great Britain will insist upon Great Britain being fairly treated in this matter."

At the conclusion of my speech the Conference evidently felt that they had had as much for that session as they could comfortably digest, and a motion was made for the adjournment of the Conference.

To my surprise the speech, which contained nothing which ought to have surprised the delegates if they had been aware of the position of the British Government as stated in the House of Commons debate, caused a great sensation. The French, Italian and Belgian Delegations had evidently come to the Conference expecting no opposition to any of the recommendations of the Report. They had assumed that the business of the Conference would be confined to drafting a protocol laying down the conditions for putting the Plan into operation. As a matter of fact, I was appalled at the ignorance which was displayed by the Delegations of these countries. They had no appreciation at all of the contributions which Great Britain had made to France, Italy and Belgium in the settlement of their War Debts to this country.

The full Conference assembled next morning (Wednesday, 7th August). It was clear that the French, Italian and Belgian delegates had kept their officials up all night preparing statements for them, which were read to the Conference. The statements were moderate in tone, but emphatic that there could be no concessions by them on the demands I had put forward. The smaller Powers who suffered to some extent from the alteration of the Spa percentage were unanimous in their criticisms of the Report. There was, however, an underlying feeling that I had thrown out a challenge which would have to be taken up, and the speeches made that morning were obviously drafted to gain time for a further exploration of the British case. At a reception given by the Dutch Government the previous evening my "bombshell" was almost the sole topic of conversation, and among neutrals the feeling was frankly expressed that the Conference would have to face up to the facts, and that a little plain speaking had been introduced into an International Conference which had been strikingly absent from the proceedings of previous Conferences.

The French and Italian Press were most violent in their remarks upon my speech, and were insistent that no sacrifice of the advantages which France and Italy derived from the Young Plan should be made.

On the next day the Conference went into Commission. It had not been my intention to speak at the first meeting of the Finance Commission, but events made it necessary that I should make a second speech and repeat in stronger language the demands of the British Delegation. It had come to our knowledge that the statement was being widely circulated that I was simply bluffing, and that a strong line of opposition would expose the bluff. The Chairman of this Finance Committee really precipitated my second speech by proposing the setting up of a number of sub-committees to draft a protocol for the putting of the Plan into operation. This proposal I strongly opposed, and said that until the Conference had come to a decision upon the three demands made by the British Government it was useless to proceed to other business. This speech, as might have been expected, "put the cat among the pigeons", and drew excited replies from the French and Belgian and Italian Delegations. In none of the speeches was any attempt made to deal with the arguments and statements I put forward. They were in the main a repetition of the phrase - "the Young Report is an indivisible whole and we cannot admit any alteration of its recommendations".

At the end of this meeting of the Financial Commission the divergence between Great Britain and the other Creditor Powers had become so marked that it was decided to adjourn for two days to see what might happen in the meantime. I agreed to this adjournment only on the condition that the next session should be devoted to a continuance of the general debate, and that Mr. Graham's speech on Deliveries in Kind should come first. The debate on Deliveries in Kind at this particular moment was really a time-killing arrangement while private consultations were going on behind the scenes on the questions I had insisted should be dealt with before other matters were discussed.

At this meeting, on Saturday the 10th, Mr. Graham made a clear statement of the British position on Deliveries in Kind. Mr. Graham's speech was moderate and persuasive, and it made a distinctly favourable impression upon the meeting.

At the conclusion of this speech, ignoring the fact that it had been agreed to confine the business of that session to the subject raised by Mr. Graham, M. Cheron rose, and without any remonstrance from the Chairman, said that he proposed to reply to the speech I had made two days before. He innocently confessed that he was doing this because the French Press had attacked him on account of the weakness and inadequacy of his earlier reply. This turn in the proceedings of the Commission had taken me completely by surprise, but I could not quite allow M. Cheron's speech to pass without an immediate reply.

M. Cheron had read his long speech, and he evidently did not expect that I should reply to him at once. I was getting rather impatient with this constant repetition of statements which were no answer to the case that I had put forward, and I did not spare M. Cheron on this occasion. It was in the course of this speech that I used the expression which became notorious, and which M. Cheron has not lived down to this day. The following is an extract from what I said:

"I hope that I shall not be considered discourteous if I say that M. Cheron's speech has taken me somewhat by surprise. I understood that the sitting was to be devoted wholly to the question of Deliveries in Kind. But M. Cheron has replied to what I said when I spoke on Wednesday. Had this been a continuation of the general debate on the whole Plan, I should have had no complaint to make about the nature of M. Cheron's intervention this morning.

"I am not going to follow M. Cheron in the points he has made, and particularly in the figures he has submitted to the Committee. I will practically confine myself to saying that I do not accept the accuracy of a single figure M. Cheron has put forward. If this were the occasion for going into details on this matter I should refute every one of the constructions which M. Cheron has placed upon his figures. It is not true to say that Great Britain did not suffer, in the proposed distribution, under the Young Plan in comparison with the distribution which she received under existing agreements. I hope that the word will not be considered offensive, but M. Cheron's interpretation of the Balfour Note is grotesque and ridiculous to anyone who understands its full character.

"It is no good going on arguing the question day after day in the Committee, one side repeating its arguments and the other side repeating its claims. It is high time that we came to grips with this matter. I have not come here to spend the rest of my days at The Hague. I want to get back to my own country. I am as anxious as any member of the Committee to come to an agreement which will be mutually satisfactory and which will place this vexed question upon a permanent foundation. But there can be no settlement unless it is a settlement based upon justice. This general debate will have to come to a close very soon. My resolution is before the Committee, and I cannot delay a decision upon that resolution very much longer."

At the close of my speech a number of delegates rose to continue the discussion, but the Chairman was of opinion that the atmosphere had become so electric that it would be well to adjourn the Conference until the debate could be continued in a calmer spirit.

After the adjournment of the Conference there was a violent reaction on the part of the French to the words "grotesque and ridiculous" which I had used in describing M. Cheron's interpretation of the Balfour Note. Although these words were not used by the interpreter in translating my speech into French (he had translated in their place the milder expression of "wholly inaccurate"), the actual words I had used became known. They were seized upon by the Press correspondents, and were prominently displayed in the Paris Press next morning. This storm was apparently due to one of those differences in the precise meaning in the two languages of words which are identical in form. But I learnt afterwards that the reason M. Cheron was so indignant at the use of this expression was because he was habitually cartooned by his political opponents in the French Press in the character of a clown.

A story is told that during a recent political crisis in Paris, there was a demonstration of students in protest against the part M. Cheron was supposed to have taken in overthrowing the previous Government. During this street demonstration the students encountered M. Cheron, seized him, and compelled him to sit down in the middle of the street. They drew a circle round him, and danced around singing: "You are grotesque and ridiculous!" Only those who know M. Cheron could imagine the full humour of that situation.

During that weekend I had a visit from two of M. Cheron's seconds, who came to demand from me an explanation of my language. I had no difficulty in assuring them that the words in English had not the offensive meaning they had in French, and were a common Parliamentary expression. At a meeting of the principal delegates next morning, called for other business, there was a delightful exchange of courtesies between M. Cheron and myself which cleared up this incident and put everybody into good humour once more.

That same Saturday afternoon an embarrassing episode occurred which might have had the effect of breaking up the Conference altogether. It appears that on this Saturday afternoon in Edinburgh Mr. MacDonald had had a long interview with two international bankers, who had impressed upon him that there was a danger that my opposition to the French might lead them to take retaliatory action against Great Britain by withdrawing French francs deposited in London.

At the end of this interview Mr. MacDonald sent the following open telegram addressed to "The Treasury, London."

"Prime Minister, Edinburgh to Treasury." Most Urgent.

"Send to Chancellor at Hague in code immediately.

"My information is worsening from all sides: even an adjournment strikes in minds of important people an ominous note. I am relying upon three of you before break occurs to get into touch with me and perhaps we could arrange to meet before any action for adjournment is taken or if you prefer that one of you should meet me in London.

"PRIME MINISTER."

This telegram reached the Treasury at three o'clock on Saturday afternoon. There was no responsible official at the Treasury on duty at that time, and the telegram fell into the hands of a young clerk who opened it. He discovered that the telephone girl on duty was not in possession of a copy of the code, so he rang up the British Delegation at The Hague, and he read the contents of the telegram to an official of the British Delegation there. When it became known to us that this telegram had been telephoned to The Hague *en clair* we were staggered at the possible consequences. It was well known to us that the telephone lines were being tapped, and it was highly probable that the contents of this important message would soon be known to all the Press correspondents at The Hague. As a matter of fact, the newspapers next morning had an account of the long interview between the Prime Minister and the bankers in Edinburgh. If this message from him to me became known to the delegates of the other Powers it would confirm the widespread impression that I was simply bluffing and had not the support of the British Government in insisting upon the demands I had made.

I immediately sent the following message to the Prime Minister. After quoting the terms of the telephoned message, I said:

> "This message was read over the telephone *en clair* by some officer in London to a junior Foreign Office official at the Delegation Office here. It looks as if a serious error of judgment has been committed in London and this I am investigating at once. But in the meantime I should like to know whether your telegram from Edinburgh to Treasury was also sent *en clair*. The consequences of any leakage of this message may

be disastrous. So far my main task has been to convince the foreign delegations that I am not bluffing and have been speaking with the full authority of His Majesty's Government and with the complete approval of the country at large. Yesterday there seemed every indication that this lesson had at last been learnt and distinct signs of cracking have been shown by both French and Belgians. To-day, as appears in the letter which I had already written before this telephone message was received and which goes by to-night's bag, there has been a very marked stiffening. The reason for this I have not so far discovered. Of course, the fact of this message having been sent and its tenor are bound to become known to other delegations, and I very much fear that my task of reconciling the Young Plan with British interests has become almost impossible. The only chance seems to me immediate issue by you of a statement that I have the fullest support both of yourself and of every member of the Government in the position which I have taken up and which I intend to maintain."

The Prime Minister responded immediately with this communication:

"The Financial Commission will make a most serious mistake and may wreck immediate prospects of a settlement unless they understand quite finally that the Experts' Report requires readjustment to meet the just claims of this country. Irrespective of party or section the country support the case you have made. Every newspaper so far as I have seen backs you. All parties in House of Commons stand by you. I hope most sincerely your colleagues on the Financial Commission will see that they have to face a position when the most elementary considerations of fair-play as between country and country compel a reconsideration of some of the recommendations of the Report. Our action hitherto in promoting the settlement of Europe on a basis of good-will is a proof that we wish this Conference to succeed both on its political and financial sides, but we have reached the limits of inequitable burden-bearing."

On the receipt of the Prime Minister's communication I got in touch with M. Jaspar, and told him that I proposed to read this at the meeting of the

Financial Commission to be held on Monday. M. Jaspar, however, urged that I should not do this as "the patient is so weak that this will kill him". I gathered from this remark that the foreign delegates were still under the impression that I was bluffing, and that to be suddenly disillusioned might give them a fatal shock. However, I did not wait until Monday, but gave the Prime Minister's message to the Press at once, and it certainly produced a marked effect upon the French delegates. For some days previous there had been rumours among the Press correspondents that M. Briand had appealed to Mr. MacDonald to come to The Hague and take charge of the British Delegation, or, failing that, M. Briand was in favour of an adjournment of the Conference to Geneva in the hope that Mr. MacDonald would be more amenable. On Monday, however, it became clear that Mr. MacDonald's original telegram had leaked out, and among the Press correspondents there was a general talk to the effect that a private message from the Prime Minister had been received instructing the British Delegation to climb down. The intractable attitude of the foreign delegates during the whole of the following week was undoubtedly due to their knowledge of the Prime Minister's first telegram.

At the end of the first week of the Conference the outlook was black. The French, Belgian and Italian delegates showed no disposition to meet us on the demands I had put forward. It had been arranged that the Financial Commission should resume its meetings on Monday (12th August) to continue the debate on Deliveries in Kind. But it was realised that this was a mere pretence to keep the Commission in existence. In these circumstances it was felt that if any progress was to be made on the matter which was holding up the Conference the principal delegates would have to meet privately and discuss the situation. At my interview with M. Jaspar on Saturday afternoon I suggested that the principal delegates should meet on Sunday morning to talk over matters. The meeting was to be strictly private, and no secretaries or officials, apart from the Secretary-General, should be present. But before this meeting took place I had arranged with M. Jaspar that the British, French, Belgian, Italian and Japanese Experts should meet informally to discuss how the British claims could be met. This was the first real advance in the way of acknowledging the substance of the British claims. The Sunday morning meeting, therefore, was of a perfunctory nature, the only incident of importance being the clearing up of the misunderstanding about the "grotesque and ridiculous" incident, and the exchange of courtesies between M. Cheron and myself. The meeting, however, was useful as it put everybody in a good humour and restored a favourable atmosphere.

The informal meetings of the Experts began at once to consider in what way the demands of the British could be met. This Committee continued its discussions until late on Sunday evening and throughout the following Monday, Tuesday and Wednesday. When the failure of this Committee to reach any conclusion was reported to me, I got in touch with M. Jaspar, and expressed my views strongly about the way in which the representatives of the other Creditor Powers were treating our demands. Following upon this conversation, next morning (Wednesday, 14th August) I addressed the following letter to M. Jaspar:

"DEAR M. JASPAR,

"Referring to my remarks to you about the deadlock on the Committee of Treasury Experts, I repeat that I must press for a definite decision on the points I have submitted to the Conference at an early date. I agree that it might be best to have a talk today among the Heads of the other Creditor Powers, and if they desire I will submit my proposals, which are definitive, in writing, but they are known to you. The time has come for a decision, and I expect this by Friday evening, or the session on Saturday will be futile.

"I repeat that on the matter of distribution I cannot accept anything less than the restitution of our share under existing agreements.

"I am very anxious that we should arrive at a friendly agreement.

"Yours sincerely,
PHILIP SNOWDEN."

The delegates of the other Creditor Powers acted upon the suggestion contained in this letter, and by midnight on Friday M. Jaspar handed to the Secretary-General a letter addressed to me covering proposals to the British Delegation by the other Creditor Powers. They had evidently been working very hard, for the memorandum of proposals accompanying M. Jaspar's letter was a lengthy document.

The British Delegation met immediately to examine these proposals from the other Creditor Powers, and it was at once realised that the document was so wholly unsatisfactory that it could not be accepted as providing even a basis for discussion. After this decision of the British Delegation I saw M. Jaspar at four o'clock the same afternoon and told him that I had received his letter and the Statement from the other Creditor Powers, and I wanted to have a few words with him before I sent the reply which was being prepared to it. I said that I thought he would not be surprised to hear from me that the Statement was quite unacceptable, and that it made no advance, indeed in some respects it was less satisfactory than the talk between the Experts in the early part of this week. I wanted to speak to him quite frankly, and at the moment between ourselves. I did not press him to give me a categorical answer to my question, but I would like to know whether I was to regard this Statement as the last word. He threw up his arms and said: "Well, I do not know. It is difficult for me to say that." To this I replied: "Quite right! Your gesture is perhaps the best answer I could have. So I will not press you any more."

He then went on to say that I must not regard it as their last word, and indicated that he was not at all satisfied with it, and added that if it rested with him there would be little difficulty in coming to an agreement. He was very anxious that there should be further time for conversations, and implied that if they were given more time they might go further. He also said that if it rested with the French he thought that they and the French could work together and do something more satisfactory, but the Italians were the difficulty. I suggested that the Japanese might help him, as they were in a much more independent position. He replied that he had already seen the Japanese, and that they would help. He left me, expressing his desire and intention to do all he could to bring about a settlement.

After my interview with M. Jaspar, the British Delegation met again the same evening (Friday, 16th August) to approve the reply and the covering letter which was to accompany it. Our reply was a very lengthy document, extending to more than two thousand words, and it is not necessary either to reproduce it here or even to summarise it, as it was in effect a restatement of the British demands.

On the next day (Saturday, 17th August) the delegates of the other four Powers were in conference considering our letter and Memorandum, and about nine o'clock that evening M. Jaspar called to see me. I had asked Mr. Graham to be present at this interview. M. Jaspar handed a Memorandum containing a proposal that the "technicians" attached to the interested Delegations should meet to determine the various allocations proposed in their previous note. In view of the inadequacy of the offer and the failure of the previous Expert conversations, Mr. Graham and myself had some hesitation in accepting this proposal. We felt, however, that it would be undesirable to risk a break-down of the Conference until further opportunity had been given for expert or other review of the available documents. We therefore agreed to M. Jaspar's proposal, on condition that there must be no going back on the central points of the British claim, and that the experts selected should not include any persons who had been members of the Young Committee; and, further, that this enquiry should not be made an excuse for further delay.

Sunday (18th August) was a comparatively quiet day. The weather during the whole time we were at The Hague had been remarkably fine. I took advantage of a brief respite to see something of the interior of Holland, and my wife and I took a long motor drive, which included a visit to the cities of Utrecht and Leyden. We were much impressed by the appearance of prosperity everywhere, and with the cleanliness of the towns through which we passed, and the evidences of a thrifty and hardworking population which were to be seen. On my return I learnt from Sir Maurice Hankey that no further crisis had developed during my temporary absence from The Hague!

The situation at this time was undoubtedly very grave. We expected no result from the meeting of the Experts, and this expectation proved correct, for, after working for two days, they produced a Report which in no respect altered the situation. The Conference now had been more or less in existence for a fortnight, and we had to seriously consider the possibility of a complete break-down of the negotiations. I may say here that during all the difficulties which we had met with in the previous fortnight I never really believed that the Conference would come to a break-down. The French, Italians and Belgians had far too much to lose by the rejection of the Young Plan to persist to the end with their opposition to any concessions being made to the British demands.

On the Monday morning (19th August) the British Delegation met to take a review of the position and to examine the possible developments. On that Monday evening, however, an incident happened which gave a new turn to events. Throughout all the negotiations which I have described, Mr. Adatci, the principal Japanese delegate, had acted as an intermediary, using his influence to try to reconcile the conflicting views. On the previous Friday, just after the Note from the other Creditor Powers had been received, Mr. Adatci and a Japanese colleague asked for an interview with me. Mr. Adatci explained that the Japanese Expert had collaborated with the Experts of the other principal Powers in drawing up this Note; but Mr. Adatci wished me to understand that, owing to the distance, it had been impossible for the Japanese Delegation to consult their Government, and they had informed the other Powers that they must reserve complete liberty of action. They intended to keep their hands free so that they could join either the one party or the other, and their object was to assist in every possible way to concert the conflicting views of the other Powers and thus secure a successful outcome of the Conference. Their relations with Great Britain had always been close and friendly, and they would be particularly glad if they could at any time be of service to the British Delegation. They hoped that if the occasion arose I would not hesitate to call upon them. I thanked Mr. Adatci warmly for his offer, and expressed my great appreciation of the motives which had inspired it.

During the weekend Mr. Adatci had not been idle, and he had taken a step which turned out to be of very great importance and which contributed in no small measure to the eventual settlement of the disagreements.

On Monday evening I received an invitation from Mr. Adatci to meet M. Briand and M. Loucheur the following day at tea in Mr. Adatci's hotel. This friendly meeting took place on Tuesday, the 20th August, at 4 p.m. The conversation between M. Briand and myself was of a most gratifying character, and was carried on in a most friendly spirit.

After this meeting M. Loucheur called at my hotel, evidently at the request of M. Briand, and he explained that M. Briand had been deeply impressed by the determined manner in which I had insisted that we must have satisfaction as regarded the Spa percentages. Both M. Briand and himself felt that it would be a tragic thing if the whole plan of the Conference broke down about the question of two millions. If the Young Plan had been still under discussion privately the French Government would have had no objection to altering the table of distribution; but, now that it had been published, any change in that table, he was afraid, in view of French public opinion, was out of the question. They were prepared, however, to arrange some compensation to Great Britain for the loss she had suffered without altering the table of the Plan; and they were trying their best to see what could be done in this way. France was prepared to guarantee to Great Britain half of the loss we complained of, and they would pay this either by means of an annuity or in a capital sum. As regarded the balance of the deficit, M. Loucheur suggested that we might arrange as best we could with the Italians, and he was under the impression that the Italians, if pressed, would be prepared to make some contribution.

Later, I saw M. Pirelli, the principal Italian delegate, but he declined to make a substantial advance beyond an offer to co-operate in putting through a general settlement of the debts for liberation and ceded properties, and to allocate to us an unspecified proportion of any rights that Italy might obtain from Czechoslovakia under such a settlement. M. Pirelli was not a free agent in this matter, and he evidently was working under strict instructions from Mussolini, who was opposed to Italy surrendering any part of the unmerited advantages offered to her under the Young Plan.

Notwithstanding the difficulty with Italy, I felt very much encouraged by the outcome of my conversation with M. Briand and M. Loucheur. I got in touch with M. Jaspar, who I found was still extremely anxious for a settlement. He said his difficulty was that the other Creditor Powers did not know what I was prepared to accept; and I said that if he could induce the Italians to make an offer similar to that of France and Belgium we could begin to talk business. My tea-table talk with M. Briand undoubtedly did improve the relations between the French Delegation and ours, and henceforth my conversations with them were of a very cordial nature.

Nothing of material importance happened during the next three days; but on Thursday, the 22nd August, we had a meeting of the delegates of the six Powers, and it was decided to push on immediately and uninterruptedly with conversations in regard to the British demands with a view to reaching a decision. These conversations resulted in a fresh offer by the other Creditor Powers, which was communicated to the British Delegation at midnight the same day. Again the offer was regarded by us as inadequate. The estimate of the other Creditor Powers was that it would give us £1,430,000 annually. The British Delegation met at ten o'clock on Friday morning and agreed to my view that the offer was quite unacceptable.

M. Jaspar was undismayed by the failure of this and all the previous offers to satisfy the British Delegation, and he begged that he might be given a little more time to produce "a final offer". So we agreed to postpone further meetings over the weekend.

In view of what seemed now a strong probability that we should come to a break-down within a few days, acting upon our instructions from the Cabinet we telegraphed to the Prime Minister, suggesting that some of the members of the Cabinet might come to The Hague for a consultation on Sunday, the 25th August. There were two courses open to us, to both of which considerable objection might be raised. The Delegation might return to London - but we felt that if we did that it would risk the disruption of the Conference. On the other hand, for the Cabinet to come to Holland would undoubtedly cause great excitement, and would give the other Powers the impression that we were weakening in our determination. During the weekend the other Creditor Powers were preparing their final offer, and it was certain that if it became known that the British Cabinet was meeting in Holland their offer would be affected adversely.

We placed the whole position before our colleagues in London, and they agreed with us that it would be inadvisable for any of them to cross to Holland. The decision in the last resort was left to the Delegation. Nothing, however, that happened could be kept secret, and on the Sunday morning the Dutch newspapers came out with sensational stories that the British Cabinet was secretly meeting in Holland. This information appears to have leaked out from London, for the reports in the Dutch newspapers were attributed to an English source. It came to our knowledge that the Note which the other Creditor Powers were preparing, and which had been finished on the Saturday night, was rewritten on Sunday morning when this sensational news about the British Cabinet coming to Holland became known. These Powers had evidently assumed that there were divisions in the British Cabinet, and that if they took a firm line they would force the acceptance of their terms. This new Note was not delivered to us until eight o'clock on Monday morning, and I at once called the other British Delegates and our Experts into consultation. The Note was submitted to careful examination, and to our surprise it made no substantial advance on the previous offer, and was in fact merely a repetition of it.

At two o'clock that afternoon I sent this letter to M. Jaspar as the agreed reply of the British Delegation:

"August 26th 1929.

"DEAR MR. JASPAR,

"We have received your communication of the 25th August conveying to us the reply to my letter of the 23rd August in which I asked for a definite settlement in writing of the final proposals which the other Creditor Powers were prepared to make.

"The British Delegation have considered your Memorandum, and they note with regret that it shows no appreciable advance on your previous offer and is altogether inadequate.

"Yours sincerely,
"PHILIP SNOWDEN."

I heard indirectly that M. Jaspar felt some annoyance at the brevity of this reply and the rapidity with which it had been dispatched after the other Powers had spent so much time in drafting their Memorandum. It was explained to him that the British Delegation saw no useful purpose in going over the same ground time after time, and the only long reply the British Delegation could have made to this last Note would be to repeat what they had already stated at great length.

I had a considerable amount of sympathy with M. Jaspar, because I felt quite sure that the tenor of this last Note must have been a disappointment to him, and represented the failure of his efforts to induce his colleagues to make some further concession. When M. Jaspar had cooled down he admitted that there was some justification for the tone of our reply.

At eleven o'clock on the morning we had received this last Note, Mr. Adatci called to see me. He said that he assumed that I had received the Memorandum containing the proposals drawn up by the other Creditor Powers for the satisfaction of the British claims. He wished to explain the position of Japan in this matter. The Japanese Delegation had attended the discussions as an observer; and they had offered their advice, but did not take part in signing the Memorandum and did not associate themselves with it. He had explained this to the representatives of the other Powers, and had obtained their consent to making this declaration to the British Government as a matter of loyalty. He further explained in order to assist at a settlement the Japanese Delegation had agreed to rebate the 7½ million Reichsmarks that they had received during the past five months of the Dawes Annuities. I thanked Mr. Adatci for his statement, and said that the Memorandum was even less satisfactory than the verbal proposals made last week. The other Creditor Powers knew quite well that an offer on these lines must be unacceptable, and that it was a waste of time to put it forward.

I told him that I had expected that if the new proposal did not satisfy our full demands it would at least represent a substantial advance on previous offers, which might furnish the basis of a new agreement. As a fact, the Memorandum actually closed the door to any agreement. Mr. Adatci said that he did not regard this last Note as a final offer. The other Creditor Powers were prepared to make further concessions, but they wanted to know what was the Chancellor's minimum. I replied that if the other Creditor Powers had made a substantial advance towards meeting our views we might have been able to say what we would in the last resort take, but I could make no suggestion upon the basis of an offer such as that contained in the Memorandum. Mr. Adatci said that he feared that we were very near a break-down at the Conference. The other Ministers were so tired that nothing could be done that morning.

In the evening of the same day Mr. Adatci paid me a further visit. It was quite evident to me that he was acting as a friendly intermediary between the parties. He told me that he had been informed that the French Council of Ministers had met that day, and had decided that the proposals put forward in the Memorandum of yesterday represented the last word so far as France was concerned. Public opinion in France would not allow their delegates to go any further. Mr. Adatci enquired whether it would be any use trying to get the other Powers to put up a proposal that would increase our share from 60 per cent to 70 per cent. I did not wish to put Mr. Adatci into a difficult position, and to encourage other people to put forward such an offer in the belief that it would be accepted.

After the receipt on Monday (26th August) of this unsatisfactory Note from the other Creditor Powers, the deadlock appeared to be complete. The Conference had now been sitting for three weeks. For nearly a fortnight there had been no meetings of the full Conference. The private negotiations between the principal delegates had, so far, resulted in no offer from the Latin Powers that the British Delegation could regard as in the least satisfactory. They themselves admitted that their offer did not represent more than 60 per cent of the British share of the Annuities of which we were being deprived by the proposals of the Young Report.

Substantial progress, it is true, had been made on the political side, and an agreement was almost complete provided a settlement could be reached of our financial claims. The matters of Deliveries in Kind, which had been in the very able hands of Mr. Graham, had also made some progress, though our requirements had not been completely met. In these circumstances the British Delegation at an early meeting on Tuesday (27th August) decided to ask M. Jaspar to summon the heads of the six principal Powers at three o'clock that afternoon, and to arrange for a meeting of the Plenary Conference on the following morning at ten o'clock. When this message was delivered to M. Jaspar we learnt that the French, Belgian and Italian Delegations had just made a similar request to him.

This meeting, which marked the turning-point in the fortunes of the Conference, assembled in a Committee Room of the First Chamber of the States-General at five o'clock.

It had been reported from Rotterdam that the French Delegation had booked the whole of the sleeping accommodation in the Paris Express for that evening.

M. Briand, up to this time, had taken no part in the conversations at previous meetings of the heads of the Delegations and of the proceedings in the Financial Committee and the Plenary Sessions of the Conference. At the opening of this meeting he became the spokesman of the Latin Powers, and rather cleverly tried to put the responsibility for the failure to come to an agreement upon the

British Delegation. He spoke of the grave political consequences which were at stake, and asked us to soar above the consideration of paltry figures! The difference was so small - not worth the break-up of the Conference!

My reply to this argument was obvious. The deadlock was due to the fact that the other Creditor Powers were determined to grasp an advantage at the expense of Great Britain, and if, as M. Briand asserted, the difference between the other Creditor Powers and Great Britain on this matter was so paltry, the matter could be settled at once if the other Creditor Powers would concede the just demands of Great Britain.

M. Briand, I said, complained that we had never stated the minimum sum that we were prepared to accept. I pointed out that we were justly entitled to the full sum of which we were being deprived, and it was for the others to say how much of that demand they were prepared to concede. The efforts they had made up to the present time, amounting to not more than 60 per cent of our just claim, did not provide a basis for bargaining. M. Briand had repeatedly admitted the justice of our case, and he had said that if the other Creditor Powers could make a concession to us without altering the Young Plan he would have been willing to do so. It was for them to state their maximum offer, and if that approached to any minimum which the British Delegation might have in mind they would examine it and see whether the gap could be bridged. Mr. Henderson strongly supported the position we were holding, and complained that we could not get the other Creditor Powers to state definitely whether their offer of 60 per cent was the final offer they could make.

The room was insufferably hot, and it was suggested that we might adjourn for ten minutes to "air the room". As it turned out, however, the ten minutes were spun out to five hours. During this ten minutes' interval the British Delegation remained in the Conference Chamber, and the other Creditor Powers went into another room. The other parties used this short interval to get their heads together.

Within five minutes M. Jaspar returned to our room to say that his friends had been talking the matter over and they were only prepared to advance 60 per cent. But he had declined to return to the British Delegation without offering 70 per cent, which he had achieved. I rejected this offer, and told M. Jaspar that he had done remarkably well in securing an advance of 10 per cent in five minutes, but I should require him to make an advance upon this.

While these consultations were going on in the other room we were discussing among ourselves whether we could help matters by making a definite offer of what we would be prepared to accept. I put down on a half-sheet of note-paper five points constituting our minimum demands. They were:

(1) Their offer of £1,400,000 to be raised to £2,000,000.
(2) Some further concession on the non-conditional annuities.
(3) Coal orders from Italy 1,500,000 tons as a minimum.
(4) International Bank to be situated in London.
(5) Existing concessions to be confirmed.

I handed this Note to M. Jaspar, who went away to submit it to his friends. He returned in half an hour with the following counter-offer:

(1) They were prepared to offer £1,750,000.
(2) They found a difficulty in granting this owing to the position of the Smaller Powers.
(3) Italy had been persuaded to increase the coal orders to 700,000 tons.
(4) They were not willing to discuss the Bank.
(5) Accepted.

This proposal was not acceptable to us, and M. Jaspar withdrew to see if he could gain any further concessions. I congratulated him upon the progress he was making, and pointed out that in half an hour he had made very considerable advance. At the same rate he would come up to our minimum demands before midnight.

He returned in a quarter of an hour with a further advance of £50,000.

"You are doing first-rate, M. Jaspar," I said; "be not weary in well-doing." During the next two or three hours he passed to and fro between the two rooms, each time bringing some small advance. Before midnight he had come to within £240,000 of the British claim. M. Jaspar was in despair. He said:

"What do you say when a horse will not run for your Derby?"

"You mean 'scratched'."

"Yes", he said, "I am 'scratched'. I cannot do more. You have emptied our pockets."

"Go through your pockets again," I said, very kindly, "I am sure you will find enough left to cover what remains between us."

"You told me you had a very kind heart," he said. "You are a bit too hard. I have never met a man like you before. You are a new type." I assured him it was out of the kindness of my heart that I wished him to continue his efforts, for I wanted him to have the satisfaction of having saved the Conference. Then someone had a brain-wave! A hitherto undiscovered means of giving us the sum we needed was found, and at midnight our demands were accepted and the Conference was saved!

All this time from noon of the previous day no delegate had had a meal. It was an intolerably hot evening. Swarms of midges and mosquitoes covered the table of the Committee Room. In the interval between M. Jaspar's wanderings from one Committee Room to the other I spent my time murdering hordes of these insects as they settled on the table. The delegates were famished. At last some Good Samaritan produced a few dry rolls and some musty cheese, and our lives were saved.

The Germans, who had taken no part in these conversations, were summoned. There was a long wait before they arrived, and when they did Dr. Stresemann was not with them, as the doctor had refused to allow him to leave his bed. For certain parts of the agreement the consent of the German Delegation was necessary. The heads of the agreement at which we had arrived were explained to them so far as they affected them.

At two o'clock in the morning this long and momentous meeting ended. When we went outside we found the square of the Binnenhof crowded with journalists who had been waiting all these hours, and who had enlivened the time by making bonfires of copies of the Young Report! The news of the agreement had already been communicated to them, and they were the first to offer their congratulations to the British Delegation.

I got back to our hotel about three o'clock in the morning, where I found my wife in a state of great anxiety about the outcome of this protracted meeting. She was greatly relieved at the good news I had to tell her. She had suffered, like all of us, from the strain of the last four weeks, and was happy that our efforts had at last been crowned with success. Throughout all this time she had been an inspiration and a consoler. No matter how black things might seem, she had a word of hope. She had never despaired of success when success seemed farthest away. Her quiet confidence was an encouragement to us all. Nor was this the only help she gave. She had attended throughout to an enormous mass of personal correspondence, and when I returned to the hotel tired in the early mornings after a day of conference she was there waiting for me to see that food and rest were immediately provided.

Three years later the Young Plan, like its numerous predecessors, was found to be unworkable, and is no longer being operated. It may be of historic interest to explain what our four weeks' strenuous struggle at The Hague for British rights gained for the time being.

We claimed an addition to our Annuity of £2,400,000 a year, a fairer share of the Unconditional Annuities, and some improvement in regard to the Deliveries in Kind. The agreement reached on the first of these three claims gave us an increase in our guaranteed Annuities of £2,000,000 a year for thirty-seven years. This payment was to be guaranteed to the extent of £990,000 by the French and Belgian Governments, and £450,000 by Italy. We received at once a lump sum of £5,000,000 - the equivalent of an additional Annuity of £360,000 a year. In addition, by a rearrangement of the dates on which the debt payments were to be made to us, we gained an additional sum of £200,000 a year. Of these sums 90 per cent were guaranteed, and were therefore placed in the category of Unconditional Annuities. This addition may be regarded as a full compensation for that small sacrifice we made from the total of our original amounts. With regard to the second point, we obtained a larger percentage of the Unconditional Annuities. On the third claim, namely, Delivery in Kind, we secured a very substantial advance. These three matters constituted our gains in what I might call the financial and commercial sphere.

The British Delegation were equally successful on the political side, the credit for which is wholly due to Mr. Henderson. An agreement was reached between France, Belgium and Great Britain on the one hand, and Germany on the other, by which the complete evacuation of the Rhineland was to be effected. The withdrawal of the British troops began at once, and our evacuation was completed before Christmas.

The next three days were spent in winding up for the time being the work of the Conference. It was necessary to hasten the conclusion of the Conference, as some of the delegates had to go to Geneva for the meetings of the League of Nations Assembly. During these three hectic days the officials attached to the delegations worked day and night in order to prepare the Protocol embodying the Resolutions of the Conference and the preliminary schemes for putting the Young Plan into operation from the 1st September.

On Saturday morning (31st August) the Financial Commission met and passed the final Protocol, and the Plenary Meeting followed an hour later. There was no time for an open public ceremony in the presence of the Press and the Diplomatic Corps, nor for long and eloquent speeches which might have been expected on such an historic occasion. A few words of mutual congratulation and satisfaction were offered, and on my motion a warm vote of thanks was accorded to M. Jaspar, who had carried out the arduous duties of President with such conspicuous tact and success. This day happened to be the birthday of the Queen of the Netherlands, and as the delegates passed from the Conference Hall into the stately square of the Binnenhof a band played the well-known hymn, "Now thank we all our God".

It had been frequently asserted in the foreign Press that the British Delegation were fighting only for some sordid material gain. It is quite true that we were demanding our just right in the matter of the distribution of Reparations, but behind our insistence upon that right there was a much more important principle involved. Our resistance to the call upon Great Britain to make further sacrifices was an indication that we had reached the limit of our quixotic generosity, and that we should not allow Great Britain any longer to be regarded as the "milch cow of Europe". And still beyond that, and of greater importance, was our assertion of our international rights and of our determination that international agreements should be respected. I am convinced that our stand made a profound impression upon our future relations with other European countries. The rights and the influence of Great Britain in international diplomacy had been reasserted. We had won the respect of the nations with whom we had been in acute controversy during these four momentous weeks.

Throughout the Conference the personal relations between the British Delegation and those of the other Powers had been of a friendly character, which was a striking contrast to the bitterness of the personal attacks which were made upon me in the French Press. These criticisms were more amusing than irritating. One of the mildest caricatures of myself which appeared in the French Press was one which represented me as the reincarnation of the men who had burned Joan of Arc, beheaded Mary Queen of Scots, and banished Napoleon! I am sure that Yorkshire had to bear a measure of the unpopularity which my determined and stubborn attitude inspired in the French Press and among the French people. When the Dutch pressmen interviewed my wife to ask her what she thought about these French attacks upon her husband, she quietly remarked: "He is a Yorkshireman, and they do not understand the Yorkshire character."

M. Cheron shared M. Jaspar's opinion that I was a new type of diplomatist. M. Cheron was asked from what part of England he would like the British delegate to come whom he might meet in a future international conference. He replied: "Show me a map of England", and when this was done he said: "Where is Yorkshire?" It was pointed out to him, and then he said, pointing to Land's End: "I would like him to come from there."

M. Jaspar remarked at a meeting in Belgium of the British Chamber of Commerce some months later:

"At The Hague recently I had some valuable lessons in English which have given me an irresistible desire to visit Yorkshire. I have learnt how an Englishman defends the interests of his country; I have learnt what it is to be firm, vigorous and expressive."

Before leaving for Geneva, M. Briand sent my wife a beautiful bouquet of orchids, accompanied by a large photograph of himself inscribed "With expressions of admiration and good wishes."

A few days later I received a very warm letter from Mr. Adatci, who had been so useful as a conciliator. He said:

"When on Saturday, August 31st, The Hague Conference adjourned its work, I was obliged to go to the station, to take the first train which would bring me direct to Geneva. It was this special circumstance which absolutely prevented me from realising my great desire; I wish to express to Your Excellency all my admiration, as well as my affection for you personally as well as for the attitude you so courageously took up in regard to Great Britain and the cause of justice and equity.

"I wish to add that, thanks to the confidence you showed in me, I was able to contribute in some small measure to the success of the Conference.

"When in Geneva I saw in the papers what an enthusiastic welcome you received in London, I leapt for joy at the thought that the heart of the British people was indeed beating in unison with yours. To-day the whole world understands completely the attitude you took up for England."

It was a great surprise to me that our stand made such an impression on world opinion. We were supported with enthusiasm by practically the whole of the British Press and British public opinion. I was given to understand later that the proceedings of the Conference were followed in England with the interest and excitement of a Test Match. Telegrams and cables of encouragement from all parts of the world came to us hourly. When the agreement had been reached we were overwhelmed with messages of congratulation upon the outcome of our stand for British interests.

Three months later the Freedom of the City of London was conferred upon me "for my courageous stand for the interests of Great Britain."

I gathered from the British Press that preparations were being made to give the British Delegation a great reception on their return to London. This prospect inspired me with more terror than all the foreign delegates I had had to fight during these four weeks. Mr. Henderson had gone direct from The Hague to Geneva, and Mr. Graham and myself and our officials decided to return by the midnight boat from The Hook of Holland which would land us at Liverpool Street at 8.30 on Sunday morning. I thought that this early hour on a Sunday would enable us to avoid a too tumultuous reception. However, when we arrived at Liverpool Street there was a great crowd of enthusiastic people. According to the Press it was the greatest welcome that had been given to British statesmen returning from an international conference since Disraeli brought back "Peace with Honour" from Berlin fifty years before.

When I reached Downing Street I found the following much-appreciated message from the King:

> "On your return home after three strenuous weeks at The Hague Conference I warmly congratulate you on an achievement which has earned for you the gratitude and admiration of your fellow-countrymen. I hope you may now have some rest, and I look forward to seeing you before long.
>
> "GEORGE R. I."

When we sat down in the quiet of my room in Downing Street, my Parliamentary Secretary said to me: "Well, what do you think about it all." I replied: "These things do not move me. I have seen too much of the fickleness of public opinion. One day the public put a halo round your head, and the next day they press a crown of thorns upon your brow. Ten years ago I was turned out of Parliament because I could not take the popular side upon the War, and you were in prison for the same reason." The only thing that had touched me on this journey was the sight of that crowd of boys and girls assembled near the line as the train came along from Harwich shouting and waving their little Union-Jacks.

Three days after our return we had the honour of an invitation from the King to visit Their Majesties at Sandringham. This was a very pleasant experience, and the honour of being admitted for twenty-four hours into the simple and beautiful home life of Their Majesties is a very happy memory. The story of the happenings of The Hague were delightfully interspersed with visits to various parts of the Sandringham estates, where we had witness of the friendly relations between the tenants and their Royal landlord. The King presented me with a reading table, and the Queen gave to my wife an afternoon tea table which had been made in the royal workshop on the estate. These are gifts which we shall always treasure.

Chapter Twenty-Seven

The Budget of 1930

In the early months of 1930 I had to turn my attention to the financial position of the country in view of the Budget Statement which was due to be made in April. The prospects were not very encouraging. I had to follow a Chancellor of the Exchequer who for four years had played "ducks and drakes" with the national finances, and had been living from hand to mouth, using capital to meet current expenditure, and "robbing every hen-roost" on which he could lay his hands. What Mr. Churchill had called the "worst economic blizzard the world had ever known" was raging and gathering force every week. The number of unemployed had risen from 1,122,700 at the time the Labour Government took office to 1,660,000 in April 1930. It was clear that there would be a considerable deficit on the 31st March when the financial year closed.

The financial year, in fact, ended with a deficit of £14,523,000 instead of a surplus of £4,336,000 which Mr. Churchill estimated in the previous Budget. Revenue fell short of the estimated yield by £11,871,000, and expenditure exceeded the original estimate by £6,748,000. The result, therefore, was a failure by £18,619,000 to realise the expectations of Mr. Churchill's Budget of 1929. This was part of the financial problem with which I was faced in framing the Budget for 1930. But, as a matter of fact, the position was much worse than these figures disclosed.

Owing to the trade depreciation the yield of the existing taxes could not be expected to reach the figure of the previous year, and additional expenditure on account of Unemployment would have to be met.

I introduced the Budget on Monday, the 14th April. The country was already painfully aware of the main facts of the financial situation, and was prepared to accept a considerable increase of taxation. I estimated that the total revenue for 1930-31 on the basis of existing taxation at £739,645,000, and the total expenditure at £781,909,000. The difference which I had to make good was

£42,264,000. The announcement of this deficit gave the House a shock from which it took them a few minutes to recover. To balance the Budget it was not, however, necessary to resort to increased taxation to meet the whole deficit as there were resources available for the current year of a fairly considerable amount.

When Mr. Churchill enacted the Derating Scheme he put on an additional Petrol Duty. The receipts from this extra duty had been allowed to accumulate for eighteen months before the expenditure on Derating began, and these receipts had accumulated in what was called the Rating Relief Suspensory Fund. I need not go into the details of a rather complicated matter. It will be sufficient to say that a sum of £16,000,000 was available from this Fund, and I proposed to apply it to meeting a proportion of the prospective deficit. This device reduced the sum I had to meet from increased taxation to £26,264,000. On strict financial principles the previous year's deficit of £14,500,000 ought to be made good in the current year, but in view of the general financial situation I did not feel justified in imposing upon the tax-payers the additional taxation which would have been necessary. I proposed to make a special provision for additional debt reduction of £5,000,000 in the current year, £5,000,000 in the next year, and £4,500,000 in 1932.

I proposed to abolish the last vestiges of Mr. Churchill's inglorious Betting Duty. That tax was introduced in 1926, accompanied by licence fees payable by bookmakers and for entry service in respect of their premises. The tax on bets was a miserable failure, and has been abandoned by its author in the previous year's Budget. There remained in force the duty of £10 payable on bookmakers' licences, and I proposed to repeal this duty so that the Statute Book would once more be entirely free from the blemish of a measure that ought never to have appeared upon it. The cost of this abolition was comparatively small, being about £200,000 a year.

In 1925 Mr. Churchill had reimposed the McKenna Duties. These duties had been imposed by him as Revenue Duties, although they were at the same time highly protective in their effect. The McKenna Duties, and the Silk Duties which Mr. Churchill had also imposed, brought in a revenue of about £10,000,000. To my great regret I was unable to repeal these duties in this Budget. In the existing financial circumstances I could not afford to sacrifice this revenue, repugnant as the duties were to me. The addition of £5,000,000 to the Debt provision brought the figure of the prospective deficit to £31,714,000.

To meet this deficit I proposed in the first place to raise the Beer Duty by 3s. per standard barrel. This was a small addition amounting to not more than 1d. per gallon, which was, of course, too small to justify any alteration in retail prices. I had been in consultation with the brewers, and I had from them an assurance that this small increase in the duty would not be passed on to the consumer either in an increase of price or a reduction in the gravity of the beer.

I looked to an increase in the Income-Tax to meet the greater part of the additional revenue I needed, and I therefore proposed an increase of 6d. in the £1 on the standard rate, raising it from 4s. to 4s. 6d. By an ingenious arrangement, however, I was able to avoid any part of this increase falling on the smaller Income-Tax payers. Instead of charging half the standard rate on the first £225 of taxable income, I gave a relief of 2s. 6d. on the first £250. This concession had very remarkable results. It had the effect that about three-quarters of the whole number of Income-Tax payers were not affected by the increase in the standard rate. There would be no increase in the Income-Tax of unmarried or widowed persons with incomes, all drawn from investment, not exceeding £485 a year, or with incomes all earned not exceeding £582 a year. In the case of a married man with a family with an income not exceeding £882 there would be no additional payment. The cost of this change in the graduation of the Income-Tax amounted to £5,000,000. In addition to the increase of 6d. on the standard rate of the Income-Tax, I had to raise the rates of the Surtax by a sum which was estimated to yield £12,500,000 in a full year. I still had to find a further sum of money, and this I raised by an increase in the Estates Duties. The increase was small. There was no increase in the rates on estates below £120,000, and the increase rose by steps to an increase of 10 per cent on estates over £ 1,000,000. In future, estates over £2,000,000 were to pay a duty of 50 per cent instead of the existing duty of 40 per cent.

The total effect of the changes in Income-Tax, Surtax and the Estate Duties which I have just described was to yield a revenue of £31,500,000 in the current year and £43,500,000 in a full year. This was the method I adopted to meet an estimated deficit of £31,714,000.

In addition to these financial changes in the Budget, I proposed two amendments in the Inland Revenue law. The avoidance of Surtax and the Estate Duties by methods which were legal under the existing law, but which could not be defended on moral grounds, had become a grave scandal. Lawyers who specialised on methods of legal avoidance of taxation had discovered that Estate Duty on landed estates and investments could be avoided through the medium of private companies. Rich landowners and wealthy industrialists formed themselves into private companies, and thus escaped taxation on more than a nominal sum. A system of avoiding Super-Tax by taking out a single-premium insurance policy was being widely practised. The announcement that I proposed in this year's Finance Bill to deal with these two instances of the avoidance of Estate Duties and the Surtax was, when I made the announcement, received with general approval, even of the Tory Party. But when we came to deal with the actual proposals in the Finance Bill I encountered a violent and persistent opposition from the Tory Party.

The Budget was received with warm approval by the Labour Party and the Liberal members, but, as was expected, with disapproval by the Tory Press and the Tory Party. In presenting this Budget Statement I spoke for an hour and forty-five minutes, which for brevity was something of a record in Budget Speeches. In the brief complimentary speeches following my statement, Mr. Churchill was kind enough to congratulate me upon the manner in which I had so tersely compressed the survey of this vast field into a moderate compass, and also upon the physical vigour which had enabled me to go through the ordeal which, both in the preparation and at the moment, is certain to tax a man's strength to the full. Mr. Lloyd George was very whole-hearted in felicitating me upon what he described as a most admirable statement, which in lucidity and compression was the same miracle of compression as a 6-inch shell, and it had the same shattering detonation in its effect upon the Tory members. The majority of the Labour members, though disappointed that I had not been able to reduce indirect taxation, fully realised my difficulties, and were prepared to wait for a Socialist Budget until trade prosperity returned. The Left-Wing Labour members, of course, expressed their dissatisfaction without reserve, and wanted to know why I had not the courage to put an additional annual taxation of at least £200,000,000 on the "idle rich". It was not sufficient for them that I had raised most of the additional revenue I required by the taxation of people with incomes over £1,000 a year, and had imposed little additional burdens upon people with incomes below that figure. They could see no Socialism in such a Budget as this - it dashed their hopes that the Labour Government would establish "Socialism in our Time".

When the House entered upon a discussion of the Finance Bill, which incorporated the Budget proposals, it became clear that the Tories were determined to use every device of obstruction to delay the progress of the Bill. They placed upon the Order Paper over one hundred foolscap pages of amendments. The first day on the Committee Stage of the bill gave a foretaste of what we might expect. The Opposition had been well organised, and the back bench members of the Tory Party had been primed to make long and irrelevant speeches. By midnight it was impossible to treat these obstructive tactics with the consideration to which an Opposition is entitled when they confine themselves to reasonable discussion. By midnight practically no progress had been made, and it was clear that we must be prepared for an all-night sitting.

An all-night sitting resolves itself into a test of physical endurance. The Tories had evidently assumed that they would be able to wear me out, but they had wholly miscalculated my powers of endurance. Hour after hour during the small hours of the morning the debate continued, but, as always happens during an all-night sitting, it degenerated into mere frivolity. Mr. Churchill was leading the Opposition, and he was not behind the back bench members in pursuing a policy of sheer obstruction. In order to waste time, motions were made every hour "to report progress", and these motions wasted further time in speeches and divisions. I could not get a vote upon any amendment except by moving the closure, and this led to further divisions and further waste of time. At five o'clock in the morning Mr. Churchill could stay the course no longer and went off to bed. At eight o'clock I announced that owing to the absence of Mr. Churchill through physical collapse I thought it inadvisable to continue the discussions, which could be resumed when the right hon. gentleman had sufficiently recovered to be able to take part in them. It was, I added, very regrettable that, in view of the promise he had made of the very vigorous part that he was going to play in the debates, he had been compelled to retire from the ring, and I felt sure that I was expressing the feelings of all hon. members in extending to him our deep sympathy and our hopes for a speedy recovery.

When Mr. Churchill returned to the House he had to submit to a good deal of good-humoured banter, which made him determined to seek an early opportunity of retrieving his reputation. The adjournment of the House over the Whitsuntide holidays gave Mr. Churchill no opportunity until the day after

Parliament reassembled. Further consideration of the Finance Bill was put down for that day. The holiday had enabled him to recover his physical strength, and he was determined to show the House that he could go through an all-night sitting without a physical collapse. We began a further consideration of the Finance Bill at half-past three on Tuesday afternoon, and the sitting continued without interruption for twenty-two hours, the House not rising until a quarter to one on the following afternoon. The adjournment of the sitting was at that time necessary in order to prepare for the ordinary sitting of the House, which was arranged to begin at a quarter before three o'clock.

This sitting was one of the longest on record. The sitting was characterised by all the disgraceful features which always accompany an all-night sitting. Disorderly scenes were frequent, and the Chairman had a hard time in keeping the debates within reasonable limits. Few members remained on the benches for the discussions, returning from the library, the smoke-room, and refreshment rooms to take part in the divisions. Not more than one-third of the full strength of the Tory Party were present at any time during the sitting. The leaders of the Tory Party were all absent. To the credit of Mr. Baldwin, Sir Austen Chamberlain and Mr. Neville Chamberlain it may be mentioned that they were absent from the House. They left these disgraceful proceedings to be led by Mr. Churchill, who on this occasion was able to stay the course, but only, it was quite evident, by sheer physical effort. He could not afford to expose himself once more to jeers and ridicule. During the whole sitting the Labour members refrained from taking any part in the talking, but they were present in considerable numbers throughout and loyally backed me up in fighting the Tory obstruction. By eight o'clock Tory reinforcements arrived after a good night's sleep, and the battered and exhausted Tories who had held the fort up to that time were relieved. In spite of all the Tory obstruction, I managed to add a number of clauses to the Bill without conceding anything except a few amendments of a minor nature.

I came through this long sitting (during which I was not absent from the bench for more than a few minutes) without feeling the least physical exhaustion. I declined to assist the waste of time by making long speeches, and only intervened with a few sentences when it was necessary to do so. The proceedings during this long sitting were a disgrace to the House of Commons, and I expressed the opinion that it was a pity that the electors had not had the opportunity of "seeing their legislators at work". If they could have done this it would have destroyed any respect they might have for the Mother of Parliaments and for their elected representatives.

Undismayed by his discomfiture on this occasion, Mr. Churchill continued to pursue obstructive tactics. Two days after this all-night sitting he uttered an extraordinary threat in a speech he was making in opposition to the provision in the Bill to prevent the avoidance of Surtax. For some days he had been boasting in the smoke-room that he would prevent me from getting the Budget through. An Act passed in 1913 lays down that the Budget resolutions, on the strength of which taxation is levied each year until the Finance Bill is passed, have force only until the first week in August. Unless the Finance Bill was passed by this date it would be illegal for the Government to levy Income-Tax or Customs or Excise Duties. Tax-payers would be able to claim their money back, for the Act lays down "that any money paid or deducted under the Budget resolutions shall be repaid or made good". Mr. Churchill had the colossal impudence in this speech to warn me that unless I would bow to his dictatorial demands to drop fifteen or twenty clauses of the Finance Bill he would not allow me to get the Bill through in the statutory time. To gratify his vanity, Mr. Churchill was prepared, if he had the power, to throw the whole revenue collection into a state of chaos, and to make the Exchequer liable to the repayment of tens of millions of pounds. I treated this arrogant threat with the contempt it deserved, and made no reply to it beyond pointing out that the clause which Mr. Churchill was then opposing had been copied word for word out of Mr. Churchill's Finance Bill of 1925. In replying to this he said that he was not contesting the principle but the propriety and expediency of doing it at the moment when I was already proceeding with so much unnecessary vigour and so much unnecessary animus against the Income-Tax and the Surtax payers. By this proposal I was running a great risk in offending the whole body of the Income-Tax and Surtax payers. Mr. Churchill had evidently exhausted his powers of obstruction, for after this I had very little trouble with him, and the Finance Bill passed into law well ahead of the time-limit.

Chapter Twenty-Eight

Internal Trouble about Unemployment

During the whole Session of 1930 the question of Unemployment dominated the proceedings of the House of Commons. Every few weeks the Tories put down a vote of censure on the Government for their failure to solve the problem. Mr. Thomas was trying energetically to do what was possible within his limited resources to provide employment on public works. In the meantime the figures of the Unemployed continued to rise month by month, until by the end of July they had passed the two million figure. Mr. Lloyd George was active urging the adoption of his programme of spending £250,000,000 on the making of roads, the improvement of bridges, the provision of small-holdings, and the development of the telephone system.

I came in for a good deal of criticism, some of it from our own supporters, because the impression had got abroad that I was the hindrance to the raising of a large public loan for these purposes. This criticism was quite unjust. Mr. Thomas, Mr. Herbert Morrison (the Minister of Transport who had charge of the roads) and Mr. Arthur Greenwood (the Minister of Health) all bore testimony to the truth that I did not oppose the expenditure of public money on the schemes of their respective Departments which they had submitted to me. It was quite true that I was opposed to floating a public loan of £250,000,000 for undefined purposes. I was quite prepared to raise the money if necessary to carry through well-thought-out schemes of public works of a useful and remunerative nature. But I set my face against a shovelling out of money to be worse than wasted to provide work of no public utility.

On the 21st May 1930, Sir Oswald Mosley, who had been associated with Mr. Thomas, resigned his post as Chancellor of the Duchy of Lancaster because a programme he had submitted to the Cabinet had not been approved. A few days later, in a debate upon Unemployment, Sir Oswald recited in the House the terms of his Memorandum, and it therefore became public property. He submitted that his proposals would find employment for 730,000 persons at a cost of £10,000,000 a year! The finance of these schemes would not stand a moment's consideration, and they inspired Mr. Lloyd George to wonder whether the Chancellor of the Exchequer would not actually make a profit if the transaction were carried through. As one instance of the absurdity of his finance he calculated that pensions of £1 a week for men at 60 with 10s. for their wives if married, would, provided they were given to 390,000 persons, over a period of fifteen years involve a net cost to the State of £2,500,000!

The resignation of Sir Oswald Mosley did not come as a surprise. He and Mr. Thomas could not get on well together, for their temperaments were wholly different. I doubt, indeed, if anybody would be able to work with Mosley unless he were prepared to meekly follow him. During the few years he had been in public life he had never remained for long in one Party nor constant to any professed views. He entered Parliament as an Independent Tory, afterwards for a short time he was an Independent Liberal, then he joined the Labour Party, and he had not been with that Party more than a few months before he furnished the Party with proposals for a new programme.

I never had any faith in the sincerity of Mosley's professions of Socialism. I was always suspicious of a rich man who came into the Socialist Movement and at once became more socialist than the Socialists. As soon as he joined the Labour Party his speeches were violent denunciations of capitalists and the idle rich, and when addressing a Socialist gathering they were interlarded with frequent references to "my dear comrades". I can understand the working-class Socialist who knows something of the hardships of working-class life sometimes expressing bitter feelings about the class which he regards as his exploiters, but such things coming from a man like Oswald Mosley, who enjoys all the luxuries which his wealth and social position can command, give me a feeling of nausea. Mr. MacDonald warmly welcomed Mosley into the Labour Party. An intimate social relationship was established such as never existed between Mr. MacDonald and the plebeian members of the Labour Party. My views of Mosley's sincerity were very generally shared by the Labour members. His past political record did not encourage a belief in the sincerity of his latest conversion. His attempts immediately after he had joined the Party to give the movement a new programme were strongly resented. It was felt that he was a man on the make, and was using the Labour Movement as an instrument for satisfying his ambition. Mosley had considerable ability. He had a striking appearance, and spoke well. He always reminded me of Ferdinand Lassalle, the founder of the German Working Man's Association which later became the Social Democratic Party. The physical resemblance of the two men was most striking, and they had other characteristics in common. In a conversation with a friend recently I mentioned this similarity between Mosley and Lassalle, and my friend said: "That is very interesting, for an acquaintance of mine who knows Mosley well tells me that Mosley is aware of his resemblance to Lassalle, and has modelled his own career largely in imitation of Lassalle." If ever Mosley had the powers of a Hitler or a Mussolini he would be more ruthless and merciless, because weaker and vainer, than those two dictators.

I must go back now to the story of his resignation from the Labour Government. The rejection by the Government of the schemes embodied in his Memorandum was given as the excuse for that action. He was evidently under the impression that he would be able to take the Labour Party with him in support of his plan, or at least disrupt the Party and form a party under his leadership out of the dissatisfied elements. Immediately after his resignation he sent to the Executive of the Parliamentary Party a resolution, which was in fact a vote of censure on the Government, and he asked that a special meeting of the Labour Members of Parliament should be called to discuss this resolution. This meeting was held, and was very largely attended. In submitting this resolution Mosley spoke for an hour, and recited the proposals embodied in his Memorandum. It was a very able speech, and would have carried conviction to those who were ready to accept the finance of his plan without investigation. The meeting was impressed, and he might have secured a considerable amount of support for his propaganda if he had not made the fatal mistake of pressing his resolution to a division. This ill-advised action caused a revulsion of feeling, for it gave the impression that he was more concerned to attack the Government than to gain support for his plan. Mr. Henderson tactfully saved the situation in a short speech, in which he expressed some sympathy with Mosley's impatience that more was not being done to deal with the Unemployment question, but pointed out that if Mosley's vote of censure were carried it might do considerable harm to the Party.

When Mosley discovered that the Party was not prepared to accept him as a new leader he left the Labour Party and attempted to form a New Party, which turned out to be a fiasco. The advent of this New Party was heralded by a flaming Manifesto in which it was announced that the New Party would run 400 candidates at the next General Election. As a matter of fact, it had about ten candidates at the 1931 Election, all of whom were defeated, including Mosley himself. After the failure of this effort he turned his attention in other directions. He went to Italy, saw Mussolini, and the Socialist of a year before became the leader of a movement to establish a Fascist State in this country. In his brief political career Mosley has been an Independent Tory, an Independent Liberal, a member of the Socialist Party, the leader of the New Party, and the leader of a Fascist movement. Where his next evolution will land him remains to be seen.

Chapter Twenty-Nine

The Serious Financial Position

By the end of 1930 the financial and trade position of the country was causing me grave concern. The world economic blizzard was then blowing with full blast. During the year the figures of the unemployed had risen from 1,303,000 to 2,230,000. Our export trade had declined by 30 per cent. The revenue was falling. The effect of this depression on the prospect for my next Budget was a very grave one. It was already clear that at the end of the financial year in March I should be faced with a very serious Budget deficit.

The previous year, it will be remembered, had ended with a deficit of £14,500,000. In my Budget in April 1930 I had made substantial increases of taxation, and the expected yield from these taxes was not being realised. So far as I could estimate, three months before the end of the financial year, I might be faced with a deficit of £40,000,000 on the current year's account.

But that was not the worst of the prospect in front of me. National expenditure was increasing, and we were borrowing for the Unemployment Insurance Fund at the rate of £40,000,000 a year, and the cost of Transitional Benefit was adding a large sum to the Exchequer expenditure. I was appalled at the prospect of having to make another large addition to taxation, and yet I felt that the country could not afford a Budget which was not balanced. There were already signs that our national finances, and especially the continuously increasing load of debt upon the Unemployment Insurance Fund, were being watched and criticised abroad.

The Bank of England was already feeling the consequences of the weakening of the confidence of foreign markets, and there was at that time a steady trickle of money from London. In these circumstances it was plain to me that it was to the expenditure side of our national accounts that we must turn our attention to secure a sound budgetary position. Unpalatable as it might be to the Labour Party to abandon for the time being expectations of an increased expenditure on the social services, that course would have to be adopted if financial stability was to be maintained. By this time I had received the first draft of the estimates of the expenditure for next year. These estimates showed no recognition of the necessity for reduction - on the contrary the Civil Estimates showed a large increase, mainly due to the alarming increase of the Exchequer charge for Transitional Benefit which had risen from £10,000,000 in 1930 to £30,000,000 in 1931. It was this liability which upset the balance of the current year's Budget, and it was the main cause of the difficulties with which I was going to be faced next year.

This, briefly stated, was the financial position and outlook at the end of 1930. It was a situation which was more or less known to outside financial and commercial experts, and a widespread demand for a drastic reduction of national expenditure was growing. Meetings were being held in the City and elsewhere with the object of enforcing an economy programme upon the Government. Placed in a position similar to but more desperate than our own, other countries were making drastic reductions of their expenditure. The British Government was pressed to follow these examples. Knowing the seriousness of our own position from the inside, and knowing that it was more desperate than these outside critics fully realised, I welcomed this agitation for a reduction of expenditure because I realised that no Government could embark upon a drastic reduction unless it were supported by a strong public opinion.

In February 1931 the House of Commons came to my assistance. The Tories put down a Motion in the following terms:

> "That this House censures the Government for its policy of continuous additions to the public expenditure at a time when the avoidance of all new charges and strict economy of the existing services are necessary to restore confidence and to promote employment."

To this Tory Motion the Liberals moved an Amendment in the following words:

> "That this House considers that, having regard to the effect of the present burden of taxation in restricting industry and employment, the Government should at once appoint a small and independent Committee to make representations to Mr. Chancellor of the Exchequer

> for effecting forthwith all practical and legitimate reductions in the national expenditure consistent with the efficiency of the services."

Sir Laming Worthington-Evans moved the Tory vote of censure, and recited an appalling list of extravagances and financial crimes of which he alleged the Labour Government had been guilty. At the conclusion of this speech I rose at once before the Liberal Amendment was called. The earlier part of my speech was devoted to an ordinary debating reply to the mover of the Tory vote of censure. I dealt vigorously with the financial record of the late Tory Government, and exposed the promises which the Tory Party had made at the General Election of 1924 to carry out expensive schemes of social reform – promises which had helped them to get their majority. During the five years of the Tory Government which we had succeeded, national expenditure had increased, and the Government had made no real effort to secure a reduction.

It seemed as though this debate was going to be confined to a Party squabble, and would end by contributing nothing towards the solution of the very formidable problems with which the country was faced. Had the debate ended with nothing more useful than the representatives of the different Parties throwing stones at each other it would soon have been forgotten. But near the end of my speech I turned away from Party recrimination to speak seriously about the actual national financial position. The House was soon hushed into a deep silence, the members realising that a statement of the utmost gravity was being made. I took the House of Commons and the nation into my confidence, and made a frank and full disclosure of the serious financial situation. As this part of my speech made a tremendous sensation in the House of Commons and throughout the country, and had an important influence on later developments, I think I must quote it fairly fully:

> "In spite of what I have said now, having pointed out the difficulties, I say with all the seriousness I can command that the national position is so grave that drastic and disagreeable measures will have to be taken if Budget equilibrium is to be maintained and if industrial progress is to be made. An expenditure which may be easy and tolerable in prosperous times becomes intolerable in a time of grave industrial depression. The right hon. gentleman made a quotation from my last

Budget speech that I was anxious to avoid the imposition of any further imposts upon industry. In view of the deeper depression since that time, I feel the importance of that statement today more than I did twelve months ago. I believe, if I may put it so bluntly as this, that an increase of taxation in present conditions which fell on industry would be the last straw. Schemes involving heavy expenditure, however desirable they may be, will have to wait until prosperity returns. This is necessary I say this more particularly to my hon. friends behind - to uphold the present standard of living, and no class will ultimately benefit more by present economy than the wage-earners. I have been in active political life for forty years, and my only object has been to improve the lot of the toiling millions. That is still my aim and my object, and if I ask for some temporary suspension, some temporary sacrifice, it is because I believe that that is necessary in order to make future progress possible...

"The Budget position, as the right hon. gentleman said, is serious. It is no secret that I shall have a heavy deficit at the end of this year. No Budget in the world could stand such an excessive strain as that which has been placed upon it by the increase of unemployment during the last twelve months. The depression has affected both sides of the Budget. Expenditure has increased, revenue has declined. There is this fact which I think we sometimes ignore. Productive capacity has now fallen off by 20 per cent. That means 20 per cent less in those resources from which the Exchequer must draw its revenue. Capital values have fallen, except in the case of gilt-edged stocks. And may I say, in reply to what the right hon. gentleman stated about British credit, that, in spite of the depression, British credit is standing higher today than it has done during the last five years. Of course, I do not mean exactly at this precise moment, but taken over a few weeks.

"We have the burden of War Debt. I do not want to give offence to anybody when I make this statement, that when the history of the War in which that Debt was incurred, its recklessness, its extravagance, commitments being made which were altogether unnecessary in the circumstances at the time, when that comes to be known, I am afraid posterity will curse those who were responsible. Though the industrial slump has affected this country so seriously, we have suffered less than others of the great industrial countries of the world. Their budgetary positions are worse than ours. I am quite familiar with what the right hon. gentleman has said about the talk which is going on in certain quarters, but I am sorry to hear that the right hon. gentleman associated that with the responsibility of a Socialist Government. This is not a situation and this is not an occasion when people should talk of taking action which might ruin the country in order to gain a Party advantage.

"There is, as the right hon. gentleman said, one vulnerable spot in our position, and that arises from the fact that we are the world's great financial centre. It is quite true, as he said, that if there were well-grounded fears that this country's budgeting was not sound, then it might have disastrous consequences, which would have their repercussions abroad. It is quite true that other countries are watching, and we must maintain our financial reputation. That we can do. Our position is fundamentally sound, sounder than that of any other country in the world, and all that is required is an effort to get over the present temporary crisis, and that can be done without any very great efforts. It will involve some temporary sacrifices from all, and those best able to bear them will have to make the largest sacrifices. In the general sacrifice, the Members of the Cabinet are prepared to make their substantial contribution. As I have said before, this is a problem which no Party can solve, but the country and the House of Commons must realise the gravity of the position. Instead of Party bickering, which we can resume later, we must unite in a common effort to take effective measures to overcome our temporary difficulties and to restore our former prosperity."

It is difficult to convey an impression of the effect of this statement. Members turned deadly serious, and listened with strained attention to this unexpected development of the debate. It was felt that a House which a few minutes before had been cheering the familiar reproaches on an ordinary Party occasion now realised that it was faced with a situation which would demand the co-operation of all Parties. The task was too big for one Party, and a united national effort would be needed to deal with the crisis.

After my statement, Sir Donald Maclean moved the Liberal Amendment in a brief speech, in which he said that my grave warning was not unworthy of some of my great predecessors. Then the House emptied, and members congregated in the Lobbies, the library and the smoke-room to discuss the statement. Its effect on the Labour members was stunning. They regarded this as the end of their hopes that the Labour Government would proceed with a policy of spending public money on extravagant schemes of social reform. I was very sorry for the Labour members. I had so phrased my statement as to prepare them gradually for the unpleasant truth, and the abandonment for the time being of schemes upon which they had set their hearts. The Left-Wing members of the Labour Party at once began to express their dissatisfaction and disgust with the statement. One of them declared: "It's bigger, not smaller, Budgets we want!" They showed not the least appreciation of the national situation, nor of the fact that the decline in revenue and in trade made it impossible to carry out a policy of increased expenditure which might have been possible when trade was booming and revenue was expanding. The more moderate members of the Labour Party expressed fears about wage standards as well as insurance benefits, and my reference to schemes, desirable in themselves, having to wait until more prosperous times disturbed some of the Liberals, who were advocating large-scale expenditure upon an employment policy. I had purposely refrained from going into details in my statement, waiting for a further opportunity to do so.

Next morning the Press of the country reflected the sensation which had been made in the House of Commons. All the newspapers appeared with large-type cross-page headings. My speech was described as the gravest statement which had been made by a British Chancellor of the Exchequer for fifty years. The Daily Herald, the organ of the Labour Party, took a very reasonable line. In an editorial article it said:

> "The country realises to the full the seriousness of the crisis which faces it, and none realise it more fully than the workers, whose sufferings from it are the heaviest. The crisis is upon us and must be met, and to meet it Mr. Snowden calls upon the whole nation for the courage to make

> sacrifices. To that call the nation will respond. It is prepared to face the crisis with that same courage and that same resolution that has long been its habit. The tenacity of the British will be shown now. That which needs to be done will be done. That which needs to be endured will be endured. But in this national struggle there must be a national solidarity."

In view of the reasonable desire of the Labour members for a fuller explanation of what was involved in the statement made in the House of Commons, we arranged the following week a meeting of the members. There was a crowded meeting, expectant and perplexed. I spoke for half an hour, and discussed the facts of the financial situation. I told them that from the best data available at the moment I expected there would be a deficit of £50,000,000 at the end of the financial year in March. In such circumstances it was perfectly idle to talk of going on as though things were normal, as there comes a time when the tactful thing to do is to retreat to advance. I told them that I felt it would be criminal upon my part not to warn the Party of the dangers ahead. The acid test of democracy was whether the leaders had the courage to tell their followers the disagreeable truth. The full blast of the economic blizzard had come on my head. I had a very disagreeable and unpleasant job, and it was not made easier if every step I took was treated with suspicion and charges of perfidy. If my critics would take my job I was perfectly ready to hand it over to them. I believed that when the Labour Movement realised that it was up against hard facts it would not shrink from facing them.

The small Left Wing element in the Party who had been so vocal outside in denouncing my House of Commons statement were very mild in the discussion which followed my speech, and could only suggest that I was trying to scare the Party. They made a demand for a further meeting of the Party so that a general discussion could take place. The meeting, however, rejected this suggestion, and further procedure was left in the hands of the Consultative Committee. My speech created a profound depression among the members, and they clearly left the meeting with a feeling that their old foundations had been swept from under them.

The Liberal Amendment to the Tory vote of censure which had called for the appointment of a small Committee to see what economies could be made in national expenditure was carried by 469 votes to 23 against. The minority consisted of Left-Wing Labour members, who recorded their votes as a protest against my speech. In consultation with the three Parties, I proceeded at once to make arrangements for the appointment of such a Committee. It had been arranged with the Liberals and the Conservatives that the Committee should consist of a Chairman and six members, two being suggested by each Party. I was able to induce Sir George May, who had recently retired from the position as head of the Prudential Insurance Company, to accept the position of Chairman. The Committee was given the following terms of reference:

> "To make recommendations to the Chancellor of the Exchequer for effecting forthwith all possible reductions in the national expenditure on Supply Services, having regard especially to the present and prospective position of the revenue. In so far as questions of policy are involved, in the expenditure under discussion, this will remain for the exclusive consideration of the Cabinet, but it will be open to the Committee to review the expenditure and to undertake the economies which may be effected if particular policies were either adopted, abandoned or modified."

The Committee got to work at once. It made a thorough investigation of the expenditure of the various Departments, and by the end of July it presented its Report, which in its thoroughness and exhaustiveness was a monument to the way in which the Committee carried out its duties.

Chapter Thirty

The First 1931 Budget

Three weeks after my speech in the House on economy, I was suddenly struck down with an internal disorder which necessitated a serious operation. This misfortune kept me away from the House and the Treasury for seven weeks, and it naturally gave rise to doubts whether I should be able to prepare and deliver the Budget Statement. The operation was very successful, and all that I needed was time to recuperate. I never had any doubt that I should be fit to present the Budget, but I fixed the date rather late in April so as to be quite sure that I should be able to undertake the task. The date was fixed for Monday, the 27th April. I went up to London on the Friday before to meet the Cabinet, to whom I gave an outline of the Budget proposals. A few of my Cabinet colleagues had been down to Tilford to see me during my convalescence, and they were not surprised to see me on this Friday looking quite fit.

We spent a quiet weekend at 11 Downing Street, and on Monday went across to my room at the House of Commons and rested until the time came for my presence on the Treasury bench.

I would like to mention that Mr. Baldwin had previously approached Mr. MacDonald with a suggestion that if the Opposition could do anything by way of making my task easier they would be delighted to do it. I very much appreciated this kindly consideration. The only divergence from the usual proceedings in presenting the Budget was that by arrangement with the Chairman of Ways and Means I omitted that long and tiresome and unnecessary exposition of the details of the income and expenditure of the previous year. I have always regarded this statement as being quite unnecessary in the Budget Speech, for all the information is contained in a Blue Paper which is in the possession of members before the Budget is opened. In the words of the chairman of a company meeting, on this occasion this part of the usual Budget Speech was "taken as read". I had, however, prepared the usual analysis, and this was incorporated in the official report of my Budget Speech.

When I entered the Chamber after seven weeks' absence I met with an extremely kind reception from all Parties. I got through my speech without feeling the least physical effect; indeed, all the newspapers remarked upon this. They all said that I looked better than I had done for a long time. One newspaper, commenting on this, said that when I took my spectacles out of the case I closed it with a snap which was heard all over the Chamber, and which seemed to say "Of course I am all right! What's all this about?" The House was unusually crowded, even for a Budget Day, the side galleries being thronged with members who could find no seats on the benches on the floor of the House, while every available place in the Peers', the Distinguished Strangers', and the Ladies' and Public Galleries was occupied.

The previous financial year had ended with a deficit of £23,276,000, instead of an estimated surplus of £2,236,000. Revenue had fallen short of the estimates by £13,550,000, and expenditure had exceeded the estimates by £11,962,000. This was a better result than I had expected some months before. The effects of the trade depression on the revenue did not for some time show itself fully, as Income-Tax and Surtax are assessed upon incomes of previous years, and new expenditure does not usually mature until the following year's Budget.

On these estimates of income and expenditure for the current year I had a prospective deficit of £37,366,000. This was sufficiently appalling, and the only consolation to be derived from it was that it was not so bad as at one time I had feared.

Having arrived at this figure, the problem that faced me was how to meet this deficit and to balance the Budget. As I had stated in my speech in the Economy Debate I was anxious, if at all possible, to avoid increasing taxation this year. In the previous year I raised the Income-Tax from 4s. to 4s. 6d., increased the rates of Surtax and of Estate Duties, and raised the Beer Duty. The state of trade was now so bad (the figures of the unemployed had risen to 2,600,000) that I must avoid a further increase of taxation, and in preparing the Budget I turned my attention to finding ways and means by which the deficit might be met without any further burdens upon the tax-payers. There was in existence a fund known as the Exchange Account, consisting of £33,000,000 advanced from votes of credits during the War. It had been used as a fund for the purchase of dollar currency for the payment of our debt to America in advance of payment at a time when the market was most favourable. This fund was now hardly necessary owing to the establishment of the Bank of International Settlements. From this fund I took £20,000,000.

Some years previously an arrangement had been made by which Income-Tax was paid in two equal half-yearly instalments in January and July. This was a concession to the tax-payers at the expense of the Exchequer. I had never been quite convinced of the fairness to the Exchequer of this arrangement, though, no doubt, it was a great convenience to the tax-payers. So I made a change by requiring that three-quarters of the Income-Tax instead of half should be paid in January, and the remaining quarter in July. This alteration would give an additional sum of £10,000,000 for the current year's revenue. I was still left with a deficit of £7,500,000, and this I wiped off by an increase in the Petrol Duty from 4d. to 6d. per gallon. This was the simple way in which I balanced the Budget.

The Budget on the whole had a favourable reception. That was probably due more to a feeling of relief that I had been able to avoid the imposition of heavy additional taxation than to the merits of the Budget itself. In view of the well-known financial position of the country, a large addition to direct taxation had been generally expected. After the feeling of relief had worn off there was some criticism that I had not followed up in this Budget the statement that I had made in February as to the need for a reduction of National Expenditure, and imposed the sacrifices which I had then suggested would be necessary if the budgetary position was to be placed permanently upon a sound foundation.

That criticism missed altogether the motive I had in producing what I admitted was a "stop-gap" Budget. It would have been quite impossible at that time to get the support of the House of Commons to drastic reductions of expenditure and to the imposition of heavy additional taxation. The question of National Expenditure had been remitted to the May Committee which was then at work, and I had no alternative but to await the Report of that Committee, when I should have its authority for proposing reductions of expenditure. I anticipated then that when the Report of this Economy Committee was made a second Budget in the autumn would become necessary. The methods by which I had managed to balance the Budget I admitted could not, perhaps, be defended by the canons of financial orthodoxy, but they could be justified as legitimate devices in those times of financial stringency, so long as they were recognised to be devices of a temporary nature.

At the time the Budget was disclosed this was the impression that was made upon the House, and it was described as an eminently sensible piece of work.

Chapter Thirty-One

Waiting for Dead Men's Shoes

I now turn to describe some incidents of the summer of 1931. The conversations between the Liberal leaders and ourselves on the subject of Parliamentary co-operation were resumed, and we met in the Prime Minister's room at the House of Commons to consider plans to that end. The Liberals were usually represented by Mr. Lloyd George, Lord Lothian, Sir Herbert Samuel and Sir Archibald Sinclair. During June and July of 1931 these meetings were held often. The Liberals were really anxious that the Labour Government should be kept in office until the Electoral Reform Bill had become law by the operation of the provisions of the Parliament Act.

For about twelve months there had been renewed activity among Free Traders. My wife, who was keenly interested in the subject, had arranged a number of luncheons at Downing Street which were attended by prominent Free Traders belonging to all political Parties. At these gatherings plans were discussed for a popular and widespread Press and platform campaign on the question.

At one of our meetings in the Prime Minister's room with Mr. Lloyd George and his friends, he suggested a wider co-operation between the two Parties, and proposed that we might agree upon a joint propaganda on a Free Trade programme. This was further discussed at subsequent meetings, and it was agreed that a small joint Committee should be appointed with two experts, one selected by each Party, to draw up a programme and to prepare literature on the subject.

Mr. Lloyd George suggested that this campaign might begin in the coming autumn with a public demonstration at which the leaders of the two Parties would appear together, and I suggested that the Prime Minister and Mr. Thomas should be the Labour Party spokesmen at this demonstration. I am afraid this was a bit of irony upon my part, for at that time I knew that both Mr. MacDonald and Mr. Thomas were inclined towards tariffs. However, this plan fell through. The national financial crisis became acute in August, and the political developments which quickly followed transformed the political situation.

In the latter part of the summer of 1930 it had come to my knowledge that Mr. MacDonald's mind was turned towards Protection. The first indication I had was a casual remark he made to me when we were sitting on the bench. He turned to me and said: "I have been thinking how we can win a clear majority at the next General Election. I would have just a three-point programme:

No reduction in the Social Services;
A forward programme on Unemployment;
A 10 per cent all-round Revenue Tariff."

I simply replied "Oh!" and the conversation was not pursued. About the same time, however, I found out from what was told to me that he was canvassing Cabinet Ministers as to their views about a tariff, and giving as a reason that the financial position was likely to be so bad next year that the choice would be between a heavy increase in direct taxation and a revenue tariff. Mr. Thomas, who was usually in the confidence of the Prime Minister, and who had always had leanings towards Protection, was supporting the Prime Minister in this matter.

From the beginning of May until July 1931 there was a sustained Press campaign against me inspired by a section of the Labour Party and encouraged by some of its leaders. Unfounded reports were constantly being circulated about the state of my health, and it was assumed that I should not be able to continue to hold my office as Chancellor of the Exchequer. Rumours appeared in the Press about divisions in the Cabinet, and I was always represented as "the devil in the machine". I was held by some to be the obstacle to the Cabinet pursuing a more socialistic policy, and by others to be preventing the Government from embarking upon a Protectionist policy. Mr. MacDonald at the same time was the victim of intrigues by a small disgruntled section of the Labour Party who were disappointed because they had not been given office in the Government. They were endeavouring to supplant Mr. MacDonald by Mr. Henderson, although I doubt if Mr. Henderson was a party to this intrigue. In anticipation of my resignation of the post of Chancellor some of my Cabinet colleagues were pressing Mr. MacDonald to give them the reversion of my office. Mr. MacDonald told me that Mr. Thomas was pressing him persistently to give him that office when it became vacant. Mr. Thomas has some good qualities, and I always liked him, but the last position for which he is fitted is that of Chancellor of the Exchequer! The one man in the Government who had qualifications to succeed to the office of Chancellor was Mr. William Graham. But he was too modest and retiring to press his own claims.

At this time the "Big Five" of the Labour Party - the Prime Minister, Henderson, Thomas, Clynes and myself - were in the habit of meeting once a week in the Prime Minister's room for a general conversation about the Parliamentary situation and the state of the Labour Party generally. At one of these meetings in May, Mr. Henderson startled us by announcing that he wanted to resign his seat and go to the House of Lords. He gave as a reason the state of his health. We assumed that he wished to retain his office as Foreign Secretary, but he was not very definite on this point. We were strongly opposed to Mr. Henderson taking the step he desired. If he went to the House of Lords a by-election at Burnley would follow, and at that time the by-elections were going against the Government, and in all probability the seat would be lost. Mr. Henderson took the opposite view, and expressed his confidence that there would be no difficulty in holding the seat for Labour. We pointed out to him that the action he proposed would make a bad impression on the Labour movement generally, and particularly in Burnley where the Labour Party would resent being put to the turmoil and expense of an unnecessary by-election. Notwithstanding the opposition to his desire to go to the House of Lords at once, he raised the question again at our meeting the following week, but when he got no support he did not press his wishes any further.

But at this second meeting the real reason for Mr. Henderson's sudden desire to go to the House of Lords transpired. Lord Parmoor, who was the Leader of the Labour Party in the Upper House, was anxious to retire from that arduous position, and this had come to Mr. Henderson's knowledge. He wanted to go to the House of Lords to succeed Lord Parmoor as Leader of the Labour Party there. Mr. Henderson had urged that the reason he wanted to go to the House of Lords was that he found the strain of the House of Commons too great.

There was really nothing in this, as Mr. Henderson had never taken an active part in the work of the House of Commons; neither in opposition nor in office had he ever helped us in the rough and tumble of Parliamentary debates. Mr. Henderson has never been a Parliamentarian. His heart has been in the work of the organisation of the Labour Party. As Foreign Minister he had to answer questions on one or two days a week in the House of Commons, and occasionally to speak in debate when some question connected with his Department was raised. On these occasions he read his statement from a brief. Whenever we asked him to help the Government in a general debate he always had the excuse that he was recovering from an attack of influenza, or he could feel an attack coming upon him. I could never understand Mr. Henderson's reluctance to take a more active part in the Parliamentary debates. It was not that he was incapable of extempore speaking, for I have heard him on many occasions in Labour Party Conferences speak on the spur of the moment with great effect. In recent years he has got into the unfortunate habit when he has a set speech to make of reading it word for word from a typed memorandum. This practice is calculated to destroy one's confidence in speaking from notes only, and it certainly lessens the effectiveness of the speech.

In the course of the talk upon Henderson's peerage, one of my colleagues asked what were my intentions in regard to the future of my own position. I had never before to anyone disclosed a decision which I had definitely reached at the time of the last General Election. I had made up my mind that I should not seek re-election. I felt that after forty years of active political work I was entitled to a quieter life. So when pressed I told my colleagues of this intention. Even if before the end of the present Parliament I gave up the office of Chancellor I did not intend to retire from the House of Commons until the General Election. I was quite willing to retire into the freedom and ease of a private member's life, but if my colleagues wished me in the event of my resigning the Chancellorship to continue in the Government to the end of this Parliament in a less arduous office I should be willing to consider such a suggestion.

And now Lord Passfield (Mr. Sidney Webb) and Mrs. Webb come upon the scene. They came over to Tilford one Sunday afternoon in May (they lived only twenty minutes' drive from us), and Mrs. Webb explained the purpose of their visit. She and Sidney, she told me, had been talking matters over, and they had come to the conclusion that I should resign my present office and go to the House of Lords. Sidney was very anxious to resign his office as Colonial Secretary as soon as arrangements could be made for a successor.

He would be willing to continue until the end of the present session, though he would like to be relieved earlier if I would fall in with the suggestion. The office of Colonial Secretary, he said, was a very easy job, and would be far less exacting than the post I then held. He said that the Labour Party in the Lords needed an accession of strength, and as Lord Parmoor had then intimated his intention to give up the leadership of the Party in that Chamber, if I agreed to resign at once I could succeed him in the leadership. That position had no attractions for me; neither had the prospect of going to the House of Lords. If I did resign the Chancellorship I should have no objection to taking his office as Colonial Secretary until the end of the present Parliament, continuing to sit in the House of Commons. I explained to Lord Passfield and Mrs. Webb that it was quite out of the question for me to resign until I had got certain work through. I was very anxious to retain the Chancellorship until I had been able to carry out the conversion of the huge block of £2,000,000,000 of 5 per cent War Loan. I had set my heart upon this. I had a complete scheme ready, but unfortunately owing to the financial position of the country the prospects of the success of such a conversion operation were not then very promising.

This suggestion by Lord Passfield was, I am sure, entirely free of even a suspicion of Party intrigue, and was prompted solely by his desire to get out of office, and at the same time, if I did intend to resign the Chancellorship, to provide me with the opportunity to continue in the Government in a less arduous position.

Chapter Thirty-Two

The Story of the Crisis

By the end of July 1931 the financial situation was beginning to assume a very serious aspect. In financial circles it was the one topic of conversation. Gold and foreign deposits in London were being withdrawn at a rate which threatened the stability of our national financial position. On the 31st July the House of Commons was to rise for the Summer Recess. The day before, Mr. Neville Chamberlain came into my room and said that he intended next day in the debate on the adjournment to speak upon the situation, but he was very anxious to say nothing which would have a disturbing effect. He was well aware of the actual financial situation, and he would make a non-partisan speech and would avoid putting any questions to me which might place me in an embarrassing position. He was anxious to be helpful, and he thought it might be well if I could make a reply to him which would impress the country with the gravity of the situation without causing a panic. I gave him a full account of the information in my possession. We agreed upon the general line that he would take in his speech, and I promised to follow with a speech which would raise the discussion above Party controversy.

Mr. Chamberlain's speech next day was singularly free from the slightest spirit of partisanship. It was couched in language which showed that his desire was not to secure a Party triumph, but how best to serve the interests of the country.

When Mr. Chamberlain sat down I rose at once, and expressed my gratitude for the spirit of his speech. I was fully aware of the difficulty of dealing publicly with the acute financial position of the country, for this was a time when a lightly spoken word or even a wrongly turned sentence might have serious consequences. Investors were naturally nervous, and the slightest suspicion regarding the non-security of their investments was apt to lead them to adopt a course which was not justified by the actual facts. Foreign credits were held in London to the extent of probably many hundreds of millions of money, and recent events had shown that serious consequences might rise through even an indefinite rumour. I then went on to examine the budgetary position, which was getting progressively worse owing to the deepening of the industrial depression. Unless very considerable economies could be effected, the outlook was indeed very grave. That day I had received the Report of the May Economy Committee. It would be published next day, and I was afraid it would come as a shock to the country. I could assure Mr. Chamberlain and the House that the Government would at once take this Report into consideration. I reminded members that the House of Commons had a special responsibility for the Report of this Committee. This Committee had been set up by the House of Commons. No Government, and especially a Government like our own, which did not command a majority of its own in the House, could expect to carry through drastic reductions of expenditure without the co-operation of all other Parties. The responsibility for carrying out any recommendations which the Government would submit in October must be assumed by the House of Commons as a whole.

I said the position of London is fundamentally sound. It still remains the best market in the world for foreign investors, and so far as I and the Government are concerned we shall take every possible step to ensure that the proud and sound position of British credit shall in no way be impaired.

This speech, delivered in a quiet, almost conversational tone, made a profound impression upon the members. Although it was the last day of the summer session, when members were anxious to get away on their holidays, the Chamber was crowded. It sent members away in anything but a holiday mood, and the general feeling of depression was increased next day when the Report of the Economy Committee was issued.

My references to the responsibility of all Parties for dealing with the crisis, and my invitation to the Opposition Parties to co-operate, were regarded in many quarters as an invitation to form a National Government to tide over the financial crisis. Such an idea was not in my mind. My remark simply stated the obvious fact that it would be impossible for a Minority Government to carry proposals for the drastic reduction of expenditure if the Opposition were to pursue Party tactics and endeavour to make Party capital out of unpopular proposals. I realised at the time that we should very likely have to face the opposition of a section of our own Party in carrying through economy schemes.

The Labour Party, or at least a section of them, had lived so long in the belief that the only function of a Labour Government was to spend money that they would not be likely to be reconciled to the opposite policy. There was not at that time the least likelihood that the Conservatives would consider the setting up of a National Government. Only a fortnight before, Mr. Baldwin had referred to this question in a public speech, and had pointed out that the insuperable objection to the Conservatives co-operating with men of other Parties was that the Conservatives believed that the restoration of prosperity could only be achieved by the protection of the home market and the development of the imperial market. He was prepared to co-operate gladly with men to whatever Party they belonged if they would agree to a policy aimed at that object.

My idea of the political future at the end of July was that when we met in the autumn and submitted our economy proposals we could count upon the support of the Conservatives and the Liberals, and the reluctant support of the majority of our own Party, though the Conservatives would probably regard our proposals as inadequate and endeavour to secure more drastic reductions of expenditure.

At the close of the sitting of the House which I have been describing, I asked the Prime Minister to call such members of the Cabinet as might be available into his room as I wanted to make known to them in brief the nature of the May Economy Report which I had just received. At this meeting an Economy Committee of the Cabinet was set up which consisted of MacDonald, Henderson, Thomas, Graham and myself. The importance of taking immediate action on the recommendations of this Committee was realised, and it was decided that the members of the Economy Committee should come back to London on 25th August and be prepared for days of continuous sittings. Meanwhile, each of the Government Departments which would be affected by the recommendations of the May Committee Report were to thoroughly examine the recommendations and to submit the results of their examination to the Treasury not later than the 18th August. This would give the members of the Cabinet Economy Committee a week before they met to examine these reports.

I had better now set out the main recommendations of the May Economy Committee. The Committee had construed its terms of reference very widely, and had gone very exhaustively into the budgetary position. After examining the prospective expenditure next year and estimating the probable revenue, including the usual provision for the reduction of debt, the Committee came to the conclusion that there would be a sum of £120,000,000 to be made good next April, either by severe taxation or by economy. On this basis the May Committee had proceeded to make recommendations for economy by reduction of expenditure. They made recommendations which would reduce expenditure by over £96,000,000. The remainder of the estimated deficit, amounting to £24,000,000, would have to be met by increased taxation. Over £80,000,000 of savings the Committee recommended would be obtained by a reduction of the expenditure on social services.

With regard to the Unemployment benefits, I may mention that at the same time a Royal Commission on Unemployment Insurance was sitting, and this Commission had presented an interim report two months before the May Committee reported. The May Committee had the advantage of considering the recommendations of this Unemployment Commission, which had proposed to reduce Unemployment benefits for adults by 2s. a week, but the May Committee proposed a rather smaller reduction.

It will be seen that the recommendations of the May Committee had given the Cabinet Economy Committee a hard task. I took no holiday, but remained in close touch with the Treasury and the Bank of England during the succeeding weeks. Within a week, however, of the publication of the May Report the financial situation had become so bad that a meeting of the Cabinet Economy Committee became urgently necessary. The first effect upon foreign opinion of the publication of the May Report and its exposure of the budgetary position estimating the deficit of £120,000,000 had been to increase the nervousness among the foreign owners of deposits in this country. The Bank of England was losing gold and foreign exchange very heavily, and day by day the withdrawals increased at an alarming rate. It was clear that if this continued the point of exhaustion would come very soon, with disastrous consequences.

The root cause of this withdrawal of gold and foreign capital was understood to be the belief of the foreigners that our budgetary position was unsound, and that until that was remedied, or until there was evidence that we were taking drastic steps to set it right, this uneasiness abroad would continue. The foreigners did not appear to realise that the budgetary position in this country taken at its worst was much better than their own, for at that time, with one exception, all the foreign countries and the Dominions had proportionately much heavier Budget deficits than we had. Whatever the foundation for this impression abroad might be, there was no doubt about its reality. The efforts of the Bank of England in arranging a £50,000,000 credit through the three Central Banks had not had the desired effect.

When the facts of the large foreign withdrawals of gold and foreign exchange came to my knowledge I felt that we could not wait until the date we had fixed for the meeting of the Cabinet Economy Committee on the 25th August. The collapse was almost certain to come before then if we delayed. So on the 7th August I sent an urgent communication to the Prime Minister (who was at Lossiemouth), and put before him a statement of the serious position, and suggested that he should try to get the Cabinet Economy Committee together as soon as possible. He came back to London at once, travelling overnight, and on his arrival the two of us spent most of the day considering the situation and interviewing a number of representative bankers who were called in to a consultation.

Immediately upon receipt of my communication, Mr. MacDonald had given instructions that the members of the Cabinet Economy Committee should be called from their holidays, and the first meeting of the Committee was held on 12th August. Our conversations were continued the following day, and we decided that next year's Budget must be balanced, that every section of the community must make proportionate sacrifices. At the time Mr. MacDonald summoned the Cabinet Economy Committee he communicated with Mr. Baldwin, Mr. Neville Chamberlain and Sir Herbert Samuel. Mr. Baldwin, who was having a holiday at Aix, immediately responded to Mr. MacDonald's request, and Mr. Neville Chamberlain interrupted his fishing holiday in Scotland to meet us in London, and Sir Herbert Samuel also returned from holiday for the purpose.

These three leaders of the Opposition Parties all showed a willingness to be helpful in this crisis, and promised to be available for any further consultations which we might desire. Mr. MacDonald returned to Scotland after these meetings of the Cabinet Economy Committee and these interviews with the Opposition leaders, but three days later came back to London for further sessions of the Cabinet Economy Committee. From that day onward meetings of the Cabinet Economy Committee, of the Cabinet as a whole, and conversations with the leaders of other Parties, kept some of us at work from early morning till late at night. What happened as the outcome of these meetings has been related in inspired newspaper reports, in speeches in the country, and in debates in the House of Commons by individuals who, more or less, took part in them. Of the members of the Labour Cabinet, Mr. MacDonald and myself were the only two who were present at all these gatherings. We conducted the conversations with the leaders of the other Parties, and reported the results of these conversations to our Cabinet colleagues. I will deal with what happened at these meetings only in so far as to give the correct version of the numerous accounts which had been made public.

As soon as the Report of the May Committee was received, I instructed the Treasury officials to go into the budgetary position with the utmost care, and to submit to me a balance-sheet of the estimated Income and Expenditure for the current financial year which would end on the 31st March 1932, and a similar statement for the following year – that is, from the 1st April 1932 to the end of March 1933.

This examination gave appalling results. Assuming that borrowing for the Unemployment Insurance payments and for the Road Fund ceased and were met out of revenue, the estimated deficit for the current year amounted to £74,679,000, and for the following year to the colossal figure of £170,000,000. This figure of £170,000,000 represented the problem the Government had to solve. This deficit would have to be met by economies and by increased taxation.

The Cabinet Economy Committee submitted to the Cabinet a first draft of economy proposals which amounted to a sum of £78,500,000. Of this sum £50,000,000 was in relation to Unemployment. But it must be understood that these were only tentative proposals suggested for consideration, and they included no cuts in the standard rates of Unemployment allowances. All these suggestions were not strictly economies. The £50,000,000 in relation to Unemployment included a sum of £10,000,000 which represented increases in the premiums of insurance paid by employers and workers. This Report from the Cabinet Economy Committee was considered by the Cabinet on the 19th August. This meeting of the Cabinet lasted for nine hours, after which the Press announced that a set of figures had been agreed upon which would provide for balancing the Budget. This statement was not strictly correct. There was a provisional agreement on economies which amounted to £56,250,000;

and ways and means of increasing this figure by a saving of £20,000,000 on Transitional Benefit was left over for further consideration.

On the following morning, in accordance with instructions from the Cabinet, Mr. MacDonald and I met the Opposition leaders. Mr. Baldwin was away on holiday, and his place was taken by Sir Samuel Hoare. The Opposition leaders at this Conference were Sir Herbert Samuel, Sir Donald Maclean, Mr. Neville Chamberlain and Sir Samuel Hoare. We put before them a full and frank statement of the budgetary position, and when we disclosed to them the figures I have just given of the appalling extent of the deficit for the current year and the following year, they were naturally staggered. The Conference adjourned to allow the Opposition leaders time for the consideration of our economy suggestions. It was agreed that we should meet again next day to hear their views on the tentative economy proposals we had laid before them. In the meantime the Cabinet sat in the morning and the afternoon, and the figures which we had put before the Opposition leaders on the previous day were considerably modified.

When we met the Opposition leaders after the Cabinet meeting we had to report to them that in regard to Unemployment the Cabinet had rejected the proposal of the Cabinet Committee, and instead of being £50,000,000 it was reduced to £22,000,000. Of that sum of £22,000,000, £14,000,000 was not an economy at all, but really additional taxation. There was to be a contribution of £10,000,000 from employers and employed, and there was also to be a levy for the Unemployment Insurance Fund of 2d. a week from those who were working. This levy was expected to yield £4,000,000. The effect of the increased contribution from employers and the workpeople and from the 2d. levy left only £8,000,000 of real savings on the Unemployment expenditure, and of that sum £3,000,000 had already been decided upon under the Anomalies Act which had been passed by Parliament. The new savings on Unemployment would, therefore, amount only to £5,000,000, and this sum was to be obtained by imposing a Means Test for Transitional Benefit. The paltry character of this economy will be realised when I mention that the estimated cost of Unemployment in the following year would amount to £119,000,000.

The Opposition leaders, after considering the proposals we had submitted to them the previous day for a total of economies amounting to £78,500,000, had been prepared to accept them as a very bold scheme and a courageous attempt to grapple with the realities of the situation. The modified statement which we had to submit to them that afternoon was not regarded as being satisfactory. It would have left about £120,000,000 to be raised by additional taxation. They regarded these proposals as altogether inadequate, and they told us that in their opinion Parliament would take the same view.

On the suggestion of Mr. Henderson, the Cabinet Economy Committee met the General Council of the Trade Union Congress, the Executive of the Labour Party, and the Consultative Committee of the Parliamentary Labour Party on the afternoon of 20th August. At that time it will be remembered the Cabinet had agreed provisionally to economies amounting to £56,000,000, but had declined to make a cut in the Unemployment allowances. I went to this meeting with the Trade Union Congress Committee with great reluctance. I had never recognised the right of the Trade Union Congress Committee to be consulted on matters of Cabinet policy. I went to this meeting, however, because, in addition to the Trade Union Congress Committee, there were present representatives of the Labour Party Executive and of the Parliamentary Labour Party. I put before this meeting a statement of the economies on which the Cabinet had already agreed, but pointed out that at present they had not decided upon a reduction in the Unemployment allowances. That statement of mine was construed by the meeting as a definite decision of the Cabinet not to make any reduction in the Unemployment payments.

That, however, was not my intention. There was a division of opinion in the Cabinet on that question, and I did not regard the matter as having been finally closed. As a matter of fact, there was a small majority in the Cabinet favourable to a reduction in the Unemployment allowances. This was disclosed at the time in the *Daily Herald*, the organ of the Labour Party, in full detail, with the names of the Ministers who took the one view or the other. My statement to this joint Conference simply amounted to this, that at that time the Cabinet had not included any reduction of Unemployment allowances in their economy proposals, but the Cabinet did on the following days reconsider seriously the possibility of increasing the total of the economies by a 10 per cent reduction in the Unemployment benefits.

Mr. MacDonald and myself were instructed to meet the Opposition leaders, and to ask them, without a definite commitment, what their attitude would be if the Cabinet agreed to a reduction in the Unemployment allowances which was estimated would yield £12,250,000, which would bring the total of the relief to the Budget up to £68,500,000. The Opposition leaders told us that if we could submit a definite proposal to that effect they might consider if it would be regarded as adequate. As a matter of fact, that figure of £68,500,000 was within £2,000,000 of the total economies which were proposed to Parliament by the National Government when they took office.

To turn back to the meeting with the Trade Union and Labour representatives. After we had left this meeting the Trade Union Congress Committee discussed the statement we had put before them, and late that evening they sought an interview with the representatives of the Cabinet. Mr. MacDonald and I received them. The spokesman of the Trade Unions were Mr. Bevin and Mr. Citrine, the Secretary of the Trade Union Committee. This deputation took up the attitude of opposition to practically all the economy proposals which had been explained to them. They opposed any interference with the existing terms and conditions of the Unemployment Insurance Scheme, including the limitation of statutory benefit to 26 weeks. We were told that the Trade Unions would oppose the suggested economies on teachers' salaries and pay of the men in the Fighting Services, and any suggestions for reducing expenditure on works in relief of unemployment.

The only proposal to which the General Council were not completely opposed was that the salaries of Ministers and Judges should be subjected to a cut! They were of opinion that no economies were needed, and all the revenue that was necessary could be obtained by additional direct taxation and the suspension of the Sinking Fund! The deputation showed no appreciation of the seriousness of the situation; their statements appeared to be based upon a pre-crisis mentality; and the objections they raised to the proposals were those which members of the Cabinet would have taken had the national financial circumstances been prosperous. I replied to all the points they raised at some length, but we had to realise that the Trade Union General Council were not prepared to play their part in the existing crisis, nor to accept even the scheme of economies which had already been provisionally agreed to by the Cabinet.

Chapter Thirty-Three

The Story Continued

During the succeeding three days, that is, from Thursday 20th August to Sunday 23rd August, Mr. MacDonald and I, with the consent of the Cabinet, had frequent interviews with the leaders of the Opposition. They maintained their attitude that if the Government could not go beyond the figure of £56,250,000 as the total of their economies, they would feel compelled to call for an early meeting of the House of Commons, when they would unite and defeat the Government. Faced with this probability, the Cabinet turned its attention to seeking whether something more could be done. I ought to add that the Opposition leaders were wholly dissatisfied with the proposals of the Cabinet for reducing the cost of the Unemployment payments. The Cabinet, therefore, turned its attention to seeing what could be done to meet the demands of the Opposition leaders on this matter. There was, as I have said, an almost equal division of opinion in the Cabinet on the question of a reduction in the Unemployment benefits.

It was, therefore, decided that Mr. MacDonald and myself should be empowered to submit tentatively to the Opposition leaders a suggestion that if we could increase the economies by £20,000,000, namely, £12,500,000 from the Unemployment Grants and £7,500,000 from other sources, they would regard that as satisfactory. We were placed in a difficult position in making this suggestion, because we had no assurance that if it were accepted by the Opposition leaders the Cabinet would agree to do it. However, we put the proposal before them, and we received the impression that if this could be done they would regard the total of our economies as satisfactory. But they urged that this was a matter upon which the bankers should be consulted, and if they were satisfied the Opposition leaders would raise no further objection.

This brings me to the position of the bankers in this crisis. The financial position was daily getting worse. A collapse of credit was imminent, and this would have had a disastrous effect. So much has been said about the dictatorship of the bankers that it is only fair to them to state clearly what their attitude was throughout all these negotiations. In order to fight the financial crisis, the Bank of England was endeavouring to raise a credit of £80,000,000, half of which would be raised in New York and the other half in Paris. The Federal Reserve Bank of New York and the Central Bank in Paris had throughout shown a sympathetic attitude to the financial difficulties in which Great Britain was placed. They had already granted credits for a sum of £50,000,000, and these credits were exhausted. Both New York and Paris were quite ready to grant a further credit of £80,000,000 provided satisfactory assurances for the security of the advances could be given. In fact, the Federal Reserve Bank of New York and the Central Bank of France had issued on their own initiative a reassuring statement as to the British Government's intentions to rehabilitate the national financial position.

Contrary to reports which were circulated that the present crisis was due to a conspiracy on the part of the bankers, the fact was that throughout the banks had shown great willingness to render financial assistance to the Government. All that the foreign banks had insisted upon was that they should be reasonably sure of the security for the advances they were ready to make. The representatives of the Bank of England made it quite clear that if the economies of £56,000,000 represented the Government's final word, the scheme would be of no value in restoring foreign confidence. They pointed out quite truly that an analysis of that figure showed that the real savings in the expenditure amounted only to about £42,000,000, the remainder being further taxation upon the employers and work-people. Mr. MacDonald and I put before the bankers the suggestion we had made to the Opposition leaders with the consent of the Cabinet that the total economies might be increased by £20,000,000 from the figure of £56,000,000 previously accepted. They thought that if this could be done it might satisfy New York, and the credits sought would be granted. I elaborate this matter because it was upon this that the Labour Government was finally broken up.

A proposal had been strongly pressed from certain quarters that the Budget might be balanced by a suspension of the Sinking Fund. To this I was strongly opposed, because I could not agree to a proposal which was a mere subterfuge to hide the true financial position. A further suggestion was pressed very strongly that we might have recourse to a 10 per cent revenue tariff. A 10 per cent revenue tariff on certain imported manufactures would, we were told, yield £20,000,000, and a further 10 per cent on food at present untaxed would probably yield a further £25,000,000.

On Saturday, the 22nd August, the situation was hectic. The Bank of England submitted to Mr. Harrison, the President of the New York Federal Reserve Bank, the tentative suggestion of a reduction of 10 per cent in Unemployment payments, and £7,000,000 from other sources. Mr. Harrison replied by telephone that, while he was not in a position to give the answer until he had consulted his financial associates, his opinion was that it would give satisfactory assurance, and the credits would be forthcoming. The reply of Mr. Harrison to the enquiry from the Bank of England after he had consulted the financial interests in New York was quite satisfactory. He said that if the proposals approved by the Bank of England were likely to receive a favourable response from public opinion in Great Britain that would be regarded as satisfactory, and there would be no further difficulty in raising the required credits in New York, and the French market would probably raise an equivalent amount.

When this opinion reached us the Cabinet was called upon to make a crucial decision. This decisive meeting of the Cabinet was held at seven o'clock on Sunday, the 23rd August. The split in the Labour Cabinet took place because unanimity could not be reached on the proposal to reduce Unemployment pay by 10 per cent. The May Committee had recommended a cut of 20 per cent. It may be mentioned that after a 10 per cent cut in Unemployment pay the recipients of these payments would be in a better position than they were under the Labour Government of 1924 when there were abounding Budget surpluses. There had been in the meantime a fall in the cost of living which was equivalent to a 30 per cent increase in the purchasing power of these benefits.

When this final test came the Cabinet would not agree to implement the authority they had given to Mr. MacDonald and myself to submit to the Opposition leaders and the bankers the suggestion for £20,000,000 further economies which would include a reduction of 10 per cent in Unemployment payments. A small majority of the Cabinet (and this became public property later) were in favour of these further economies, but as we could not have carried a united Cabinet in adopting them, and half the Cabinet would have resigned, the break-up of the Labour Government was inevitable. A cut in the Unemployment pay was repugnant to us all, but we had no choice in the matter.

Chapter Thirty-Four

The Formation of the National Government

When this final disagreement occurred it was evident that the Prime Minister had anticipated such a development, and had made his plans to deal with it. He asked the members of the Cabinet to place their resignations in his hands. This was done, and the Prime Minister immediately left the meeting to seek an audience with the King to acquaint him with the position, and to advise His Majesty to hold a conference with Mr. Baldwin, Sir Herbert Samuel and himself next morning. The Cabinet agreed to this course. Mr. MacDonald left at 10.p.m., and the members of the Cabinet remained in the room to await his return. He came back at 10.40, and told us that His Majesty had accepted his advice to meet Mr. Baldwin, Sir Herbert Samuel and himself next morning at 10 o'clock.

The Prime Minister, quite properly, had kept the King fully informed of the conversations with the Opposition leaders and of the difficulties within the Labour Cabinet. During the week before the resignation of the Labour Government the King had left Sandringham for Balmoral, but on the Saturday before the resignation of the Government the Prime Minister informed His Majesty of the critical situation, and that probably a change of Government might become necessary. His Majesty at once returned to London, and arrived there at eight o'clock on Sunday morning.

Two hours after the arrival of the King from Balmoral, Mr. MacDonald had an audience with him at the Palace, and after this interview a statement was issued from 10 Downing Street, which read: "On the Prime Minister's advice the King has asked Mr. Baldwin and Sir Herbert Samuel to see him, because His Majesty wishes to hear from them themselves what the position of their respective Parties is."

In accordance with this statement, Sir Herbert Samuel and Mr. Baldwin had, separately, audiences with the King that Sunday afternoon.

That evening the fateful Cabinet Meeting was held when the resignation of the Labour Cabinet was agreed upon.

What took place at the meeting with the King and the three Party leaders at the Palace at ten o'clock on Monday morning I do not know beyond what was reported to us by Mr. MacDonald on his return. A meeting of the Labour Cabinet was called for twelve o'clock noon (24th August), and to this meeting Mr. MacDonald reported that it had been decided to form a Government of individuals whose task would be confined to dealing with the financial emergency. Mr. Baldwin and Sir Herbert Samuel were prepared to join such a Government, with Mr. MacDonald as Prime Minister.

The resignations of the Labour Ministers had already been given to Mr. MacDonald, and it was agreed that he should place them in the hands of the King that afternoon.

The developments from that Monday morning's audience with the King came to me quite unexpectedly. I left the Cabinet Meeting at 10.40 p.m. on the Sunday under the belief that the outcome of the resignation of the Labour Cabinet would be that Mr. Baldwin would be asked to form a Government, and with the help of the Liberals would carry through measures of economy and additional taxation which would balance the Budget and restore national stability. Whatever, at that time, may have been in Mr. MacDonald's mind as to a National Government with himself as Prime Minister he kept to himself, for at a meeting he had with the Opposition leaders at 11 p.m. on Sunday after his return from the Palace he gave them no hint of such a possible development. Mr. Neville Chamberlain, who was present at that meeting, stated publicly a few days later that he went to bed that night expecting that next day Mr. Baldwin would be called upon to form a Government.

Mr. MacDonald at the Palace meeting on the Monday morning agreed to the formation of a National Government, with himself as Prime Minister, without a word of previous consultation with any of his Labour colleagues. He knew he would have the great majority of the Labour Cabinet against him, and practically the whole of the Parliamentary Labour Party. He had, in fact, at that time, no assurance that he could take any of his late colleagues with him. Mr. Baldwin and Sir Herbert Samuel were in a different position. They could count confidently on carrying their Parties with them. Mr. MacDonald at the best could not hope to have the support of more than a mere handful of Labour members.

It was a very strange thing that Mr. MacDonald should have taken this grave step without informing some at least of his Labour colleagues of his intention. He did tell his Cabinet, as I have mentioned, that he intended to advise the King to call the Opposition leaders into consultation, but this was not understood either by them or the Labour Cabinet as the prelude to a National Government.

Mr. Baldwin and Sir Herbert Samuel at once called their supporters together to endorse their action, which they promptly did. Mr. MacDonald, on the other hand, never sought to meet the Labour Party. Two days after the formation of the National Government he sent a private letter to each Labour member of Parliament in which he stated the reasons for the resignation of the Labour Government and the formation of the National Government. This letter was not intended to be published, but some Labour member who received it must at once have handed it to the Press, for it appeared in the evening newspapers the same day.

A meeting of the Parliamentary Labour Party was held on 28th August. Mr. MacDonald did not attend it, nor did he send any message or appeal. This was naturally taken as an indication that he had finally separated himself from the Party and did not want its support. I do not know if Mr. MacDonald had an invitation to attend this meeting. I was not aware of it until after it had been held. Labour members have since complained that Mr. MacDonald and myself did not attend this meeting. Even had I known of it my presence would have been useless, for the day before the Trade Union Council and the Committee of the Parliamentary Labour Party had issued a public manifesto which made any change in their attitude to the National Government impossible. I deal with this manifesto later.

When the members of the Labour Cabinet were leaving after the Prime Minister's announcement that he had agreed to form a National Government, he asked me and Mr. Thomas and Lord Sankey to remain behind. We then had a frank conversation about the new situation which had so unexpectedly arisen. He asked us if we were prepared to join him in the Government which was to be formed. In view of my position as Chancellor of the Exchequer, and the exceptional responsibility I had for helping to get the country out of its difficulties, I felt that there was no other course open to me than to assist the new Government, provided I could get certain assurances as to its character and its purpose.

I had not the least expectation then of the developments which followed later. It never entered my mind that this meant the permanent separation from my former colleagues in the Labour Party. I expected that, though we had differed on what, after all, was a comparatively minor matter, we should be able to resume our former cooperation in the Labour Party when the emergency legislation had been passed.

These views as to the purpose of the National Government were publicly expressed at the time by Mr. MacDonald, Mr. Baldwin and Sir Herbert Samuel. The official statement issued from Downing Street the day the National Government was formed contained the following passage:

> "The specific job for which the new Government is being formed is to deal with the national emergency which now exists. It will not be a Coalition Government in the usual sense of the term, but a Government of co-operation for this one purpose When that purpose is achieved the political parties will resume their respective positions."

The following day in a broadcast address Mr. MacDonald repeated this view. He said:

> "It is not a Coalition Government. I will take no part in that. It is not a Government which compels any party to change its principles or to subordinate its individuality. I should take no part in that either. It is a Government of individuals, formed to do this work. If the work takes little time the life of the Government will be short. When that life is finished the work of the House of Commons and the general political situation will return to where it was last week, and those who have taken risks will receive either our punishment or our reward. The Election which will follow will not be fought by the Government. There will be no coupons, and, I hope, no illegitimate prejudices."

Mr. Baldwin, speaking at a Conservative meeting called to endorse the action of their leaders, repeated in substance what the Prime Minister had said in the quotations I have given. Sir Herbert Samuel, at a meeting of the Liberal members called for the same purpose, after stating that the leaders had the acquiescence of Mr. Lloyd George in the course they had taken (Mr. Lloyd George was ill at the time and had been unable to take part in the consultations with the Labour Cabinet), said:

> "This Government is a temporary combination, but in my own view it cannot abandon the task which it has undertaken until it has seen it well on the way to completion."

I had thrown in my lot with the National Government with considerable regret, but from a sense of duty. It was no pleasant experience to be separated, even if only temporarily, from old colleagues and from a Party with which I had been closely associated for nearly forty years. I did not then realise that later developments would exacerbate the relations between ourselves and our late colleagues, and lead to a permanent alienation.

On the 27th August a general manifesto was issued by the Trade Union Council, the National Executive of the Labour Party and the Consultative Committee of the Parliamentary Labour Party which removed any doubt I might have felt as to the wisdom of my action in joining the National Government. This manifesto was a shameful travesty of the facts which had led to the resignation of the Labour Government, and a gross misrepresentation of the purpose for which the National Government had been formed. This manifesto stated that the motives which impelled the National Government in its policy of drastic cuts in social expenditure were that this country was setting a bad example to other countries in taxing the rich to provide for the necessities of the poor; that Unemployment benefit was being attacked on the ground that it strengthens resistance to wage reductions; and that the new Government was an attempt to reverse the social policy which provided for the unemployed, the aged and the sick, the disabled, the orphaned and the widows.

This was the first indication of the line the Labour leaders were going to take in repudiating responsibility for economies to which the Labour Cabinet as a whole had agreed. This manifesto did much to change my views about the political honesty of my late Labour colleagues, and to make me doubt whether any future coming together would be possible.

As I have already said, I do not think that Mr. MacDonald felt any regret that the break with his Labour colleagues had come to pass, and later developments have amply confirmed this belief. The day after the National Government was formed he came into my room at Downing Street in very high spirits. I remarked to him that he would now find himself very popular in strange quarters. He replied, gleefully rubbing his hands: "Yes, to-morrow every Duchess in London will be wanting to kiss me!"

It is not for me to say what were the motives which had determined the majority of the late Labour Cabinet to take the course they did, but if I might venture to suggest a reason I should say that the opposition of the General Council of the Trade Union Congress was largely responsible for their action. Mr. Arthur Henderson had taken the line that a Labour Government should not carry through a policy in opposition to the views of the Trade Unions. It was a favourite saying of his that "we must take the Trade Union movement with us". Opposition to cuts in the Unemployment payments was given as the reason for their action, but at least half of the Labour Cabinet Ministers who now took up the attitude of opposition to the new Government had been willing, reluctantly I admit, to agree to this 10 per cent cut being included in the economy proposals.

At the time the Labour Cabinet broke up it was understood that a General Election would follow in the course of a few weeks, and I think it is true that the Labour Ministers were afraid to face the electors with a record of having reduced the Unemployment pay. From information which came to me, I understood that Mr. Henderson and his colleagues were confident that their action in declining to make a reduction in the Unemployment benefits would secure them a majority at the forthcoming Election. They argued that there were about three million unemployed voters, and these with their families and the Trade Union movement as a whole would vote solidly for the Labour Party. This belief showed how little they understood the national character, and how little they realised the force of the case which could be made against them.

My feelings and expectations at the time I joined the National Government could perhaps best be given by reproducing correspondence I had with the Chairman of the Labour Party in my constituency. The first of these letters was written late on the Saturday before the resignation of the Labour Government on the Monday. It was written then because of my expectation that the resignation of the Labour Government would be followed by the acceptance of office by Mr. Baldwin, and that a General Election would ensue. The following is a copy of the letter I addressed to the Chairman of the Divisional Labour Party in Colne Valley:

"11 DOWNING STREET, WHITEHALL, S.W.,1

"22nd August 1931.

"DEAR MR. HEYWOOD,

"I have intended ever since I recovered from my recent illness to inform you that it will not be possible for me to seek election to the next Parliament. Although I have had a remarkable recovery, I am compelled to realise that at my age (I am turned 67) I cannot expect to be able to continue the strenuous life I have lived for the last forty years. I must seek relief from the arduous work of the House of Commons with its long hours and late sittings.

"The political situation makes it necessary that I must, without further delay, convey my decision to you so that you may take steps to seek a new candidate.

"I need hardly add that I have reached this decision with great regret. I shall always remember with pleasure and gratitude my association with Colne Valley, and the confidence and consideration I have received from the constituency.

"Yours sincerely,
"PHILIP SNOWDEN."

Chapter Thirty-Five

The Emergency Budget

As the National Government had been formed for the specific purpose of dealing with the national emergency, it was considered desirable to have a small Cabinet consisting of ten persons. Four of the members of the late Labour Government - Mr. Thomas, Lord Sankey, Lord Amulree and myself - had followed Mr. MacDonald. Lord Amulree had held the office of Secretary for Air in the late Government since the tragic death of Lord Thomson, who was killed in the disaster to the R101 airship on its first trip in October 1930. Lord Amulree continued to hold office in the first National Government, though he was not a member of the Cabinet. Lord Sankey, Mr. Thomas and I retained the offices we had held in the Labour Government. The new Cabinet, as I have said, consisted of ten members, and of these four were Labour men, four were Conservatives and two were Liberals.

The new Cabinet got to work at once, and from its formation up to the meeting of Parliament a fortnight later daily meetings were held. One can never get a true appreciation of the character and qualities of political opponents from contact with them in Parliamentary controversy only. I had formed an opinion of Mr. Baldwin from this experience which was changed by closer association with him. I had regarded Mr. Baldwin as an honest man, by no means brilliant, but possessing a measure of common-sense, which is more useful in politics than mere intellectual gifts. My twelve months' association with him in the Cabinet gave me a high opinion of his personal character and of his general capacity. I came to understand the reason he was held in high regard by his Tory colleagues and by the Tory Party generally. In the Cabinet discussions he wasted no time on mere talk. He listened to what was being said, and at the conclusion of the discussion he summed up the issue in a brief but impressive speech.

It is more difficult to give an impression of Mr. Neville Chamberlain. We had been colleagues on the Liquor Control Board which had been set up during the War. He took little part in the discussions on this Board, and he seemed to me to be held back by a natural modesty. Both Mr. Neville Chamberlain and Mr. Baldwin are instances of men being associated with a political Party by the accident of birth and upbringing. Mr. Baldwin is essentially liberal in his outlook, and Mr. Neville Chamberlain's association with the Tory Party has not destroyed his passion for social reform which he inherited from his distinguished father. Before he entered Parliament he had made a local reputation for progressive ideas on municipal government. He once told me that he was not deterred from extending municipal and public enterprise because some people called it Socialism. His tenure of office as Minister of Health in the Tory Government of 1924–29 was the outstanding success of that Administration. Except upon the question of tariffs I had little occasion during the time I was associated with the National Government to disagree either with Mr. Baldwin or Mr. Neville Chamberlain, and I think I may say that the respect I felt for both of them was reciprocal.

The work of the first National Government was confined to preparing measures for dealing with the national crisis. By common agreement all controversial legislation was suspended. The Tory members of the Cabinet played the game. A small Committee, consisting of myself, Mr. Chamberlain, Sir Herbert Samuel and Lord Reading, was appointed to prepare a plan for the Emergency Budget, which must be submitted to Parliament as soon as it met. As an instance of the non-party spirit which animated the National Government in its early weeks I may perhaps be permitted to mention that, when I submitted to this Committee measures for raising additional revenue by taxation, Mr. Neville Chamberlain remarked: "I suppose that a revenue tariff is ruled out of consideration?" I answered that that was so, and Mr. Chamberlain replied: "I have nothing to say. I do not press it."

The Cabinet decided that it was very necessary that Parliament should be called together as soon as possible in order to get its support for the measures of economy and taxation which would balance the Budget. This was necessary to steady foreign opinion, which was still rather shaky – in fact the withdrawal of gold and foreign currencies continued. After the formation of the National Government the Treasury raised credits in New York and Paris to the extent of £80,000,000. This credit was rapidly being exhausted, and something had to be done at once to stop the drain.

So Parliament was called together for the 8th September, a fortnight after the formation of the National Government. The measures necessary to balance the Budget had been fully prepared. This expedition in dealing with the crisis was without precedent.

When Parliament met, the House of Commons presented a new and strange appearance. The Labour Party had transferred themselves to the Opposition benches.

Only about a dozen Labour members were supporting the National Government. The whole of the Liberal Party had associated themselves with the new Government, and they, with the whole strength of the Conservative Party, occupied the Government side of the House.

When Mr. MacDonald and I entered the Chamber we were received with jeers and ironical cheers from a small section of the Labour Party, but the majority of the party refrained from any hostile demonstrations. It was not a pleasant experience for me to find myself facing as an Opposition the Party which I had in the previous session reckoned as my supporters.

Mr. MacDonald opened the proceedings of the sitting with a long explanatory statement of the reasons for the resignation of the Labour Government and the formation of the National Government. On the whole he was listened to without interruption from the Labour Party. When he sat down Mr. Arthur Henderson, who had been appointed the Leader of the Labour Party, rose to reply. He expressed his deep regret that circumstances had arisen which led to the resignation of himself and his friends from the Labour Government, and to the separation from three or four of their colleagues who had been in the forefront of the Labour battle, and who, especially in two cases, had been associated with the building up of the movement. "I want to say this, that whether the withdrawal of our colleagues be long or short, whether it be temporary or permanent, it is a direct loss to the Labour Movement." He went on to express his dissent from the claim of the new Government to be a National Government. It could not be regarded as a "National" Government when it was opposed by the largest Party in the House of Commons. The Labour Party had decided to act as an Opposition so long as this Government lasted, and they had to do their best to maintain that position.

He then went on to state at great length the history of the resignation of the Labour Government. He admitted that a serious crisis existed, and claimed that the Labour Government had never denied the fact nor refused to consider it. He went into the greatest detail of what had happened in the days immediately preceding the downfall of the Labour Government, and disclosed the fact that the Labour Government had provisionally accepted economies to the sum of £56,000,000, but had declined to agree to an increase in this figure by cuts in Unemployment payments. These and further disclosures by Mr. Henderson of what happened in the Cabinet was the beginning of a perfect orgy of Cabinet revelations which reached a culminating point during the General Election which followed. He claimed that the reason the Labour Government fell was because a number of its members were not willing to call for sacrifices from the unemployed. Many of his statements were hotly disputed in interruptions by Liberal and Labour members who had at least as full a knowledge of the facts as Mr. Henderson himself.

This debate had taken place on a Motion by the Prime Minister that on Thursday (two days later) the House would resolve itself into Committee for the presentation of an Emergency Budget. The general debate on this motion was continued next day, and on Thursday, 10th September 1931, I presented the most momentous Budget ever submitted to the House of Commons in peace time. I managed to compress it into a speech of only an hour's duration. The House of Commons and the country had been prepared for severe measures, but when I submitted a full statement of the actual position and of the drastic taxation which would have to be imposed to balance the Budget the House was stunned into a painful silence. Even the usually exuberant Labour members forgot to interrupt, and it was only when I reached the concluding sentences that a few of them had so far recovered as to interrupt and jeer.

As this Budget is of historic importance, I will give a short summary of its main provisions. The revised estimates for the current financial year 1931-32, before taking account of economies and new taxation proposals, were as follows:

Revenue:	£744,200,000
Ordinary Expenditure:	£772,579,000
Amortisation of Debt:	£40,300,000
Estimated Deficit:	£74,679,000

That was the estimated Deficit on the 31st March 1932. That was a sufficiently appalling figure, but the worst had still to be told. I estimated that next year, that is the financial year from the 1st April 1932 to 31st March 1933, again before taking into account all economies and new taxation proposals, the deficit would amount to the colossal figure of £170,000,000. That figure was arrived at after allowing for the usual provision for Sinking Fund of £50,000,000.

The economy proposals were estimated to give a total relief to the Budget of 1932-33 of approximately £70,000,000. I estimated that the savings in the six months of the current year which had still to run would be about £22,000,000. I proposed to reduce the sum set aside for Debt Remission from £50,000,000 to £32,500,000, which was the sum required to meet our obligations to provide specific sums annually for the reduction of certain debts. This proposal set free for the general purposes of the Budget £13,700,000 in the current year and £20,000,000 in the following year. This saving of £20,000,000 in the next financial year and the economy proposals amounting to £70,000,000 left me with £79,500,000 to be raised by increased taxation. 70 per cent of the increased taxation was direct, and 30 per cent indirect.

The following table shows how the Budget for the current year and for the succeeding year were balanced:

	1931-32	1932-33
Estimated Deficit on existing basis	*£74,679,000*	*£170,000,000*
Economies	£22,000,000	£70,000,000
Saving on Debt Amortisation	£13,700,000	£20,000,000
New Taxation - Inland Revenue	£29,000,000	£57,500,000
New Taxation - Customs and Excise	£11,500,000	£24,000,000
Total	£76,200,000	£171,500,000

I concluded my Budget Speech in these words:

> "I have finished what I described as my very unpleasant task. These proposals are admittedly drastic and disagreeable. They are justified

only by the regrettable necessity urged upon us by the present financial position of the nation, but I have received during the last few weeks the most amazing evidence of the willingness of the nation, men and women of all classes, to make their contribution to this effort. This morning my post was like the post of every day for a week past. Old age pensioners have returned their pension books. War pensioners have offered to forgo their pensions for the year. National War Savings Certificates have been returned cancelled. Postal orders, large and small, pour in. Children, even, have sent from their savings-boxes shillings and half-crowns to help the nation in its need. Factory girls have come to me with collections taken in the workshops; and today, following many other similar gifts, I received a 5 per cent War Loan bond for £1,000 to be cancelled.

"These proposals that I have submitted give everybody the opportunity of contributing. I have tried as best I could to spread the burden of the sacrifice as fairly and as evenly as human ingenuity can devise. To balance a Budget with a deficit of £170,000,000, to spend as we are doing this year, at the expense of the Exchequer, something like £100,000,000 for the relief of Unemployment, is an achievement which no country in the world has ever attempted. The House of Commons will, I believe, accept these proposals, the country will accept them, and in so doing they will show to the world an example of the indomitable British spirit in the face of difficulty.

"'All our past proclaims our future: Shakespeare's voice and Nelson's hand,
Milton's faith and Wordsworth's trust
In this our chosen and chainless land,
Bear us witness: come the world against her, England yet shall stand.'"

The scene which followed when I sat down was unprecedented in Parliamentary history. Perhaps I might be allowed to describe it in the words of a Parliamentary sketch-writer:

"Such a scene as that in the House of Commons today has not been produced by any Budget Speech of modern times. Having unfolded a scheme of heavy sacrifices to balance his Budget, Mr. Snowden sat down with the cheers of united Unionists and Liberals ringing in his ears. Backbench members rose to their feet to acclaim him. They waved order papers and handkerchiefs, and shouted applause to this little man with the pinched figure, the pallid, almost fleshless face, and the steely eyes, who had demanded from them and the nation new and heavy contributions in the middle of a financial year. But it was not that on which thoughts were centred. When others had run away from the crisis provoked by their policy he stood on the bridge to ride the storm. 'Bear us witness: come the world against her, England yet shall stand.' He made the words of Swinburne ring out with a new meaning. Every patriotic impulse was stirred. The appeal was irresistible. For several minutes the ranks behind stood cheering. Front benchmen were compelled to abandon official dignity and join in the applause. It was an amazing scene with these Unionist Protectionists making a hero of a Socialist Free Trader. The House has known many changes, but surely none so dramatic as this. It was not only the temporary emotion that made one think of Mr. Snowden as just the man for such a moment. Martyr or hero is in his make-up. The frail figure with the strong personal force, brought to the front at a time of rare national crisis, dominated the House. The preliminary jeers of his old colleagues and associates left him unaffected. His break with them for the sake of the nation had been the big thing. Their little petulant cries now mattered nothing. But soon he dominated even them so that they had to listen in compulsory silence. Summoning all his physical reserves, he spoke with remarkable clearness and even stridently. 'And now', he said, as he held his hand on his forehead, 'I have balanced my Budget.' It was a great personal triumph.

"Mr. Snowden had had his hour, and has bidden such a farewell to politics as is given to few men for their retrospect. He could take the memories of his last Budget into retirement and live in content."

Never before in the history of Parliament had members risen to cheer an increase of taxation! This was the last of four Budgets I had introduced.

It was known that it would be my last, for a fortnight before I had announced that I should not seek re-election at the close of the present Parliament.

It was evident that at that time the relations between myself and all my late Cabinet colleagues had not become embittered, for at the close of my speech two of them handed across the table notes expressing warm congratulations upon it.

The day following the introduction of this Budget, the Prime Minister had the disagreeable duty of putting the economy proposals before the House of Commons. I have mentioned that these economies in the aggregate amounted to £70,000,000. This was about £14,000,000 more than the figure to which the Labour Cabinet had agreed. The increase from the Labour Party's £56,000,000 was accounted for by a proposal to reduce the weekly Unemployment benefit by 10 per cent.

The economies were strongly opposed by the Labour Opposition. One would have thought that ordinary decency would have prevented them from opposing those particular economies to which the Labour Cabinet had unanimously agreed. But that was not the case. They criticised practically every item of this programme, regardless of their inconsistency. For instance, the Labour Government had agreed to a reduction of 15 per cent in teachers' salaries. The new Government proposed to reduce them by 10 per cent. But this did not prevent the official spokesman of the Labour Party, who had agreed to the 15 per cent in the Labour Government, from making a violent attack upon the proposal to reduce teachers' salaries at all. I must say that the opposition of the Labour Party to the economies as a whole was not only unprincipled but very feeble. They made it quite clear that they were going to make their opposition to the cuts in Unemployment pay their main plank at the forthcoming General Election. How sadly they misread the national situation and the spirit of the people was shown by the result of the General Election which followed shortly after.

I had very little difficulty in getting my Budget through the House. The Labour Opposition miserably collapsed, and on one occasion during the Committee Stage of the Finance Bill the House had to adjourn because the Labour Party could not continue the debate. Mr. Henderson, though Leader of the Labour Party, and Mr. William Graham, nominally a deputy leader and the Party's expert on financial matters, were scarcely seen on the benches after the first two days of the session.

The Finance Bill, in addition to the economy and taxation proposals, included clauses designed to facilitate the conversion of the 5 per cent War

Loan to a lower rate of interest. I had been, as I have said, for some time very anxious to deal with this question, but the disturbed monetary conditions had prevented this gigantic operation, involving £2,000,000,000, from being carried out. In order to take advantage of a favourable opportunity, I incorporated in this Finance Bill a complete scheme for the conversion. I did not remain in office long enough to have the satisfaction of carrying through this long-cherished desire. Nine months later the financial and monetary position had greatly improved. Interest rates were lower, and on the 30th June 1932 my successor to the Chancellorship, Mr. Neville Chamberlain, announced that he had decided to embark upon the gigantic task of converting the whole of this War Loan into a Stock at 3.5 per cent. This operation was estimated to give a net saving to the Exchequer of £23,000,000 a year. This vast operation was unparalleled in its magnitude and its success.

I now turn back to the financial and monetary position as it existed in September 1931. The Budget had had the immediate effect of restoring confidence abroad. For some days after its introduction the withdrawals of foreign deposits from London fell sharply. Unfortunately, however, that did not continue. Foreign confidence was again shaken by speeches that were made and articles written by prominent people advocating inflation and repudiation. The opposition of the Labour Party to the Budget proposals had given the impression abroad that the country was not united. In the world atmosphere of nervousness difficulties developed in foreign countries. This was as much due to nervousness about their own position as to a loss of faith in sterling.

In order to protect sterling, the Bank of England had on the 1st August raised a credit of £50,000,000 in Paris and New York, and this was very quickly exhausted. Further credits to a total of £80,000,000 had been raised by the British Government a day or two after the National Government was formed, but in the prevailing world conditions even this credit had not proved sufficient to stem the tide of withdrawals of foreign deposits from London. By the middle of September the situation had become so serious that there was no other course open but to suspend the Gold Standard.

On 19th September the Bank of England addressed a letter to the Prime Minister and myself stating the serious financial situation, and representing to us that in their opinion it was expedient in the national interests that they should be relieved of their obligation to sell gold under the Gold Standard Act of 1925.

The Prime Minister and I spent that weekend in London in consultation with the Bank of England and other financial bodies. We came to the conclusion that we must at once ask Parliament to suspend the gold convertibility of the currency. The amount of foreign assets held in London largely exceeded the amount of the bankers' gold. If the Bank of England in these circumstances remained under a legal obligation to pay out gold on demand the security of the currency might have disappeared.

The next day (Monday, the 21st September), amid great excitement, I introduced into the House of Commons a Bill to suspend the Gold Standard. We were well aware that the initial effect on the exchange value of sterling might be serious, but we believed that this effect would be temporary, and that those who had confidence in sterling would not find that confidence misplaced. But we also realised that it was one thing to go off the Gold Standard with an unbalanced Budget and uncontrollable inflation, and another thing to take that measure, not because of internal financial difficulties, but because of the excessive withdrawal of foreign deposits. We had balanced our Budget, and there remained no danger of having to print paper, which leads to uncontrolled inflation. I made an appeal to everybody to keep cool, and not to aggravate the situation by panic. The suspension of the Gold Standard had not the serious consequences that might have been expected. There was a depreciation in the exchange value of sterling, but this had the result of improving our competitive power in our export trade, though, on the other hand, it placed us at a disadvantage in our imports. Since then, most other countries have departed from the Gold Standard, and at the time I write, economists, financiers and business men are talking about a new monetary system; but, personally, I have not yet seen any practical plan to supersede the Gold Standard, and when international confidence is fully restored and international trade recover, I believe the countries will return to an improved Gold Standard.

Chapter Thirty-Six

The 1931 General Election

During the month from the time when the House of Commons assembled on 8th September to the Dissolution of Parliament on the 7th October, the relations between the Labour Opposition and their late colleagues who were now in the National Government became increasingly strained. A section of the Labour members subjected the Labour Ministers to daily insults; the most offensive insinuations, innuendoes and expressions were constantly flung across the floor. But I am glad to say that these actions were not approved by the more sensible members of the Opposition. I received a number of letters from members of the Labour Party expressing their disapproval of this conduct of the minority of their colleagues. A letter from my old friend, Sir Ben Turner, was typical of these communications. He wrote to me as follows:

> "DEAR PHILIP,
>
> "I want to write to you expressing my regret at the turn of events. Nobody can throw a stone at you for your courage and devotion to principle and duty. Those who would throw stones may be those who did it when you took a high stand in 1914. I am, of course, convinced we have to stand with the Labour Party, but that should not prevent any of us having, as I have, a high admiration of your great services to our movement. You are deeming it your duty as you see it. My wife and I know your past. It is a past of bigness and service, and while I have to go with the Party, believing that the new Coalition is not the best way, I recognise that what you have done is from the very best of motives and with the knowledge that we ordinary men could not possess. Believe me it is a wrench, but not one that is going to divide our friendship.
>
> "Yours sincerely,
> "BEN TURNER."

I ignored the offensiveness of a section of the Labour Party until the Third Reading of the Finance Bill, when the official spokesman of the Labour Party, who had been a minor Minister in the Labour Government, made a speech which gave me the opportunity to say frankly what I thought about their attitude and their action in running away from their duty to deal with the financial situation. My speech on this occasion deserves a little comment because it was the last speech that I made in the House of Commons. It was delivered on the 2nd October 1931, five days before Parliament was dissolved. I had hoped up to that time that it might be possible, when the work for which we had joined the National Government had been completed, for us to come together once more. But if the Opposition speech which I have mentioned represented the spirit of the Labour Party generally, I saw such a hope must be abandoned.

It was known amongst members that this would probably be the last occasion upon which I should address the House of Commons. When the word was passed round that I was on my feet, members trooped into the House to hear my "swan song". What they expected I do not know. Did they expect something in the nature of a farewell reconciliation, with perhaps a touch of sentiment? I think I will let the members of the Press Gallery tell the story of this strange and tragic farewell to the House of Commons.

"But Mr. Snowden said nothing about farewells, and less about forgiveness. It was the valediction of a great fighter making one last deadly onslaught before he left the arena, not of a man for whom antagonisms were now bathed in the warm delusive light of sunset.

"In recent days Mr. Snowden has found it more than ever difficult to remain patient under Socialist questioning and interruption. The acid austerity of the Iron Chancellor's speech provides the answer to those who think that it cost him nothing to part with his lifelong political associates. His final speech was at least artistically in keeping with his whole career. It was an uncompromising performance delivered in a voice which attained unsuspected volume. He went out from the House of Commons which he entered a quarter of a century ago fighting hard, as he had always fought, sparing no one and asking for no quarter. He stood at the table as he had so often stood before, intense, electric, dominating, and aimed his well-directed bolts at his political opponents. But these bolts were not aimed at his old antagonist, Mr. Winston Churchill, but at those with whom he had worked for many years. Mr. Snowden made it clear at once when he rose that he intended to make the sparks fly. Fixing his eye on the almost deserted Front Opposition Bench, he said that the absence of the so-called Leader of the Opposition (Mr. Henderson) had been a marked feature of the debates in the House during the last few weeks. He waited for the uproar to subside. Mr. Henderson has led his Party from some recess behind the Speaker's Chair and his example has been followed by the deputy leaders of the Party. He had been criticised by Labour spokesmen for not imposing new taxation in his Budget of the previous April. In reply to this taunt he said: 'Last February I tried to warn the country about the financial position, but I never received one word of public support for the position I put forward from any member of the late Government.' He had not only put the position before the House of Commons, but he had put it also much more frankly before a special meeting of the Labour Party. What support did he get? Not any. Leaning across the table, he levelled an accusing finger at the members opposite, and said contemptuously: 'All they did was to talk their usual claptrap about going to the super-tax payer.' (A voice: 'You taught us that!') 'Yes', said Mr. Snowden, 'I tried to teach you, but I am terribly disappointed that my teaching has neither been understood nor appreciated.' (Labour uproar.) The Chancellor then attacked Mr. Henderson, who had said that he was in favour under certain conditions of a revenue tariff. Mr. Henderson was not quite sure whether he was in favour of a 10 or a 20 per cent tariff, but he was in favour of a tariff. They had been told that fifteen out of the twenty members of the late Cabinet had voted for a revenue tariff. A further statement was made that a number of them were in favour of a whole-hog policy including the taxation of food and raw materials. Mr. Henderson's tariff proposal was that instead of cutting employment benefit by 10 per cent he was willing to impose a 10 per cent tariff on the cost of living of the unemployed and every other section of the community. The Labour Party was now enrolled under a tariff banner. Dealing with a remark which had been made from the Labour benches that the only way to save the situation was to abolish capitalism, he said he was sorry he could not introduce into the Finance Bill a proposal for the abolition of capitalism. He would have to leave that for someone else. He added emphatically 'any catastrophic attempt to abolish capitalism would bring greater disasters to the people than those from which they were suffering.' 'We all know that,' shouted a Labour member. Well, that was at least something he had managed to teach his late colleagues of the Labour Party. He had been criticised for not having taxed the resources of the rich much more heavily.

His difficulty with the Labour Party had always been that they could not understand a wink. He had always had to explain to them what was behind the proposal he was making. They could never be satisfied with accepting smaller things as a steppingstone to something else. Referring to the Labour Party programme as set forth in *Labour and the Nation*, he confessed that he had never read that document, but had read the summary of the proposals, and he had calculated that the cost of all they asked would be something like £1,000,000,000-a-year additional on the national expenditure. Could the Labour Party not see that he was not taxing the rich up to 20s. in the £ because he wanted to leave some treasure in the locker that would be available for the carrying out of the £1,000,000,000-a-year programme of the Party!

Mr. Snowden concluded: 'This Budget, with all its hardships, has been welcomed with unparalleled acceptance by the whole country. It places the internal resources of the nation on a sound financial basis. On that basis we can build. It is an example of the determination of the British people to face up courageously to adversity.' Before the conclusion of the speech the Labour Party had been stunned to silence, and on the Government side there was at first unconcealed glee at the drubbing he gave the Labour Party. But this mood presently changed to one of strained astonishment at the unlimited capacity of Mr. Snowden's invective. At the close of this speech the Speaker rose to put the motion for the Third Reading of the Finance Bill, but the Labour members were so stupefied that they did not challenge a division, and the Finance Bill passed the House of Commons apparently with unanimous approval."

This was my last speech in the House of Commons. It was the strangest leave-taking the House had ever seen. I never dreamt that I should leave the Parliamentary arena in which for over a quarter of a century I had fought so many hard and grim battles for Labour and Socialist principles under such tragic circumstances. Apart from the temporary enjoyment which one gets from attack, it was no pleasure to me to leave the House of Commons estranged from my late colleagues and my old Party.

But this farewell speech was really the measure of my deep disappointment with the action which the Labour Party had taken in this national crisis. I felt keenly that they had made a grave mistake. They had shown themselves to be incapable or unwilling to put aside what they considered to be Party interests and to face a disagreeable and necessary national duty. I was outraged by their hypocritical conduct in disowning proposals to which the majority of them agreed as members of the late Government. I resented deeply their weak surrender to the dictation of the Trade Union Congress. By that action they had shown that they were not a National Party, but the servants of an outside caucus.

Until the Labour Party throws off this outside domination and regards itself as responsible to its constituents and the country generally, it can never expect to be regarded as anything more than a class Party. I believed then, and still believe, that if the Labour Government supported by the Labour Party had had the courage to do in this crisis disagreeable, unpleasant, but necessary things, they would have carried the country with them as the National Government did, and raised the Labour Party in the respect and confidence of the nation.

The week following the incident I have been recording, the House of Commons rose for the General Election. Again I will let the Press describe the scene of my final departure from the House of Commons:

"For about fifteen minutes Mr. Snowden sat in his place on the Treasury Bench in a deserted House of Commons.... He sat there stiffly upright with his arms folded across his chest, and his lips tightly closed.

"Of what was he thinking? Was he thinking of the many fights he had waged, of how the crowded House had hung on his every word, or how hard it was to leave a place where he had spent so many years? For the last time he would rise from the bench from which he had often risen with zest to hurl invective at his political opponents. For the last time he would walk past the Speaker's Chair out of the House.

"What did he see as he looked at the deserted House? Did he see the figure of the member for Blackburn, burning with zeal for the Labour cause, rise from a backbench opposite in 1906 to make his maiden speech? Or were there other ghosts jostling each other on the vacant benches?

"What did he hear as he sat there in the silent House? Did he hear the cheers of his own people ringing down the years, or the harsher sound that came from the backbenches when he ended his last great speech with the brave words- 'England yet shall stand'?

"No-one could say. He sat there like an image carved out of stone.

"The grimness left his face as he approached the Speaker. Smiling, he shook hands and stayed for a few moments still clasping the Speaker's hand to say farewell.

"Then, leaning on his stick, he walked slowly out of the House."

Within a fortnight of the formation of the National Government a section of the Tory Press began an agitation for a General Election. At the same time this question was being discussed in the Tory Party, and particularly among the Tory members of the House of Commons. Near the end of September, the pressure upon Mr. Baldwin from his supporters for an immediate Election became so strong that he could no longer resist the demand. The reason put forward was that the National Government had only a majority in the House of Commons of about 70 members, and that the House as at present constituted did not truly reflect the support for a National Government in the country, with such a comparatively small majority in the House of Commons it was urged that foreign opinion was doubtful about the stability of the National Government.

This was the reason put forward for a General Election, but it did not in truth explain why the Conservative Party were pressing this. The purpose behind this Conservative demand was stated by Lord Hailsham as early as 3rd September in calling for a "constructive programme of tariffs and Imperial development".

Lord Hailsham's demand was taken up by the rank and file of the Conservative members of the House of Commons, and on 22nd September these members sent to Mr. Baldwin a Resolution demanding an immediate Election on the issue of a general tariff, and stating that the Conservative Party should pledge themselves to give full support to Mr. Ramsay MacDonald as the head of the National Government if he would go to the country with their policy. Under this pressure from their party, the Conservative members of the Cabinet raised this issue. Mr. Baldwin came into my room at the House and gave me a frank statement of the position in which he was placed by this decision of his Party. He, himself, was very anxious to stand by the conditions upon which the National Government had been formed, but Party pressure was too strong for him. It will be remembered that the National Government was formed on a distinct pledge that the Government would confine itself to settling the financial crisis, and then the Parties composing it would revert to their former positions of independence. It was at that time clearly understood that there would be no General Election until the work for which the National Government had been created had been completed, and that the General Election which would follow on the completion of that work would be fought upon the usual Party lines.

When the suggestion was first made that there should be an immediate General Election fought on an appeal by the National Government, the Liberal leaders were strongly opposed to the idea, and I entirely shared their views. So was Mr. Lloyd George, who had not fully recovered from his recent operation. Sir Herbert Samuel and Lord Reading, the two Liberal members of the National Cabinet, were in close touch with Mr. Lloyd George, and they communicated his views to the Cabinet. However, it became quite clear to us that the Tory members of the Cabinet were determined upon their demand for an immediate General Election; and, recognising the futility of further opposition, finally the Liberals and myself reluctantly accepted the position. If a General Election could not be prevented, I felt that the sooner it came the better.

During the last week in September and the first week in October the Cabinet met daily to consider this question. The fact that these discussions were taking place in the Cabinet was well known, and also the differences which were dividing the Cabinet. Efforts were being made to see whether it would be possible for the divergent views in the Cabinet to be reconciled on an agreed formula dealing with the question of tariffs. Sir Herbert Samuel and Lord Reading were unwilling to commit the Liberal Party to any concessions on the question of tariffs without getting the consent of their Party, and they submitted to a meeting of the Liberal members of the House of Commons the formula which had been proposed by the Conservative members of the Cabinet. After this meeting of the Liberal members, the discussions which were taking place in the Cabinet became public property. The formula which had been submitted for the consideration of the Liberal members of Parliament was not acceptable, and an amended formula was put forward by Sir Herbert Samuel and Lord Reading, which was equally unacceptable to the Conservatives. The question at issue was whether the National Government should go to the country and ask for a mandate for the control of imports, while leaving the widest discretion as to the means by which such control should be exercised.

During these discussions I worked with the two Liberal members and entirely shared their views. We were prepared to go to the country as a National Government and ask for a mandate to complete our work; but we were not prepared to go to the country on the tariff issue. It was found to be quite impossible to agree upon a formula, and it was finally decided that the Prime Minister, in announcing the Dissolution of Parliament, should issue a manifesto setting forth the reasons for the appeal to the country, and that it should contain a statement of the policy upon which the Cabinet were agreed, namely the stabilisation of the pound sterling and the restoration of British credit; and should ask for a free hand to deal with the question of the balance of trade.

Parliament was dissolved on the 7th October. On the same evening Mr. MacDonald issued his manifesto to the nation. This manifesto was on the lines it had been decided he should take.

In view of the action of the National Government following this General Election, it is important to examine to what extent the question of tariffs figured as an issue at this General Election. The farthest the Prime Minister went on the question of tariffs was contained in the following sentences in his broadcast manifesto:

> "As it is impossible to foresee in the changing conditions of today what may arise, no one can set out a programme of appeal on which specific pledges can be given. The Government must, therefore, be free to consider every proposal likely to help, such as tariffs, expansion of exports and contraction of imports, commercial treaties and mutual economic arrangements with the Dominions."

Mr. Baldwin spoke at Leeds on the 20th October. He said:

> "After all, what is the fundamental issue? It is not Socialism. It is not Individualism. It is not Free Trade. It is not Protection. But it is this. Will you in the hour of your country's need entrust her destinies to a Government selected from all the great parties in the State who are willing to work together harmoniously in the interests of the country, who are trying to pull together and pull the country through without disaster to your money, to your food or to your employment. Will you give them when you send them

> to Parliament that free hand for which we ask? Will you allow us to employ whatever measures after deliberation we may decide to be the best?"

Sir Herbert Samuel in his election speeches took the same line. In his election address he used these words:

> "The people are not called upon now to decide for or against a general and permanent system of tariffs. This is not the issue at this Election. That is not included in the Prime Minister's appeal."

These extracts from the speeches of political leaders during the Election show that a mandate to establish a system of general Protection was neither sought by nor given to the National Government. There had been a good deal of talk about the alleged adverse balance of trade, and what the National Government sought was a mandate to consider tariffs among other suggestions as a means of redressing the adverse trade balance if, after exhaustive examination, it was found that an adverse balance of trade actually existed, and, if so, that tariffs would be a suitable means of dealing with it.

But, as a matter of fact, the question of tariffs was not at all an important issue at this General Election. The issue upon which the electors voted was whether the government of the country should be handed over to the Labour leaders who had failed in their duty at a time of national crisis, or whether the National Government should be continued in office until it had completed the work of rehabilitating the national financial position. Assured by the declarations of the National Party leaders, as Mr. Baldwin had put it, that Free Trade or Protection was not an issue, millions of Free Trade votes were cast for Conservative candidates at the Election.

I think I may modestly claim to know something of the mind of the electorate and of the considerations which determined their votes. Owing to the state of my health, I was not able to take the platform, but I used the microphone and the Press with what the newspapers described as "devastating effect" to expose the inconsistency of the Labour Party and their lack of courage in facing their duty in a grave national emergency. Every day from the first day of the Election campaign to the eve of the poll I launched attacks upon my late Labour colleagues. I did this in no vindictive spirit, but because I was firmly convinced that it would be a national disaster to give power to a Party which had shown itself unworthy to be trusted with the responsibility of office.

The British Broadcasting Corporation placed the microphone at the service of the leaders of the three political Parties. I gave one of the talks, and my effort was universally believed to have had a great influence on the result of the Election. The Labour Party gave me the credit, or, as they put it, discredit of being responsible for the tragic fate which overtook them. I am inserting in the Appendix a full report of this talk.

Mr. Henderson, Mr. Graham and Mr. Clynes broadcast appeals for the Labour Party, and I am sure that their appeals did more harm than good to their Party.

After each of these Labour broadcasts I followed them up with replies in the Press exposing their inaccuracies and giving the facts about their commitment to economies which they were now repudiating. From the beginning of the campaign the Labour leaders were in a hopeless position. Their attempts to wriggle out of their commitments, when members of the Government, to most of the economies the National Government had imposed carried no conviction, but served to emphasise the public impression of their own insincerity.

There never had been any doubt that the result of the General Election would give a large majority for the National Government, but the actual result surpassed the wildest expectations. The Labour Party were not merely defeated, but decimated. After the polls had closed, I sat in my room at Downing Street until three o'clock in the morning to receive the Election results by wireless. It seemed almost incredible that Labour seats which had been held at previous Elections by enormous majorities should have fallen to the assaults of the National candidates. Every member of the late Labour Cabinet, with the exception of Mr. George Lansbury, was defeated, and of the minor Ministers only a few were successful. The Labour Party returned only 52 members, and the total Labour vote fell from 8,380,000 to 6,650,000 votes. Nobody had expected such a result. The most optimistic forecast had given the National Government a majority of not more than 200 seats. The actual result had given the National Government a majority of 493 members!

Immediately after the result of the Election was known, the Prime Minister set to work to reconstruct the Cabinet. Since the formation of the National Government the Cabinet had consisted of ten members only, but it was now restored to the usual number, and Ministers holding important Ministerial offices were now included in the reconstructed Cabinet. Lord Reading, who had held the post of Foreign Secretary since August, asked to be relieved from office for business reasons, and Sir John Simon, who had hitherto not held office in the National Government, succeeded Lord Reading.

As I was no longer a member of the House of Commons, it was essential that I should resign my office as Chancellor of the Exchequer. Representations were made to me from the highest quarters that I should remain in the Government and take a post which had no Departmental duties, and at the same time go to the House of Lords to strengthen the Government Bench in that Chamber. I took the office of Lord Privy Seal, on the understanding that I should be available for any special duties which might arise. It had been assumed that Mr. Neville Chamberlain would succeed me as Chancellor of the Exchequer, a post which he had held for a few months in 1923.

It was known, of course, that tariffs would be one of the matters which would receive the consideration of the new National Government in connection with the question of the balance of trade. Sir Philip Cunliffe-Lister had been President of the Board of Trade, and I felt strongly that the two key posts in the Government on the question of tariffs should not be held by two such pronounced Protectionists as Mr. Neville Chamberlain and Sir Philip Cunliffe-Lister. I made representations to the Prime Minister to this effect when he was reconstructing the Cabinet, and I suggested to him that Mr. Walter Runciman might be appointed President of the Board of Trade. The Prime Minister agreed to this suggestion.

I had suggested Mr. Runciman for this position because of his pronounced views on Free Trade. He had been regarded as one of the strongest Free Traders in the country, holding his views with an unshakable tenacity. How tragically mistaken I was later events proved! Mr. Runciman was not at first disposed to accept office. When the Prime Minister offered Mr. Runciman this position he came to see me and explained that his business connections made it difficult for him to take office in the Government. I explained to him how anxious I was that he should go to the Board of Trade to hold the fort for Free Trade against the assaults of the strong Protectionist elements in the Government. He said that he quite realised the importance of the Free Trade position being represented in the Government, and promised to consider the matter for a day or two. He finally agreed to accept the office of President of the Board of Trade. I hope that the Recording Angel has kept no note of my responsibility for Mr. Runciman's appointment to this office!

The announcement of my elevation to the peerage was made on the 17th November. This was a step which had been generally anticipated, and the announcement, therefore, caused no surprise. There were, of course, the expected comments in the Press about the strange turn of events which had brought the former Socialist agitator and unsparing critic of the capitalist system into the House of Lords, but almost without exception the Press comments were favourable and complimentary.

The reason for my acceptance of a peerage were quite well understood. I hope I shall be believed when I say that a peerage had no attraction for me, and if I could have remained in the Government without going to the House of Lords I should very much have preferred that course. But, being no longer a member of the House of Commons, there was no other means by which I could do that than to go to the House of Lords. Even if I were no longer a member of the Government I did not wish to drop out of politics altogether, for after forty years of political activity it had become part of my life, and I felt that a seat in the House of Lords would give me the opportunity, when I felt disposed to do so, to use the House of Lords as a political platform.

Chapter Thirty-Seven

A Constitutional Revolution

The new Parliament was summoned immediately after the result of the General Election was known. The King's Speech was delivered on the 10th November, and the debate on the Address in reply occupied the House of Commons for a week. In view of what followed, attention should be called to this statement in the King's Speech:

> "The Nation was also invited by my Ministers to empower them to pursue a policy designed to fully establish confidence in our financial stability and to give them authority to frame plans for ensuring a favourable balance of trade."

It is clear from this that at that time the Government interpreted the mandate they had received from the country to give them authority not to carry out a general scheme of Protection, but to frame plans for dealing with the alleged adverse balance of trade. If, after a full examination of the problem, the Government came to the conclusion that temporary tariffs might be advantageous in this connection, they were entitled to apply them under the declarations which had been made at the Election by the Prime Minister, Mr. Baldwin and Sir Herbert Samuel.

The fact that Mr. Runciman, the President of the Board of Trade, had a Bill for the application of temporary tariffs ready for introduction immediately the debate in the Address was concluded shows that no examination into the problem of the balance of trade had been made by the Government. It had been assumed without any examination that drastic measures should be taken at once to restrict imports by means of tariffs. It is quite true that the imports of certain articles had increased considerably in the previous two months, but the explanation of that was obvious. British importers had naturally assumed from the speeches of Ministers preceding and during the General Election that tariffs might be imposed, and they were anxious to forestall this possibility by replenishing their stocks before this should happen.

Mr. Runciman's Bill, which became the Abnormal Importations Act, was hurriedly rushed through Parliament, and it came into force on 20th November. This Bill empowered the Treasury to issue Orders imposing duties not exceeding 100 per cent on commodities which the Board of Trade considered were being imported into this country in abnormal quantities.

Free Traders did not oppose these measures, as they were temporary in their operation. The Act was to continue in force for a period of six months, and no longer. Mr. Runciman had defended these Acts on the ground that they were designed to deal with an emergency, and were not intended to prejudice the Government's fiscal enquiry. Free Traders could not take the responsibility of breaking up the National Government at that stage, and were willing to wait until the outcome of the promised full examination into the existing economic emergency had been made. They had accepted the declarations made by the Party leaders at the Election, and affirmed in the quotation I have given from the King's Speech that any proposals which might be made after an impartial enquiry would be for the purpose of the present emergency, and would not commit the country to a permanent system of Protection.

Mr. Runciman assured me that if the Government decided to impose tariffs on imported iron and steel he would resign rather than support the proposal. His assurance, however, did not satisfy me, but left the impression that he could no longer be relied upon to offer opposition to an extension of tariffs, on which the Protectionist members of the Government were clearly determined.

I consulted with my Free Trade colleagues, and we agreed that the situation was serious, and that we must see the Prime Minister and put before him our views.

In reply to our letter the Prime Minister wrote to say that he shared my feelings and would be very glad to see us. He asked me to invite the members who were growing disturbed, and said I should invite Runciman to come to the meeting, which he suggested should be of the nature of a deputation to him. Sir Donald Maclean, Sir Herbert Samuel, Sir Archibald Sinclair and myself were on this deputation, and Mr. Runciman was present. We talked for half an hour. The Prime Minister, as usual, was discursive and incoherent, and when we left the meeting we asked each other what he had said and where he stood, but none of us could give the answers to these questions. The only clear impression we had gathered from the meeting was that we could not rely upon the Prime Minister to resist the policy of his Tory colleagues.

Just before Christmas a Committee called the Balance of Trade Committee was appointed to examine this subject and to submit proposals. Before the Committee met, Mr. Runciman had been active in trying to get the support of members of the Committee to a plan for a general revenue tariff of 10 per cent. His main motive appears to have been to get a revenue which would enable a reduction of the Income-Tax to be made. He talked about a reduction of a shilling in the standard rate. He had to my knowledge been pressing this on his Liberal colleagues. Sir Herbert Samuel and Sir Donald Maclean came to see me before Christmas and put this proposal before me.

A few days later Mr. Runciman came down to Tilford at his own request, and urged me to accept this proposal. He argued that this plan might be accepted by the Protectionist members of the Balance of Trade Committee, and thus we should avoid more extreme tariff proposals. He pressed strongly the precedent of Holland, practically a Free Trade country, which had a low general tariff for revenue purposes. We had a long talk, and the outcome was that I said that he could not expect me to commit myself to such a proposal, but I would think it over. I gave him no encouragement to believe that I should support it, but I learnt later that he had given both his Liberal colleagues and the Chancellor to understand that I was in favour of it, and that they could count upon my support. He had no ground for saying this from anything I had said to him. Mr. Chamberlain some time before had publicly expressed himself against a mere revenue tariff as being of no use from the Protectionist standpoint. The Balance of Trade Committee held several meetings during the Parliamentary recess in January. The memoranda prepared by the Board of Trade under Mr. Runciman's directions were all directed to supporting the tariff proposals.

At the final meeting of this Committee I announced that I could not subscribe to the Majority Report, and would submit a Note of Dissent. The morning of the final meeting of this Committee Sir Herbert Samuel came to me and told me that he too could not agree to the Majority Report, and would submit alternative proposals. The Majority Report had recommended an all-round *ad valorem* duty of 10 per cent, with additional duties on the recommendation of an Import Duties Advisory Committee in cases which appeared to them to be either articles of luxury or articles of a kind which are being produced or likely within a reasonable time to be produced in the United Kingdom in quantities which are substantial in relation to the United Kingdom consumption.

In my memorandum of dissent from the recommendations of the Committee, I stated at length my objections to their conclusions. I was not convinced that it had been proved that an adverse balance of trade really existed. If it did, the results would be shown in the depression of the exchange value of sterling, but as a matter of fact the pound had kept fairly steady since the departure from the Gold Standard at a figure round what we were told was its real external value. I expressed the view that the Majority Report without proof assumed an adverse balance of trade, and that we were in danger of applying medicine to cure a suspected disease which had not been thoroughly diagnosed, and about whose existence we were not quite sure. The recommendations of the Committee travelled far beyond its terms of reference, which were to find means of restoring the balance of trade if it was proved that an adverse balance existed. The recommendations were for a complete and permanent reversal of our fiscal policy; they laid the foundations of a Protectionist system upon which a complete structure could be built. How true this forecast was is abundantly proved by the experience of two years of the working of the recommendations of this Committee, which were incorporated in an Act of Parliament.

My memorandum of dissent and Samuel's memorandum were submitted to the Cabinet with the Report of the Majority, to which all the members of the Committee had agreed except Samuel and myself. The Cabinet sat for the whole day (21st January) for the consideration of the Report and the memoranda submitted by Samuel and myself. It was quite evident from the beginning of the meeting that agreement on the Report could not be secured. Samuel and myself were strongly supported in our attitude by Sir Donald Maclean and Sir Archibald Sinclair.

When the Cabinet broke up, the four dissentients grouped themselves together to take counsel. The Prime Minister joined us and expressed his desire to talk things over with us. It was arranged in this conversation that the five of us (the Prime Minister, Sir Herbert Samuel, Sir Archibald Sinclair, Sir Donald Maclean and myself) should meet at my flat at 8.30 that night. They all came. The Prime Minister stressed his personal position. If we resigned he would carry on, but his position would be embarrassing and humiliating. He made the suggestion that the resignations might be averted by conceding to the dissentient Ministers the liberty to publicly express their dissent. This was considered, but dismissed as impracticable and Gilbertian. Mr. MacDonald left us after an hour and a half's talk in the belief that there was no means of reconciling the differences.

The Cabinet met next morning, and in order to avert the resignations of the dissenting Ministers a suggestion was made which was ultimately adopted and which created a revolutionary precedent in Cabinet procedure. The suggestion was the one the Prime Minister had mentioned to us the previous evening, namely, that the difficulty might be overcome and the resignations averted by suspending the practice of Cabinet responsibility and allowing the dissenters a free hand on the tariff proposals. They might be left free to speak and vote against them in Parliament and in public.

Sir Donald Maclean said that we were bound to give serious consideration to any suggestion which would avert the break-up of the Government, and we asked to be allowed to retire to consider this proposal. We did so. Maclean summed up the situation with much force. I said I was not enamoured of the idea, but if we did not accept it we should be open to the charge that we had rejected an unprecedented offer of personal freedom, and that we were determined to break up the Government and were indifferent to the consequences of such action. I had all along urged that if we had to resign we should be assured that our position was impregnable and that we had been driven to that by the attitude of the Tories. Sinclair and Samuel agreed, and after a few minutes we went back to the Cabinet and stated our decision.

We asked for and obtained a clear understanding of what the agreement to differ meant and involved. We would accept the offer on condition that we were to be free to vote and speak against any tariff proposals, whether purely Protectionist or under the guise of a revenue tariff. This freedom was to extend to Members of Parliament supporting the National Government. The Party Whips were not to exert any influence to get M.P.s to vote for tariff proposals. Freedom was to be given to Liberals to run Free Trade candidates at the elections if they promised general support to the Government.

Our Cabinet colleagues accepted this interpretation of the agreement, and five members of the Cabinet were appointed to draw up a Press announcement, which appeared a few hours later. It was issued from 10 Downing Street on the 22nd January, and read as follows:

> "The Cabinet had had before it the Report of its Committee on the Balance of Trade, and after prolonged discussion it had been found impossible to reach a unanimous conclusion on the Committee's recommendations.
>
> "The Cabinet, however, is deeply impressed with the paramount importance of maintaining national unity in the presence of the grave problems now confronting this country and the whole world.
>
> "It has accordingly determined that some modification of usual Ministerial practice is required, and has decided that Ministers who find themselves unable to support the conclusions arrived at by the majority of their colleagues on the subject of import duties and cognate matters are to be at liberty to express their views by speech and vote.
>
> "The Cabinet being essentially united on all other matters of policy believes that by this special provision it is best interpreting the will of the nation and the needs of the time."

This announcement aroused considerable interest in the country, and on the whole was received with satisfaction. A few sticklers saw in this departure from precedent a constitutional revolution which might have disastrous consequences. Mr. Lloyd George, who was now in opposition to the Government, confessed that he had not a ghost of an idea what it meant. A few other Liberals who were hostile to the Government and who were anxious that the Liberal members should withdraw, expressed their amazement at this departure from constitutional usage.

When the House of Lords met on the 10th February, this question was raised by Lord Banbury in the form of a direct vote of censure upon the Government for abandoning the doctrine of Cabinet responsibility. As one of the Ministers responsible for this innovation, I was expected to defend the action of the Cabinet. This was my maiden speech in the House of Lords. In expectation that

I should speak upon this motion, there was a very large attendance of peers, and the visitors' galleries were packed. The newspapers were interested to see how I should accommodate myself to the strange atmosphere of the Gilded Chamber. I was not in the slightest degree nervous, and felt as much at home as if I were addressing the House of Commons. The House of Lords, however, is a very different place to speak in from the House of Commons. One who has long been accustomed to the turmoil and the excitement of the House of Commons debates might find the frigidity of the House of Lords rather disconcerting. The peers, apparently, consider it to be beneath their dignity to give vocal expression to their agreement with or dissent from the sentiments which have been expressed by a speaker. A newspaper correspondent, commenting upon my first intervention in the House of Lords debates, wrote:

> "Lord Snowden has become almost a cult in latter-day politics. He exercises the subtle fascination of what repels. In triumph he remains the dourest, bleakest, loneliest silhouette on the Westminster skyline. The subject which ushered this noble figure into a fresh arena could not have been better chosen. The motion guaranteed an incidental discussion on Free Trade, and when Lord Snowden talks on Free Trade he is on ground that renews his strength like Antaeus, and his arrogant prowess grows magnificent.
>
> "In the same comfortable lounge suit he wore in the Commons, the ex-Chancellor awaited the occasion with calm, sometimes folding his arms and sometimes sticking his thumbs in the arm-holes of his waistcoat-two variations of a yeoman attitude. His nearest colleagues - Protectionists both - left a wary gap on either side."

I explained the reasons the Free Trade Ministers had accepted the offer of the agreement to differ. I did not on this occasion deal with the question of Free Trade, except in so far as it was the controversial issue on which the Free Trade Ministers had offered to resign. I emphasised the fact that this idea did not come from us but from the Protectionist members of the Government. I declared that we remained in the Cabinet solely on condition that we had the same freedom to express our views on this question as those who took the opposite view. We would not be content to remain silent and allow the Protectionists to carry on in the country a raging propaganda in favour of Protection. Upon this vital matter we certainly would not be tongue-tied. We might be mistaken, I said, but we held with the fullest conviction that the tariff proposals of the Government would be disastrous to the economic and industrial life and prosperity of this country. This question will be the issue of the next Election, and it would not be fair to expect that Free Traders could leave the field between now and the General Election for the Protectionists to entrench their position, and that we should allow the question of Free Trade to go by default.

The outcome of the Ottawa Economic Conference held in August 1932 brought about a situation which made it impossible for the Free Trade members of the Government to be any longer associated with it. I was not a member of the British Delegation to Ottawa, and I cannot, therefore, write from personal knowledge of what took place. But I know sufficient from confessions that were made to me by members of the Delegation that the delegates had, in the words of one of the British delegates, "a hell of a time". It would be very illuminating if we could get from the British Delegation a frank account of their experiences and their views of some of the Dominion representatives. Mr. Neville Chamberlain gave us a sidelight upon the harmony of the proceedings at Ottawa when he said that he had found the bonds of Empire had worn very thin. The "harmonious" proceedings at the Conference were on the point of breaking up at two o'clock on the morning of the day when the British Delegation was due to leave Ottawa. A complete break-up was only averted by further concessions made by the British Delegation.

All the Dominion delegates were obsessed by the idea of economic nationalism, and they threatened that if the British Delegation would not agree to their demands they would make arrangements with foreign countries. The principal Australian delegate publicly stated that unless Great Britain was willing to concede their demands "we should have to go outside to foreign countries and we should take away the preference from you".

The Free Trade members of the Cabinet had been reduced to three by the regrettable death of Sir Donald Maclean, which had occurred two months before. Sir Donald's sudden death was an irreparable loss, not only to Free Trade but to the Liberal Party. The Prime Minister appointed a Tory Protectionist to succeed him as President of the Board of Education.

On the publication of the Ottawa Report I felt it was necessary that the remaining Free Trade Ministers should get together to consider the situation.

A meeting of the Cabinet to receive the Report of the British Delegation to the Conference was held on Saturday, 27th August, and after this meeting I sent the following letter to the Prime Minister:

"MY DEAR MACDONALD,

"I do not know what impressions you carried away from the Cabinet Meeting on Saturday, but you seemed very unconscious or complacent about the troubles which were obviously ahead of you. You cannot be so innocent as to imagine that the Free Trade members of the Government are going to acquiesce in the Ottawa agreements. I do not know if the Press has been prompted, but on Sunday it was practically unanimous in announcing that there had been complete agreement in the Cabinet, and that the Free Trade Ministers had accepted the tariff proposals for the increased food taxes. This, as you know, is not the case. Samuel, speaking for all of us, expressly reserved a declaration of our attitude until the further papers had been produced. But there is no doubt as to what that declaration will be when Samuel returns from the Channel Isles. If you have any impression that we shall agree to the proposals already known to us or that we shall be satisfied with the 'agreement to differ', you are under a strange delusion.

"The Ottawa agreements are the final and complete triumph of the Tory Protectionists, and if the Free Trade members of the Government were to be now content to 'disagree', and remain in a Government which was carrying through a permanent policy of full Protection, they would be justly objects of contempt and derision. The reasons which induced us unwillingly to accept the compromise last February no longer have any weight with us, nor has any appeal to my personal loyalty to you so long as you acquiesce in such a policy, and are used by the Tories as their instrument for carrying out a Tory policy. You appeared to realise this in the letters you sent to me three weeks ago. You then seemed anxious to have a talk with me, but you have sought no opportunity for such a conversation. I had arranged to hold myself at your service all this last weekend, and to remain in London over Sunday if you wished to see me. But you appear to have preferred to spend that day with Simon and Baldwin. I have not had three minutes' private talk with you this year. I should have thought on such a momentous matter as these Ottawa agreements, and you knowing my views, you would at least have sought to find out what I was thinking and likely to do.

"Samuel's absence will delay the announcement of our resignations, and we shall have to consult with the minor Free Trade Ministers so that our resignations can be simultaneously announced.

"This letter is not a formal offer of my resignation, as I am acting in full harmony with my colleagues, and I do not want to appear to have precipitated their action. But I thought it only fair that I should warn you of what is coming.

"In view of your own declarations, and even those of Baldwin, at the General Election, I can hardly imagine this letter will come as a surprise to you.

"Yours sincerely,
"SNOWDEN."

To this letter I received a reply by return of post in which Mr. MacDonald said that he was under no delusions at all, but doubted very much if I would agree with Ottawa. He had not had time to examine the Report very closely, but he was concerned about the national situation which would be left if there were political changes. He asked me not to overlook the fact that we, the Labour Ministers, have heavy responsibilities for the last Election and the present distribution of political power. He did not seem to realise that these "heavy responsibilities" were to carry out the pledges given at the last Election, and prevent the Tories from using the National Government for Party advantage.

During the following days I kept in close touch with Sir Herbert Samuel, and we were in complete agreement as to the course we should follow. On the Prime

Minister's return to London on the 5th September I made a further request that we should meet to talk over the situation. He came to my flat on Friday afternoon, 8th September, and we had a talk for an hour and twenty minutes.

He was evidently disturbed about his personal position, and kept on repeating: "I do not know what to do", but he thought that after the World Economic Conference [June-July 1933] an opportunity for resigning might come, when he could say "We have done our work". But I pointed out to him that if that Conference were a success he would be heartened and not inclined to resign, and if it were a failure he could only resign by admitting failure. It was very difficult to bring him to the point of discussing the resignations of the Free Trade Ministers. I gathered by inference that he was not very much troubled about it. In fact he gave me the impression that he would be relieved if we went, as then he would have a united Cabinet.

That same evening I had a telephone message from Samuel to say that there had been a meeting of the Liberal Ministers, and they all agreed to fall in with the recommendation of himself and Sinclair to withdraw from the Government. He expected the resignations would number twelve.

Next morning, Friday, 9th September, Samuel called to see me. He repeated what he had told me over the telephone the previous evening, and seemed very pleased with the result of the Liberal meeting. We discussed the future procedure. The Liberals would issue a joint letter of resignation setting out their reasons, and also a memorandum summarising the objections to the Ottawa agreements. He quite agreed that we must consult the convenience of the Prime Minister as to the time of announcing the resignations. Meanwhile we would let him know what was going on so that he could be prepared to fill our places, and so that the names of the new Ministers could be published almost immediately after the public announcement of our resignations.

During all this time I was in constant communication with the Liberal Ministers and worked in full co-operation with them. After my interview with the Prime Minister which I have described, I had no further personal communication with him. The Liberal Ministers met him on two occasions, and they reported the result of the interviews to me. The dissenting Ministers were very anxious that the announcement of their resignations should not be delayed, but the Prime Minister said that he did not want the formal resignations until about the end of the month, as it was desirable to have a Cabinet Meeting, which it was not possible to have sooner. For various reasons he made excuses for delaying to summon this meeting.

As I pointed out to Samuel, there was "tactics" in this, as it would enable the Tory members to carry on a campaign to raise prejudice against the Free Trade Ministers. Although, as I have said, I had no personal communication with the Prime Minister after the interview I have reported, he did write to me a long letter on the 14th September, the purport of which can be gathered from my reply to it, which was as follows:

"TILFORD,

"FARNHAM,

"15th September 1932.

"MY DEAR MACDONALD,

"I have your letter of the 14th. The point you put to me as to the effect of a break-up of the present Government by a large number of resignations, especially on the International situation and the forthcoming World Economic Conference, is not new to me. It has been urged upon us every time there has been dissension through the determination of the Tories to force a full Tory policy. Your own personal position, which I agree is difficult and will be still more difficult if you continue as the Prime Minister of what must be a Tory Government, has always hitherto made an appeal to our loyalty. You would like to get out, you say, but feel bound in honour to stick it. But there is a limit to the response to this appeal to personal loyalty, and others, too, must consider their honour. Has it not occurred to you the proper people to whom this appeal should be made to consider national interests, and to subordinate personal views on principle in those interests, are your Tory colleagues? They have sacrificed nothing, but have used the enormous Tory majority we gave them at the Election to carry out a Tory policy and to identify us with it. We have sacrificed our Party and ruined the political careers of a score of young Labour M.P.'s.

"I am not in the least influenced by the talk of the effect the break-up of the Government will have upon the World Economic Conference. There never was any prospect of that doing much good, and any such prospect has been destroyed by the decisions of the Ottawa Conference which has closed the door to any international tariff arrangements.

"You, I know, realise as well as I do, and indeed as well as the Ottawa delegates do, that the agreements are a piece of colossal humbug. There has been nothing so dishonest as the pretensions of the delegates about the 'great success' of the Conference and the campaign in the Tory Press to deceive the public about it. The sooner the new official paper containing the Schedules is published the better it will be for political decency. You will then get such an exposure of the Schedule E Tariff rates as will surprise you.

"To turn to your suggestions about the date of our resignations. I want to go as soon as possible, and before the whole Ottawa conspiracy is exposed. From what I have already said, you will gather that I could not contemplate the expedient of making the Economic Conference an excuse for delaying my resignation. The Tories have destroyed that Conference already. This, I believe, will be one of the main reasons the Liberals will urge as a reason for their resignations.

"I am seeing the Liberals tomorrow, and the date of our resignations will be considered. They are in the difficulty that their National Executive meets next week to consider Ottawa, and the Ministers, who have acted so far on their own views, do not want to appear to have been forced to it by their Executive.

"Then there is another strong reason for our early resignation. You say you have made 'discreet enquiries' about the effect of our resignations. *The Times* leader yesterday showed they knew what was going on, and if we delay we are just giving the Tories a fortnight's run to raise public opinion against us while we have no chance of replying. 'Thrice is he armed who gets his blow in first.'

"I do not know what the Liberals will decide on this point. It is a pity so many Ministers are away, but if the matter is so important as to need a Cabinet Meeting they ought to be called back as soon as possible. A fortnight's delay while the Press is attacking us is not fair to us. I think you ought to consider getting an early meeting, if you really think it is necessary.

"You ask me to let you have my views on the matters you raise in your letter, and I have tried to give them with perfect frankness.

"Yours sincerely,
"SNOWDEN."

"P.S.-I shall draft my letter of resignation after the meeting with the Liberals tomorrow. so it will be ready whenever it is convenient for you to receive it."

The Prime Minister got his way, and the Cabinet was not called together until 28th September. In the meantime, out of deference to the Prime Minister, we withheld our resignations. I was the first to arrive at the Cabinet Meeting. Mr. Baldwin came in next, and said he understood we were going, and he would like to express his deep regret and to say how happy he had been to work with me, and should always feel kindly towards me. On personal grounds I reciprocated these sentiments, for I always found Mr. Baldwin a very agreeable person with whom to work, and I had learnt to appreciate his straightforwardness.

It was assumed from the beginning of the Cabinet Meeting that our resignations were irrevocable, and the business was confined to explanations on our part of the reasons a separation had become inevitable, and on the part of the other members of the Cabinet to expressions of regret that we had decided to leave them.

The meeting was very friendly, and nothing acrimonious was said by anybody. When the Cabinet rose after a general handshaking and expressions of regret at parting with us, I handed to the Prime Minister my letter of resignation with an intimation that I was sending a copy for publication in the Press. Samuel was getting the signatures of all his resigning colleagues, and would hand the letter to the Prime Minister that afternoon. I was sorry for Runciman. He seemed to be a very unhappy man. When we got outside he turned back and made a cryptic remark that he might be able to drink again at the fountain.

The same afternoon an official announcement was made from 10 Downing Street of the appointment of the new Ministers. The three Cabinet Ministers who had resigned were Sir Herbert Samuel, Sir Archibald Sinclair and myself, and, in addition, eight Junior Liberal Ministers resigned. The new Ministers were two Tories and a Simonite-Liberal. The Simonite-Liberals had by this time become quite indistinguishable from the Tories, so that with the withdrawal of Sir Herbert Samuel and Sir Archibald Sinclair (whose action was enthusiastically approved by the Liberal Party in the country) the National Government was transformed into a Tory Government.

My resignation had no Party significance. I had no Party. On the afternoon of our resignations the Prime Minister made a statement to the Press. It is well worthwhile placing on record. He said:

> "The position of the National Labour Ministers-Lord Sankey, Mr. Thomas and myself-is that we put our hands to a very big job twelve months ago. We knew what it meant.
>
> "The same determination to disregard the ordinary partisan interests which were showed then we shall show still. The work is not finished. It cannot be finished until, one way or another, there is a Reparations and Debt Settlement and there is a World Economic Conference. We go on until these things are done.
>
> "We make the same appeal to the electors as we did twelve months ago - that the nation needs a non-Party Government, and that purely Party considerations would weaken our national influence in the world and would be a blow to the movements now at work towards world recovery."

Could there be a clearer instance of mental delusion or of disingenuous misrepresentation?

The next day I received the following letter from the Prime Minister:

"MY DEAR PHILIP,

"I was very sorry yesterday to have your letter of resignation, and I shall make no attempt to say again what I have already said to you about it.

"With kind regards,

"Yours always sincerely,
"J. R. MACDONALD."

The same day I handed in my seals of office to the King. I was a free man once more.

Appendix

Broadcast to the Nation on the General Election

17th October 1931.

In front of me, as part of the wireless arrangement, is a red light, and a red light is a warning of danger to be avoided. I am going to give you this warning tonight. I am going to talk to you for a few minutes about this General Election. I don't think I can say much that is new to you. The issue is very simple, and it has been stated through the wireless this week with admirable clearness by Mr. Baldwin and Sir John Simon. This in an unusual Election, and I can well understand that you feel rather puzzled about it. An ordinary General Election is quite a simple matter. We have the three Parties running independently. Each has its distinct programme of ordinary political questions. Most of us are Party men and women, and we vote the Party ticket. But at this Election the old Party divisions have been largely obliterated. New and strange issues have to be decided.

I have been a strong Party man, and I never expected to find myself in the political company I am keeping today. But I never had a shadow of doubt about the wisdom and rightness of my action. I joined the National Government to carry out the financial policy I pressed on my late colleagues in the Labour Government. They knew this policy was necessary. But when it came to the point of having to face up to it they hadn't the courage to face the unpopularity and opposition which necessary measures of economy would naturally meet within certain quarters. To call a halt in expenditure on the social services and to make cuts in the dole and reductions in pay here and there seemed, in the absence of knowledge of how necessary they were, to be inconsistent with Labour policy.

So it would have been in ordinary times. But these are not ordinary times. However anxious we may be to advance the social services we cannot do it when the resources from which the cost must come are drying up. A nation, like an individual, cannot go on increasing expenditure when income is falling, unless it wants to be landed into bankruptcy. It became clear to me in the early part of this year that we were on the edge of national bankruptcy, and drastic measures would have to be taken if that catastrophe were to be averted.

The vast increase in unemployment with its enormous cost to the Exchequer, the rapid fall in revenue through the decline in the profits of industry, had upset all Budget calculations. In a speech in the House of Commons in February I called attention to the position and urged Parliament to give serious consideration to it. I pointed out that we had committed ourselves to expenditure which might be tolerable in a time of prosperity and abounding revenue, but which we could not stand in a period of intense depression. Economy in expenditure was absolutely necessary. It was the only way in which we could conserve our resources and prevent a complete collapse of our social services.

I may mention the fact now because no harm is likely to be done since we have balanced the Budget, but the situation was so serious that by the middle of November, if we had allowed things to drift, there would have been no money to pay the unemployment benefits. What we have done has saved the unemployed from that plight.

You have been told by a spokesman of the Labour Party this week that the resources of the country are enormous and that we have money enough to go on spending to our hearts' content. This is appalling ignorance or wilful deception. It is true the resources of the country are great; but the fact is that they cannot continue to be mortgaged for current expenditure. Let me give you a few striking facts. When I first entered Parliament in 1906, twenty-five years ago, the total national expenditure for the year, excluding the Post Office, was £123,000,000. This year it is £804,000,000 - nearly seven times more. The Income-Tax then was 1s. in the £1; today it is 5s., with an additional Surtax running up to 5s. 6d. in the £1. In 1906 the whole cost of the social services was only £18,000,000. This year it is £237,000,000 - over thirteen times more. In 1906 there was no unemployment benefit. This year the country is paying £132,000,000 for this item - more than the whole national expenditure twenty-five years ago. In 1906 national and local taxation took one-thirteenth of the national income - that is, the incomes of everybody in the country aggregated together. This year nearly one-third of the national income is taken in rates and taxes. Only two-thirds is left to maintain the population and to provide capital and wages for industry. We are far away the most heavily taxed nation in the world. All this taxation has to come out of industry. There is nowhere else it can come from.

In July our own financial difficulties were aggravated by the serious financial panic on the Continent. I need not go into that story. It has been told to you often in the last few weeks. In August the situation became so pressing that measures had to be taken at once. The majority of the Labour Government, after agreeing to most of the economies, shirked the responsibility of placing the proposals before Parliament, so the Prime Minister dissolved the Government.

It became necessary to form a new Government at once. So the National Government was formed to deal with the situation. By drastic economies, and by heavy taxation spread fairly over the whole population, the Budget has been balanced. I know that the economies we have had to make are disagreeable. It has been no pleasure to impose them. They were necessary to prevent a far more serious reduction in working-class conditions. They are far less drastic than reductions which the Labour Government of Australia has been compelled to make, and far less than the economies made in Germany. After the cuts have been made the unemployed in this country are far more generously provided for than in any other country. In America they are left to private charity or to beg or starve. After the reductions in unemployment pay the benefits now are 17 per cent more in value than the Labour Government in 1924 considered adequate, and at a time when there was a Budget surplus of £30,000,000 - not a deficit of £170,000,000.

It is being said that the National Government has failed to save the pound. It is true we have been driven off the Gold Standard, and the external value of the pound has fallen. But its internal value has not depreciated. The purchasing power of the pound at home is still worth 20s. The action of the National Government in balancing the Budget has prevented a tremendous increase in the cost of living.

The question is being asked: Why have a General Election now? The answer is that the National Government was formed without any direct mandate from the nation. The crisis was urgent and acute. There was no time to appeal to the country. Now that we have secured a certain measure of stability we desire to give the electors the opportunity to express their opinion on the National Government and to give it their definite authority to continue and complete its work. The Government has not put before the electors a programme for the establishment of a new earth in the new Parliament. It leaves that to others who have no responsibility and who know they are not likely to be called upon to redeem their promises.

I would warn the electors against being influenced by other considerations than the one issue. That one issue on which you should vote is, as I have stated elsewhere, whether we should have a strong and stable Government in this time of national crisis, or whether we shall hand over the destinies of the nation to men whose conduct in a grave emergency has shown them to be unfitted to be trusted with responsibility. I regret that other issues are being raised in this Election. The position is too serious to have the national unity threatened by divisions on a subject which is no essential part of the work in front of the National Government.

There is no more stern and unbending Free Trader than I am. If Free Trade or Protection were the issue at this Election I should be on the side of Free Trade. We all joined the National Government on the understanding that controversial Party questions were to be set aside until we had completed the task of restoring national solvency. I do not believe that the Conservative leaders would regard a majority obtained in the circumstances of this Election as giving them a mandate to carry a general system of Protection in the new Parliament. Such a radical departure from our established fiscal system could not be made without an emphatic and unequivocal decision of the electorate. But I would warn Free Traders that if they do attach importance to this question at this Election, if they follow the advice of Mr. Lloyd George and vote for the Free Trade candidate, they will not be doing that by voting for the Labour Party.

The Labour Party is not a Free Trade Party. Its candidates are saying that from a thousand platforms. They have issued an Election programme which involves the most extreme form of Protection. Immense subsidies are to be given from the taxes to keep up the prices of agricultural produce; the staple manufacturing industries and the transport services are to be taken over and subsidised from the same source. A month ago the Trade Union Council was preparing a tariff policy. When the General Election became imminent they dropped that in order to pose as an anti-tariff Party.

Mr. Henderson is quoted in the *Daily Herald* this morning as having said that if he were faced with a large cut in unemployment pay or a 20 per cent revenue tariff as an emergency expedient he was going to try the value of that expedient. Now he is denouncing tariffs as an expedient to raise prices and lower wages. He was prepared a month ago to raise the cost of living to the unemployed and to all employed workers by 20 per cent rather than adopt the straightforward course of reducing the benefits by 10 per cent. This is the Party which Mr. Lloyd George recommends the Electors to support as a sound Free Trade Party.

I hope you have read the Election programme of the Labour Party. It is the most fantastic and impracticable programme ever put before the electors. All the derelict industries are to be taken over by the State, and the tax-payer is to shoulder the losses. The banks and financial houses are to be placed under national ownership and control, which means, I suppose, that they are to be run by a joint committee of the Labour Party and the Trade Union Council. Your investments are to be ordered by some board, and your foreign investments are to be mobilised to finance this madcap policy. This is not Socialism. It is Bolshevism run mad.

I have been an advocate of a sane and evolutionary Socialism for forty years, but I have always attacked such a revolutionary policy as is set out in this manifesto. Well might Mr. Lloyd George say the other evening that there is no likelihood of the country giving this programme a majority. Nothing could better show the utter lack of understanding of the national and international financial situation than such a programme as this. At a time when national retrenchment is vital, when above all else confidence in our sanity is needed, this programme is issued, a programme which, were it taken seriously, would destroy every vestige of confidence and plunge the country into irretrievable ruin.

May I say a word in conclusion to my old friends in the ranks of the Labour Movement? My recent action may seem to them inconsistent with my past. I assure them it is not. I am supporting this National Government as a temporary expedient to do the work which I would fain have seen a united Labour Government undertake. I am doing this because I do not want to see the work of a life-time brought to rack and ruin. To none more than to the working-classes is it more vital that a strong National Government should be returned. I ask them to believe that I give them this advice under a profound conviction that in doing so I am still serving the best interests of the working-classes and safeguarding their future progress. Goodnight.

Index

Alexander, A. V., 212, 213
Amulree, Lord, 295
Asquith, Herbert Henry, x, 51, 55, 64, 66-7, 71, 86, 88-90, 98-100, 107, 112, 124, 126-7, 133, 137-8, 141, 148, 151-3, 164, 181-2, 187, 191

Baldwin, Stanley, 59, 127, 131-2, 134, 137-9, 148, 158, 167-9, 178, 191, 192, 196-200, 207-8, 254, 268, 278, 280, 282, 288-92, 294-6, 310-13, 317, 326, 330, 333
Balfour, Arthur, 52-5, 64, 96, 119, 127, 216
Balfour Note, 216, 224, 227-8
Barnes, George, 22, 32, 75, 107
Beaverbrook, Lord, vii, 22-3
Bevin, Ernest, 284
Blackburn, 36-47, 81-4, 108-11, 121-3
Bondfield, Margaret, 69, 137, 208, 214
Bradford, 16, 27
Burns, John, 32-3, 42, 51

Campbell-Bannerman, Henry, 48, 51, 55, 64, 119, 131
Chamberlain, Sir Austen, 53, 143, 180, 206, 254
Chamberlain, Joseph, 11, 47, 52-5
Chamberlain, Neville, 192-3, 254, 276-7, 280, 282, 289, 295-6, 303, 315, 319, 324
Churchill, Winston, vii, x, 51-3, 66, 127, 192-5, 205-7, 212, 214, 217-8, 249-55, 306
Clynes, J. R., 22, 75, 106-8, 125-6, 134, 136, 138, 142-3, 178, 207, 273, 314
Colne Valley, 121-3, 125, 191, 206, 294
Cowling, 1-10, 15, 18-20, 47, 172

Fawcett, Milicent, 63, 72-3

George, David Lloyd, viii, x-xi, 51, 66-7, 74, 86, 89, 98-102, 106-12, 124, 127, 129, 133, 137, 153, 184, 207, 220-21, 252, 256-7, 271, 292, 311, 322, 336-7
George V, 98, 125, 138, 207, 213-4, 247-8, 288-90, 332
Glasier, Bruce, 17, 25, 119, 203
Graham, William, 161, 169-72, 212, 226, 234, 240, 247, 273, 278, 302, 314

Haldane, Lord, 51, 136, 140-1
Hankey, Sir Maurice, 139, 214, 220, 234
Hardie, Keir, X, 17, 21, 23-4, 30-5, 41, 47, 50-1, 59, 68-9, 75-9, 104, 119, 203
Henderson, Arthur, 50-1, 86-7, 99-103, 108, 126, 134-8, 141, 178, 207-11, 213, 215, 241, 244, 247, 258, 272-4, 278, 283, 293, 297-8, 302, 307, 314, 336

Ickornshaw, xi-xii, 1-10, 15

Jowett, F. W., 32, 43, 47, 75

Keighley, 1, 18-20, 25, 29

Lansbury, George, 140-1, 209, 213, 314
Law, Andrew Bonar, 98, 107, 125, 131, 161
Leeds, 4, 42-3, 92, 104, 173, 312

MacDonald, Ramsay, ix-xi, 21, 32-4, 40, 47, 50, 82-3, 93, 108, 125-6, 129, 134-39, 141-3, 151, 172, 174-5, 181, 184-9, 191, 197-8, 207-11, 228-31, 257, 268, 271-3, 278, 280-93, 295, 297, 310, 312, 321, 325-32
Maclean, Sir Donald, 265, 282, 318-21, 324
Mann, Tom, 18, 24
Marx, Karl, 17, 27, 119
Maxton, James, 128, 177, 204
Mosely, Sir Oswald, 213, 256-9
Morrison, Herbert, 213, 256

Nelson, 10-12
Norman, Montagu, 144-5

Pankhurst, Emmeline, 59-67
Parmoor, Lord, 140-1, 214, 273, 275
Passfield, Lord, *see* Webb, Sidney

Reading, Lord, 296, 311, 315
Redmond, John, 86
Runciman, Walter, 51, 98, 112, 315-9, 331

Samuel, Sir Herbert, 51, 98, 112, 271, 280, 282, 288-92, 296, 311, 313, 317-21, 325-8, 330-1
Sankey, Lord, 290, 295, 331
Shackleton, David, 48, 50, 66, 75
Shaw, G. B., 22, 110
Shaw, Tom, 138, 142, 154
Simon, Sir John, 88, 112, 127, 178, 180-1, 315, 326, 331, 333
Sinclair, Sir Archibald, 271, 318, 320-1, 327, 331
Smillie, Robert, 22, 92-3, 108
Snowden, Lady Ethel (wife of Philip), xi, 43, 46, 68, 73, 81, 109, 122-3, 160, 172, 234, 243, 246, 248, 271

Thomas, J. H., 46, 129, 134-7, 186, 198-9, 207-14, 256-7, 271-3, 278, 290, 295, 331
Thorne, Will, 32, 118

Tillett, Ben, 18, 22
Trevelyan, C. P., 124, 138, 140,
Turner, Sir Ben, 22, 305

Wakefield, 41-3

Walsh, Stephen, 70-1, 75, 138
Webb, Sidney, 80, 134-7, 142, 212, 274-5
Wheatley, John, 128, 152, 181, 208